Neglected Aspects of American Poetry

The Greek Independence War and Other Studies

by

Aaron Kramer

Dowling Studies in the Humanities
and the Social Sciences

Library of Congress Cataloging-in-Publication Data

Aaron Kramer, *Neglected Aspects of American Poetry: The Greek Independence War and Other Studies*

    1. *American Poetry*
    2. *Literature*
    3. *History*

ISBN 1-883058-17-1

Announcement

Dowling Studies in the Humanities and the Social Sciences (DSHSS) has been established to further research in the humanities and the social sciences. Manuscripts submitted undergo an external review and need not reflect the views of the Editorial Board.

On behalf of the Editorial Board, I am pleased to express appreciation for the support we have received from the Dowling College administration; we especially thank President Victor P. Meskill, Provost and College Secretary, Albert E. Donor, and Dean of Arts and Sciences, James E. Caraway.

Robert M. Berchman
Editor in Chief

Dowling Studies in the Humanities
and the Social Sciences

Sponsor
Victor P. Meskill, *ex officio*

Editor in Chief
Robert M. Berchman

Managing Editor
Parviz Morewedge

Editors

Joseph Behar

Joan Boyle

James E. Caraway

Jeffrey Cole

Andrew Karp

John D. Mullen

Byron Roth

Susan Rosenstreich

Martin Schoenhals

James O. Tate

Neglected Aspects of American Poetry

The Greek Independence War and Other Studies

by

Aaron Kramer

Dowling College Press

Note

These essays, though basically united in emphasis, were created over a very large span of time and under a variety of circumstances. The Emma Lazarus study, for example, is excerpted from my master's thesis submitted to the English Department of Brooklyn College in 1951; the *Columbiad* analysis was written for my doctoral mentor Nelson Adkins of New York University in 1963; shortly thereafter I wrote most of what is now "A Matter of Centennial Interest" as part of my dissertation proposal; the comparative study of Burns and Hughes was invited and published by *Freedomways* shortly after Langston Hughes' death in 1967; my Melville paper was presented at the 1976 NEMLA conference in Burlington, Vt.; the five Whitman pieces were published between 1979 and 1985 in the *West Hills Review;* my Giovannitti paper was delivered at the 1982 NEMLA conference in New York City; the Dodson tribute appeared in *Freedomways* soon after after his death in 1983; my paper on the Greek War for Independence was presented at the 9th Mediterranean Institute Conference, held at Athens in 1983; my Funaroff/Bergman study was heard at the 1985 NEMLA meeting in Hartford; the Wheelock essay was invited and published in 1991 by the *North Atlantic Review;* and the Rukeyser memoir, written for what would have been her 80th birthday, appeared in two parts in 1993.

Contents

Introduction

In 1977, undaunted by the infestation of tourists in every London cranny, I undertook a second visit to the Samuel Johnson Museum, once his home. My 1956 foray had been a total frustration: each room so crowded, I could not get close enough to examine a single showcase; the lines at the souvenir desk so huge, I left empty-handed.

Braced for another mob-scene, I stepped inside. But no other guest was there. After a leisurely sampling of treasures, I approached the desk. This time the same two ladies, I could swear, 21 years older, but still in love with the ghost of that house, lavished their graciousness entirely on me. Contrasting the two visits, I asked for an explanation. One of them, eyes filling with tears, murmured: "He isn't on examinations any more." All I could do was buy every item on display and leave the door behind, that door once greeted as a shrine, now marked with an invisible X — X for leprosy, for quarantine, for no longer being on examinations.

That incident was by no means my first experience with the actual machinery by which neglect can be decreed and mass-produced, but it remains with me: emblematic of the taste-setters' raw power and the public's acquiescence.

I am no sentimentalist, no Don Quixote tilting at windmills. It is in the very nature of Time that the old will somewhat give way to the new, even when the old is superior. And the struggle of the old to keep from being shoved aside is no fiercer than that of the new to establish a foothold. It is, indeed, one and the same struggle.

Where then, if not at Oxford and Harvard, will the chief productions of recent decades elbow their way into curricula, onto examinations? And how is this to be accomplished except at the expense of — say — a Samuel Johnson, or, worse yet, the whole Age of Johnson? Preferably in a civilized way — through the screamless, bloodless good fortune called attrition.

One imagines the literature faculty at a staff meeting or an informal tea; the last of the Johnsonians (he who considered the résumés of these very people when green applicants, these Joyce and Woolf and Yeats specialists now graying and at last in power) is about to retire. Is it by silent agreement or blatant vote that the new era begins, that the last of the Johnsonians will be replaced not by another of his ilk, if another such exists, but by the first of the Ted Hughes and Philip Larkin and Seamus Heaney specialists?

The precedents are awesome and still within memory. It was thus that the pre-Raphaelites faded — from examinations, from memory; exquisiteness had not saved them. Thus too the giants fell — Tennyson, Wordsworth — assaulted with double fervor because their largeness so formidably blocked the way for the young.

I don't believe this oligarchic system has prevailed in the concert hall, where audiences have the privilege to decide — with their purchase of tickets and cries of "Bravo!" — that Mozart and Beethoven and Brahms will survive most 20th century music, despite the clout of the conservatories. When Mendelssohn is banished, or Shostakovich's *Lady Macbeth,* it is by government edict. Nor will those who frequent the museums allow a great painter or a whole age of painting to be displaced in the galleries by new work simply because today's professors and critics of art declare it superior.

In the realm of poetry the public can vote only by buying or shunning new books. And the century now concluding has witnessed a diminution of purchase so extreme that most publishers have no poetry list at all. Past their academic years, according to polls, few do any serious reading; fewer still, by far, read poetry. It is impossible not to notice that the poets in highest critical favor today and therefore most likely to be taught in colleges, explored in critical and biographical volumes, reviewed in journals, purchased by libraries, featured in anthologies, are those least accessible to the public, most interested in communicating with one another; while the poets sinking deeper and deeper into neglect — if not contempt — are those whose work, in form and content, is most widely accessible and would be most likely to win readers if it could come to them. The comment I hear most frequently at readings is: "I didn't know poetry was something I could understand." After a long lifetime in the field, I am left with the impression that a cold algebraic equation holds sway: A poet who does not need to be elucidated in advanced courses and accompanying guidebooks cannot possibly be great. Sometimes, in ultra-patrician, ultra-aestheticist hands, the equation is altered: A poet who uses his craft to denounce, to arouse, to utter prophecy (i.e., Whittier in his abolitionist years) cannot be worth serious attention.

I hope the note sounded here does not strike the reader as desperate. That most artistic creations will sink into shadow is inevitable; after all, entire ages of history have fallen into neglect along with their art. And it is likely that most of the works no longer read a century later are inferior in artistic merit and of less interest in content than most of what survives.

But this is a likelihood I for one have persistently refused to accept on faith in my own roles as reader, teacher, anthologist, essayist, and broadcaster. This refusal has often been rewarded by exciting discoveries, shared without concern for the raised eyebrows of those whose misjudgments I embarrass. On the other hand, after blowing the dust off a volume once well regarded, I have usually found its oblivion warranted; but the decision is mine, not Time's or some faceless, nameless critic's. By such means I have also become better able to understand what kinds of poetry were deemed admirable by a generation, for example, that rejected Whitman and Melville, that caused Higginson to advise Emily Dickinson against seeking publication. Finally, reading such poets has helped me to appreciate more fully the heroism of Whitman, Melville, and Dickinson, whose singing was not muted by neglect.

If I did not believe unjust oblivion to be reversible, I would not have written these essays. If my publishers did not agree that unmerited neglect can and should be challenged, they would not have committed themselves to this collection. There are, moreover, here and there, independent-minded librarians who acquire books by and about untrumpeted poets, who do not periodically remove the seldom-borrowed collections of yesterday to make shelf-room for the favored collections of today. There are, if few and far between, anthologists who do more than rehash one another's menu of contents, who clearly examine the whole book of a poet and choose pieces not hitherto reprinted. There are, in a handful of classrooms across the land, professors who enlist their students in campaigns of discovery, assigning poets once well known, now in obscurity, leading their charges on treasure-hunts, transforming the research paper from a dry requirement to a thrilling involvement full of aesthetic and other surprises, as education should be. If this were to happen year after year on a hundred campuses, each student sharing with his or her classmates the essence of a dust-freed book, the stranglehold of curriculum committees, book review magazines and standard anthologies would begin to be broken, and much that is wonderful would emerge from shadow to be embraced by the audience it deserves.

A final word: neglect takes many forms and comes in varying degrees. Thus, Barlow's "Hasty Pudding" is still quite popular and readily available in anthologies. Even more so is Emma Lazarus' "New Colossus." But their extraordinary lives are a cipher, and their major works remain virtually unknown. In the case of poets now conscientiously studied, such as Whitman and Langston Hughes, certain aspects receive repeated attention, while significant facets of their work are generally ignored. Melville's poetry as a whole — though increasingly anthologized — is seldom taught or publicly discussed. In 1976, invited to lecture on his neglected poems at the University of Kansas, I was privately informed that only three of the 61 department members had known Melville wrote poetry. So the essay in this volume challenges a two-fold neglect.

The same was the case in a 1979 broadcast honoring Edna St. Vincent Millay; while excoriating anthologists and professors for an unconscionable quarter-century of downgrading, I omitted all of her once widely anthologized poems and presented only selections from her brilliant, utterly ignored posthumous collection of 1954, *Mine the Harvest*.

In the case of Giovannitti and Wheelock, poets long by-passed, as well as Funaroff and Bergman, whose dynamic group never had its moment, I have chosen, as with Melville, one overlooked aspect that seems especially worth study — again, neglect within neglect. With Giovannitti, in my selection of his poetry itself, I am making the most of this opportunity and am including still another, even more totally ignored segment of his *oeuvre,* a group of poems inspired by the Russian Revolution. Clearly, their explosive content would keep any anthologist now successful from daring to give them a few pages even if he secretly finds them of artistic merit. I, on the other hand, would not consider excluding them — partly because they pertain to my correspondence with Giovannitti's son (see Appendix I), and partly because — whether one approaches the subject with enthusiasm, disgust, embarrassment or disillusion — one cannot question its historic interest or the fact that his is probably a richer response than that of any poet then alive.

Finally, in focusing on the verse inspired by Greece's 1821–34 independence war against Turkey, I am assaulting not only the neglect into which a fascinating epoch has fallen, but also the disappearance of numerous writers once considered significant voices in American poetry.

Joel Barlow's *Columbiad*

From 1782 to 1802

In 1782, while writing *The Vision of Columbus*,[1] Joel Barlow was a New England chaplain; twenty years later, reshaping that poem into *The Columbiad*,[2] he was a deistic citizen of the world. A comparison of the two versions can be useful in gauging the poet's development.

For a brief study it may be best to analyze a single section. Book VII of *The Vision*, reworked as Book VIII of *The Columbiad*, was chosen because the number and nature of the differences are striking. Almost two thirds of the lines are new, and a hundred old lines are excluded. The retained passages have undergone scores of lesser but frequently revealing changes. Since Barlow's declared object was "altogether of a moral and political nature,"[3] *The Columbiad* calls for attention as a statement of ideas.[4] Its creator made no claims of poetic excellence; yet he had toiled for years, with tremendous energy, to achieve what he hoped "would be considered his masterpiece."[5] The alterations should therefore be examined with respect to form as well as content.

I. Language

Failing to follow Blake, Wordsworth, and Coleridge in their revolt from the heroic couplet,[6] and being doubly imprisoned within the framework and tone of a youthful production long alien to him, Barlow was apparently constrained to register his romantic outbursts through line-by-line fireworks, sometimes with disastrous results.[7]

Seldom could the poet, in constructing his new couplets, pass by a noun without attaching modifiers that range from hackneyed, prosaic or dull — to redundant, excessive or outlandish. Clichés abound: *bright galaxy, deathless deed, unnumber'd foes, bold breast, fierce war-*

riors, matchless might, avenging sword, enchanting lyre, wild confusion, pearly tear, etc. One plods through such prosaisms as *proper base, broad plain truths, obvious wants,* and *mutual aids,* and such colorless phrases as *sage experience, dreary trance, sordid ceaseless hate, vile spirit, senseless rank, dread voice,* and *generous hand.* The redundancies include *mingling rays unite, flashing flames, dark intolerance,* and *"houseless hordes, their smoking walls that fly."* It is hard to overlook the fulsome rhetoric of *symphonious strains, tremendous triumph, hideous howl, gory waves, misery's pains, corse-encumber'd plains,* or the strained effort resulting in *nascent prize, adolescent grace,* [Order's] *cerulean robes, time's anterior world,* [the universe's] *renovated globes, flamy wall,* and *forky tongue.* Possibly he sensed that, unadorned, his noun would be inadequate; often there was a need to "fill up" the pentameter; most adjectives were intended to lend visual and aural support, but their cumulative attack succeeds in benumbing the reader, leaving him unresponsive when a well-made line is reached.

Yet there are more than a few admirable strokes in the new version, and Jeffrey was not altogether far-fetched in declaring Barlow "a giant" compared with many of his contemporaries.[8] Some lines display a vitality and rightness beyond almost anything in the innocuous, totally derivative *Vision.*[9]

PRISONERS OF WAR:
   "From the black prison ships, those groaning graves"

PAINTING OF LEAR:
   "Insults the tempest and outstorms the skies"

GEN. WARREN DIES:
   "And leaves a victory to the wasted foe"

REVOLUTIONARY HEROES:
   "Whose holy hands our banners first unfurled"

DRAGON GUARDING GOLDEN FLEECE:
   "Then, with one sweep of convoluted train,
   Rolls back all Greece, and besoms wide the plain"

MEDEA:
> "But the sly Priestess brings her opiate spell"

DESPOTIC POWER:
> "Blots with his breath the trembling disk of day,
> Treads down whole nations every stride he takes"

SMUG AMERICANS:
> "Thy pride to pamper, thy fair face to show . . .
> And lurks no spot in that bright sun of thine?"

AFRICA TO AMERICA:
> "Enslave my tribes! then boast their cantons free"

BARBARY SLAVES:
> "And the chain clanking counts the steps they tread"

MASTER RACES:
> "Rove through the world and hunt the nations down . . .
> Rome chains the world, and wears herself the chains"

AMERICA'S MISSION:
> "Restore their souls to men, give earth repose"

and the entire passage, lines 293 to 304, describing a Second Flood.

Lines of this caliber are perhaps less easy to find than are the blemishes; and it has evidently become the custom to overlook them, even among scholars friendly to Barlow, as is seen in Appendix I.

By 1885 the poem as a whole had "long since passed out of the category of books that are read."[10] Parrington, heartily endorsing the tradition of merry-making over *The Columbiad*, says: "It was a mistake to return to it."[11] Davis calls the poem "abominable."[12] Howard asks "Whether these revisions were merely bad or worse than the originals."[13] To Woodress "the youthful blemishes are more attractive than the middle-aged remodeling."[14] Even Todd, a devoted admirer, admits that "the poem contains too many grave defects to be considered a classic."[15]

The new lines display an odd conglomeration of virtues and offenses; it is safe to conclude that Barlow, after years of poetic inactivity, returned to the Muse with no firmly individual style such as he had achieved briefly with "Hasty Pudding" ten years earlier and was again to achieve, at the very gate of death, with "Advice to a Raven in Russia," ten years later. A comparison of the minor changes in retained lines, however, leads to a judgment less harsh than that generally accepted today. One finds a fairly consistent effort to replace outworn, vague, and pompous words with fresher, clearer, and simpler ones:

guidance: finger	toils: wires
dread: dark	toils: deeds
unpleasing: turgid	rocks: shells
sounding: soothing	hosts: crews
beauteous: verdant	hosts: troops
o'er: on	unnumber'd: thousands
hapless: lamented	keen-eyed: lynx-eyed

The deftness of such minor improvements is demonstrated more dramatically in phrases than in single words:

spread destruction round:	shake the sheeted ground
beauteous banks:	war-beat banks
threatening blast:	every tempest
exhaustless store:	native store
heart-felt sighs:	fraternal sighs
each far clime:	every land
wakes the tender tear:	still renews my tear
ascending crowds:	men
round the turrets rise:	midnight war supplies
master's mind:	painter's mind
modest mansions:	modest walls
thy turrets, York:	Manhattan's mart
greet the skies:	grace the land

Finally, some entire lines are reworked. "... the dangerous labors dare" becomes "drag forth the shining gewgaws into air"; "Along the strand unnumber'd keels arise" is transformed into "There couch the keels, the crooked ribs arise"; "Thro' all the realms their seats of science rear" gives way to "Young schools of science rise along the shore"; for "People the shoals and fill the exhaustless tide" we are given "Repeople still the shoals and fin the fruitful tide"; and sculpture, instead of being "Warmed with the scenes that grace their various clime," is "Caught from the cast of every age and clime."

Not all of these are successful; but what he changed needed to be changed. The poet's direction is toward concreteness, modification, and life. Unfortunately his choice often depended on alliteration, too. With justice the *Philadelphia Port Folio* "damned" *The Columbiad* for its "ludicrous alliteration."[16] This device is used relentlessly, slavishly, missing the intended mark of sensuous appeal.

Would Todd include the following lines among the "many ... eloquent and melodious passages"[17] he finds?

> Heaves his hoar head and shakes the heaven he bears:
> — Son of my sire! Oh latest brightest birth
> That sprang from his fair spouse, prolific earth!
> Great Hesper, say what sordid ceaseless hate ...

Of twenty stressed syllables, seven begin with "s," six with "h," three with "b," two with "l." This record is hard to beat (outside of Quince's "Pyramus and Thisbe" playlet in *A Mid-summer Night's Dream*). There is much alliteration in the *Vision*, but not this much. One senses the poet straining to give the project all he had in terms of dexterity, as if to compensate for the fact that he was toiling without authentic poetic impulse. What should not be ignored, however, is that the new alliterative patterns are purposeful, unlike those in the *Vision* (*tender tear, beauteous banks, master's mind, modest mansions*, etc.) which Barlow wisely eliminated.

II. Versification

The rhymes of *The Columbiad*, while less imperfect than some in the *Vision*, are equally tame and monotonous.[18] It therefore seemed more meaningful to place alongside the carefully wrought couplets of 1802–1806, those dashed off in a frivolous moment at an inn while Barlow sought election as deputy from Savoy in December of 1792.

"Hasty Pudding," composed in 187 sets of rhyme, has 74 different rhyme sounds, of which thirty appear only once. The four most common occur a total of only thirty times. The most often repeated rhyme words ("thee" and "song" — five times each) are excusable as refrains. Almost its equal in length, a new passage of Book VIII (see

Appendix Two) has 66 rhyme sounds, of which twenty are used only once. The four most common occur a total of 38 times. "State" and "shore" appear as rhymes six times each; "main," "man," "tide," "mankind," "earth" and "birth" are used five times each. Many end-words in "Hasty Pudding" are colorful, concrete, appropriate. Those in the new passage of *The Columbiad* — obviously called upon repeatedly for convenience's sake — are almost uniformly flat and heavy, of an abstract, rhetorical-philosophical nature.[19]

Of the 35 other new couplets in Book VIII only five introduce rhyme sounds not in the above-analyzed passage. Among the thirty repeated rhyme sounds, 24 end-words are to be found frequently in the long passage. Of the 127 couplets carried over from the early poem, only four are given new rhyme sounds, and all four sounds appear in the long passage, in which certain of the "new" rhyme words are repeatedly employed. In five other couplets retained from the *Vision*, one rhymed word is kept, one altered. Of the five altered words, two are used again as rhymes in the long passage. The conclusion may be drawn that Barlow, as a rhymer, had become either exhausted or indifferent after one relatively strong performance in 1792: indifferent, if his introductory declaration is to be trusted.

In two other areas of versification, however, he shows signs of a rebellion from the strictness of his earliest period. The *Vision*'s entire Book VII contains only one instance of enjambment (a thought continuing past the couplet and terminating in the middle of the next line); in our one long Book VIII addition alone, ten such run-ons appear, equalling the number in "Hasty Pudding." Further, there is a considerable difference in the lengths of thought-units. In the *Vision*'s first 98 couplets, 36 thoughts are complete in one couplet, 14 in two, seven in three, one in four, and two in five couplets. On the other hand, the *Columbiad* passage (lines 69–266) includes 17 thoughts complete in one couplet, 16 in two, eight in three, two in four, two in five, and one in seven couplets.

If these changes were part of a conscious program, the statistics would probably be much more remarkable; it is likelier that Barlow was by this time capable of handling larger and more complex ideas than those in the *Vision*, and that the gusto of his thinking thrust aside the old metronomic pattern. True, "he chose to imitate the least enduring qualities of contemporary verse,"[20] but even his master, Southey, was making important metrical experiments at this time,[21] and in the '60s Charles Churchill had definitively disarranged the Popeian measure.[22] Such winds of change apparently passed him by, or swayed him only slightly.

Yet in 1809 it was no mean compliment for the *Port Folio's* critic, displeased though he was, to rank *The Columbiad* with Southey's *Madoc*.[23] Modern scholars ignore those technical improvements which help to make the later poem far more animated and readable than its predecessor. They are perhaps disappointed that, while Barlow's ideas had undergone a dramatic transformation, as a bard "he was still stuck in the bog of provincial poetry."[24]

III. Religion

Even before one arrives at the crucial passage on religion which is almost totally discarded by the later Barlow, one discovers enough slight changes to realize that the change is not at all slight. Spiritual words are generally muted, modified, or eliminated. The Seraph is now called "my son" or "guardian power"; "Hesper" replaces the "Angel"; Dwight's voice is no longer "divine," nor is Jacob "Heaven-taught"; "zeal" becomes "hope"; souls are not "ardent" but "searching"; his brother's soul approaches "homeward" rather than "approving" skies; the "wide heavens" turn into a "dim void"; beauties are not "immortal" but "unfading"; "joys above" shrink to "promised joys above." "The expanse" replaces "the heavens," as "death's dread summons" replaces "Heaven's . . ." "The Almighty's mind" loses identity to become "his beamful mind." Three pointedly modified lines deserve special study. For "The sacred task unnumber'd sages claim" Barlow substitutes "The preacher's task persuasive sages claim." "Heaven in their view" no longer "unveils the eternal plan"; instead, the poet apostrophizes: "Lead, light, allure them thro the total plan." The youthful chaplain rhapsodized: "On glory's wing to raise the ravish'd soul"; the deist's voice is subdued: "On wings of faith to elevate the soul."

Twelve more lines on religion are melted down to six, and those six significantly altered. An enthusiastic picture of the church's triumph in his nation is eliminated; and, instead of a proselytizer's tribute to the clergy — leading "whole nations in the walk of truth," shedding "the bright beams of knowledge on the mind," — Barlow coldly allows his preachers "to mould religion to the moral mind."

Finally the reader of the 1782 epic reaches an exuberant 66-line passage in which the young poet delivers a Calvinist sermon. This climactic point of Columbus' vision shows America, thanks to its "unnumber'd sages," leading mankind to the harmony of "social compact.... To life, to happiness." Though of "different faiths," the clergy — including the poet-preacher — are united in zeal. Columbus is permitted to hear the Almighty's resonant voice defining His omnipotence and warning any would-be offender that "his guilty soul" will be overwhelmed. "Poor distrest mankind" is a "darkling race" always groping "for bliss," blind "to virtue." The first thinkers "rose from the darksome dust ... to trace the eternal Cause" and discover that love is "the all-ruling plan" linking man to God. Universal harmony is on the way; salvation from pain and guilt is available. "Be babes on earth, be seraphs in the skies," the Lord coaxes. Merciful, he heeds "the cries of grief." In the form of Christ, "God descends," His "stern vengeance" having softened. Atoning on the Cross for man's sins, He seals "the pardoning grace." Thus, washed in Christ's blood, man can achieve splendor on earth and in heaven. This is "the eternal plan" which humankind must learn to follow.

In *The Columbiad* all but eight of the 66 lines are omitted, and the eight are toned down, especially in two key lines describing the clergy: from "Yet one blest cause, one universal flame" to "Yet one their voice, their labors all combined"; from "Lights of the world and messengers of God" to "Lights of the world and friends of humankind."

Replacing the fullblown Calvinist vision are four sharply critical verses that stress the difference between the positions of religion in America and in nations where church and state are one:

> No dark intolerance blinds the zealous throng,
> No arm of power attendant on their tongue;
> Vext Inquisition, with her flaming brand,
> Shuns their mild march, nor dares approach the land.

As early as 1792 Barlow had said as much in prose:[25]

> Nations are cruel in proportion as they are guided by priests.
> ... In the United States of America there is no church; and this
> ... ensures the unembarrassed exercise of religion.

The horrified charges of atheism levelled at *The Columbiad*, even by
such old friends as Noah Webster and Henri Gregoire,[26] are scarcely
supported by anything in the work itself, as the poet was quick
to declare.[27] They may have derived from memories of his 1792
Advice, or the circulation of a private letter praising Paine's *Age of
Reason,*[28] or his translation of Volney's *Ruins,* an intensely anti-
religious work.[29] The alterations in the sections under study, while
very significant, do not bear out Sheldon's contention that Barlow
had no place for religion in his scheme of things,[30] or Howard's
conclusion that "in his private beliefs he was more nearly an atheist
than ... Ethan Allen and Tom Paine," while "in his published
writings" he paid "the highest tribute to Christianity."[31]

If Barlow could wear a hypocritical mask in 1802, he might just
as well have done so twenty years before; and his "pronounced ...
predilection for Calvinism"[32] may simply have been good business in
the world of Timothy Dwight. The letters (1782–86)[33] contain no
reference, not even one rhetorical phrase, to show the slightest
Christian sentiment or interest; on the other hand, he mentions
having spoken "in the chapel to admiration ... and what is more
shall have six dollars for it when I get it"[34] — a perfect statement in
miniature of his two literary motives: glory and money. In 1783 he
left his post without regretting "that he would never preach sermons
again, nor enjoy the privileges of a chaplain."[35] And, his 1785 edition
of Watts' *Psalms* not proving "a very lucrative venture," the poet
decided that he'd "had enough of such work."[36]

The *Columbiad* revisions, made with obvious care, express a
modified belief in God. What the reader senses is "a lessening of in-
terest" in heaven "in favor of earth and ... the daily lives of men."[37]
Barlow's radicalism of the '90's had softened "about the turn of the
century."[38] Though Sawford sees no evidence of this in *The Colum-
biad,* the new approach to religion may represent just such a soften-
ing. In 1792 he had written:[39]

> It is men who are corrupted by the church; for the very existence
> of a church ... is founded on a lie ... the practising of ... sorceries.

Can he now have taken the cue from Jefferson's newly-delivered Inaugural Address and echoed it as closely in his *Columbiad* as a follower can echo a leader?

> ... enlightened by a benign religion, professed indeed and practiced in various forms yet all of them inculcating honesty, truth, temperance, gratitude, and the love of man.[40]

IV. Politics

The minor political shifts are subtler and harder to find than are the religious changes. The aborigine is no longer "lurking" but "frequent." An admiring comment on the labors of "whole realms of slaves" is eliminated, and the dangers they face are criticized. "Virginian Muses" now "meet" on the James River campus where "royal spires" formerly ascended. The "sway" of empire is no longer called "peaceful." Britain's role in the Revolution is portrayed bitterly. The poet has discarded his neutral tone, so that "proud Albion's sons" become "Britain's soil'd sons"; the "crimson stain" they create is now a "guilty stain"; their "rolling fire" is characterized as "hostile fire." Discarding his impartial picture of war, "Blind carnage raves, and great Montgomery dies"; the poet now presents the moment through partisan eyes: "The assailants yield, their great Montgomery dies." Barlow, the republican, substitutes "equal rights" for "freedom" and strikes out an unmerited tribute to "liberal sires" who had apparently not been rearing schools "with guardian care." Education, instead of pointing "the paths of fame," must "fashion freedom's lore," — and how different is "the solid prize" when it is seized not by "youths unnumber'd" but by "homebred freedmen"!

A few touches, however, are not nearly enough: the old couplets simply cannot hold the weight of Barlow's richly specific 1802 vision. Additions of extraordinary length are required. It is too easy to say merely that both poems are "pregnant with the views he entertained at the time of the composition of each."[41] *The Vision* contains its quite conventional beliefs very neatly, but *The Columbiad* actually bursts at the seams with a fifteen-year harvest of high-powered thinking and living.[42] It is equally untrue that *The Columbiad* "does not admit of detailed comparison in every way with his prose works."[43] The huge Book VIII additions parallel, idea by idea, what can be found in Barlow's other writings. It is almost as if he had set out to paraphrase himself in rhyme:

23–26, 43–46: The horrors of war "convulsed" his nerves and agonised" his "soul." The tone is fearful; he alludes to impressment and naval turmoil.

"I see two great nations rushing on each other's bayonets without any cause . . . but a misunderstanding. I shudder at the prospect, and wish to throw myself between."[44]

67–76: warm tribute is paid to the revolutionary warriors who "conquer'd freedom for the grateful world."

". . . that epoch of light and liberty has freed one quarter of the world . . ."[45]

77–94: The battle for liberty never ends; internal enemies may "divide" them or send a "soft infection through the land," to "dazzle . . . corrupt . . . inflate" them with "state . . . power . . . pomp" and "construct a throne" while the patriots sink into "one lethargic sleep."

"If you really have no talents . . . than . . . to copy precedents from old monarchies, I pity you."[46] "I doubt the patriotism of those who lead your leaders . . . I see the most perfidious measures . . . adopted . . . for hurling you from the exalted station . . ."[47]

95–130: The rape of the golden fleece illustrates the danger to liberty: Medea's "opiate spell" overcomes "the guardian's sleepless ire."

Howard: "He did intend . . . introducing philosophic comments in the guise of old stories . . . All these mythological researches proved of little use."[48]

131–54: In peacetime, the Son of Liberty has a "superior task": he "fashions and improves mankind" through education in democracy. In America he can "mould a fair model for the realms of earth." By reverting to the "great social plan" of "moral nature," America can restore "the sober sense of man."

"If we wish to preserve the principles and practice of liberty . . . we must proceed by instruction."[49] "It begins to be the fashion there now [England] to look to America for examples of good government."[50]

155–78: "Despotic power" destroys civilization. Just as Order overcame the "wild confusion" of Anarchy and "stock'd with harmoni-

"What an inconceivable mass of slaughter" is caused by "dark, unequal government!"[51] "Kings can do no good."[52] ". . . nations,

ous worlds" the universe, so it is the mission of America, by its example, to "snatch this earth" from kings, who "convulse the moral frame," and "to raise regenerate man."

179–394: Rather than "mislead" himself, and "perhaps mislead mankind," the poet criticizes the "blemish" of slavery which proves America hypocritical in its protestations of freedom and equality. Africa has retaliated by enslaving Americans in Barbary; Atlas threatens that nature will eventually revolt. But such superstitious threats are wasted in a land where "Science/Strips the heavens of love and hate,/Strikes from Jove's hand the brandisht bolt of fate." Nor can "pathos" help, though a description of the slave-system might "gain/Full many a voice to break the barbarous chain." Only the voice of "strong self-interest" can be effective: all masters become tyrants, and "tyrants are never free." To avoid the ruin that has overtaken feudal Europe, America must grant "Equality of Right" — which is "nature's plan." Under the "holy Triad" of EQUALITY, FREE ELECTION and FEDERAL UNION, America will lead mankind to a future of peace and plenty (a vision "Columbus well enjoy'd.")

509–16: The basis of "the social plan" is "the common sense of man."

521–24: Democracy in action: the constituents "watch their delegates" formulate flexible laws

rising from their lethargy, will reclaim the rights of man."[53] "... A general revolution is at hand, whose progress is irresistible."[54]

"I shall not relinquish this right, nor neglect this duty [of criticism] whoever may be the men, and whatever the party ..."[55] "[Slavery] ... in every point of view, moral, political and economical, is perhaps the greatest blemish and may become the greatest scourge to our country."[56] "... our captive citizens who have survived the pains and humiliation of slavery in this place [Barbary] ... said that without me ... they would all have perished."[57] "[Enemies] ... we find ... useful ... in supplying our wants ... we cease to regard them as enemies."[58] "A race of hereditary masters cannot be a race of republicans."[59] "Such a revolution cannot stop short of fixing the power of the State on the basis allotted by nature, the unalienable rights of man, which are the same in all countries."[60] "You can't imagine what a garden it [National Institute] would make of the United States."[61]

"Establish government universally on the individual wishes and collective wisdom of the people."[62]

"It is not intended that every citizen should be ... a legislator. But every citizen is a voter;

which they will "obey, but scru-
tinize."

it is essential to your institutions
that he should be a voter."[63]

The political shift in Barlow, as evidenced in these new passages of Book VIII, is from a Hamiltonian to a Jeffersonian view of man and society. The midway point, violently French in its stress, is by now far behind him — thanks to the imperial excesses of Napoleon and the defeat of the Federalists at the polls. Freedom and equality have become his passion: they are the base of nature's moral plan. Only when this plan is thwarted does evil overwhelm the world. Man's hope is a restoration of the natural social order, and America must lead the way. Thus, the elimination of a big religious passage and the addition of a much fuller political one are two sides of the same coin: man is no longer a creature cringing in darkness and guilt, pleading with God for salvation; a world in darkness and guilt is pleading with man for salvation, and — "following nature" — man marches forth to answer the call.

V. Arts and Sciences

Aside from religion and politics, other areas touched upon in Book VII of the *Vision*, particularly the arts and sciences, are handled differently in Book VIII of *The Columbiad*. During his seventeen years in Europe, Barlow had greatly expanded his knowledge of both fields by encyclopedic study as well as by friendship with artists and scientists.[64] This growth is reflected in several ways.

Most obvious is the introduction of new words such as embryon, fulminants, satellites, avulsion, fissure, meteor, compendium, tint, and panorama. More noteworthy, however, are the poet's shifts in outlook. America's contributions to the arts and sciences, for example, are given far less sweeping praise now than in 1782, a sure sign of cosmopolitanism. Such prominent figures as Franklin and Rittenhouse, Dwight and Humphreys, are subtly but surely downgraded; several strident passages claiming world leadership in both fields are eliminated; only when America becomes morally just can she bear superior cultural fruit (line 407).

Most significant is the greater richness in Barlow's subject matter. His work with Robert Fulton, for instance, is reflected in his vision of the future: canals, tunnels, dikes, ports, irrigation systems; his work in geology shows in vivid descriptions of the cosmos (lines 13–18) and of an earthquake followed by a flood (lines 271–304); artists are dealt with in detail now, their productions enthusiastically described, obviously from first-hand knowledge. Some of their best work had probably not been done when the *Vision* was written. It is interesting that not a single name in the original group of scientists and artists was omitted from *The Columbiad* (though at least one had become his enemy), and not one new name appears, not even Robert Fulton.

Clearly the poem of 1802 represents not only Barlow's individual preferences, but also "the manifold intellectual aspirations of the time in which he lived, its scientific progress, its mechanical ingenuity and daring, its wish to reject all degrading forms of faith."[65]

* * * *

If the section here studied is typical, certain conclusions can be drawn. First, although no claim of technical excellence is warranted, Barlow's revisions are more often to his credit than is generally allowed, with a few spectacularly ruinous exceptions. The hardened tradition of denying any taste or skill to Barlow is undoubtedly justified in considering the total structure of the poem — a structure twenty years older than its new passages; but that tradition is challenged by a serious analysis of specific details.

Second, as for content, although very little of value is offered which cannot also be found scattered throughout his prose, *The Columbiad* is a storehouse of high republican thought and passion. Those friends of his prose who regret that "Joel Barlow will live . . . because he was the author of" *The Columbiad*,[66] might think of it instead as a "huge political and philosophical essay in verse, the writing of which formed the one real business of Barlow's life."[67] Several sturdy passages, Whitmanesque in their warmth of spirit and loftiness of vision, have lain buried for almost two centuries — thanks largely to the malicious guffaws of Federalist critics. Their quarrel, really, was not with his rhymes but with his views.[68]

NOTES

1. The poem was planned as early as 1779.

2. The revision was begun in the 1790's.

3. Joel Barlow, *The Columbiad* (Philadelphia: C. & A. Conrad, 1807), Introduction.

4. "... as a philosophical and moral poet, we think he has talents of no ordinary value." Francis Jeffrey, *Edinburgh Review*, quoted by James Woodress, *A Yankee's Odyssey* (Philadelphia: Lippincott, 1958) 269.

5. Theodore Zunder, *The Early Days of Joel Barlow* (New Haven: Yale University Press, 1934) 231.

6. Yet he "at least planned to obtain a copy of Coleridge's Poems," according to Leon Howard, *The Connecticut Wits* (Chicago: Univ. of Chicago Press, 1943) 308.

7. Nevertheless the *London Monthly Magazine* called the revision "magnificent ... beyond anything which modern literature has to boast, except the *Paradise Lost* of Milton." (Woodress, p. 268).

8. *Ibid.*

9. Zunder, on p. 218, offers a detailed negative opinion of the *Vision*. Howard R. Sawford, in *A Comparison and Contrast of the Ideas Expressed by Joel Barlow in The Vision of Columbus and in The Columbiad*, calls the poem "an inferior performance" (p. 16) but refers to its revised version as "the object of perpetual humor" (iii).

10. Charles B. Todd, *Life and Letters of Joel Barlow* (New York: G. P. Putnam's Sons, 1886) 214.

11. Vernon L. Parrington., *Main Currents in American Thought*, I (New York: Harcourt Brace, 1930) 387.

12. Joel Barlow, *Advice to the Privileged Orders in the Several States of Europe* (Ithaca: Cornell Univ. Press, 1956) vii.

13. Howard, p. 310.

14. Woodress, p. 246.

15. Todd, p. 215.

16. Howard, p. 322.

17. Todd, p. 215.

18. Zunder (p. 218) complains of certain end-rhymes in the *Vision* that "annoy even the most sympathetic reader." Some of these are revised in *The Columbiad*, and few appear in the new passages.

19. This is so despite Barlow's adherence to the Erasmus Darwin doctrine that poetry should be visually effective.

20. Howard, p. 311.

21. *Thalaba the Destroyer* (1801) influenced the metrics of Shelley's *Queen Mab*.

22. The Churchill influence can be traced in the writings of Barlow's colleagues, particularly Trumbull. (See Howard, p. 54)

23. Woodress, p. 268.

24. Sawford, pp. 42–43.

25. *Advice*, pp. 30–31, 35.

26. Webster's brief but "severe censure" and Barlow's very long letter to Gregoire (defining his religious position) are given in full by Todd, pp. 220–33.

27. Jefferson called Barlow's defense "a sugary answer" which Gregoire did not deserve, since there was no ground for "offense" in the poem.

28. "I rejoice at the progress of Good Sense over the damnable imposture of Christian mummery." (Howard, p. 299) Barlow had rescued and published the manuscript when Paine was arrested.

29. He undertook the task at the suggestion of Jefferson, who had abandoned it due to political discretion or lack of time.

30. F. Sheldon, "The Pleiades of Connecticut," *The Atlantic Monthly*, XV (1865) 195. "One government, one reverend sire elect, and no religion, was his theory of the future of mankind."

31. Howard, pp. 324–25. But Nelson Adkins, in a private note, astutely comments: "... Howard's use of the word atheist is incorrect. A man is either an atheist or not. There is no more or less."

32. Parrington, p. 359. This reference includes the entire Yale group.

33. Zunder, pp. 140 ff.

34. *op. cit.*, p. 144.

35. *op. cit.*, p. 168.

36. *op. it.*, p. 185.

37. Sawford, p. 82.

38. *op. cit.*, p. v.

39. *Advice*, p. 32.

40. Thomas Jefferson, *The Life and Selected Writings* (New York: Modern Library, 1944) 323.

41. Sawford, p. iv.

42. This may, indeed, be a large part of its trouble as a poem. Yet Sheldon calls it "a dilution" of the *Vision*. (*Ibid.*)

43. Sawford, p. 121.

44. Woodress, p. 201. The descriptions of war are far more graphic and indignant in *The Columbiad* than in the *Vision*. See the discussion on the nature of war (*Advice*, p. 42). This quotation is from a letter to George Washington, 1798.

45. *Advice*, p. 21.

46. Woodress, p. 205. (Open letter to the citizens of the United States, 1799.)

47. Todd, p. 172. (Another part of the same letter.)

48. Howard, p. 309. In discussing the influence of E. Darwin's *Botanic Garden*, he overlooks the application of this principle in *The Columbiad.* The Golden Fleece myth is used for a contrary effect in Book Five, with reference to Kosciusko and Lafayette.

49. Woodress, p. 240. (Letter on public education in Vermont, 1798.)

50. Todd, p. 198. (Letter to Robert Fulton, 1802, including significant remarks on British admiration for President Jefferson.)

51. *Advice*, p. 44.

52. Woodress, p. 128. (*A Letter to the National Convention*, 1792.)

53. *Ibid.*, p. 131. (Same letter as above.)

54. *Advice*, p. 10.

55. Todd, p. 173. (Open letter quoted above, 1799).

56. Woodress, p. 224. (Letter to Wolcott on Louisiana Purchase).

57. Todd, pp. 135, 137. *The Columbiad's* words: "... the weeping bride,/The home, far sunder'd ..." (Book VIII, 249–50) recall his 1796 letter to Mrs. Barlow: "Many ... have wives at home ... from whom they have been much longer separated." (Woodress, p. 171)

58. *Advice*, p. 113. Bentham's utilitarian doctrines are echoed elsewhere. The Revolutionary War heroes are called a "self-devoted Band" in *The Columbiad*, Book VIII, line 67.

59. Woodress, p. 224. (Letter to Wolcott quoted above.)

60. *Advice*, p. 50.

61. Todd, pp. 208–09. (Letter to his brother-in-law, Senator Baldwin, 1800.) His prospectus for a great national educational center won the support of Jefferson and others; its various schools encompassed many fields of sciences, arts, and technology discussed in *The Columbiad*. Education is at the core of his hope for a grand universal future of peace and plenty: "Till men shall wonder.... How wars were made, how tyrants were endured." (Book VIII, lines 405–406)

62. *Advice*, p. 102.

63. Howard, p. 332. (July Fourth Oration, Washington, 1809.)

64. Todd, p. 93, discusses his association with Copley, Trumbull and West.

65. Moses C. Tyler, *Three Men of Letters* (New York: G. P. Putnam, 1895) 169–70.

66. Charles Angoff, *A Literary History of the American People*, II (New York: Knopf, 1931), 156.

67. Tyler, p. 170.

68. According to *Allibone* (p. 122) "Barlow bore these attacks without making any formal defence, yet with less dignity than became a philosopher, attributing them all to political enmity."

Appendix I

Soon after the Mexican War, Hawthorne (through a crazy fictional character) satirized Barlow and his epic machinery.[1] In 1865 Sheldon, in a totally jaundiced account of Barlow's life and work, sneered: "Few men in these degenerate days have the endurance to read the 'Columbiad' through."[2] Six years later, in a hostile biographical sketch, *Allibone* quoted a particularly damaging paragraph of the Jeffrey review and this from the *Analectic Magazine:* "His verses bear no sign of poetical inspiration; it is evident that they have all been worked by dint of resolute labour."[3] J. B. McMaster delivered a savage attack in 1893 against "the scribbler who defiled the English language by writing 'The Columbiad.' "[4]

Beers in 1920 boasted, "I am one of the few men — perhaps I am the only man now living who have read the whole of Joel Barlow's 'Columbiad.' "[5] In 1931 Angoff referred to it as "one of the most pretentious and most unreadable poems ever written in the United States ... and one of the most worthless." He considered four anniversary poems "the only ones of all his verses that are at all worth reading."[6] "Advice to a Raven in Russia" did not appear in print until seven years later; but for so thorough a scholar to overlook "Hasty Pudding" is surprising. Even more puzzling is his statement, after quoting McMaster's assault, that "No literary historian, since the time this judgment was made, has dared controvert it."[7] Tyler's masterly essay, "The Literary Strivings of Mr. Joel Barlow," did in fact appear two years after McMaster.

Tyler's treatment of *The Columbiad* stands alone as a remarkably balanced piece of criticism based on a careful, complete, and unbiased reading. While acknowledging severely all that the poem lacks (tenderness, delicacy, humor, charm, etc.), and declaring it a catastrophe as an epic, he also recognizes its didactic power and places it thematically within the great American tradition "as an involuntary expression ... of the American consciousness and even of the American national character itself, as sincere, and as unflinching as were ... the renowned state-papers of Jefferson, the constitution of 1789, and Washington's farewell address."[8]

NOTES

1. Quoted by H. A. Beers, *The Connecticut Wits and Other Essays*, p. 10.
2. F. Sheldon, "The Pleiades of Connecticut," *Atlantic Monthly*, XV (1865), 195.
3. *Allibone's Critical Dictionary of English*, I (1871) 122.
4. Quoted by Angoff, II, 161.
5. Beers, p. 10.
6. Angoff, 156, 161, 167.
7. *op. cit.*, p. 161.
8. Tyler, p. 170.

Appendix II

Following are several new passages in Book VIII of *The Columbiad:*

1) Lines 13–18, on Science:[1]

> Led forth the systems on their bright career,
> Shaped all their curves and fashion'd every sphere,
> Spaced out their suns, and round each radiant goal,
> Orb over orb, compell'd their train to roll,
> Bade heaven's own harmony their force combine,
> Taught all their host symphonious strains to join . . .

2) Lines 23–26, on Impressment of Sailors and Naval Turmoil:

> From blazing towns that scorch the purple sky,
> From houseless hordes, their smoking walls that fly,
> From the black prison ships, those groaning graves,
> From warring fleets that vex the gory waves . . .

3) Lines 43–46, on Fear of War with France:

> The drum's rude clang, the war wolf's hideous howl
> Convuls'd my nerves and agonis'd my soul,
> Untun'd the harp for all but misery's pains,
> And chased the Muse from corse-encumber'd plains.

4) Lines 509–516, on Republicanism:

> Fixt in small spheres, with safer beams to shine,
> They reach the useful and refuse the fine,
> Found, on its proper base, the social plan,
> The broad plain truths, the common sense of man,
> His obvious wants, his mutual aids discern,
> His rights familiarize, his duties learn,
> Feel moral fitness all its force dilate,
> Embrace the village and comprise the state.

5) Lines 521–524, on the New Republic:

> They watch their delegates, each law revise,
> His faults designate and its merits prize,
> Obey, but scrutinize; and let the test

Of sage experience prove and fix the best.

6) Lines 531–542, on Religion:[2]

No dark intolerance blinds the zealous throng,
No arm of power attendant on their tongue;
Vext Inquisition, with her flaming brand,
Shuns their mild march, nor dares approach the land.
The different creeds their priestly robes denote,
Their orders various and their rites remote,
Yet one their voice, their labors all combined,
Lights of the world and friends of humankind.
So the bright galaxy o'er heaven displays
Of various stars the same unbounded blaze;
Where great and small their mingling rays unite,
And earth and skies exchange the friendly light.

7) Lines 587–604, on Benjamin West:[3]

West with his own great soul the canvas warms,
Creates, inspires, impassions human forms,
Spurns critic rules, and seizing safe the heart,
Breaks down the former frightful bounds of Art;
Where ancient manners, with exclusive reign,
From half mankind withheld her fair domain.
He calls to life each patriot, chief or sage,
Garb'd in the dress and drapery of his age.
Again bold Regulus to death returns,
Again her falling Wolfe Britannia mourns;
Lahogue, Boyne, Cressy, Nevilcross demand
And gain fresh lustre from his copious hand;
His Lear stalks wild with woes, the god defies,
Insults the tempest and outstorms the skies;
Edward in arms to frowning combat moves,
Or, won to pity by the queen he loves,
Spares the devoted Six, whose deathless deed
Preserves the town his vengeance doom'd to bleed.

8) Lines 611–616, on John Singleton Copley:[4]

He bids dread Calpe cease to shake the waves,

While Elliott's arm the host of Bourbon saves;
O'er sail-wing'd batteries sinking in the flood,
Mid flames and darkness, drench'd in hostile blood,
Britannia's sons extend their generous hand
To rescue foes from death, and bear them to the land.

9) Lines 69–430:

On fame's high pinnacle their names shall shine,
Unending ages greet the group divine,   70
Whose holy hands our banners first unfurl'd,
And conquer'd freedom for the grateful world.
And you, their peers, whose steel avenged their blood,
Whose breasts with theirs our sacred rampart stood,
Illustrious relics of a thousand fields!
To you at last the foe reluctant yields.
But tho the Muse, too prodigal of praise,
Dares with the dead your living worth to raise,
Think not, my friends, the patriot's task is done,
Or Freedom's safe, because the battle's won.   80
Unnumber'd foes, far different arms that wield,
Wait the weak moment when she quits her shield,
To plunge in her bold breast the insidious dart,
Or pour keen poison round her thoughtless heart.
Perhaps they'll strive her votaries to divide,
From their own veins to draw the vital tide;
Perhaps, by cooler calculation shown,
Create materials to construct a throne,
Dazzle her guardians with the glare of state,
Corrupt with power, with borrow'd pomp inflate,   90
Bid thro the land the soft infection creep,
Whelm all her sons in one lethargic sleep,
Crush her vast empire in its brilliant birth,
And chase the goddess from the ravaged earth.[5]
The Dragon thus, that watch'd the Colchian fleece,
Foil'd the fierce warriors of wide-plundering Greece:
Warriors of matchless might and wondrous birth,
Jove's sceptred sons and demigods of earth.
High on the sacred tree, the glittering prize

Hangs o'er its guard, and fires the warriors' eyes;   100
First their hurl'd spears his spiral folds assail,
Their spears fall pointless from his flaky mail;
Onward with dauntless swords they plunge amain;
He shuns their blows, recoils his twisting train,
Darts forth his forky tongue, heaves high in air
His fiery crest, and sheds a hideous glare,
Champs, churns his poisonous juice, and hissing loud
Spouts thick the stifling tempest o'er the crowd;
Then, with one sweep of convoluted train,
Rolls back all Greece, and besoms wide the plain,   110
O'erturns the sons of gods, dispersing far
The pirate horde, and closes quick the war.
From his red jaws tremendous triumph roars,
Dark Euxine trembles to its distant shores,
Proud Jason starts, confounded in his might,
Leads back his peers, and dares no more the fight.
But the sly Priestess brings her opiate spell,
Soft charms that hush the triple hound of hell,
Bids Orpheus tune his all enchanting lyre,
And join to calm the guardian's sleepless ire.   120
Soon from the tepid ground blue vapors rise,
And sounds melodious move along the skies;
A settling tremor thro his folds extends,
His crest contracts, his rainbow neck unbends,
O'er all his hundred hoops the languor crawls,
Each curve develops, every volute falls,
His broad back flattens as he spreads the plain,
And sleep consigns him to his lifeless reign.
Flusht at the sight the pirates seize the spoil,
And ravaged Colchis rues the insidious toil.   130
      Yes! fellow freemen, sons of high renown,
Chant your loud paeans, weave your civic crown;
But know, the goddess you've so long adored,
Tho now she scabbards your avenging sword,
Calls you to vigilance, to manlier cares,
To prove in peace the men she proved in wars:
Superior task! severer test of soul!

Tis here bold virtue plays her noblest role
And merits most of praise. The warrior's name,
Tho peal'd and chimed on all the tongues of fame,   140
Sounds less harmonious to the grateful mind
Than his who fashions and improves mankind.
    And what high meed your new vocation waits!
Freedom, parturient with a hundred states,
Confides them to your hand; the nascent prize
Claims all your care, your soundest wisdom tries.
Ah nurture, temper, train your infant charge,
Its force develop and its life enlarge,
Unfold each day some adolescent grace,
Some right recognize or some duty trace;   150
Mould a fair model for the realms of earth,
Call moral nature to a second birth,
Reach, renovate the world's great social plan,
And here commence the sober sense of man.
    For lo, in other climes and elder states,
What strange inversion all his works awaits!
From age to age, on every peopled shore,
Stalks the fell Demon of despotic power,
Sweeps in his march the mounds of art away,
Blots with his breath the trembling disk of day,   160
Treads down whole nations every stride he takes,
And wraps their labors in his fiery flakes.
    As Anarch erst around his regions hurl'd
The wrecks, long crush'd, of time's anterior world;
While nature mourn'd, in wild confusion tost,
Her suns extinguisht and her systems lost;[6]
Light, life and instinct shared the dreary trance,
And gravitation fled the field of chance;
No laws remain'd of matter, motion, space;
Time lost his count, the universe his place;   170
Till Order came, in her cerulean robes,
And launch'd and rein'd the renovated globes,
Stock'd with harmonious worlds the vast inane,
Archt her new heaven and fixt her boundless reign:
So kings convulse the moral frame, the base

Of all the codes that can accord the race;
And so from their broad grasp, their deadly ban,
Tis yours to snatch this earth, to raise regenerate man.[7]
　My friends, I love your fame, I joy to raise
The high toned anthem of my country's praise;   180
To sing her victories, virtues, wisdom, weal,
Boast with loud voice the patriot pride I feel;
Warm wild I sing; and, to her failings blind,
Mislead myself, perhaps mislead mankind.
Land that I love! is this the whole we owe?
Thy pride to pamper, thy fair face to show;
Dwells there no blemish where such glories shine?
And lurks no spot in that bright sun of thine?
Hark! a dread voice, with heaven-astounding strain,[8]
Swells like a thousand thunders o'er the main,   190
Rolls and reverberates around thy hills,
And Hesper's heart with pangs paternal fills.
Thou hearst him not; tis Atlas, throned sublime,
Great brother guardian of old Afric's clime;
　High o'er his coast he rears his frowning form,
O'erlooks and calms his sky-borne fields of storm,
Flings off the clouds that round his shoulders hung,
And breaks from clogs of ice his trembling tongue;
While far thro space with rage and grief he glares,
Heaves his hoar head and shakes the heaven he bears: 200
— Son of my sire! Oh latest brightest birth
That sprang from his fair spouse, prolific earth!
Great Hesper, say what sordid ceaseless hate
Impels thee thus to mar my elder state.
Our sire assign'd thee my more glorious reign,
Secured and bounded by our laboring main;
That main (tho still my birthright name it bear)
Thy sails o'ershadow, thy brave children share;
I grant it thus; while air surrounds the ball,
Let breezes blow, let oceans roll for all.   210
But thy proud sons, a strange ungenerous race,
Enslave my tribes, and each fair world disgrace,
Provoke wide vengeance on their lawless land,

The bolt ill placed in thy forbearing hand. —
Enslave my tribes! then boast their cantons free,
Preach faith and justice, bend the sainted knee,
Invite all men their liberty to share,
Seek public peace, defy the assaults of war,
Plant, reap, consume, enjoy their fearless toil,
Tame their wild floods, to fatten still their soil,   220
Enrich all nations with their nurturing store,
And rake with venturous fluke each wondering shore. —
Enslave my tribes! what, half mankind imban,
Then read, expound, enforce the rights of man!
Prove plain and clear how nature's hand of old
Cast all men equal in her human mould!
Their fibres, feelings, reasoning powers the same,
Like wants await them, like desires inflame.
Thro former times with learned book they tread,
Revise past ages and rejudge the dead,   230
Write, speak, avenge, for ancient sufferings feel,
Impale each tyrant on their pens of steel,
Declare how freemen can a world create,
And slaves and masters ruin every state. —
Enslave my tribes! and think, with dumb disdain,
To scape this arm and prove my vengeance vain!
But look! methinks beneath my foot I ken
A few chain'd things that seem no longer men;
Thy sons perchance! whom Barbary's coast can tell
The sweets of that loved scourge they wield so well.[9]   240
Link'd in a line, beneath the driver's goad,
See how they stagger with their lifted load;
The shoulder'd rock, just wrencht from off my hill
And wet with drops their straining orbs distil,
Galls, grinds them sore, along the rampart led,
And the chain clanking counts the steps they tread.
    By night close bolted in the bagnio's gloom,
Think how they ponder on their dreadful doom,
Recall the tender sire, the weeping bride,
The home, far sunder'd by a waste of tide,   250
Brood all the ties that once endear'd them there,

But now, strung stronger, edge their keen despair.
Till here a fouler fiend arrests their pace:
Plague, with his burning breath and bloated face,
With saffron eyes that thro the dungeon shine,
And the black tumors bursting from the groin,
Stalks o'er the slave; who, cowering on the sod,
Shrinks from the Demon and invokes his God,
Sucks hot contagion with his quivering breath,
And, rack'd with rending torture, sinks in death.[10]   260
Nor shall these pangs atone the nation's crime;
Far heavier vengeance, in the march of time,
Attends them still; if still they dare debase
And hold inthrall'd the millions of my race;[11]
A vengeance that shall shake the world's deep frame,
That heaven abhors, and hell might shrink to name.
Nature, long outraged, delves the crusted sphere,
And moulds the mining mischief dark and drear;
Europa too the penal shock shall find,
The rude soul-selling monsters of mankind: 270
    Where Alps and Andes at their bases meet,
In earth's mid caves to lock their granite feet,
Heave their broad spines, expand each breathing lobe,
And with their massy members rib the globe,
Her cauldron'd floods of fire their blast prepare;
Her wallowing womb of subterranean war
Waits but the fissure that my wave shall find,
To force the foldings of the rocky rind,
Crash your curst continent, and whirl on high
The vast avulsion vaulting thro the sky,   280
Fling far the bursting fragments, scattering wide
Rocks, mountains, nations o'er the swallowing tide.
Plunging and surging with alternate sweep,
They storm the day-vault and lay bare the deep,
Toss, tumble, plough their place, then slow subside,
And swell each ocean as their bulk they hide;
Two oceans dasht in one! that climbs and roars,
And seeks in vain the exterminated shores,
The deep drencht hemisphere. Far sunk from day,

It crumbles, rolls, it churns the settling sea, 290
Turns up each prominence, heaves every side,
To pierce once more the landless length of tide:
Till some poised Pambamarca looms at last
A dim lone island in the watery waste,
Mourns all his minor mountains wreck'd and hurl'd,
Stands the sad relic of a ruin'd world,
Attests the wrath our mother kept in store,
And rues her judgments on the race she bore.
No saving Ark around him rides the main,
Nor Dove weak-wing'd her footing finds again; 300
His own bald Eagle skims alone the sky,
Darts from all points of heaven her searching eye,
Kens, thro the gloom, her ancient rock of rest,
And finds her cavern'd crag, her solitary nest.
    Thus toned the Titan his tremendous knell,
And lash'd his ocean to a loftier swell;
Earth groans responsive, and with laboring woes
Leans o'er the surge and stills the storm he throws.
    Fathers and friends, I know the boding fears
Of angry genii and of rending spheres 310
Assail not souls like yours: whom Science bright
Thro shadowy nature leads with surer light;
For whom she strips the heavens of love and hate,
Strikes from Jove's hand the brandisht bolt of fate,
Gives each effect its own indubious cause,
Divides her moral from her physic laws,
Shows where the virtues find their nurturing food,
And men their motives to be just and good.
    You scorn the Titan's threat; nor shall I strain
The powers of pathos in a task so vain 320
As Afric's wrongs to sing: for what avails
To harp for you these known familiar tales?
To tongue mute misery, and re-rack the soul
With crimes oft copied from that bloody scroll
Where Slavery pens her woes; tho tis but there
We learn the weight that mortal life can bear.
The tale might startle still the accustom'd ear,

Still shake the nerve that pumps the pearly tear,
Melt every heart, and thro the nation gain
Full many a voice to break the barbarous chain.   330
But why to sympathy for guidance fly,
(Her aids uncertain and of scant supply)
When your own self-excited sense affords
A guide more sure, and every sense accords?
Where strong self-interest, join'd with duty, lies,
Where doing right demands no sacrifice,
Where profit, pleasure, life-expanding fame
League their allurements to support the claim,
Tis safest there the impleaded cause to trust;
Men well instructed will be always just.   340
      From slavery then your rising realms to save,
Regard the master, notice not the slave;
Consult alone for freemen, and bestow
Your best, your only cares, to keep them so.
Tyrants are never free; and, small and great,
All masters must be tyrants soon or late;
So nature works; and oft the lordling knave
Turns out at once a tyrant and a slave,
Struts, cringes, bullies, begs, as courtiers must,
Makes one a god, another treads in dust,   350
Fears all alike, and filches whom he can,
But knows no equal, finds no friend in man.
      Ah! would you not be slaves, with lords and kings,
Then be not masters; there the danger springs.
The whole crude system that torments this earth,
Of rank, privation, privilege of birth,
False honor, fraud, corruption, civil jars,
The rage of conquest and the curse of wars,
Pandora's total shower, all ills combined
That erst o'erwhelm'd and still distress mankind,   360
Box'd up secure in your deliberate hand,
Wait your behest, to fix or fly this land.
      Equality of Right is nature's plan;
And following nature is the march of man.[12]
Whene'er he deviates in the least degree,

When, free himself, he would be more than free,
The baseless column, rear'd to bear his bust,
Fails as he mounts, and whelms him in the dust.
    See Rome's rude sires, with autocratic gait,
Tread down their tyrant and erect their state;   370
Their state secured, they deem it wise and brave
That every freeman should command a slave,
And, flusht with franchise of his camp and town,
Rove thro the world and hunt the nations down;
Master and man the same vile spirit gains,
Rome chains the world, and wears herself the chains.[13]
    Mark modern Europe with her feudal codes,
Serfs, villains, vassals, nobles, kings and gods,
All slaves of different grades, corrupt and curst
With high and low, for senseless rank athirst,   380
Wage endless wars; not fighting to be free,
But cujum pecus, whose base herd they'll be.[14]
    Too much of Europe, here transplanted o'er,
Nursed feudal feelings on your tented shore,
Brought sable serfs from Afric, call'd it gain,
And urged your sires to forge the fatal chain.
But now, the tents o'erturn'd, the war dogs fled,
Now fearless Freedom rears at last her head
Matcht with celestial Peace, — my friends, beware
To shade the splendors of so bright a pair;   390
Complete their triumph, fix their firm abode,
Purge all privations from your liberal code,
Restore their souls to men, give earth repose,
And save your sons from slavery, wars and woes.
    Based on its rock of Right your empire lies,
On walls of wisdom let the fabric rise;
Preserve your principles, their force unfold,
Let nations prove them and let kings behold.
EQUALITY, your first firm-grounded stand;
Then FREE ELECTION; then your FEDERAL BAND;   400
This holy Triad should forever shine
The great compendium of all rights divine,
Creed of all schools, whence youths by millions draw

Their themes of right, their decalogues of law;
Till men shall wonder (in these codes inured)
How wars were made, how tyrants were endured.
　　Then shall your works of art superior rise,
Your fruits perfume a larger length of skies,
Canals careering climb your sunbright hills,
Vein the green slopes and strow their nurturing rills,　　410
Thro tunnel'd heights and sundering ridges glide,
Rob the rich west of half Kenhawa's tide,
Mix your wide climates, all their stores confound,
And plant new ports in every midland mound.[15]
Your lawless Mississippi, now who slimes
And drowns and desolates his waste of climes,
Ribb'd with your dikes, his torrent shall restrain,
And ask your leave to travel to the main;
Won from his wave while rising cantons smile,
Rear their glad nations and reward their toil.　　420
　　Thus Nile's proud flood to human hands of yore
Raised and resign'd his tide-created shore,
Call'd from his Ethiop hills their hardy swains,
And waved their harvests o'er his newborn plains;
Earth's richest realm from his tamed current sprung;
There nascent science toned her infant tongue,
Taught the young arts their tender force to try,
To state the seasons and unfold the sky;
Till o'er the world extended and refined,
They rule the destinies of humankind.　　430
　　Now had Columbus well enjoy'd the sight
Of armies vanquisht and of fleets in flight,
From all Hesperia's heaven the darkness flown,
And colon crowds to sovereign sages grown.[16]

NOTES

1. This passage, and an extended one beginning on line 271, illustrate Barlow's
fascination with science. See Todd, p. 201, on his mineral collection. According to
Howard (p. 313), "Barlow seems to have had a sufficient grasp of the principles of
modern geology to make his account of the creation much more up to date than

even the one given by Erasmus Darwin." Howard points out that the poet's "exten-
sive interest in . . . astronomy and physics" is reflected in his substitution of contem-
porary theory for "the biblical version" of creation "used in the *Vision of Colum-
bus.*"

2. This passage not only challenges Catholicism but may also carry a veiled
comment on the political "Inquisition" his country had just experienced under the
Alien and Sedition Laws, whose chief targets had been Jeffersonians of Barlow's
color. The laudatory view of his own land as a superior society in 1802 underscores
the absence of such praise for France, which had won his accolades in the prose
published a decade back, prior to the Reign of Terror.

3. Robert Fulton, Barlow's friend and collaborator, had studied with West.
After a flare-up between them, the poet had acted as mediator. See Todd, p. 203.

4. Todd (p. 193) includes a long, detailed letter from Barlow to Fulton on a
Copley painting.

5. This salvo is aimed at those Barlow perceives as betrayers of the Revolution,
including the military-minded Society of the Cincinnati and others of royalist orien-
tation who wanted Washington to be crowned.

6. Barlow discusses Anarchy in *Advice to the Privileged Orders*, pp. 18–19.

7. This passage also reflects Barlow's mastery of scientific knowledge; here he
uses natural occurrences as an analogy to political upheaval. The condemnation of
kingship (lines 175–178) is a far cry from his grovelling letter to Louis XVI on the
1782 epic. He calls his *Vision of Columbus* ". . . in part . . . the offspring of these
reflections which your conduct has taught me to make. With reverence and grati-
tude I embrace your Majesty's permission to claim for it your royal protection."
(Zunder, p. 186.) The implied call for a world revolution (lines 177–178) is reminis-
cent of his prophecy, "a general revolution is at hand, whose progress is irresistible"
(*Advice*, introduction, p. 10)

8. Although Barlow was by no means alone in his poetic assault on slavery (see,
for example, Freneau's "To Sir Toby," a passage in Timothy Dwight's *Greenfield
Hill* and another in Cowper's "The Task") nothing in his day compares in magni-
tude and thoughtfulness to this remarkable protest and warning (lines 189–394).

9. Barlow's superlative achievement as diplomat was the release of many U.S.
citizens held captive on the Barbary Coast while he was consul in Algiers. His vivid
description of their incarceration is a valuable eye-witness account.

10. This haunting picture of the plague is corroborated in his letters from
Algiers (Todd, pp. 132–33).

11. It is not unlikely that, in composing these lines, Barlow was inspired by the
daring slave rebellion of 1800 led by Gabriel Prosser.

12. This confident declaration is an expression of French necessitarianism, dis-
cussed by Howard (pp. 313–14). There is much more of the same in Book IX.

13. Such allusions — to Rome, the Jews, the Incas, the Egyptians, the Normans,
and the Saxons — are a result of his encyclopedic reading. (See *Advice*, p. 20)

14. Barlow's intensive study of feudalism is also reflected in *Advice*, Chapter
One.

15. With Robert Fulton, Barlow had projected a work in four books: *The Canal:*

A Poem on the Application of Physical Science to Political Economy. (Woodress, 215–16)

16. In 1805 the infant U.S. Navy forced Tripoli to make peace. At this moment the American empire was pushing westward; like Whitman later, Barlow ignored the mistreatment of the natives.

Appendix III

Since the early '60s, when this paper was written, there has been a remarkable upsurge of critical attention to Barlow, and the two versions of his epic in particular. I should like to indicate at least in part the scope and variety of publications produced in recent years:

I. Volumes

William C. Dowling, *Poetry and Ideology in Revolutionary Connecticut* (Athens: Univ. of Georgia Press, 1990)

To make sense of the Connecticut Wits, Dowling reads them as conscious inheritors of Pope and Swift, warring against a degraded social and economic order and urging for the new republic a return to the ideals of the classical "Golden Age." He shows how, imbibing Europe's revolutionary ideas, Barlow broke from the other "Wits" to take the bold stance of demystifier. In a thorough reading of *The Columbiad* he finds the poet challenging all ideologies, including those he had previously promulgated. He now sees Federalism, for example, as "an American variant of the outworn ideologies of the European ancien régime." He rejects the cyclical theory of history, the grim Augustinian view of existence, in favor of a progressive history leading to a "commonwealth of man." He dares to arrive at a materialistic vision of mankind alone in a godless universe, perfectable because of an innate morality. He unmasks as myth Original Sin and the Fall, and clears the decks for a free future. But he hymns a new ideology — that of progress, of commerce, of the emerging capitalism which was to become just one more means by which people "oppress one another and desecrate the world." Approaching Barlow on his own terms rather than on 19th or 20th century expectations of what poetry should be, Dowling probes deeply and fruitfully. Surprisingly, most references to *The Vision of Columbus* show points of agreement with the revised work, which critics wrongly see as a "doctrinal reworking" rather than as a strenuous effort to unmask "the illusory appearances thrown up by ideology" to hide "the grim world of economic and power relations."

II. Articles in Books

Lewis Leary, "Joel Barlow: the Man of Letters as Citizen," in *The Humanist as Citizen*, eds. John Agresto and Peter Riesenberg, National Humanities Center (Univ. of North Carolina Press, 1981) 37–56.

Part One of this festschrift volume groups Socrates, Newton, Barlow and Lincoln; but Leary claims no excellence for his chosen subject: "the American ... revolution produced" no "distinguished man of letters" (such as Milton). Seldom listening to his "inner voice," Barlow "gave his day what in his judgment his day most needed." Others were saying much the same — "he sang in chorus" and "is not a person to return to." Like Woodress (1958) Leary feels that "Barlow would have been a major poet" if *The Columbiad* had been "livened with passion" and Reason had been "put aside as in 'Advice to a Raven in Russia,'" composed a month before his death. Even *The Vision of Columbus* fares better with Leary, as it had with Leon Howard (1943), who claims that in the later version he "had lost the impulse of the poet and become a scholar," positioning himself "outside the poem, so that the ardent voice of the younger man is muted." Most valuable is Leary's unswerving focus on Enlightenment religion and Barlow as its advocate even in *The Vision of Columbus*, whose tributes to Voltaire must have appalled Barlow's mentor Timothy Dwight, and whose celebration of Manco Capac's "benevolent and pacific" Inca religion is a far cry from Dwight's Old Testament blood and thunder in The *Conquest of Canaan* (1785). Excerpts from all the works, both prose and verse, underscore Barlow's religious consistency, with the sun as prime symbol, providing even "The Hasty Pudding" with a new dimension.

Charlotte Kretzoi, "Puzzled Americans: Attempts at an American National Epic Poem," in *The Origins and Originality of American Culture* (Budapest: Akademiai Kiado, 1984) 142–44, 145, 148

Kretzoi's focus is on Barlow, Longfellow (*Hiawatha*), and Benét (*John Brown's Body*). The notes show she dealt directly only with the Benét poem. Her brief study of Barlow, and her citations, depend entirely on literary historians Pattee (1935), Pearce (1961), Spiller (1987) and Parrington (1954). There is nothing new. She wrongly declares "*The Columbiad* was obviously considered by his contemporaries as the first American national epic poem." Without reading it, she finds that "not much can be said in favor of Barlow's epic.... The poem is heavy and monotonous ... Barlow was unable to find a new, more elastic form to express the exciting experiment of creating a new nation." Still, it is not "a complete failure as a national epic. *The Columbiad* moved on an adequately magnificent plane and its scope was great." Simplistically ignoring such factors as its radicalism (while citing Noah Webster's hatred of its "atheistical principles") and an ever-hardening tradition of mockery by influential critics who shunned the poem itself but merely echoed each other, she wrongly concludes: "The reason why it could not gain popularity as an American classic is entirely due to its artistic deficiencies."

Carla Mulford, "Radicalism in Joel Barlow's *The Conspiracy of Kings* (1792)," in *Deism, Masonry, and the Enlightenment*, J. A. Leo Lemay, ed. (Newark, Del.: Univ. of Delaware Press, 1987) 137–57.

The Columbiad is ignored except for a passing endnote reference, and *The Vision of Columbus* is discussed only once, as evidence of the poet's early interest in comparative religion and mythology (a religious system "renders political institutions sacred," giving them "immediate energy and duration.") But this study shows how far from *The Vision* Barlow had traveled by 1792 on his way to *The Columbiad*, how high he stood in the ranks of Europe's revolutionary thinkers. Already in *The Conspiracy* (misjudged as "utterly lifeless" in the *Dictionary of Literary Biography*) Barlow replaces Christ with "a religion of man's worship of man's own ability." The author finds that Barlow here fulfills Diderot's poetic aesthetic, offering in verse that is emblematic and suggestive rather than analytical and discursive the revolutionary message that the people have the power to reinvent their world. Here is the antecedent to Emerson, Thoreau and Whitman. Rather than being "utterly lifeless," *The Conspiracy* "utters life." This essay readies us for the even more egregiously misjudged *Columbiad.*

John McWilliams, "The Epic in the Nineteenth Century," in *The Columbia History of American Poetry*, Jay Parini, ed. (New York: Columbia Univ. Press, 1993) 34, 37–41, 61.

McWilliams traces the mockery of *The Columbiad* by critics who probably hadn't read it, from Poe to Benét, and himself refers to it as "verse, not poetry," and "relentless bombast." But in content he gives it its due, as "thoughtful and innovative," and claims that Barlow's "visionary affirmation … later later shared by Whitman, may contain the most practicable path of man's survival yet devised." He shows that while *The Vision of Columbus* narrates incidents, *The Columbiad* is a gigantic expansion of the Prospect Poem, unfolding "the progressive future of the entire Western world."

III. Articles in Journals

Alice P. Kenney, "America Discovers Columbus: Biography as Epic, Drama, History." *Biography*, IV, 1 (Winter, 1981) 45–65.

The developing myth of Columbus, from Robertson (1777) to Samuel Eliot Morison (1942), is traced, beginning with Barlow's Robertson-inspired *Vision of Columbus*, begun in the dark days of 1779 "to inspire his disheartened countrymen" to keep struggling for independence. Though extremely concise, Kenney's summary of *The Columbiad*, and later references, demonstrates a conscientious reading of the entire poem, observing astutely: "He … passed beyond the figure of the discoverer to make America itself the real hero of his epic, though neither his talents nor the resources of poetic convention available to him permitted him to do this directly." She explains that by "starting with Columbus' discovery, Barlow tried to create for the new nation a cultural tradition distinct from that of England." However, she makes no effort to deal with the "major revisions" between the 1786 publication that "went through four editions" and the 1807 version that was either hated or ignored, and never sold.

John Bidwell, "The Publication of Joel Barlow's Columbiad," *Proceedings of the American Antiquarian Society*, XCIII, 2 (1984) 337–80.

The focus is not on the poem but on how Barlow financed the book, saw it through the press, and distributed it. The artistic involvement of Fulton, Fuseli, etc., is thoroughly detailed (Blake was once thought to be involved as well). How he actually did the remaking of *The Vision* is of some interest in comparing the two works (340–42). We learn that for an 1806 British essay on Barlow, the preview chosen from the poem was the fiery Book VIII denunciation of slavery, and that he continued revising "until the last moment." A few fine examples are given (346) of improved Book V lines. Francis Jeffrey, the most notorious of all "poet-killers" (Wordsworth, Coleridge, Byron, Shelley, Keats, etc.), "found kind things to say about the poem ... but nothing whatever to justify its epic pretentions." A stinging 1811 comment in the *Alexandria Gazette* demonstrates the burning political malice at the core of anti-*Columbiad* "opinion." Barlow is condemned as a dangerous Francophile, a known atheist, who was "induced ... to supply the poetical deficiencies of his *Columbiad* by the richness of paper and elegance of type and engravings, greatly ... to the injury of his private purse."

Gregg Canfield, "Joel Barlow's Dialectic of Progress," *Early American Literature*, XXI (1986) 131–43.

Taking off from Emory Elliott's (1982) suggestion that "contradictions and inconsistencies make.... *The Vision of Columbus* interesting in spite of itself," Canfield notes similar contradictions in two political pamphlets preceding *The Columbiad*, after his conversion "from Calvinism to Deism and from Federalist conservatism to Jeffersonian progressivism." While ignoring *The Columbiad*, this approach illuminates the epic, seeing Barlow as "aggressively" indulging "in paradox rather than" being "a victim of changing opinions." He counters Griffiths' (1975–76) complaint that the poet was "not a profound nor even very original thinker," pointing out that Barlow "wrote political manifestos, not philosophy, and ... concerned himself more with stimulating political action than with writing the truth." Canfield sees his originality "in his leaps over conventional dilemmas using conventional thought," celebrating (like Locke) the possibility of social progress through education: man is not "fallen" by nature but is perfectable, as is society. Barlow sees "human nature, human society and human history in terms of progressive, synthetic improvements engendered by the competition of opposites" (such as "good" and "evil").

James McCord, "West of Atlantis: William Blake's Unromantic View of the American War," *The Centennial Review*, XXX, 3 (Summer 1986) 383–99.

A glimpse at *The Vision of Columbus* (and Freneau's poems of the American Revolution) as inspirations for Blake's *America*, stressing the fear they shared that he who triumphs over tyranny may become a tyrant in his turn. Only Book IV of *The Vision* is specifically referred to and very briefly cited.

Terence Martin, "Three *Columbiads*, Three Visions of the Future," *Early American Literature*, XXVII (1992) 128–33.

Obviously motivated by the cinquecentennial, Martin brings together three Columbus epic-poets: a Frenchwoman (1756), a Britisher (1798) and Barlow (1787, 1807). Despite his facilely snide comments about all three, Martin's disinterment of DuBoccage and Rev. Moore is admirable. A conscientious reading allows him to find the essence of each poem, present telling excerpts, and compare them. The others see Columbus' discovery as an adventure that energized an ongoing history; Barlow sees it as an event that fostered a national beginning. His "geographical and political panoramas are ... grander in conception and scope." Martin also contrasts *The Vision of Columbus* and *The Columbiad*, citing Elliott's view: "Less confident" in the later poem, "caught between changing religious assumptions and Enlightenment attitudes, Barlow 'seems obsessed with asserting a collective national identity.'" Martin concludes that the maturing poet "with studied determination salutes the advent of republican institutions" in history — transforming Columbus into "the aspirations of the world he discovered." Assured "that he will be fulfilled by history," the great explorer "is subsumed by his vision, at once the occasion, the receptor, and the embodiment of Barlow's faith in the developing United States."

Among other recent volumes that deal seriously with Barlow, some of which are cited in the works examined above, are E. L. Tuveson's *Redeemer Nation: The Idea of America's Millennial Role* (Univ. of Chicago Press, 1968), Henry F. May's *The Enlightenment in America* (Oxford Univ. Press, 1976), Cecilia Tichi's *New World, New Earth: Environmental Reform in American Literature from the Puritans Through Whitman* (Yale Univ. Press, 1979), Mason I. Lowance's *The Language of Canaan: Metaphor and Symbol in New England from the Puritans to the Transcendentalists* (Harvard Univ. Press, 1980), Emory Elliott's *Revolutionary Writers: Literature and Authority in the New Republic, 1725–1810* (Oxford Univ. Press, 1992), and Ruth Bloch's *Visionary Republic: Millennial Themes in American Thought, 1756–1800* (Cambridge Univ. Press, 1985). Stuart Curran, in *Poetic Form and British Romanticism* (Oxford Univ. Press, 1986), suggests that Barlow developed an aesthetic of epic poetry from Hayley's *Essay on Epic Poetry,* and that *The Vision of Columbus* and *The Columbiad* influenced Shelley in writing *Queen Mab.*

I should also mention two of the more significant articles dealing with one or both of the Barlow poems. Gregg Canfield (see comments above) disputes John Griffiths' 1975–76 essay in *Early American Literature* X, "*The Columbiad* and *Greenfield Hill:* History, Poetry and Ideology in the Late Eighteenth Century." In the same journal, XIII, 1978, Robert D. Richardson, Jr., reassesses Barlow's literary and ideological impulses, indcating his avant-garde religious, mythological and political motifs ("The Enlightenment View of Myth and Joel Barlow's *Vision of Columbus*")

The Greek Independence War
in American Poetry

An Introductory Note: parts of this essay were presented at the 9th Mediterranean Institute, held in Athens. Afterward a Greek scholar informed me that a volume on the same topic had been published in Thessaloniki in 1971,[1] but that my approach and much of my content were altogether different. Had I known that such a work already existed, I would not have undertaken this exploration. But I am glad that I did not know, since at least half of my material, including large anthologized poems by several prominent poets, is untouched by Professors Raizis and Papas, and — what both studies consider — gains, I trust, from a second point of view. I have therefore decided to let my 1983 essay stand without a single change (except for the addition of Lunt's "The Grave of Byron" and several footnotes).]

It is not surprising that by the close of the turbulent 19th century Greece's independence war had shrunk to one full poem and a few retrospective references in the anthologies. Now, almost another century later, only that same poem, Halleck's "Marco Bozzaris," and a single brief passage in Whittier's "Snowbound," give occasional evidence of the response by American poets to that dramatic twelve-year conflict.

One assumes that there must have been more. In the first place, the generation that had fought for American independence was still alive and aware of itself as the inspirer of other subjugated nations throughout Europe and Spanish America. Second, for the poets emerging from Harvard, Yale and Princeton, steeped in the glories of Hellenic culture and history, Greece held a unique place in heart and mind. Third, the overpowering influence of Byron, as poet and man, reached its crescendo with his death at Missolonghi. Fourth, a strong Christian strain pervaded American life and thought, praised in poets, often insisted upon by the moralistic arbiters of taste; this crusading spirit must have been ignited by the one element that set Greece apart from Spain, Italy, Mexico and Brazil: hers was a struggle of oppressed Christians against Moslem tyranny.

A definitive investigation, while desirable, would be close to impossible 160 years later. Many publications in which the instant verse responses appeared have vanished or are inaccessible. Some poets of stature, whose collected works later achieved publication, omitted (probably as tendentious or shrill) the political outbursts of their earlier days; while the anthologists, favoring innocuous verses on religion, nature, and domestic sentiment, included only a handful on such violent themes as the Greek revolution. Still, it is possible without too much trouble to discover a fair-sized cluster of poetic responses long neglected.

The values of even a modest study are manifold. First, it can corroborate or challenge the assumptions stated above. Then too, it can serve as an interesting comparison with the poetry on Greek independence then being produced throughout Europe, including Greece. Further, it can be considered side by side with such bodies of literature as the poetic response 110 years later to Spain's struggle against Franco and his Axis allies. It can also illuminate the issues and incidents of an important but hazily remembered moment in history. In addition, it can introduce us to poets long submerged, and perhaps reward us with the discovery of one or more whose oblivion is unjustified, whose art is on a par with that of Halleck, at least, and whose voices still deserve to be heard. Finally, it allows us to deal with the problems of ethics and aesthetics — why, for example, poets such as Longfellow, whose commitment to a free Greece is evident in their actions, letters and journals, refused to deal with the subject in their poems, while others, such as Percival, seemed to leap at the opportunity, as if repeated references to Thermopylae and Marathon would give their verses the grandeur toward which they strove.

We will examine first some poets little known even in their own day but well-enough regarded to be anthologized. If they produced no literary gems inspired by the struggle, we can hope at least to determine from them what approaches were recurrent.

On Washington's birthday, February 22, 1825, fifty years after Lexington and Concord, Ebenezer Bailey's prize ode, "The Triumph of Liberty,"[2] was recited at the Boston Theatre. An 1817 Yale graduate and now principal of the Boston Young Ladies' High School, Bailey introduced several major themes. First, he linked the Greek war with the "Spirit of Freedom" abroad throughout the planet, including "the Andes' fronts of snow" where "victorious Bolivar" must "faint not — in the war/Waged for the liberty of nations!" Second, he linked it with the American Revolution: "Ye hail the name of Washington; pursue/The path of glory he has mark'd for you." Third, he linked the new yearning for freedom with that of the past:

> Those sons have broke
> Their fetters, — spurn the slavish yoke,
> And emulate their fathers' glory . . .
> The clash of arms rings in the air,
> As erst it rung at Marathon . . .

He also raised a double note of condemnation: against the Greeks themselves, "should their recreant limbs submit once more" (a realistic fear in 1825), and against the betrayal of the Greek cause by the leaders of the "unholy alliance" — Russia, Britain, and especially Austria, "Whose sacrilegious leagues have twined/Oppression's links around" the rebel provinces — the very same "unholy alliance" Byron had condemned since the Congress of Vienna. "When shall another Byron sing and bleed/For you!" he asks Greece, a year after the poet's death at Missolonghi. A final theme, barely touched at here, is the religious aspect of the struggle. To the Turks Bailey merely refers cleverly as the waning "Crescent," while rebuking the "christian kings and potentates" who (he implies) betrayed Christian Greece on behalf of Moslem tyranny.

Katherine A. Ware's patriotic odes caused a stir in the mid-'20's. Her "Greece"[3] expands Bailey's tribute to the newly dead poet in a 12-line passage: "Immortal Byron! thou, whose courage planned/The rescue of that subjugated land . . ." Unlike Bailey, she characterizes the Moslems as "barbarous bands" against which the poet, had he lived, would have "bid the Christian cross triumphant wave." With the same religious emphasis she adds a new theme, that of Turkish cruelty: "Where Scio's isle blushes with Christian gore,/And recreant fiends still yell around her shore." Finally, there is an implied appeal to the world to assist the rebellion. Jove himself "bids creation save/Minerva's 'first born,' from a barbarous wave."

George Washington Doan's "Thermopylae"[4] includes no directly modern references, but the time and spirit are right as an invocation to the Greeks' heroic ancestors. The intentions of George Hill, however, are unmistakable.[5] In "The Might of Greece," from "The Ruins of Athens," he brings "The might of Greece" solidly into the 19th century; its story is "a fire /Unquench'd, unquenchable"; the tone of its "free mountain-air" is now "Shaking earth's tyrant race through every distant zone!"; its triumph "shall be/Thrones, dungeons swept away ..." Although Hill's sonnet "Liberty" pales beside Wordsworth's "Toussaint" and Byron's "Chillon," it makes a strong statement on the world-wide implications of the Greek upsurge: "There is a spirit working in the world ..." And the Muses are declared viable in their home-land again:

> By Delphi's fountain-cave, that ancient choir
> Resume their song; the Greek astonish'd hears,
> And the old altar of his worship rears ...

At 21, James G. Brooks, perhaps the most talented of this now unknown group, wrote "Greece — 1822."[6] Anthologist Griswold's serious blunder in titling it "Greece — 1832" utterly destroys the historic value of the poem as a denunciation of cowardly Greeks betraying the heroic Greeks led by Ypsilanti in 1821. Recalling "the gallant Spartan few" who "Bled at Thermopylae," he fiercely calls Greece "Land of dead heroes! living slaves!" The land of Leuctra and Marathon is now "Despised — degraded in the dust!" Like Bailey he exhorts Greece to awake from its trance, to follow "A gallant chief," Ypsilanti no doubt; but "in vain the hero calls ... /His banner ... falls/In ruin, Freedom's battle-shroud." He accuses the modern Greeks of lacking soul; 1821 has left only "a meteor's glare." The land of glory is "blighted, lost, degraded."[7]

The final poet, George Lunt, illustrates a typical scholarly problem. A Cambridge graduate in 1824, he published two years later *The Grave of Byron and Other Poems*. According to Griswold (1852) he was then nineteen. Claiming "considerable merit" for the title poem, Griswold concurs with his fellow-anthologist Samuel Kettell, who wrote in 1829: "He has evidently high powers as a poet."[8]

Unfortunately, the sections Kettell excerpted are little more than echoes of *Childe Harold;* without getting hold of the rare volume, it is impossible to guess whether Byron's involvement with Greece is mentioned in the poem, and whether any pieces about the Greek struggle appear in the book. The excerpts before us include only an occasional line that may apply (i.e., "Free as the martyr's last prayer when to die/Is glorious gain . . .")[9]

[I have recently had the good fortune to unearth a microfilm of Lunt's 1826 volume (published in Boston by Hilliard, Metcalf & Co.). The small group of accompanying lyrics are thoroughly Byronesque — in his earliest, most sentimental vein; and none of them refer to Greece. But the title-poem, with its apt motto from *Childe Harold,* deserves serious attention not only as a prodigious youthful effort, but because its central segment is a lofty and impassioned response to the war then raging. An elegy of almost 900 lines, in Spenserians except for two songs, "The Grave of Byron," though somewhat overblown, certainly surpasses John Neal in art as well as length.

Bits of the segment are predictable: the "half decayed" ruins are "Memorialists of Freedom" that offer "some fading trace/Of all that Athens, Thebes, and Sparta was/Ere tyrants gave to sons of Grecian fathers laws." The cause is Christianity:

> Then did they hurl the crescent from on high,
> And where the infidel insulting trod,
> Planted the flaming red-cross banner of our God.

But the long passage is otherwise remarkably free of anti-Moslem rhetoric, and it is a Greek fighter, not Lunt, who refers to the Turks as "dastards." The overriding purpose of the segment is to depict the "poet-hero's" historic power, in death as in life, to inspire revolutionary fervor among the Greeks.]

We turn next to five poets now generally ignored but who were considered major figures in the 1820's and for several decades beyond.[10]

Immensely popular, Lydia Huntley Sigourney was known as "the sweet singer of Hartford." But there is nothing sweet about her "Missolonghi";[11] it is in fact as bloody a portrayal of the events and as racist a war-cry as her most unsophisticated followers could hope for. The poem's loftier elements include allusions to the Greek past ("Sons of Miltiades, arise! . . . Rise, soul of Pindar!") and some touching vignettes of heroism by the families of the fallen: "Aged men" who "haste to the battle fray," widows who "mount the tower," "little sons" who "lift their martyr'd father's lance," and maidens who dare "The iron strife." Although it was not at Missolonghi that Marco Bozzaris fell in 1823, his brave last words are recalled, flowing "Sadly sweet from those lips of rose." Oddly, there is no mention of Byron, who died there a year later.

Unlike those words of Bozzaris, the rhetoric of Mrs. Sigourney is overwhelmingly violent. "By red Scio's wrongs and groans,/By Ipsara's unburied bones," she demands vengeance against the foe. But *her* crusade has nothing to do with freedom from foreign oppression; it is based utterly on religious and racial difference. "Ibraham's host" are "wild . . . swarthy . . . turban'd . . . accursed." They "thirst for blood." Elatedly their "jewell'd Sultan" counts "The blood-pools around" Missolonghi's "ruin'd wall." The Turk is an "infidel," Mahomet "a false prophet," while leading the Greek cause is the "God of Christians." Like Ebenezer Bailey, she denounces Greece's so-called Christian "sister nations" who "with hearts of stone/ . . . close the leaden eye" to Greece's agony, letting her stand "alone/In the dire crusade." And the anti-swarthy poem ends in a way that must have pleased the most bigoted and self-righteous elements of New England Puritanism:

> Go! — angel-strengthen'd to the field of blood,
> Raise thy white arm, — unbind thy wreathed hair,
> And God's dread name upon thy breastplate wear,
> Stand in *His might*, till the pure cross arise
> O'er the proud minaret, and woo propitious skies.

Mrs. Sigourney was very well advised to omit "Missolonghi" from her *Poetical Works* (London, 1850); it is a poem which underscores her lack of stature, and it helps us to appreciate the virtue of "Marco Bozzaris,"[12] the sole surviving American poem on the Greek war, and one of the two poems on which Fitz-Greene Halleck's reputation has rested for 160 years.

Bozzaris fell in 1823. The piece appeared in Bryant's *New York Review* in 1825. Halleck must have toiled long and hard to make his poem worthy of its subject. Rather than relieve himself of all his Greek impulses, thereby creating a misdirected hodgepodge, he chose to relate one heroic moment so vividly that the reader experiences it, and to extol it so lyrically that it achieves the level of high elegy. At midnight the Turks dream of crushing Greece; their dream is shattered by a small band under Bozzaris, conscious of their ancestors' stand against mighty Persia. He falls victorious; it is a death welcome to him and cherished by those who love him most. For he is "... Freedom's now, and Fame's:/One of the few, immortal names,/That were not born to die."

There is one religious reference. Bozzaris exhorts his men: "Strike — for the green graves of your sires;/God and your native land!" At this "They piled the ground with Moslem slain." But the passage does not reverberate with strident adjectives, and is embedded within a lofty context of heroic action. To appreciate the degree of restraint Halleck imposed upon himself for the sake of artistic integrity, one need merely look at the ninth stanza of "Alnwick Castle," the title poem of his first collection (1827).[13] Here he rages at Britain in particular, and Christian Europe in toto, for betraying Greece:

> ... to-day the turbaned Turk ...
> Is England's friend and fast ally;
> The Moslem tramples on the Greek,
> And on the Cross and altar-stone,
> And Christendom looks tamely on,
> And hears the Christian maiden shriek,
> And sees the Christian father die;
> And not a sabre-blow is given
> For Greece and fame, for faith and heaven,
> By Europe's craven chivalry.

Only a name now, John Neal in the 1820's was held in high international esteem. From 1823 to 1827 he lived in England, publishing novels and contributing to the best journals. "Among the most remarkable of our writers, whether of poetry or prose," he was, according to anthologist Kettell,[14] "gifted with an almost magical facility of literary composition. What to others is a work of careful study, and severe labor, is to him a pastime ... thrown off with a rapidity that almost surpasses belief." He produced his "best novel," *Seventy-Six,* at "odd hours . . . in less than a month."

That characteristic, of which he was obviously as proud as Kettell was in awe, is astoundingly demonstrated in a 352–line elegy, "The Sleeper: Written the Day After the Funeral of Byron."[15] Unfortunately, "The Sleeper" is more remarkable for the facility of its creation and the general elegiac effect it manages to sustain than for the richness of individual lines or passages. Perhaps it deserves to be known as the most ambitious elegy attempted by an American poet up to that time and until the death of Lincoln. [This was written before I found George Lunt's "Grave of Byron."] Though longwinded, it is graced by simplicity, dignity and musicality; perhaps, as Neal believed of all his revisions, the lament for his beloved[16] Byron would have lost its spontaneity and warmth had he taken scalpel or shears to it.

The references to the Greek war are no less facile, predictable, and forgettable, than the poem's phrasing. The "warrior-poet" resembles the "Grecians of the past, — /To whom the battle and the chase . . . /Were pastime and repose. . .," the young Spartan who "set/His foot — and met/The Persian in array . . ." Like the heroes of old, Neal's poet chose "to die/In martyrdom to Liberty . . ." But the cause is larger than Greece: Byron was called "to break/The thraldom of the nations . . ." and will be honored wherever "There's freedom in the air . . ." Nor does Neal avoid the usual slurs against "The Moslem foe . . . The heathen. . . ." One can imagine Byron's comment if Neal's cry could indeed have roused him from death: "Awake! Strike down the infidel. . . ." Twenty-four years later, in "A Fable for Critics," Lowell gives John Neal six times as many lines as Poe; but the latter is judged three-fifths genius, whereas Neal is dismissed as a man of talent who might have become a poet if he had worked at it rather than believe that he was one already. The Byron elegy, if nothing else, demonstrates Lowell's astuteness.[17]

Lowell bypassed James G. Percival, whose reputation during the Greek war was matched only by Bryant's. A generation later Griswold still spotlighted his work, finding in him the "natural qualities of a great poet . . . a brilliant imagination, remarkable command of language, and an exhaustless fountain of ideas . . . and his genius is versatile."[18] Leader of an establishment that would never have allowed Whitman, Melville, or Emily Dickinson a hearing, and whose British counterparts blocked Browning's reputation till the 1860's, Griswold was right at least in pointing to Percival's 1827 volume as a primary expression of America's enthusiasm for the Greek revolution. But, interestingly enough, the only Greek poem he anthologizes, "Liberty to Athens,"[19] is omitted by Percival from his two-volume *Poetical Works* (Boston, 1859). It is well-wrought, but no more or less significant in content than the extraordinarily large number of Percival poems reprinted in 1859,[20] beginning with "Ode on the Emancipation of Greece," which — along with odes on the emancipation of Spain and South America — had been in his first volume (1821) and now appeared in a section called "Juvenile Poems."

That early ode recalled Persia and Marathon, Xerxes and Sparta; the same allusions, along with Thermopylae and Leuctra, appear in "The Senate of Callimachi." We return to "the Persian tents" in "The Sunian Pallas," while "The Greek Mountaineers" and "Liberty to Athens" introduce Harmodius, "hero of the Panathenian games," who wreathed his "avenging sword" in his myrtle. Marathon and Bozzaris are linked in "The Last Song of the Greek Patriot," which celebrates "The heart that holds the Spartan fire...."

Most of the other themes found in the responses of the time are also touched upon by Percival. There are exhortations to the oppressed: "Is there no hand/To grasp the avenging sword?" ("Greece, From Mount Helicon"); execrations against the "heathen Turk" ("The Last Song of the Greek Patriot"); praise of the responding heroes: "Blest be the sword each Maynote draws/To lop away his bonds and shame" ("The Senate of Callimachi"); condemnation of "a cold and coward world" that leaves Greece "to work" its "way alone" ("The Sunian Pallas"); insistence that the struggle is international: "Freedom's *last, best* hope is here!" ("Hellas"); and exultation at independence achieved:

> 'Tis a nation's cry of joy, —
> None to ravage and destroy, —
> Not a foreign foot is found
> On our consecrated ground.   ("Grecian Liberty")

A few elements are less familiar. In several poems Percival names

Greece's earlier oppressors, "Goth and Frank," along with the Turk; elsewhere he begs the factions: "Your ancient wrongs and feuds forget . . . Unite! unite!" ("The Senate of Callimachi") and in an 1827 "Greek Appeal to America" he appeals for assistance from the "chosen land":

> Open wide thy helping hand, —
> Pour thy corn and wine, like sand . . .
> Quick, before the flame expire, —
> Feed, O, feed the holy fire!

This poem probably succeeded in raising funds for Greece. That Percival adopted the stanza form and rhetoric of Burns' beloved battle-cry, "Scots, Wha Hae," must have added to its impact. Today we can admire the poet for his ardor, his noble stance, and his imitative skill, while recognizing that here, as in the other ten poems inspired by the Greek war (as also in the 4,000 lines of his *Prometheus*, whose Spenserians once dazzled critics but can now be seen as a creditable copy of *Childe Harold*), he fails to achieve a voice of his own, he fails to touch us deeply, transformingly. Through him, however, we can feel how much 1821 meant to a liberal New Englander:

> Now the nations are waking
> From slavery's night;
> Their manacles breaking,
> They haste to the fight,
> Where tyrants shall make their last stand for their thrones.
> ("Ode on the Emancipation of Greece")

Through him, too, we can see how inextricably interfused, even among the most enlightened Americans, were the causes of liberation and anti-Mohammedanism:

> . . . nations
> Who bear the name of Christian, and are proud
> Of light and truth and mercy. Arm ye; take
> The cross and sword; move to the war of death
> Stern and devoted; pause not, till the Turk
> Has lost the power to harm . . .
> ("Greece, From Mount Helicon")

Thirteen years — to the day — after its massacre, Scio finally found its poet.[21] Greece was independent; the time of appeals and rebukes had passed. Touring the Aegean, Boston's fiery poet-preacher John Pierpont received a bitter birthday gift: a rough sea forced the ship to dock for an unscheduled day at the harbor of blood. Apparently determined to transmit the impact of that experience, Pierpont for once shed the lofty, generalized style typical of himself and his contemporaries. As colloquial, natural, casual, free of poeticisms as Frost eighty years later, he suddenly allows the ghosts of the island to invade us as unbearably as they invade him.

The poem operates on a series of ironies and contrasts. Pierpont's birthday had been Scio's deathday. An unlucky number of years had passed: thirteen. He "blessed" the rough sea-swell for giving him what was to be an excruciating day on Scio. As for the gorgeousness of the locale:

> Oppression's rod
> Wrought its worst work, where the good hand of God
> Seems to have wrought its fairest and its best.

The storehouses, once glutted with rich and exotic wares — a catalog rivalling Keats' "St. Agnes Eve" — "All empty now, lie open to the sky:/Nothing to sell here, and no one to buy!" Of the once-radiant college nothing remains but a "formless mass of prostrate walls"; yet the girl who leads him to it is unaware of what she and her nation have lost:

> … joy and wonder sparkle in her eyes,
> As, with true Greek appetite for gains,
> She pockets a piastre for her pains.

Riding into the country, he finds "mile after mile" of "Mansions that once vied/With those of Venice …" now "Roofless and windowless … fire/Here had its perfect work." They seem to beg the perusing Yankee for restoration, and he imagines himself sitting "at ease" in his "palace hall," seeing "a paradise" blooming around him. But would he take it? The cliffs of Mount Opus "Ring with the answer … No!"

It is here, after this picturesque, often playful, marvelously leisurely preparation of 116 lines, that the poem suddenly reverses itself in texture, tone, and pace, as the mountain tells its story:

> When, from our height, we saw the swell,
> And heard the rush, of war's infernal flood
> Through all that city's bleeding lanes,
> O'er all the villas of those blooming plains;
> We opened, then, our dens and caves
> To the poor peasants. Behold, here, their graves!
> The fleet of foot to these, our caverns, sped;
>   To these our heights and cavern-depths, alike
>   The hell-hounds followed where the blood-hounds led,
> The brutes to mangle, and the fiends to strike!
> We trembled then, at the deep death-note
> Pealed from the panting bull-dog's throat, —
>   The flash, — the echo and the smoke, —
>   The yell, — the stab, — the sabre stroke, —
>   The musket shot, — the frenzied shriek, —
>   The death-groan of the hunted Greek, —
> Till our white feet with streams of gore were dyed,
> And mangled limbs were strown on every side, —
> With many a skull by Turkish sabre cleft;
> Our vultures finished what their blood-hounds left!

As the ship moves away, the farewell to Scio "From one who ne'er shall look on thee again" is touching: "... nothing lonelier lies beneath the sun,/And nothing lovelier doth he look upon!" Pierpont tells her not to envy Syra, which "awhile" may replace her as the center of commerce. In an Isaiah-like vision he sees a new Scio arise "as soon as the sceptre of Islam is broken":

> And vine-leaves and roses thy temples shall deck,
>   And some of thy children shall cling to thy breast,
> While some pluck the clusters that hang round thy neck,
>   And — *thy lap-full of oranges feed all the rest!*

Is "A Birthday in Scio" really a fine poem worth serious consideration, or is one startled into admiration because it is so different from, and so much more modern than, the large cluster of poems surrounding it, including Pierpont's own sixty-year creative span? If a poet's most blatant verses are born of a craving to 'reach,' perhaps his most effective focus is the falling of a sudden shadow on simple human activity. This focus is Pierpont's exactly, and one is forced to qualify an earlier impression that the Boston abolitionist "apparently requires a sensational event to set him in motion."[22]

It remains for us to look at the six major poets who reached maturity either before or during the Greek War — Bryant, Emerson, Whittier, Longfellow, Holmes and Poe — and the three born in 1819 — Whitman, Lowell and Melville — who were thirteen when independence finally came. Only the eldest, Bryant, included modern Greece in poems written during the war.

From 1824 on, Emerson's known poems are philosophical, lyrical, a-political. The 1833 pieces composed in Naples and Rome could have been done anywhere; no interest is expressed in the current mood. The 1834 tribute to Webster is general and noncommittal; he *may* have in mind the famous oration on Greek independence when he writes: "Seemed, when at last his clarion accents broke,/As if the conscience of the country spoke." That he does not share the prevailing anti-Moslem hysteria is evidenced in "Saadi" ("The heaven where unveiled Allah pours/The flood of truth, the flood of good") and "Song of Seyd Nimetollah of Kuhistan" ("What are Moslems? what are Giaours?/All are Love's, and all are ours"). "Greek Epigram" and the famous 1846 "Ode" help explain his silence on aesthetic grounds. In the first: " 'A new commandment,' said the smiling Muse,/'I give my darling son. Thou shalt not preach.' " The second goes further: "If I refuse/My study for their politique,/Which at the best is trick,/The angry Muse/Puts confusion in my brain." Finally, the same poem explains, in terms of his philosophic credo, Emerson's unwillingness to crusade or become agitated:

> The over-god . . .
> . . . who exterminates
> Races by stronger races . . .
> Knows to bring honey
> Out of the lion;
> Grafts gentlest scion
> On pirate and Turk.[23]

Four years younger, Longfellow and Whittier also omitted the Greek struggle while it went on, although Longfellow lived close by (France, 1826; Spain, 1827; Italy, 1828) and Whittier had no queasiness about bringing the day's headlines into his verse, particularly on the issue of liberation. In the case of Longfellow, whose habit was to let major historical moments ripen in his imagination before poetizing them, often in allegorical form, we examine with interest "The White Czar," an 1878 poem on Russia's leadership in a Christian crusade against the Turks, *apparently* under Peter the Great, who ruled from 1692 to 1725, but readily applicable to the Russian role in support of the Greeks a hundred years later:

> "And the Christian shall no more
> Be crushed, as heretofore,
> Beneath thine iron rule,
> O Sultan of Istamboul!
> I swear it! I the Czar,
> Batyushka! Gosudar!"[24]

It might be noted that when war broke out with Turkey in April of 1828, Pushkin — the Byron of Russia — asked permission to join the army.

Whittier's references, all coming after independence, are more numerous and more direct.[25] The first, "Expostulation" (1834), excoriates his hypocritical countrymen for supporting Greek emancipation while defending slavery at home:

> Go, let us . . .
> . . . beg the lord of Mahmoud's line
> To spare the struggling Suliote;
> Will not the scorching answer come . . .
> "Go, loose your fettered slaves at home,
> Then turn and ask the like of us!"

In "Garibaldi," without mentioning Greece by name, he expresses a sense of worldwide liberation "in the air"; the Italian leader hears "sea-winds burdened with a sound/Of falling chains, as, one by one, unbound,/The nations lift their right hands up and swear/Their oath of freedom."

Two retrospective references are accidental; at the unveiling of Halleck's statue, Whittier honors both the initial local impact of "Marco Bozzaris" and its permanent value:

> The Greek's wild onset Wall Street knew ...
> Let Greece his fiery lyric breathe
>   Above her hero-urns.

Later, celebrating the extraordinary life of his friend Samuel E. Howe, he finally gives serious treatment to the Greek war in nine lively stanzas that are the heart of the poem and could stand as an independent ballad; but he would not have created this passage had Howe not served in youth with the Greek rebel forces. It works well because, like Halleck's poem, it limits itself to one splendid act — the saving of a wounded Greek at great personal risk — and it sets the mood quite well:

> Once, when over purple mountains
>   Died away the Grecian sun ...
>
> Fell the Turk, a bolt of thunder,
>   Cleaving all the quiet sky,
> And against his sharp steel lightnings
>   Stood the Suliote but to die.

Whittier's final retrospective reference comes in "Snowbound," recognized, even by critics who hold him in low esteem, as a genuine American classic. Approaching sixty, he evokes a boyhood moment: a blizzard that hit the farm when he was fourteen. After days of enforced isolation, the storm ends and civilization once more reaches his threshold:

> At last the floundering carrier bore
> The village paper to our door.
> Lo! broadening outward as we read,
> To warmer zones the horizon spread.
> In panoramic length unrolled
> We saw the marvels that it told ...
> And up Taygetos winding slow
> Rode Ypsilanti's Mainote Greeks,
> A Turk's head at each saddle-bow!

Of course it matters that Whittier should have recalled this item forty-five years later; but, whatever he ultimately thought of

Ypsilanti's cause, as a boy it was the picturesqueness that entranced him, and he catalogs the Turks' heads along with other "marvels" of the "warmer zones" such as "painted Creeks,/And daft McGregor on his raids/In Costa Rica's everglades."

There should be no expectations from Holmes, though he published a good deal of verse in his undergraduate days at Harvard while the long war raged on. There are Greek references aplenty, but none are contemporary. Of all his early work, in fact, only "Old Ironsides" goes beyond light verse on homely subjects — his choice and his strength. One ambitious, unusually serious production, "Poetry: a Metrical Essay," was read before Harvard's Phi Beta Kappa Society in 1836. Here too he avoids the recent events in Greece; but in a significant passage he introduces the recurrent theme of ancient Greek heroism as a model for all liberation wars, including the American Revolution:

> Where'er the hireling shrinks before the free,
> Each pass becomes "a new Thermopylae"!
> Where'er the battles of the brave are won,
> There every mountain "looks on Marathon"![26]

In a mean-spirited and inaccurate biographical note by Poe's future literary executor, Rufus Griswold, one sentence is amazing: "Mr. Allen refused to pay some of his debts of *honour*, and he hastily quitted the country on a Quixotic expedition to join the Greeks, then struggling for liberty. He did not reach his original destination, however...." Even if this were true, even if he only *dreamt* of emulating his hero Byron on behalf of "the glory that was Greece," a poem from Poe on a current issue would be more than unlikely, since his stated goal was "supernal beauty," and he eschewed the use of poetry for moral statements. Thus, we can see why he would mask the very poor but fiery battle-cry, "Hymn to Aristogeiton and Harmodius," as a "Translation from the Greek." The style is that of a bright child or a mediocre adult, but the content could reflect a personal commitment to the *current* Greek struggle:

> In fresh myrtle my blade I'll entwine,
> > Like Harmodius, the gallant and good,
> When he made at the tutelar shrine
> > A libation of Tyranny's blood.[27]

Young Poe studied Greek as well as other languages, and won praise from his professors as a verse translator. He also wrote a number of original poems, according to schoolmates. Unfortunately, two and two add up to five. Despite its frequent inclusion in Poe collections, Mabbott denies that the "Hymn" is by Poe; despite Griswold's assertion, Mabbott and others call the expedition to Greece "fiction," and accuse the poet of having invented such stories himself.[28]

This leaves us with Bryant, by far the oldest of the group, and in the 1820's held to be America's first great poet. Like Emerson, he preferred to express his political views in his actions and his prose, but Greece was a notable exception.[29] From the first, he involved himself passionately both as poet and editor, opening the pages of his publications to poems such as "Marco Bozzaris." Invited to recite the 1821 Phi Beta Kappa poem at Harvard, he read "The Ages," a confident statement in 35 Spenserian stanzas of mankind's gradual improvement. The penultimate stanza does not name newly awakened Greece, yet declares:

> Europe is given a prey to sterner fates,
> And writhes in shackles; strong the arms that chain
> To earth her struggling multitudes of states;
> She too is strong, and might not chafe in vain
> Against them, but might cast to earth the train
> That trample her, and break their iron net.
> 　　　　　　... the moment set
> To rescue and raise up, draws near — but is not yet.

In the years that followed his zeal overflowed in several pieces, such as "To a Cloud":

> But I would woo the winds to let us rest
> 　　O'er Greece, long fettered and oppressed,
> Whose sons at length have heard the call that comes
> 　　From the old battle-fields and tombs,
> And risen, and drawn the sword, and on the foe
> 　　Have dealt the swift and desperate blow,
> And the Othman power is cloven, and the stroke
> 　　Has touched its chains, and they are broke.

Even more ardent are the concluding lines of "The Conjunction of

Jupiter and Venus," written in 1826, when Greece stood alone and many of her friends despaired. Bryant, however, assures her:

> Thou shalt arise from midst the dust and sit
> Again among the nations. Thine own arm
> Shall yet redeem thee.

Bitterly he declares that Europe, which is "stirred throughout her realms" when despot battles despot for a throne, sits on her hands in "a war for liberty." He implicates the United States as well: "I fear me thou couldst tell a shameful tale/Of fraud and lust of gain; thy treasury drained,/And Missolonghi fallen." But Greece will grow stronger by being wronged: God and its own "good sword shall yet work out . . . a terrible deliverance."

Along with these passages Bryant also produced four poems: "Song of the Greek Amazon," "The Greek Partisan," "The Greek Boy," and "The Massacre at Scio." Though noble in spirit and felicitous in phrase, shaped with an appropriately Grecian restraint and simplicity, none of the four ranks among his most memorable achievements, and it is understandable that they have not found a place in the anthologies. Perhaps "The Massacre at Scio," with its prediction that "the last link of slavery's chain" will one day "be shattered, to be worn no more," is the most moving:

> Weep not for Scio's children slain;
>   Their blood, by Turkish falchions shed,
> Sends not its cry to Heaven in vain
>   For vengeance on the murderer's head.
>
> Though high the warm red torrent ran
>   Between the flames that lit the sky,
> Yet, for each drop, an armed man
>   Shall rise, to free the land, or die.

The three major poets born just before the war began were all wide-ranging in their sympathies and knowledge. Yet Whitman, a celebrant of heroism and liberty if we ever had one, omits even the slightest reference to the twelve-year agony of Greece that must have resonated through his boyhood. Both ancient and modern Greek, ancient and modern Moslem, are incorporated into his cosmic embrace. Lowell, like Emerson and Whitman, was not caught by the anti-Moslem contagion; his respect for Mohammedan culture is expressed in "Mahmood the Image-breaker" and "Yussouf" ("called through all our tribes 'The Good' "). There is much on Halleck, satiric but with some praise, in "A Fable for Critics"; he points approvingly to the Robert Burns tribute, but ignores "Bozzaris." In the same poem Apollo makes a very sarcastic reference to the Greeks, linking them unflatteringly to America: "Hem! your likeness at present, I shudder to tell o't,/Is that you have your slaves, and the Greek had his helot." But the "likeness" is quite different in his "Ode (Read at the One Hundredth Anniversary of the Fight at Concord Bridge)" as he describes Freedom:

> . . . in the glory-guarded pass,
> Her haughty and far-shining head
> She bowed to shrive Leonidas
> With his imperishable dead . . .

Lowell's most relevant retrospective comment comes in Section IX of his 1848 "Ode to France" recalling his feelings in boyhood:

> Since first I heard our North-wind blow . . .
> I loved thee, Freedom; as a boy
> The rattle of thy shield at Marathon
> Did with a Grecian joy
> Through all my pulses run . . .[30]

The many extended mid-century tours of Europe by Bryant, Long-fellow and Lowell apparently resulted in no such remembrance of the Greek war as Pierpont's "A Birthday in Scio." Only Melville, during his great 1856–1857 pilgrimage, sought out a Greek location that corroborated his sense of the human condition. To a remarkable degree "Syra"[31] emerges as a companion piece to the unique travel poem produced a generation before. Melville employs the same slow-paced naturalness and anti-sentimental clarity that give the Pierpont poem its special power. The older poet noted a Greek girl's pleasure at receiving a piastre, oblivious to the perished glory around her; Melville describes the entrepreneurs of Syra, equally unaffected by their golden past:

> Above a tented inn with fluttering flag
> A sunburnt board announced Greek wine
> In self-same text Anacreon knew,
> Dispensed by one named "Pericles."

Ironically, while on Scio, Pierpont ends by contrasting the ruined island with its prosperous successor. Ironically, on Syra, Melville begins by contrasting the prosperous island with its ruined predecessor. Both strategies are effective. Each poet releases the ghosts of Scio flooding him, and depicts the terror of Turkey that remains in the minds of survivors even after independence. What sets Melville apart, even in a minor poem, from Pierpont and all the others who dealt with the anguish of Greece is that for him Scio becomes more than an isolated event. Like all great poets, he depicts memorably and signifies deeply. "Entering Syra harbor, I was again struck by the appearance of the town on the hill," he wrote in his journal. "The houses seem clinging round its top, as if desperate for security, like ship-wrecked men about a rock beaten by billows."[32]

What the refugees huddled on Syra's hilltop feel is what those hurled out of Izmir will feel in 1922, what those driven from their Cypriot villages will feel in 1974, what refugees of every century and nation have felt. The survivors of Scio are, in fact, a symbol of human complexity: terror, tenacity, resourcefulness, flamboyance — in the teeth of annihilation:

> Fleeing from Scio's smouldering vines
> (Where when the sword its work had done
> The Turk applied the torch) the Greek
> Came here, a fugitive stript of goods,
> Here to an all but tenantless isle,
> Nor here in footing gained at first,
> Felt safe. Still from the turbaned foe
> Dreading the doom of shipwrecked men
> Whom feline seas permit to land
> Then pounce upon and drag them back,
> For height they made, and prudent won
> A cone-shaped fastness on whose flanks
> With pains they pitched their eyrie camp,
> Stone huts, whereto they wary clung;

> But, reassured in end, come down . . .
> Begin to thrive; and thriving more
> When Greece at last flung off the Turk,
> Make of the haven mere a mart.

Almost a score of years after "Syra" and a full half-century after Byron's funeral had inspired John Neal's 352–line elegy, Emma Lazarus was stirred to one of her most distinguished youthful utterances, "On the Proposal to Erect a Monument in England to Lord Byron."[33]

Once again familiar themes emerge as she praises heroism ("On the martial bier/They laid a sword, a helmet, and a crown —/Meed of the warrior . . ."), defines the cause to which Byron and Greece were committed (". . . to disenthrall/The slaves of tyranny . . ."), expresses the universality of the struggle ("in all foreign hearts"), condemns Britain's rejection of her poet and, by implication, Greece ("England, slow and last to wake . . . /Hers is the shame . . .") and links the Greek Independence War to her ancient glory; while Byron's "brethren" denied him a place in Westminster Abbey, the Greeks believed "his sole, fitting tomb/Were Theseus' temple or the Parthenon." In ten lines, Emma Lazarus achieves precisely the elegiac force missing in John Neal:

> Fair was the Easter Sabbath morn when first
> Men heard he had not wakened to its light;
> The end had come, and time had done its worst,
> For the black cloud had fallen of endless night.
> Then in the town, as Greek accosted Greek,
> 'Twas not the wonted festal words to speak,
> "Christ is arisen," but "Our chief is gone,"
> With such wan aspect and grief-smitten head
> As when the awful cry of "Pan is dead!"
> Filled echoing hill and valley with its moan.

This survey is of necessity incomplete, but it is unlikely that the many poems awaiting rediscovery would yield new themes or attitudes, although one might be rewarded with a gem ignored for the wrong reasons when it first appeared. Apparently, fewer American poets acknowledged the Greek struggle in their work than might be expected; and those who did speak out generally echoed one another in content and style.

On the other hand, how much, and how much of permanence, was produced in Europe? Aside from the pre-war stanzas on Greece in *Childe Harold*, Canto II, and *Don Juan*, Canto III, both of them castigating his Greek contemporaries as "A land of slaves," what poetry did Byron give to the cause other than seven lines in his suicidal last poem, declaring the Greek battleground suitable for an "honorable death."[34] As for the greatest Byronic poets of Europe, political rebels all, what do we find in their work? From Mickiewicz of Poland, an image of Turkish defeat in battle ("turbans and severed heads/clattered to earth like hail! The Mussulman hordes/that had not fled sprawled lifeless in the sand"), another of Turkish defeat by Time ("turbans carved in frozen stone/ ... unknown/But for the names incised by Christian slaves") — neither pertaining to the Greek struggle; and one possible glimmer of allusion in describing a statue of Saturn whose "eyes beam" in the Greek salon of a Polish princess: "Is it the genius/of a renascent Hellas?"[35]

From Heine of Germany[36] only an exquisite twelve-line elegy, "Childe Harold," describing the dead poet's sea-voyage to England, without a hint of where or why he had died:

> Strong and dark, there sails a bark
> Sorrowful upon the wave.
> Watchers bowed above the shroud
> Bear his body to its grave.

A prose reference in a letter says little more: "While I am writing this, I hear that my cousin, Lord Byron, is dead at Missolonghi. So that great heart has stopped beating ... I have proclaimed universal mourning." From Pushkin of Russia, apparently nothing. Anthologies of 19th century German poetry include less than America's "Marco Bozzaris" — namely, nothing. The same is true of British anthologies, except for the great choruses from Shelley's *Hellas*[37] and a single innocuous reference in Matthew Arnold's "Memorial Verses" of 1850 ("Greece,/Long since, saw Byron's struggle cease ... When Byron's eyes were shut in death,/We bowed our head and held our breath.")[38] Elizabeth Barrett Browning produced a poem on "The Greek Slave," a famous statue depicting a girl on sale in a

Turkish slave market, nude and manacled. But that poem was not anthologized.[39]

Wordsworth's utter silence on the war, through a productive decade full of poems on current affairs, is doubly significant when one considers a pair of generally overlooked 1815 sonnets, "On a Celebrated Event in Ancient History," deploring the Greeks' subservience in his time:

> Yet so ye prop,
> Sons of the brave who fought at Marathon,
> Your feeble spirits! Greece her head hath bowed ...

We must wait till 1892 for a solitary stanza in William Watson's "Shelley's Centenary," which ignores *Hellas* but pays tribute to Byron:

> A fierier soul, its own fierce prey
> And cumbered with more mortal clay,
> At Missolonghi flamed away,
> And left the air
> Reverberating to this day
> Its loud despair.

In the end, Shelley seems to have achieved the sole major response, grand in magnitude, spirit, and art. But perhaps his most fiery and incisive words can be found in the prose introduction, dated November 1, 1821. It shows the complexity and significance of the struggle, and the repressive intellectual climate gripping Europe in the shadow of the anti-Greek "Holy Alliance" when poets such as Pushkin, Mickiewicz, Heine and Shelley were censored, policed and exiled:

> Should the English people ever become free, they will reflect upon the part which those who presume to represent their will have played in the great drama of the revival of liberty.... This is the age of the war of the oppressed against the oppressors, and every one of those ringleaders of the privileged gangs of murderers and swindlers, called Sovereigns, look to each other for aid against the common enemy, and suspend their mutual jealousies in the presence of a mightier fear. Of this holy alli-

ance all the despots of the earth are virtual members. But a new race has arisen throughout Europe, nursed in the abhorrence of the opinions which are its chains, and she will continue to produce fresh generations to accomplish that destiny which tyrants foresee and dread.[40]

Quite another climate prevailed in 1848, when an impressive world-wide response by poets greeted the revolutionary upsurge, and again in the 1930's, when dozens of American poets and many abroad took up the cause of Loyalist Spain — in some cases wielding sword as well as pen. To measure the distance traveled by American poetry in those 110 years, one might consider side by side Bryant's address to a Greek boy and Norman Rosten's to a Spanish mother:

> Boy! thy first looks were taught to seek
>   Their heaven in Hellas' skies;
> Her airs have tinged thy dusky cheek,
>   Her sunshine lit thine eyes;
> Thine ears have drunk the woodland strains
> Heard by old poets, and thy veins
> Swell with the blood of demigods,
> That slumber in thy country's sods.
>
> Now is thy nation free — though late —
>   Thy elder brethren broke —
> Broke, ere thy spirit felt its weight,
>   The intolerable yoke.
> And Greece, decayed, dethroned, doth see
> Her youth renewed in such as thee:
> A shoot of that old vine that made
> The nations silent in its shade.[41]

*　*　*　*　*

> In Guernica the dead children
> were laid out in order upon the sidewalk,
> in their white starched dresses.
>
> On their foreheads and breasts
> are the little holes where death came in

as thunder, while they were playing
their important summer games.

Do not weep for them, *madre.*
They are gone forever, the little ones,
straight to heaven to the saints,
and God will fill the bullet-holes with candy.

NOTES

1. M. Byron Raizis and Alexander J. Papas, *American poets and the Greek revolution 1821–1828* (Thessaloniki: Institute of Balkan Studies, 1971).

2. Samuel Kettell, *Specimens of American Poetry,* III (Boston: S. G. Goodrich, 1829) 308–11.

3. *Ibid.,* II, 291–93.

4. Rufus Griswold, *Poets and Poetry of America* (Philadelphia: Carey & Hart, 1852) 232.

5. *Ibid.,* "The Might of Greece," p. 238; "Liberty," p. 239.

6. *Ibid.,* pp. 240–41.

7. Raizis and Papas quote from three more Greek poems by Brooks, "The Greek Struggle," "Freedom," and "The Turkish Crescent," which seem loftier in spirit but lower in literary quality than the bitter stanzas of "Greece." Kettell gives the correct title, "Greece — 1822."

8. Kettell, III, 341.

9. *Ibid.,* p. 342. The quotations that follow come from *The Grave of Byron,* pp. 28, 35–36.

10. To this category also belong Park Benjamin ("The Battle of Navarino"), Nathaniel P. Willis ("The Grecian Hero"), Edward C. Pinkney ("Ille, non ego"), and Samuel Woodworth ("Fashions"), who are quoted or mentioned by Raizis and Papas.

11. Kettell, II, 210–12; Raizis and Papas discuss this poem in depth, but are unaware of its authorship; on the other hand, they quote from or mention a significant number of Mrs. Sigourney's unanthologized Greek poems.

12. *The Poetical Works of Fitz-Greene Halleck* (New York: D. Appleton, 1847) 19–25. There is a moving note about Bozzaris on p. 289.

13. Edmund C Stedman, *An American Anthology* (Boston: Houghton Mifflin, 1900) 37–39.

14. Kettell, III, 86–87.

15. *Ibid.,* 100–109.

16. *The Complete Poetical Works of James Russell Lowell* (Boston: Houghton Mifflin, 1897) 134. In the same poem Lowell also pokes fun at the excessive wave of Byronism in America. "I myself know ten Byrons, one Coleridge, three Shelleys ..." (p. 145)

17. *Poets and Poetry of America* (Philadelphia: Carey & Hart, 1842) 160–61.

18. *Ibid.*, p. 161.

19. James Gates Percival, *Poetical Works* I (Boston: Ticknor & Fields, 1859) 91–93, 239–50, 372; II, pp. 241–42, 404–06.

20. John Pierpont, "A Birthday in Scio," *Airs of Palestine and Other Poems* (Boston: J. Munroe, 1840) 91—98. That this poet's wrath is focused on a particular tyrant rather than all Moslems is made clear in the reference to "The iron sceptre of Mahmoud," and "Mahmoud, the red handed Padischa," which Pierpont translates in a final bitter footnote as " 'Man-Killer,' one of the titles of the present Soultan, and the one by which, it is said, he is particularly pleased to be addressed."

21. Aaron Kramer, *The Prophetic Tradition in American Poetry, 1835–1900* (Rutherford, N.J.: Fairleigh Dickinson University Press, 1968) 203.

22. Ralph Waldo Emerson, *Works*, IX (Boston: Houghton Mifflin, 1883) 300–301, 312, 114–19, 250, 244, 72–74.

23. *The Complete Poetical Works of Henry Wadsworth Longfellow* (Boston: Houghton Mifflin, 1893) 341. It needs to be added, however, that the dating of this poem coincides with Russia's entrance into the Balkan people's victorious war against Turkey, and that other poets (such as Richard W. Gilder, in his "The White Tsar's People," and Emma Lazarus, in "Sic Semper Liberatoritus") applied Peter's old nickname to Alexander II, who ruled from 1855 to 1881.

24. *The Complete Poetical Works of John Greenleaf Whittier* (Boston: Houghton Mifflin, 1894) 268, 205, 211, 192–93, 406.

25. *The Poetical Works of Oliver Wendell Holmes* (Boston: Houghton Mifflin, 1895) 22. In his 1857 "Poem at the Dedication of the Halleck Monument" he makes no mention of the Bozzaris poem.

26. *The Works of Edgar Allan Poe* (New York: Walter J. Black, 1927) 49–50. Byron's footnote to his Harmodius reference in *Childe Harold*, Canto III, Stanza XX, recommends Denman's as "the best English translation of the famous song."

27. Thomas O. Mabbott, *Collected Works of Edgar Allan Poe*, I (Cambridge: Harvard Univ. Press, 1969) 507, 543–44. On p. 384 Mabbott suggests that Poe's 1845 "The Divine Right of Kings" may well be an allusion to Hiram Powers' celebrated statue, "The Greek Slave." If so, the cute use of such words as "throne . . . tyrant . . . reigns . . . subject . . . power . . . governs . . . rule . . . kingly state" indicate a total insensitivity to the oppression of the Greeks portrayed by the sculptor.

28. *Poetical Works of William Cullen Bryant* (New York: D. Appleton, 1878) 19. 100–101, 153, 156–59, 170, 58–59.

29. Lowell, *Works*, 315, 318–19, 145, 137, 361, 94–95.

30. Herman Melville, *Works*, XVI (1924) 250–51.

31. *Ibid.*, p. 478.

32. *The Poems of Emma Lazarus*, I (Boston: Houghton Mifflin, 1899) 152–54.

33. Great credit must be given to Raizis and Papas for their Appendix I, in which all of Byron's significant pre-war references to Greece are listed.

34. Adam Mickiewicz: *New Selected Poems*, ed. Clark Mills (New York: Voyages Press, 1957), "The Tomb of the Seraglio," p. 40; "In the Greek Salon," p. 46.

35. *The Poetry and Prose of Heinrich Heine*, ed. Frederic Ewen (New York: Citadel Press, 1948) 129, 353. The translation of the poem is mine.

36. Curtis H. Page, *British Poets of the Nineteenth Century* (Boston: B. H. Sanborn, 1904) 713.

37. *Selected Poems of Matthew Arnold* (London: Macmillan, 1900) 203.

38. Mrs. Browning's poem is discussed in Mabbott, p. 384. The Wordsworth sonnets can be found in *The Poetical Works of Wordsworth*, rev. ed. Ernest de Selincourt (London: Oxford Univ. Press, 1965) 248. Watson's poem appears in *Poetry of the Victorian Period*, rev. ed. George B. Woods and Jerome H. Buckley (Chicago: Scott, Foresman, 1955) 900–901.

39. *The Complete Works of Percy Bysshe Shelley*, III (New York: Gordian Press, 1965) 9.

40. "The Greek Boy," *Poetical Works*, p. 171.

41. *The Fourth Decade* (New York: Farrar & Rinehart, 1943) 45.

Appendix: Poems of the Greek Independence War

EBENEZER BAILEY:	The Triuph of Liberty
KATHERINE A. WARE:	Greece
GEORGE HILL:	The Might of Greece
	Liberty
JAMES G. BROOKS:	Greece — 1822
GEORGE LUNT:	The Grave of Byron — excerpts
LYDIA H. SIGOURNEY:	Missolonghi
FITZ-GREENE HALLECK:	Marco Bozzaris
JOHN NEAL:	The Sleeper
JAMES GATES PERCIVAL:	Incantation
	Liberty to Athens
	Ode on the Emancipation of Greece
	The Senate of Callimachi
	Greece, From Mount Helicon
	The Sunian Pallas
	The Greek Mountaineer
	The Last Song of the Greek Patriot
	Greece, From Mount Helicon — excerpt
	The Greek Song of Victory
JOHN PIERPONT:	A Birthday in Scio
JOHN GREENLEAF WHITTIER:	The Hero
HERMAN MELVILLE:	Syra
EMMA LAZARUS:	On the Proposal to Erect a Monument in England to Lord Byron

THE TRIUMPH OF LIBERTY

Ebenezer Bailey

Spirit of Freedom, hail! —
Whether thy steps are in the sunny vale,
Where peace and happiness reside
With innocence and thee, or glide
To caverns deep and vestal fountains,
'Mid the stern solitude of mountains,
Where airy voices still prolong
From cliff to cliff thy jocund song, —
We woo thy presence: Thou wilt smile upon
The full heart's tribute to thy favorite Son,
Who held communion with thee, and unfurl'd
In light thy sacred charter to the world.
We feel thy influence, Power divine,
Whose angel smile can make the desert shine;
For thou hast left thy mountain's brow,
And art with men no stranger now.
Where'er thy joyous train is seen
Disporting with the merry hours,
Nature laughs out, in brighter green,
And wreathes her brow with fairy flowers:
Pleasure waves her rosy wand, —
Plenty opens wide her hand —
On Rapture's wings,
To heaven the choral anthem springs,
And all around, above, below,
Exult and mingle, as they glow,
In such harmonious ecstasies as play'd,
When earth was new, in Eden's light and shade.
But not in peaceful scenes alone
Thy steps appear, — thy power is known.
Hark! — the trump! its thrilling sound
Echoes on every wind,
And man awakes, for ages bound
In leaden lethargy of mind:

He wakes to life! — earth's teeming plains
Rejoice in his control;
He wakes to strength! — and bursts the chains
Whose rust was in his soul;
He wakes to liberty! — and walks abroad
All disenthrall'd, the image of his God.
The stifled sob of mighty souls
Rises on the glowing air,
And the vow of vengeance rolls,
Mingled with the dying prayer:
"Now, by the spirits of the brave,
Sires, who rode on glory's wave,
By red Scio's wrongs and groans,
By Ipsara's unburied bones,
Our foes beneath these reeking stones,
Shall find a grave."
Earth heaves, as if she gorged again
Usurping Korah's rebel train,
She heaves, with blast more wild and loud,
Than when with trump of thunders proud,
The electric flame subdues the cloud,
Torn and dismember'd frames are thrown on high,
And then the oppressor and oppress'd in equal silence lie.
Come, jewell'd Sultan, from thine hall of state!
Exult o'er Missolonghi's fall,
With flashing eye, and step elate
The blood-pools count around her ruin'd wall. —
Seek's thou thus with glances vain
The remnant of thy Moslem train? —
Hither they came, with haughty brow,
They conquer'd here, — where are they now?
Ask the hoar vulture with her new-flesh'd beak,
Bid the gaunt watch-dog speak,
Who bay'd so long around his murder'd master's door, —
They, with shriek and ban can tell
The burial-place of the infidel,
Go! bind thy turban round thy brow of shame,
And hurl the mutter'd curse at thy false prophet's name.

Ancient and beautiful! — who stand'st alone
In the dire crusade, while with hearts of stone
Thy sister nations close the leaden eye
Regardless of thy agony.
Such friends had He, who once with bursting pore,
On sad Gethsemane a lost world's burden bore. —
Leave, leave the sacred steep
Where thy lone muses weep,
Forth from thy sculptured halls,
Thy pilgrim-haunted walls,
Thy classic fountains' crystal flood,
Go! — angel-strengthen'd to the field of blood,
Raise thy white arm, — unbind thy wreathed hair,
And God's great name upon thy breastplate wear,
Stand in *His might,* till the pure cross arise
O'er the proud minaret, and woo propitious skies.

GREECE

Katharine A. Ware

Where time is ranging with remorseless tread,
Amid the trophies of the mighty dead,
There, Grecia's genius hovers o'er the scene
Of ruin'd grandeur — glories that *have been* —
Views the vast wreck of power with kindling eye,
And kneels beside the tomb of Poesy.
Where fame's proud relics strew her classic ground,
In gloomy majesty she glides around,
Pausing, with rapt devotion, to survey
The prostrate splendors of her early day.
Those ancient courts, where erst with wisdom fraught,
Her senate listen'd, and her sages taught;
Where that bold patriot, firm in virtue's cause,
The immortal Solon, thunder'd forth his laws!
The temple raised to Theseus' mighty name —
The storied arch of Hadrian's deathless fame!

Raises her eye to where, with beams divine,
Apollo blush'd upon the Delphic shrine —
As bow'd that chief, to learn a nation's fate,
Who gave his royal life, to save a state.
All dark and tuneless are those laurel shades,
Which once enshrined Castalia's classic maids —
For barbarous hands have raised their funeral pyre
And hush'd the breathings of their seraph lyre —
Save when the light of heaven around it plays,
And wakes the hallow'd chant of other days!
Oh! then, 'mid storied mounds, and mouldering urns,
Once more, the flame of inspiration burns!
Here, pilgrim Genius comes to muse around,
To wake one strain o'er consecrated ground!
From prostrate fanes, and altars of decay,
He learns the glory of their former day —
And, in the tender blush of twilight gloom,
He writes the story of some ruin'd tomb;
From dark oblivion snatches many a gem,
To glisten in his own fair diadem.
Immortal Byron! thou, whose courage plann'd
The rescue of that subjugated land —
Oh! hadst thou lived to rear thy giant glaive,
Thou 'dst bid the Christian cross triumphant wave!
Mark'd the pale crescent wave 'mid seas of blood,
And stamp'd proud Grecia's freedom in the flood.
But, Oh! 'twas fate's decree thou should'st expire,
Swan-like, amid the breathings of thy lyre —
Even in the sacred light of thine own song —
As sinks the glorious sun amid the throng
Of bright robed clouds, the pageantry of Heaven —
Thy last retiring beam to earth was given.
Where Scio's isle blushes with Christian gore
And recreant fiends still yell around her shore;
Where Missolonghi's bloody plain extends,
'Mid war's red blots, Athena's Queen descends.
Mark, where she comes — in all the pomp of woe —
Darkling around her sable vestments flow —

With throbbing bosom in the tempest bare —
Wild, on the breeze, floats her unwreathed hair,
Though learning's classic diadem is there.
Where fate's dark clouds the face of heaven deform —
With steadfast brow — she meets the bursting storm,
Turns to Olympus with imploring eye,
And claims the aegis of her native sky.
Hark! round its base th' eternal thunders roll,
And Jove's own lightnings flash from pole to pole —
His voice is *there*! he bids creation save
Minerva's "first-born" from a barbarous wave.

THE MIGHT OF GREECE

George Hill

The might of Greece! whose glory has gone forth,
Like the eternal echo of a lyre
Struck by an angel, to the bounds of earth,
A marvel and a melody; a fire
Unquench'd, unquenchable. Castalia's choir
Mourn o'er their altars worshipless or gone;
But the free mountain-air they did respire
Has borne their music onward, with a tone
Shaking earth's tyrant race through every distant zone!

A never-dying music, borne along
The stream of years, that else were mute, and fraught
— A boundless echo, thunder peal'd in song —
With the unconquerable might of thought:
The Titan that shall rive the fetters wrought
By the world's god, Opinion, and set free
The powers of mind, giants from darkness brought;
The trophies of whose triumph-march shall be
Thrones, dungeons swept away, as rampires by the sea.

LIBERTY

George Hill

There is a spirit working in the world,
Like to a silent subterranean fire;
Yet, ever and anon, some monarch hurl'd
Aghast and pale, attests its fearful ire.
The dungeon'd nations now once more respire
The keen and stirring air of Liberty.
The struggling giant wakes, and feels he's free.
By Delphi's fountain-cave, that ancient choir
Resume their song; the Greek astonish'd hears,
And the old altar of his worship rears.
Sound on, fair sisters! sound your boldest lyre, —
Peal your old harmonies as from the spheres.
Unto strange gods too long we've bent the knee,
The trembling mind, too long and patiently.

GREECE — 1822

James G. Brooks

Land of the brave! where lie inurn'd
The shrouded forms of mortal clay,
In whom the fire of valour burn'd,
And blazed upon the battle's fray:
Land, where the gallant Spartan few
Bled at Thermopylae of yore,
When death his purple garment threw
On Helle's consecrated shore!

Land of the Muse! within thy bowers
Her soul-entrancing echoes rung,
While on their course the rapid hours
Paused at the melody she sung —
Till every grove and every hill,
And every stream that flow'd along,

From morn to night repeated still
The winning harmony of song.
Land of dead heroes! living slaves!
Shall glory gild thy clime no more?
Her banner float above thy waves
Where proudly it hath swept before?
Hath not remembrance then a charm
To break the fetters and the chain,
To bid thy children nerve the arm,
And strike for freedom once again?

No! coward souls, the light which shone
On Leuctra's war-empurpled day,
The light which beam'd on Marathon
Hath lost its splendor, ceased to play;
And thou art but a shadow now,
With helmet shatter'd — spear in rust —
Thy honour but a dream — and thou
Despised — degraded in the dust!

Where sleeps the spirit, that of old
Dash'd down to earth the Persian plume,
When the loud chant of triumph told
How fatal was the despot's doom? —
The bold three hundred — where are they,
Who died on battle's gory breast?
Tyrants have trampled on the clay
Where death hath hush'd them into rest.

Yet, Ida, yet upon thy hill
A glory shines of ages fled;
And fame her light is pouring still,
Not on the living, but the dead!
But 'tis the dim, sepulchral light,
Which sheds a faint and feeble ray,
As moonbeams on the brow of night,
When tempests sweep upon their way.

Greece! yet awake thee from thy trance,
Behold, thy banner waves afar;

Behold, the glittering weapons glance
Along the gleaming front of war!
A gallant chief, of high emprize,
Is urging foremost in the field
Who calls upon thee to arise
In might — in majesty reveal'd.

In vain, in vain the hero calls —
In vain he sounds the trumpet loud!
His banner totters — see! it falls
In ruin, Freedom's battle-shroud:
Thy children have no soul to dare
Such deeds as glorified their sires;
Their valour's but a meteor's glare,
Which gleams a moment, and expires.

Lost land! where Genius made his reign,
And rear'd his golden arch on high;
Where Science raised her sacred fane,
Its summits peering to the sky;
Upon thy clime the midnight deep
Of ignorance hath brooded long,
And in the tomb, forgotten, sleep
The sons of science and of song.
Thy sun hath set — the evening storm
Hath pass'd in giant fury by,
To blast the beauty of thy form,
And spread its pall upon the sky!
Gone is thy glory's diadem,
And freedom never more shall cease
To pour her mournful requiem
O'er blighted, lost, degraded Greece!

THE GRAVE OF BYRON (excerpts)

George Lunt

That country was before me, — and this flag
Of Freedom's late-roused champions on the brow
Of fortressed mountains heavily seemed to drag
Down midway from its staff, as if in show
Of mourning for some mighty chief laid low
Or hero bound for his untimely tomb:
The broad land lay robed in unwonted woe
And silence, save when burst upon the gloom
Solemn and minutely the cannon's long deep
    boom . . .

And soon came armed warriors footing slow
To the complaining music's wailing peal,
While, as they tramped, the echoing soil below
Still sung responsive to the clanging steel;
And their stern eyes now could not all conceal
Their grief though they had mocked at deadly fear
And met unmoved the tide of woe or weal, —
But glancing frequent towards that sable bier,
Dropt ever and anon one agonizing tear.

With arms reversed they marched, and after came
With look sedate and manly foreheads bland,
In seemly wise and decent fitting frame
And grave slow steps, a venerable band
Who were the ancient magnates of the land,
The fathers of the people; — their ripe age
Recalled afresh the memory of the grand
Features and forms which still the Grecian sage
Owns in the chiselled block or on the classic page.

Then as I marvelled, suddenly a tune
Melted amongst those glittering sea-green isles . . .
Soft and yet sad, — till now that slow lament
Down the melodious stream came clear and strong,

Near where the grove's pomegranate foliage sent
Of youths and virgins soon a vocal throng; —
And, ever as they swelled the funeral song
Laurels and myrtles were the flowers they flung,
Wreathed with undying amaranth, along; —
And vales and sullen woods responsive rung,
Till blue Parnassus heard the mournful lay they sung:

O virgin daughters of the budding isles
Which crowning purple o'er the deep Aegean,
Whose folded foliage met those first-born smiles
Which made groves, streams, and rocks sing Io Paean!
Wail, island-daughter, him whose day is done, —
And tear the ivy garland from your head; —
Apollo's last and mightiest son
Is with the mighty dead . . .

Come, father of the morning, come and shake
Adown thy flowing ringlets' golden store,
But he whom thou didst love to wake
Shall see thy face no more.

. . . Nor summer airs, nor vintage suns shall hail
His unreturning footstep, — for the brave,
The young, the noble, whom we wail,
Is wedded to the grave.

Freedom! so richly bought, thou shouldst be sweet:
Yet would that he thy victim had but died
Floating down battle's crimson flood to meet
Red from thy strife the Stygian tide: —
How gladly then in glory's flowers we'd sheathe
His sword, and round his consecrated brow
We'd mingle with the poet's wreath
One deathless laurel bough.

Sons of the Greeks, 'mid the tumultuous flame
Of the fierce shock ye shall remember well
Who gave his life, his fortune, and his fame,
Yea his whole hope to break the accursed spell

Which ye must end; — but o'er his silent bier,
Till ancient Freedom smiling hovers nigh,
Ye may not waste another tear,
Nor one lamenting sigh.

What though his life was brief; — his young career
Was run in glory; — happy that his last
Act was the best and noblest: time may sere
And blight the nations with his withering blast,
But has no power to rend his monument
From out the hearts of men; — perchance still more
Happy, that he so early went
Down to the gloomy shore.

But year by year shall Grecian girls renew,
When spring returns, the story of his woes . . .
And often shall Aetolian sires relate,
Weeping, his melancholy tale, —
Their poet-hero's fate.

The rest was all confused, save that I heard
Sudden and quick the volleyed thunder peal
Above the soldier's grave, and the stern word,
And saw anon the marshalled squadrons wheel;
Then rushed the ringing clang of vengeful steel,
As notes of distant war came far along
The freshening breeze, and sounds of woe or weal,
Shoutings and shrieks; when from the funeral throng
Came one who ere they marched sung loud this battle-
    song:

To the charge; — if ye value the joy of the strife,
When its tumult surpasses the rapture of life:
Strike the spurs that have reeked with the blood of the
    steed, —
Bare the blades that have served you before at your need:
      Let us swear by the mothers who bore us, —
      By the blue-arching heaven that's o'er us, —
That we'll conquer the dastards we scorn in the fight,
Or our brows shall be cold in the damp dew to-night:

Forward, men! on this battle plain, gory
We'll slumber or stand in our glory.

To the charge; — should we linger, in fight for the fires
Of our altars and hearths, and the tombs of our sires, —
His spirit, who sung them and mourned for our woe,
Would rise to reproach every look from the foe:
    And we swear by the heart that he gave us, —
    By that right hand too cold now to save us, —
At his rallying name shall our sabres be keen; —
May our fame glance as bright and our graves grow as
    green.
        Ravens, — come to the feast, — ye shall share it,
        Our swords are athirst to prepare it.

MISSOLONGHI

Lydia H. Sigourney

Famine hath worn them pale, that noble band; —
Yet round the long beleaguer'd wall,
With wasted frame, and iron hand,
Like watching skeletons they stand,
To conquer or to fall.

Hark! — Hark! the war-cry. Swells the shout
From wild Arabia's wandering rout,
From turbid Nilus' swarthy brood,
From Ibrahim's host who thirst for blood,
'Tis answer'd from the echoing skies,
Sons of Miltiades, arise! —

Aged men, with temples gray! —
Why do *ye* haste to the battle fray? —
Home to the couch of ease, and pray. —
But ah! I read on those brows of gloom,
That your sons have found a gory tomb,
And ye with despair and grief opprest,

Would strike ere ye share their clay-cold rest. —

With features pale, yet sternly wrought
To all the agony of thought,
Yon widow'd mothers mount the tower
To guard the wall in danger's hour: —
Fast by their side in mute distress,
Their little sons unwavering press,
Taught from their cradle-bed to know
The bitter tutelage of woe,
No idle fears in their bosoms glow,
But pride and wrath in their dark eyes glance,
As they lift their martyr'd father's lance.

Yet more! — Yet more! — At beat of drum
With wildly flowing hair,
Helle's beauteous maidens come,
The iron strife to dare. —
Sadly sweet from those lips of rose,
The death-song of Bozzaris flows,
It is your dirge, ye turban'd foes! —
Rise, soul of Pindar! strike the shadowy lyre,
Start from your sculptured tombs, ye sons of fire!
Snatch, snatch those gentle forms from war's alarms,
And throw your adamantine shield around their
    shrinking charms.

Louder swells the battle-cry;
God of Christians! from the sky
Behold the Turk's accursed host
Come rushing in. — 'Tis lost! 'Tis lost! —
Ye bold defenders, die! —
O thou, who sang'st of Ilion's walls the fate,
Unseal thy blinded orbs, *thine own* are desolate.

MARCO BOZZARIS

Fitz-Greene Halleck

At midnight, in his guarded tent,
The Turk was dreaming of the hour
When Greece, her knee in suppliance bent,
Should tremble at his power:
In dreams, through camp and court, he bore
The trophies of a conqueror;
In dreams his song of triumph heard
Then wore his monarch's signet ring:
Then pressed that monarch's throne — A king;
As wild his thoughts, and gay of wing,
As Eden's garden bird.

At midnight, in the forest shades,
Bozzaris ranged his Suliote band,
True as the steel of their tried blades,
Heroes in heart and hand.
There had the Persian's thousands stood,
There had the glad earth drunk their blood
On old Plataea's day;
And now there breathed that haunted air
The sons of sires who conquered there,
With arm to strike and soul to dare,
As quick, as far as they.

An hour passed on — the Turk awoke;
That bright dream was his last;
He woke — to hear his sentries shriek,
"To arms! they come! the Greek! the Greek!"
He woke — to die mid flame, and smoke,
And shout, and groan, and sabre-stroke,
And death-shots falling thick and fast
As lightnings from the mountain-cloud;
And heard, with voice as trumpet loud,
Bozzaris cheer his band:
"Strike — till the last armed foe expires;

Strike — for your altars and your fires;
Strike — for the green graves of your sires;
God — and your native land!"

They fought — like brave men, long and well;
They piled that ground with Moslem slain;
They conquered — but Bozzaris fell,
Bleeding at every vein.
His few surviving comrades saw
His smile when rang their proud hurrah,
And the red field was won;
Then saw in death his eyelids close
Calmly, as to a night's repose,
Like flowers at set of sun.

Come to the bridal-chamber, Death!
Come to the mother's, when she feels,
For the first time, her first-born's breath;
Come when the blessed seals
That close the pestilence are broke,
And crowded cities wail its stroke;
Come in consumption's ghastly form,
The earthquake shock, the ocean storm;
Come when the heart beats high and warm
With banquet-song, and dance, and wine;
And thou art terrible — the tear,
The groan, the knell, the pall, the bier,
And all we know, or dream, or fear
Of agony are thine.

But to the hero, when his sword
Has won the battle for the free,
Thy voice sounds like a prophet's word;
And in its hollow tones are heard
The thanks of millions yet to be.
Come, when his task of fame is wrought —
Come, with her laurel-leaf, blood-bought —
Come in her crowning hour — and then
Thy sunken eye's unearthly light

To him is welcome as the sight
Of sky and stars to prisoned men;
Thy grasp is welcome as the hand
Of brother in a foreign land;
Thy summons welcome as the cry
That told the Indian isles were nigh
To the world-seeking Genoese,
When the land wind, from woods of palm,
And orange-groves, and fields of balm,
Blew o'er the Haytian seas.

Bozzaris! with the storied brave
Greece nurtured in her glory's time,
Rest thee — there is no prouder grave,
Even in her own proud clime.
She wore no funeral-weeds for thee,
Nor bade the dark hearse wave its plume
Like torn branch from death's leafless tree
In sorrow's pomp and pageantry,
The heartless luxury of the tomb;
But she remembers thee as one
Long loved and for a season gone;
For thee her poet's lyre is wreathed,
Her marble wrought, her music breathed;
For thee she rings the birthday bells;
Of thee her babe's first lisping tells;
For thine her evening prayer is said
At palace-couch and cottage-bed;
Her soldier, closing with the foe,
Gives for thy sake a deadlier blow;
His plighted maiden, when she fears
For him the joy of her young years,
Thinks of thy fate, and checks her tears;
And she, the mother of thy boys,
Though in her eye and faded cheek
Is read the grief she will not speak,
The memory of her buried joys,
And even she who gave thee birth,

Will, by their pilgrim-circled hearth,
Talk of thy doom without a sigh;
For thou art Freedom's now, and Fame's;
One of the few, the immortal names,
That were not born to die.

THE SLEEPER
(written the day after the funeral of Byron)

John Neal

I stood above the sea. I heard the roar
Of waters far below me. On the shore
A warrior-ship, with all her banners torn,
Her broad sails flying loose, lay overborne
By tumbling surges. She had swept the main,
Braved the loud thunder — stood the hurricane;
To be, when all her danger was o'erpast,
Upon her native shore, in wreck and ruin cast.

I thought of Greece — the proud one dead;
Struck — with his heart in flower;
Wreck'd — with his bright wings all outspread,
In his descent,
From that forbidden firmament,
O'er which he went,
Like some Archangel in his power:

The everlasting ocean lay
Below my weary eyes;
While overhead there roll'd away
The everlasting skies:

A thousand birds around me flew,
Emerging from the distant blue,
Like spirits from the summer deep, —
Then, wheeling slowly, one by one,
All disappearing in the sun,

They left me — and I fell asleep:

But soon a loud, strong trumpet blew,
And by, an armed angel flew,
With tresses all on fire, and wings of color'd flame:
And then the thunder broke
About me, and I woke —
And heard a voice above proclaim
The warrior-poet's name!
The island bard! that came
Far from his home, to die
In martyrdom to Liberty:

I started — wonder'd — where was I? —
Above me roll'd a Grecian sky;
Around me Grecian isles were spread,
O'erpeopled with great shadowy dead,
Assembled there to celebrate
Some awful rite:
Again the iron trump was blown
With overpowering might;
And lo! upon a rocky throne,
Appear'd a dead man that I knew;
His hair unbound, his forehead wet with dew,
And then the angel, standing o'er him, said
This incantation, with her wings outspread.

INCANTATION

Bard of the ocean, wake!
The midnight skies
Of solid blue,
That roll away above thee, shed
O'er thy unshelter'd head
A most untimely dew!
Wake, Sleeper, wake!
Arise!
And from thy marble forehead shake

The shadow of the dead!
Arise! Arise!
Thou last of all the Giants! Tear
Thy silken robes away —
Shake off the wine-dew from thy hair —
The crush'd and faded roses there,
And let it play,
A glittering shadow on the air, —
Like the young Spartan's when he set
His foot — and met
The Persian in array:
Byron, awake!
Stand up and take
Thy natural shape upon thee! bare
Thy bosom to the winds that blow —
Not over bowers,
Heavy with scented flowers —
But over drifted snow;
Not o'er the perfumed earth,
Sweltering in moonlight rain,
Where even the blossoms that have birth,
Breathe on the heavens a stain —
But o'er the rude,
Cold Grecian solitude:

Up, Byron, up! with eyes
Dark as Egyptian skies,
Where men may read their destinies!
Up! in thy golden panoply complete
Transfigured — all prepared to meet
The Moslem foe!

What! still unmoved, thou Sleeper! still
Untroubled by the sounds that fill
Thy agitated air!
Thy forehead set —
Thy bosom wet —
Still undisturbed!
Thy proud lip curb'd —

The death-dew on thy hair!

Awake thee, Byron! Thou art call'd,
Thou man of power! to break
The thraldom of the nations — wake!
Arise!
The heathen are upon thee! Lo, they come
Without a flute, or bell, or drum,
Silent as death,
Holding their breath;
Appall'd . . .
And see! another hand appear,
Unarm'd with helm, or sword, or spear,
Or buckler, guard, or shield;
A hand of giants! on they go,
Each — by himself — to meet the foe,
Alone in yonder field:
Three hundred Spartan shadows they,
I know them by their flying hair,
Rejoicing as it floats away,
A lustre on the troubled air:

Behold! they gather round
The marble Sleeper, where he lies
Reposing on the scented ground, —
His head with dripping roses bound —
A shadow in his eyes:
Behold them slowly trace,
With sorrow in each noble face,
The print of naked feet about the holy place:
Awake! awake!
Thou sleeping warrior-Bard! O break
Thy trance profound!
The Spartans are about thee —
They will not go without thee —
Awake!

They claim thee for the last
Of all that valiant race;

The Grecians of the past, —
To whom the battle and the chase,
The war-ship tumbling to the blast,
The stormy night,
The thunder and the fight,
Were pastime and repose!
Up, then, and take thy stand
Amid the shadowy band!
Outspread thy banner o'er them,
Go, as thou should'st, before them;

Hear thou their call,
Awake! and fall
Like the bright thunder on their foes!

On with thy helmet! set thy foot
Where'er thou art —
Strike down the infidel, and put
Thy mailed hand upon thy slumbering heart,
Or on the nearest altar, where,
Unstain'd with revel, blood, or wine,
Stands many an everlasting shrine,
Wrapp'd in perpetual cloud,
For ever echoing loud,
And sounding to the mountain air,
With voices wild, remote, and high,
Like fanes of ancient prophecy —
Built by the cherubim, of solid rock,
Into the broad blue heaven — to mock
The thunder and the Moslem shock —
The armies of the earth and sky! . . .

Up from thy charmed slumber! break
Thy long and sorrowful trance!
Now! Now!
Advance!
Ye of the snowy brow,
Each in her overpowering splendor!
The young and great,

Superb and desolate,
The beautiful and tender!
Advance!
Ye shadows of his child and wife,
And thrill the sleeper into life!

* * *

Now heaven be thanked! he lies
Regardless of our cries.
Rejoice! Rejoice!
Children of Greece, rejoice!
No change nor trouble shall come again
To the island-bard of the deep blue main;
Nor blight nor blast
To overcast
The brightness of his name;
Rejoice! Rejoice!
All ye that have loved the man, rejoice,
Throughout the world!
He cannot, now,
From the precipice brow
Of Glory's hill be hurl'd!
And you, ye men of Greece,
For his heart is yours
While time endures —
A flame
That will burn eternally —
And sound that will never cease!
And ye that have loved him, where
There's freedom in the air,
O peace!
For his beautiful eyes,
Under Grecian skies,
Were shut by the hands of Grecian men
And the voice of his heart
Will never depart
Away from the land of the brave again ...

His voice will sound with a warlike tone,
Like the distant cry
Of trumpets when the wind is high:
O peace!
Peace to the ancient halls!
Peace to the darken'd walls!
And peace to the troubled family,
For never again shall one of them be
A moment on earth alone;
A spirit, wherever they go,
Shall go for ever before them;
A shelter from every foe,
A guardian hovering o'er them;

O peace!
For every trace
Of his glorious face
Shall be preserved in the sculptured stone!
Embalm'd by Greece,
And multiplied
On every side,
Instinct with immortality —
His rest for aye in the warrior-grave —
His heart in the tomb of the Grecian brave;
His marble head
Enthroned on high, to be
Like the best of her ancient dead,
A sculptured thought of liberty —
A boding forth of Poesy
To wake the youthful ages hence, —
The gifted of Omnipotence.

LIBERTY TO ATHENS

James Gates Percival

The flag of Freedom floats once more
Around the lofty Parthenon;
It waves, as waved the palm of yore,
In days departed long and gone;
As bright a glory, from the skies,
Pours down its light around those towers,
And once again the Greeks arise,
As in their country's noblest hours;
Their swords are girt in Virtue's cause,
MINERVA's sacred hill is free —
O! may she keep her equal laws,
While man shall live, and time shall be.
The pride of all her shrines went down;
The Goth, the Frank, the Turk, had reft
The laurel from her civic crown;
Her helm by many a sword was cleft:
She lay among her ruins low —
Where grew the palm the cypress rose,
And, crushed and bruised by many a blow,
She cower'd beneath her savage foes;
But now again she springs from earth,
Her loud, awakening trumpet speaks;
She rises in a brighter birth,
And sounds redemption to the Greeks.

It is the classic jubilee —
Their servile years have rolled away;
The clouds that hover'd o'er them flee,
They hail the dawn of Freedom's day;
From heaven the golden light descends,
The times of old are on the wing,
And Glory there her pinion bends,
And Beauty wakes a fairer spring;
The hills of Greece, her rocks, her waves,

Are all in triumph's pomp array'd;
A light that points their tyrant's graves,
Plays round each bold Athenian's blade.

The Parthenon, the sacred shrine,
Where Wisdom held her pure abode:
The hill of Mars, where light divine
Proclaimed the true but unknown God;
Where Justice held unyielding sway,
And trampled all corruption down,
And onward took her lofty way
To reach at truth's unfading crown:
The rock, where liberty was full,
Where eloquence her torrents roll'd,
And loud, against the despot's rule,
A knell the patriot's fury toll'd:

The stage, whereon the drama spake,
In tones that seem'd the words of Heaven,
Which made the wretch in terror shake,
As by avenging furies driven:
The groves and gardens, where the fire
Of wisdom, as a fountain, burned,
And every eye, that dared aspire
To truth, has long in worship turned:
The halls and porticoes, where trod
The moral sage, severe, unstain'd,
And where the intellectual god
In all the light of science reign'd:

The schools, where rose in symmetry
The simple, but majestic pile,
Where marble threw its roughness by,
To glow, to frown, to weep, to smile,
Where colours made the canvas live,
Where music roll'd her flood along,
And all the charms that art can give,
Were blent with beauty, love, and song:
The port, from whose capacious womb

Her navies took their conquering road,
The heralds of an awful doom
To all who would not kiss her rod:

On these a dawn of glory springs,
These trophies of her brightest fame;
Away the long-chain'd city flings
Her weeds, her shackles, and her shame;
Again her ancient souls awake,
HARMODIUS bares anew his sword;
Her sons in wrath their fetters break,
And Freedom is their only lord.

ODE
ON THE EMANCIPATION OF GREECE

James Gates Percival

O'er Greece a dawn is rising;
The clouds that shroud her break away:
Again, behold! the immortal day,
When Persia's hosts chastising,
In Marathon's unequal fight,
The demigods of old arose,
And, mantled in the patriot's might,
Drove back in shame their myriad foes,
And crowned their brows with civic wreaths of light.

That day shall never perish!
The grass grows green above their graves;
But Liberty will cherish
The turf for ages trod by slaves.
She sounds her trumpet: "Greeks, arise!
Be men once more! O, let the hallowed stream
That flows to you from Lacedaemon, glow
With new-waked ardor; let the beam
Of independence purge your eyes,
And, waking from your long, long dream

Of prostrate thraldom, front the skies,
And bear, with onward breast, against your tyrant foe."

She stands on mangled Parthenon,
And in her raised, commanding hand
She waves aloft her thirsty brand,
And points to fields your hardy parents won,
When not a foe dared touch their land,
Who fled not, clothed with blood and shame:
O, what a pure, unmingled flame
Of high, enduring, jealous freedom shone
In hearts of stern, but fine-wrought mould, —
Hearts that spurned at power and gold,
And scorned the proudest monarch on his throne!

Though few, they shrunk not when the prowlers came
In countless swarms, like locusts, to devour
Their harvest and destroy their name,
And o'er their much-loved country shower
Blood and havoc, tears and flame:
Yes, in that dark and awful hour,
When Xerxes, with his ravening host,
Hung, threatening vengeance, on their coast,
No eye was dim, no cheek was pale;
Their blood was up, their hearts were glowing,
And, like a storm-fed torrent flowing
With foam and fury through the echoing vale,
From their rude battlements of rocks they rushed,
And with their giant tread the awe-struck Persian crushed.

Greeks! arise, be free!
Arm for liberty!
Men of Sparta! hear the call,
Who could never bear the thrall
Of coward Frank or savage Turk!
From those mountains where you lurk,
Send the voice of Freedom forth,
Spread it through the fettered North,
And from Morea tear the funeral pall.

Now the nations are waking
From slavery's night;
Their manacles breaking,
They haste to the fight,
Where tyrants shall make their last stand for their thrones:
O, by your stripes, your tears, your groans,
Now gird your loins with vengeance! let the fire
Of high achievement heart and soul inspire;
Be nerved to die or conquer, fixed to fall,
Like Sparta's sacred band before the wall,
Which stood a bulwark to the invading swarm!
O, be your hearts thus bold, thus warm,
Devoted to your country's cause!
Be there no stay, no rest, no pause!
Once more the sun of Liberty shall pour
Its brightest glories on the Aegean shore.

THE SENATE OF CALLIMACHI

James Gates Percival

In Callimachi's halls are met
The chieftains of a noble line;
The fathers' spirit lingers yet,
To aid them in their high design;
The spirit that, in ancient days,
Called forth the boldest Spartan band,
With their own shields and breasts to raise
A living bulwark round their land.

The sound that erst in Hellas rang,
When War his brazen trumpet blew,
When shields returned the hollow clang,
And ready feet to battle flew, —
That sound in Sparta's vale is raised;
The Turkish bar and bolt are riven;
The fire that erst on Oeta blazed,

In bolder eddies curls to heaven.
That flame o'er Spartan valor burned,
The brave three-hundred's funeral pyre!
Though now in Grecian earth inurned,
Their fame shall Grecian hearts inspire;
It blazes on the sacred rock,
It flashes o'er the hallowed glen;
Advance, ye Greeks! and breast the shock,
And show the world ye still are men.

The sons of sires, who knew no fear
When threatening foemen scaled their walls,
The light shall see, the sound shall hear,
And throng to Callimachi's halls:
The altar of their country burns;
They pledge their oath to liberty;
Their fathers answer from their urns,
"Be like us, sons, and ye are free."

On old Messene's soil are met
The sons of Aristomenes;
Your ancient wrongs and feuds forget
In wrongs so foul, so deep, as these:
A new Aristodemus flings
His iron gauntlet on the foe;
At once, a nation's valor springs
To deal the liberating blow.

Who would not glow in such a cause?
Who not exult in such a name?
Blest be the sword each Maynote draws
To lop away his bonds and shame:
The fire is kindled in his soul;
The spirit flashes in his eye;
A nation's blended voices roll
The vow of freedom to the sky.

Leap from your tombs, ye men who stood
At Pylae and at Marathon;
The sire shall find his boiling blood

Throb in the bosom of his son:
Haste, demigods! with shield and spear,
And hover o'er the coming fight;
O, let the rocks of Sparta hear
The gathering word, "Unite! unite!"

THE SUNIAN PALLAS

James Gates Percival

By Sunium's rock I took my way
Along the blue Aegean sea,
That bright in golden sunset lay
Round the fair islands of the free:
A form of more than mortal mould
On the high rock sublimely rose;
The bosses of her buckler rolled
Like eyes of lightning on her foes:
I looked, — the blue-eyed goddess there
Stood glorious in the evening air.
She stood and raised her brazen lance,
That glittered like a meteor's beam;
Its light below in quivering dance
Flashed gayly on the ocean stream:
Round her tall casque her plumy crest
Shook with a terrible sign of power,
And the grim Aegis on her breast
Told to the Turk his destined hour:
She spake, — and like the rush of flame
Her voice in awful murmurs came.

"Sons, worthy of your warrior sires!
Yours is the cause of earth and heaven;
Shame to the heart that faints or tires,
Till the last sacrifice is given!
Go fearlessly along your path, —
It mounts to liberty and fame;

Go, with an unrelenting wrath,
And conquer till the Turk is tame:
When the red fires of battle glare,
Remember — I am with you there.

"These rocks that rise so rudely round
Were consecrate to me of old;
Here the Athenian sternly bound,
For rapid fight, his mantle's fold:
He saw the Persian tents below;
They filled and blackened all the plain:
He rushed, — and, like a torrent's flow,
Swept them, and hurled them to the main:
This was the wrath that made him free,
The fearless wrath of Liberty.

"What if a cold and coward world
Leave ye to work your way alone;
Be the new banner never furled
Till Liberty is all our own.
Tell them we ask no other aid
Than our own hearts in such a cause;
No, none but Freemen's hands were made
To fight and win for equal laws.
Go, with a firm, confiding breast, —
Go, fight, and win the conqueror's rest."

THE GREEK MOUNTAINEER

James Gates Percival

Now bind in myrtle wreaths the avenging sword,
Like him who, at the Panathenian games,
With the bold heart no tyrant quells nor tames,
The bosom of the proud usurper gored.
We have a sterner foe to wake our wrath, —
Centuries of darkness have not dimmed us quite, —
We have the heart to feel, the hand to smite.

Woe to the wretch who dares to cross our path!
Our souls are gathered to the effort, — free
We have been, and we will be, and our sires
Shall look from heaven, and see us light the fires
On thy eternal altars, Liberty!
Though the proud fanes of ancient glory lie
Crushed by the hand of havoc and of time,
Still tower, with front as lofty and sublime,
Yon hoary peaks, the pillars of the sky.
There lived the Suliote free, when all below
Bowed to the Ottoman, — the Mainote there
Wandered as wildly as his mountain air,
And dealt at will his vengeance on his foe.
These are thy temples, Liberty! — these heights
Nursed the first hardy Dorian in his cave;
And there, when Sparta sank, the free and brave
Hung on the unconquered rocks their beacon lights.
There stood thy altars, and the eternal flame
Burns round the cloudy summits, with a glow
As bright as when it cheered the plains below,
And lit the sacred band to death and fame.
We too will have our glory, — we will light
Our torches in the fire that never dies;
And with a terrible and solemn rite
Devote us to our country's liberties.
We bind our swords in myrtle, and we go
To meet the proud oppressor on his way:
Let but the tyrant sink beneath the blow,
Gladly we die, — our foes can only slay.
They cannot rob us of that wreath of fame,
The glorious chiefs of ancient Athens bear:
O, how they come to meet us in the air,
Borne on their chariots and steeds of flame!
We hasten to our vengeance and we die, —
Wide to the winds, our blood, our lives, are given;
In the mid-joy of fight they hurry by,
Seize us, and bear us to the Patriot's Heaven.

THE LAST SONG OF THE GREEK PATRIOT

James Gates Percival

One last, best effort, now!
They shall not call us slaves, —
These iron necks shall never bow
To barter for a hated life,
But we will tell, in mortal strife,
What wrath a freeman braves:
A few short years, and we have known
The pride and joy — to live alone.

Our ancient land was free;
We washed its stains in blood:
Again the hymn of Liberty
Rose from the high Athenian shrine,
And virgin hands did often twine,
In the dark olive wood,
Their garlands for the youthful brow
Who taught the heathen Turk to bow.
These have been glorious days:
Let come what will, our fame
Is like the sun's eternal blaze,
And when they tell of Marathon,
And all the fields our fathers won,
They too shall name
Bozzaris, and the few who died,
Victims of glory, by his side.

The world has told our doom, —
'Tis liberty or death!
The tree we planted must not bloom,
For Turk and Christian — all unite,
And royal hands our sentence write,
And yet our breath,
When trampled by the ruffian herd,
Shall never breathe one recreant word.

If we must die, then die!
And let the foul disgrace
Cling to their names eternally,
Who, when they had the power to save,
Doomed to a dark and bloody grave
A high, devoted race.
Awhile the sweets of life to know,
O God, and then to perish so!

But freedom has one shore:
Would we could shelter there
The tender ones we value more
Than life or fame! O generous men!
Be with us, as ye long have been,
And we will share
All the poor fruit of toils and pains, —
Our hearts, our lives, perhaps our chains.

Come, at this fatal hour,
Ye last of high-born souls;
Come, when the crushing weight of power
Has all but bent our necks to earth;
We will not shame our glorious birth;
Nor Turk nor Hun controls
The heart that holds the Spartan fire,
The sacred relic of his sire.
We know ye cannot fear,
We know that ye are brave, —
To us, your very name is dear:
O, by that name, and all its light,
We bid you join the murderous fight,
To win and save!
O, come, if it be only time
To fall with us, in death sublime!

GREECE, FROM MOUNT HELICON
(excerpt)

James Gates Percival

                                        ... Parnassus
Has not yet lost the glory and the blaze
That suit the heaven of song. There let me pause;
There fix my latest look. How beautiful,
Sublimely beautiful, thou hoverest
High in the vacant air! Thou seemest uplifted
From all of earth, and like an island floating
Away in heaven. How pure the eternal snows
That crown thee! yet how rich the golden blaze
That flashes from thy peak! how like the rose,
The virgin rose, the tints that fade below,
Till all is sweetly pale! Are there not harps
Warbling above thee? voices, too, attuned
To an unearthly song? Methinks I hear them
Breathing around me, with a charm and spell,
That melt my heart to weeping. It is sad,
That song of heaven, — the funeral symphony
Of ancient worthies, for the murdered peace
And glory of their land. They greet the heroes,
Who rise to meet them in these iron times,
And hail them as their sons; and yet they weep
Their unavailing toil. Is there no hand
To grasp the avenging sword, and tear the knife
From the assassin? Must these generous hearts
Pour out their blood like water, till the flood
Of rage and power has swept them from the earth,
And buried all their bright and hallowed land
In death and darkness? O, forbid it, nations
Who wear the name of Christian, and are proud
Of light and truth and mercy. Arm ye; take
The cross and sword; move to the war of death
Stern and devoted; pause not, till the Turk
Has lost the power to harm; then give to Greece

Her ancient liberty, and ye shall live
Immortal, in your fame.

THE GREEK SONG OF VICTORY

James Gates Percival

The red day of slaughter is done;
The rose tint is pale in the west;
The triumph of liberty won,
Joy swells each Athenian breast:
We have buried our foes in the wave
That rolls on our iron-bound shore;
And the foot of the Ottoman slave
Shall dare scale our ramparts no more:
They came in their pride and their pomp to the fight,
But have scattered like dust, in the rush of our might.

They came with the dawning of day;
The sun brightly glanced on their sails,
And their fleet, on its conquering way,
Bore forward with favoring gales:
Like a dark cloud of tempest they came;
Already they uttered their yell, —
When we let loose our arrows of flame,
And the pride of the Mussulman fell:
Then the waves with the fire and the slaughter were red,
And our prows hurried on through the dying and dead.

They are gone, — and the sea rolls again
In peace on our iron-bound shore;
They have left but the wreck and the stain,
Where the green waves heaved purple with gore.
As the last light grows dim in the west,
O God of the brave and the free!
How the fulness that swells in each breast
Is poured forth in blessings to thee!
For we trusted in thee, — and the arm of thy might
Has scattered our foes in the perilous fight.

A BIRTHDAY IN SCIO

John Pierpont

I landed there on the day of my birth, —
The day that the city was swept from the earth;
Though thirteen years had floated away
On the stream of time since that bloody day.

There had been a strong southeaster blowing,
The night before and afternoon;
And the clouds, as night came on, were throwing
So much of mystery round the moon,
That, — what above, and what below, —
Things looked so squally, all on board
Concurred in thinking Captain Ford
Spoke wisely, when he said, "No, no;
I shall put in, and try to keep
Where the ladies, who're aboard, may sleep."

So I'd slept on board, the night before,
In the snug little port; while, round the isle,
The breakers thundered on the shore,
Like a line of sea-dogs, chafed and hoar,
Bounding and barking for many a mile.

Yet, though "outside" those dogs might prowl,
We lay where the wave was "calm as a clock";
And, though afar off we could hear the dogs howl,
And sometimes their nearer and hoarser growl,
I could sleep, and I *did* sleep, "like a rock."
But morning came! — an April morn;
And, though the winds were felt no more,
The waters still were landward borne,
And still the waves came combing o'er,
And fringed with foam the eastern shore;
And there rolled along so heavy a swell,
Between the Island and Tshesmé,
That the captain thought he might as well

Not venture round Phanae Point, that day.

O, how I blessed the restless deep,
That it sunk not with the winds to sleep!
For it gave me a day on Scio's isle, —
A day that I shall not soon forget;
For the earth's sweet face, and the blue heaven's smile,
And the sea that glittered all round, the while,
As I then beheld them, haunt me yet.

Well, we're ashore! Here hath Oppression's rod
Wrought its worst work, where the good hand of God
Seems to have wrought its fairest and its best.
That guardian mountain, towering in the west, —
His fertile flanks, — the plains that stretch away,
East and southeast, — all basking in the ray
Of such a sun! How could there ever be
A lovelier island lifted from the sea!
Yet here hath Ruin driven her ploughshare deep!
Few here survive, the many slain to weep,
And few now wander, lonely, on this shore,
Their captive sons and daughters to deplore.

These magazines, — once glutted with the stores
Of what the Euxine down the Bosphorus pours, —
Of Brusa's silks, — of stuffs from Angora's looms,
Of all the colors of the peacock's plumes, —
Of cotton goods from Europe's Island Queen, —
Of Samian wine, — of oil from Mitylene, —
Of corn, that from the coast of Barbary comes, —
Of dates from Egypt, and Arabian gums, —
All empty now, lie open to the sky:
Nothing to sell here, and no one to buy!

"Paithiske, (damsel,) canst thou tell me where
The College stood?" She answers, with the air
Of one who feels unequal to the task,
"Ohe," (I cannot,) "but I'll run and ask."
And back she comes with knowledge in her eye,
And leads me round, through places wet and dry, —

O'er heaps of brick, one clambers up with pain,
Round open cellars partly filled with rain, —
Until, at last, "Ethó!" ('Twas here!) she cries;
And joy and wonder sparkle in her eyes,
As, with the true Greek appetite for gains,
She pockets a piastre for her pains.

And is this formless mass of prostrate walls
All that remains of Scio's college halls?
Those halls to which the children of the isles,
For Panayéa's and Minerva's smiles,
Thronged, till their spreading light, like kindling morn,
Flashed on the waters of the Golden Horn,
And broke the slumbers of Mahmoud's Divan?
Yes, this is all! and the wayfaring man
Who, after thirteen years, would see the spot,
Finds, it was never known, or is forgot;
While every peasant, who is not a fool,
Will lead me, if I wish, to HOMER's school.

I mount a mule, and to the country ride.
High walls confine the road on either side;
Mile after mile presents the same sad scene,
Of princely seats, with orange groves between;
Mansions of merchant princes, that once vied
With those of Venice, both in grace and pride;
But now those mansions speak of Moslem ire.
Roofless and windowless, they show that fire
Here had its perfect work. The walls yet stand,
And seem to whisper, "Lend us, friend, a hand!"
Ay, had a Yankee, — had even I, — this "place,"
How soon I'd make it wear another face!
New floored, new roofed, and thoroughly new glazed,
The battered court-yard gate and fences raised,
The garden dressed, all trimmed the mastic trees,
I, in my palace hall, might sit at ease,
And see a paradise around me bloom;
And, as the fragrant night-breeze filled my room,
Flowing through open casements; and the moon

Silvered the scene around me; or, at noon,
As in an hour like this, in blooming spring,
I heard my marble fountain murmuring,
And saw my noble orange groves unfold
Their snowy blossoms and their fruit of gold, —
Say, "For this palace must I thank *thee*, War!"
Well, — I may have it for the asking for!

But, would I *take* it? When I turn my eye
Where yon Mount Opus swells into the sky,
Those cliffs that look down on the plains below,
Ring with the answer, — "Would'st thou take it? — No!
For 'come up hither!' — we can tell
A tale to freeze a Western freeman's blood; —
When, from our height, we saw the swell,
And heard the rush, of war's infernal flood
Through all that city's bleeding lanes,
O'er all the villas of those blooming plains;
We opened, then, our dens and caves
To the poor peasants. Behold, here, their graves!
The fleet of foot to these, our caverns, sped;
To these our heights and cavern-depths, alike,
The hell-hounds followed where the blood-hounds led, —
The brutes to mangle, and the fiends to strike!
We trembled then, at the deep death-note
Pealed from the panting bull-dog's throat, —
The flash, — the echo and the smoke, —
The yell, — the stab, — the sabre stroke, —
The musket shot, — the frenzied shriek, —
The death-groan of the hunted Greek, —
Till our white feet with streams of gore were dyed,
And mangled limbs were strown on every side, —
With many a skull by Turkish sabre cleft;
Our vultures finished what their blood-hounds left!
The arm that, thirteen years ago,
Bathed, elbow-deep, in Sciote blood,
Still sways, o'er us and all below,
The iron sceptre of Mahmoud!

And would'st thou, stranger, — were all free, —
Take any villa thou canst see,
To dwell therein? Beware! Beware!
The sword hangs o'er thee by a hair!"

Fair Scio! as I pass along thy shore,
Through waters that the brave Kanaris bore,
Where, at one blow, thou wast avenged so well,
And where the Butcher of thy children fell;
Ere yet I lose thee in the deepening blue,
So lone, so lovely, art thou to my view, —
(For nothing lonelier lies beneath the sun,
And nothing lovelier doth he look upon!)
I pray thee, listen to a parting strain,
From one who ne'er shall look on thee again:

Farewell to thee, Scio! it is but a day
That I've seen thee, and yet I shall love thee for ever.
Thy children are slain, and thy crown torn away,
And thy jewels and gold shall return to thee never.

Thou sittest, no longer, a queen in thy bower,
But a widow, — of sons and of daughters bereft;
Yet despair not, thou desolate one! for thy dower,
Lovely Scio, — thy lands and thy beauty, — is left.

And though Syra, thy proud "little sister," awhile
Thy pearls round her bold little forehead may twine,
Yet, envy her not, for she hath not a smile,
Nor hath she a face, or a bosom, like thine.

And, as soon as the sceptre of Islam is broken,
Or Mahmoud, the red-handed Padischa, dead,
The word shalt thou hear, that thy Maker hath spoken;
"Thou shalt put on thy garments, and lift up thy head."

And vine-leaves and roses thy temple shall deck,
And some of thy children shall cling to thy breast,
While some pluck the clusters that hang round thy neck,
And — *thy lap-full of oranges feed all the rest!*

THE HERO

John Greenleaf Whittier

*(The hero of the incident related in this poem was
Dr. Samuel Gridley Howe, the well-known philan-
thropist, who when a young man volunteered his
aid in the Greek struggle for independence.)*

"Oh for a knight like Bayard,
Without reproach or fear;
My light glove on his casque of steel,
My love-knot on his spear!

"Oh for the white plume floating
Sad Zutphen's field above, —
The lion heart in battle,
The woman's heart in love!

"Oh that man once more were manly,
Woman's pride, and not her scorn:
That once more the pale young mother
Dared to boast 'a man is born'!

"But now life's slumberous current
No sun-bowed cascade wakes;
No tall, heroic manhood
The level dulness breaks.

"Oh for a knight like Bayard,
Without reproach or fear!
My light glove on his casque of steel,
My love-knot on his spear!"

Then I said, my own heart throbbing
To the time her proud pulse beat,
"Life hath its regal natures yet,
True, tender, brave, and sweet!

"Smile not, fair unbeliever!
One man, at least, I know,

Who might wear the crest of Bayard
Or Sidney's plume of snow.

"Once, when over purple mountains
Died away the Grecian sun,
And the far Cyllenian ranges
Paled and darkened, one by one, —

"Fell the Turk, a bolt of thunder,
Cleaving all the quiet sky,
And against his sharp steel lightnings
Stood the Suliote but to die.

"Woe for the weak and halting!
The crescent blazed behind
A curving line of sabres,
Like fire before the wind!

"Last to fly, and first to rally,
Rode he of whom I speak,
When, groaning in his bridle-path,
Sank down a wounded Greek.

"With the rich Albanian costume
Wet with many a ghastly stain,
Gazing on earth and sky as one
Who might not gaze again!

"He looked forward to the mountains,
Back on foes that never spare,
Then flung him from his saddle,
And placed the stranger there.

" 'Allah! hu!' Through flashing sabres,
Through a stormy hail of lead,
The good Thessalian charger
Up the slopes of olives sped.

"Hot spurred the turbaned riders;
He almost felt their breath,
Where a mountain stream rolled darkly down
Between the hills and death.

"One brave and manful struggle, —
He gained the solid land,
And the cover of the mountains,
And the carbines of his band!"

"It was very great and noble,"
Said the moist-eyed listener then,
"But one brave deed makes no hero;
Tell me what he since hath been!"

"Still a brave and generous manhood,
Still an honor without stain,
In the prison of the Kaiser,
By the barricades of Seine . . .

"Wherever outraged Nature
Asks word or action brave,
Wherever struggles labor,
Wherever groans a slave,

"Wherever rise the peoples,
Wherever sinks a throne,
The throbbing heart of Freedom finds
An answer in his own.

"Knight of a better era,
Without reproach or fear!
Said I not well that Bayards
And Sidneys still are here?"

SYRA
(a transmitted reminiscence)

Herman Melville

Fleeing from Scio's smouldering vines
(Where when the sword its work had done
The Turk applied the torch) the Greek
Came here, a fugitive stript of goods,

Here to an all but tenantless isle,
Nor here in footing gained at first,
Felt safe. Still from the turbaned foe
Dreading the doom of shipwrecked men
Whom feline seas permit to land
Then pounce upon and drag them back,
For height they made, and prudent won
A cone-shaped fastness on whose flanks
With pains they pitched their eyrie camp,
Stone huts, whereto they wary clung;
But, reassured in end, come down —
Multiplied through compatriots now,
Refugees like themselves forlorn —
And building along the water's verge
Begin to thrive; and thriving more
When Greece at last flung off the Turk,
Make of the haven mere a mart.

I saw it in its earlier day —
Primitive, such an isled resort
As hearthless Homer might have known
Wandering about the Aegean here.
Sheds ribbed with wreck-stuff faced the sea
Where goods in transit shelter found:
And here and there a shanty-shop
Where Fez-caps, swords, tobacco, shawls,
Pistols, and orient finery, Eve's —
(The spangles dimmed by hands profane)
Like plunder on a pirate's deck
Lay orderless in such loose way
As to suggest things ravished or gone astray.

Above a tented inn with fluttering flag
A sunburnt board announced Greek wine
In self-same text Anacreon knew,
Dispensed by one named "Pericles."
Got up as for the opera's scene,
Armed strangers, various, lounged or lazed,
Lithe fellows tall, with gold-shot eyes,

Sunning themselves as leopards may.

Off-shore lay xebecs trim and light,
And some but dubious in repute.
But on the strand, for docks were none,
What busy bees! no testy fry;
Frolickers, picturesquely odd,
With bales and oil-jars lading boats,
Lighters that served an anchored craft,
Each in his tasseled Phrygian cap,
Blue Eastern drawers and braided vest;
And some with features cleanly cut
As Proserpine's upon the coin.
Such chatterers all! like children gay
Who make believe to work, but play.

I saw, and how help musing too.
Here traffic's immature as yet:
Forever this juvenile fun hold out
And these light hearts? Their garb, their glee,
Alike profuse in flowing measure,
Alike inapt for serious work,
Blab of grandfather Saturn's prime
When trade was not, nor toil, nor stress,
But life was leisure, merriment, peace,
And lucre none and love was righteousness.

ON THE PROPOSAL TO ERECT A MONUMENT
IN ENGLAND TO LORD BYRON

Emma Lazarus

The grass of fifty Aprils hath waved green
Above the spent heart, the Olympian head,
The hands crost idly, the shut eyes unseen,
Unseeing, the locked lips whose song hath fled;
Yet mystic-lived, like some rich, tropic flower,
His fame puts forth fresh blossoms hour by hour;

Wide spread the laden branches dropping dew
On the low, laureled brow misunderstood,
That bent not, neither bowed, until subdued
By the last foe who crowned while he o'erthrew.

Fair was the Easter Sabbath morn when first
Men heard he had not wakened to its light:
The end had come, and time had done its worst,
For the black cloud had fallen of endless night.
Then in the town, as Greek accosted Greek,
'Twas not the wonted festal words to speak,
"Christ is arisen," but "Our chief is gone,"
With such wan aspect and grief-smitten head
As when the awful cry of "Pan is dead!"
Filled echoing hill and valley with its moan.

"I am more fit for death than the world deems,"
So spake he as life's light was growing dim,
And turned to sleep as unto soothing dreams.
What terrors could its darkness hold for him,
Familiar with all anguish, but with fear
Still unacquainted? On his martial bier
They laid a sword, a helmet, and a crown —
Meed of the warrior, but not these among
His voiceless lyre, whose silent chords unstrung
Shall wait — how long? — for touches like his own.

An alien country mourned him as her son,
And hailed him hero: his sole, fitting tomb
Were Theseus' temple or the Parthenon,
Fondly she deemed. His brethren bare him home,
Their exiled glory, past the guarded gate
Where England's Abbey shelters England's great.
Afar he rests whose very name hath shed
New lustre on her with the song he sings.
So Shakespeare rests who scorned to lie with kings,
Sleeping at peace midst the unhonored dead.

And fifty years suffice to overgrow
With gentle memories the foul weeds of hate

That shamed his grave. The world begins to know
Her loss, and view with other eyes his fate.
Even as the cunning workman brings to pass
The sculptor's thought from out the unwieldy mass
Of shapeless marble, so Time lops away
The stony crust of falsehood that concealed
His just proportions, and, at last revealed,
The statue issues to the light of day,

Most beautiful, most human. Let them fling
The first stone who are tempted even as he,
And have not swerved. When did that rare soul sing
The victim's shame, the tyrant's eulogy,
The great belittle, or exalt the small,
Or grudge his gift, his blood, to disenthrall
The slaves of tyranny or ignorance?
Stung by fierce tongues himelf, whose rightful fame
Hath he reviled? Upon what noble name
Did the winged arrows of that barbed wit glance?

The years' thick, clinging curtains backward pull,
And show him as he is, crowned with bright beams,
"Beauteous, and yet not all as beautiful
As he hath been or might be; Sorrow seems
Half of his immortality." He needs
No monument whose name and song and deeds
Are graven in all foreign hearts; but she
His mother, England, slow and last to wake,
Needs raise the votive shaft for her fame's sake:
Hers is the shame if such forgotten be!

Melville

"The Dire Vox Clamans of Our Day"

Melville's refusal to remain the darling of an escapist audience cost him heavily indeed. During the quarter-century before 1876 his reputation underwent a steady decline; by the time his immense poem *Clarel: a Pilgrimage* appeared, he was utterly without readers and in an eclipse so profound that it prevailed for almost fifty years more. To appreciate the pungent criticism leveled by this poet, unheeded but undaunted, one might begin by juxtaposing *Clarel* against other 1876 productions: the long-winded, ultra-nationalistic centennial odes of Bayard Taylor, Richard H. Stoddard, George Woodberry, and Cleveland Coxe, as well as Lanier's "Psalm of the West"; threnodies for Custer by John Hay, Edmund C. Stedman, Joaquin Miller, Walt Whitman, and others who should have known better; an amazingly venomous assault on the Sioux tribesmen by Longfellow — who was ordinarily gentle, balanced, and careful not to produce a poem in the heat of the moment, and William Dean Howells, whose Custer-like barrage in the May 1876 *Atlantic Monthly* called for "The extermination of the red savages ... whose malign traits can hardly inspire any emotion softer than abhorrence."

Despite his alienation from America, his increasing hopelessness, and his conviction that poets should know evil rather than fight it, Melville offered America an intensely unsettling image of itself. In the very hour of his countrymen's centenary pride, he issued a crushing jeremiad against Anglo-Saxon crime. This he could do despite his fear that no one would listen, and despite his knowledge of the wrath that would descend upon him if, by some miracle, his grim truths were heard out. He remembered well the penalty imposed upon him by America for having written *Mardi* instead of an exotic entertainment, but this did not dissuade him from the herculean labor of creating *Clarel*.

With a courage matched only by Thoreau, he places religious arrogance at the root of the white man's difficulties "in Pequod wilds" long ago: "Hittites — foes pestilent to God/His fathers old those Indians deemed. . . ." To the Anglo-Saxons of 1876, still pushing on "in the name of Christ," he says that their conversion dream is doomed, for they lack the grace "To win the love of any race." As the most keen-eyed and bold-tongued incarnation of the Bible seers, he renounces, precisely at the centennial moment, his "birthright . . . in hope," his "sanguine country's wonted claim." Only Melville, at the time of Custer's fall, dares to identify the sickness at the root of the American psyche:

> . . . Anglo-Saxons. What are they?
> Hated by myriads dispossessed
> Of rights — the Indians East and West.
> These pirates of the sphere! grave looters —
> Grave, canting, Mammonite freebooters . . .
> Deflower the world's last sylvan glade!

Thirty years earlier, as the war against Mexico raged, Melville first raised his denunciatory voice. In *Mardi,* especially in the superb, significantly titled chapter, "A Voice From the Gods," his antipathy to "the evils of imperialist expansion" finds both artistic and prophetic expression: "Be advised; wash your hands . . . And be not too grasping . . . It is not freedom to filch . . . Neighboring nations may be free without coming under your banner."

The verse in *Mardi* emphasizes his disgust. At times the satire foreshadows Gilbert's "When the Foeman Bears His Steel":

> Hack away, merry men, hack away.
> > Who would not die brave . . . ?
> Thwack away, merry men, thwack away!
> > 'Tis glory that calls,
> > To each hero that falls . . .

Elsewhere the joy in slaughter is more grimly exposed. In "Song of the Paddlers," the shark serves as model: "Like him we prey;/Like him we slay . . . " Best of all is "Song of Arms," which precedes

Whitman's free verse and offers a very different response to the rape of Mexico than is found in Whitman's bloodthirsty *Brooklyn Eagle* editorials of the same year:

> Our clubs! our clubs! . . .
> Skull breakers! Brain spatterers!
> Wielded right, and wielded left;
> Life quenchers! Death dealers! . . .
>   To the fight . . .
> Sons of battle! Hunters of men!
> Raise high your war-wood!

In this early work Melville already puts his finger on the Mammonite lust driving the white man westward, a very different approach than the lofty, unselfcritical stance of Bryant in "Oh Mother of a Mighty Race" and Whitman in "Pioneers! O Pioneers!"

> The Golden Number rules the spheres!
> Gold, gold it is, that sways the nations:
> Gold! gold! the center of all rotations! . . .
>   Gold-hunters' hearts with golden dreamings!
> With golden arrows kings are slain . . .

One can understand America's disapproval of this audacious and vexing work, after having taken *Typee* and *Omoo* to its heart. But if rejection by critics and public offered him a prompt and unmistakable lesson, that lesson must have incited him to take an even more subversive position in the novels and stories and followed, culminating in *The Confidence-Man.*

Once the prose was behind him, he could really be "his own man"; to mine his richest vein of dissent, therefore, we must approach the poems, undismayed by Richard H. Fogle's prediction that "The poems of Melville will doubtless never be widely read" and James E. Miller's judgment that *Clarel* is "the only really significant appearance of Melville in print from the publication of *The Confidence-Man* in 1857 to his death in 1891."

Emerson, in an early version of "Merlin," had satirized the poets who "tinkle a guitar" in accordance with the expectations of "pretty people in a nice saloon," and who read them a "pretty tale" instead of forcing the truth upon them. Such a poet is a seller of a commodity —

a "grocer green," Melville calls him — who thrives with the "fulsome face/Of a fool serene," rather than "the wronged one's knight," which he should be. The consequences are only too clear: a true poet, one of conscience, must find a way of surviving without the laureate's coin; if he refuses to "sing for his supper," he must expect to starve; indeed, the consequences can be far more severe than penury and snubbing; Melville's pilgrimage in Europe leads him to the ghosts of poets martyred for their truth — Silvio Pellico, dungeoned beside the Bridge of Sighs in Venice; Torquato Tasso, immured in Ferrara's tower; Camoëns, a forgotten pauper, fevering to death in a Lisbon hospital. Out of this pilgrimage comes the definition of a poet's torment and triumph, and it is this definition, restated in a score of his noblest poems as well as many lesser ones, which keeps Melville lyrically alive for the next 35 years.

Timoleon includes a piece called "Pausilippo (In the Time of Bomba)" which is clearly an extract from the otherwise then-unpublished long poem "Naples in the Time of Bomba." Melville may have included it in the 1891 collection precisely because it illustrates, along with so much else in *Timoleon,* what can happen to a poet whose mind is (as he says of another poet in an 1885 letter) "utterly untrameled [sic] and independent":

> Clandestine arrest abrupt by night;
> The sole conjecturable cause
> The yearning in a patriot ode
> Construed as treason; trial none;
> Prolonged captivity profound . . .

But throughout Melville the artist-hero is contrasted with the laureate, the patron's darling, who pleases on commission. In lyric after lyric he pits those "discreet" ones who "trudge where worldlings go," against those "lone" ones who will not "shrink from Truth . . . Mid loud gregarious lies" ("The Enthusiast"); those who earn the "plum-pudding," against those who "in a garret/As void as a drum" prefer to "paint the plum!" ("Fruit and Flower Painter"); those who "turn with weather of the time" against those who "Stand where Posterity shall stand" ("Lone Founts"); those who heap "Gems and jewels" against those who "grapple from Art's deep/One dripping trophy!" ("In a Garret"); the Rose Farmer who boasts a sure market for his "heaps of posies" — against his unpopular, impractical neighbor, "lean as a rake," who

> with painstaking throes
> Essays to crystallize the rose.

The commitment is solemn. Bearing it in mind, one cannot turn to his poetry with anything less than total attention. It becomes clear at once that as the Golden Age recedes, as the Gilded Age advances, Melville expands his attack, begun in *Mardi*, on the gold-hunters

> raking arid sands
> For gold more barren meetly theirs
> Sterile, with brimming hands.
>
> ("Disinterment of the Hermes")

But now the demoniac obsession of his countrymen is exposed with greater lyric force:

> Gold in the mountain
> And gold in the glen,
> And greed in the heart,
> Heaven having no part,
> And unsatisfied men.
>
> ("Gold in the Mountain")

On a lush spring day "The Golden Age returns" to fields "at least," if "never to the town . . ." — but even the fields are in danger:

> . . . alack and alas
> For things of wilding feature!
> Since hearsed was Pan
>
> Ill befalls each profitless creature —
> Profitless to Man!
>
> ("When Forth the Shepherd Leads the Flock")

Gone now are such "hearts-of-gold" as the poets Hafiz, Horace, and Beranger; in their place he beholds "genius, turned to sordid ends . . . Our arts but serve the clay" ("In the Hall of Marbles"). In Anacreon's language a Greek shop announces its tourist wares, sold, ironically, by "one named 'Pericles' " Bitterly the poet recalls

"Saturn's prime/When trade was not, nor toil, nor stress,/But life was leisure, merriment, peace,/And lucre none and love was righteousness" ("Syra"). Despoiled, thanks to the swift leap of 19th century "progress," are the Pacific islands — "Authentic Edens" that were "not yet overrun" in his youth, "Ere Paul Pry cruised with Pelf and Trade . . ." ("To Ned"). The theme hammers at us in poem after poem. Venice's Grand Canal will be improved "to a huckster's street"; where "Utility reigns," greatness is replaced by "The picture that fetches a picturesque price!" ("At the Hostelry"). "Indignity" is offered to "the arch majesty" of a perished monarch; "The atoms of his pomp no prouder/Than to be blown about in powder,/Or made a muddy clay!" ("The Dust Layers"). Perhaps Melville's cleverest protest occurs in "A Railroad Cutting Near Alexandria in 1855":

> Too long inurned, Sesostres's spurned,
>   What glory left to Isis?
> Mid loud acclaim to Watts his name
>   Alack for Miriam's spices!

At his most impatient and direct, he calls New York "the Nineveh of the North" ("The Released Rebel Prisoner"). But his challenge to the Gilded Age takes subtler forms as well. Often it chooses, as we have seen, symbols from the Mediterranean world — Italy, Egypt, Greece. Sometimes (as in Hardy's much later "The Convergence of the Twain") an overconfident present is brought to heel by accident or the underestimated power of nature ("The Berg," "The Haglets," "The Admiral of the White," "The Aeolian Harp," etc.). In an especially memorable stanza "The Young Master of a Wrecked California Clipper" offers "Old Counsel":

> Come out of the Golden Gate,
> Go round the Horn with streamers,
> Carry royals early and late;
> But brother, be not over-elate —
> All hands save ship! has startled dreamers.

When describing the tainted leaders of modern society, he is merciless. A "Jesuit grave" is "genteely sleek/In dapper small-clothes and fine hose/Of sable silk, and shovel-hat." His partner, a doctor of the law, is "useful . . . to lawless power,/Expert to legalise the wrong"

("Naples in the Time of Bomba"). The industrialists and merchants
are "shoddyites" who profited from the Civil War:

> In mart and bazaar Lucre chuckled the huzza;
> Coining the dollars in the bloody mint of war.
>
> ("Bridegroom Dick")

Melville's hatred of war, as seen in *Mardi,* is expressed with even
greater strength in his Civil War poems. This can not have been easy
for a poet who, while despising the Mexican adventure, strongly
favored the Union cause and worked hard to be the epic singer of
1861–1865. Always willing to dive for the truth, that bitter "tuft of
kelp," he takes a typically unpopular position, airing the charge "That
meddlers" on both sides "kindled the war's white heat" ("Lee in the
Capitol"). Both sides "warred for Sway ... but named the name of
Right"; both carried the cross "While crossing blades profaned the
sign ..." ("Battle of Stone River, Tennessee"). In later times, he
predicts, "much of doubt ... /Shall cling, as now, to the war" ("Stone-
wall Jackson II"). At night, "sleepy and full of spleen," the Union
troops hunting a rebel band begin to "curse the war. 'Fools, North and
South!' " ("The Scout Toward Aldie").

Wilfred Owen was to learn in the last year of World War I that
"The poetry is in the pity." In this respect, Melville's war poems
match the best of Whitman's later *Drum-Taps* pieces. Families are
split apart: "Ah! black blood/Was his 'gainst even child and wife
... Such the strife." And how swiftly the young are educated:

> By the hospital-tent the cripples stand —
> Bandage, and crutch, and cane, and sling ...
> Yet these were late as bold, as gay ...
>
> ("The Scout Toward Aldie")

A number of other poems, notably "The College Colonel," "On the
Slain Collegians," "Commemorative of a Naval Victory" and
"Shiloh," deal hauntingly with this theme. Elsewhere the anonymity
of the thousands is compared with the fame of their commanders:

> It is the pathos deep.
> There is glory for the brave
> Who lead, and nobly save,

> But no knowledge in the grave
> Where the nameless followers sleep.
>
> ("Sheridan at Cedar Creek")

In a tone almost unique for his time, not to prevail until Owen and Sassoon half a century later, he spells out the private aftermath of victory-announcements:

> But others were who wakeful laid
> In midnight beds, and early rose . . .
> Snatched the damp paper — wife and maid.
>   The death-list like a river flows
> Down the pale sheet.   ("Donelson")

His words in *Mardi* were Isaiah-like: "Be advised; wash your hands ." Just so, almost a score of years later, instead of celebrating victory along with every other Northern-hearted poet, he prays in the voice of the old prophet:

> Ah God! may Time with happy haste
> Bring wail and triumph to a waste,
>   And war be done;
> The battle flag-staff fall athwart
> The curs'd ravine, and wither; naught
>   Be left of trench or gun . . .   ("Donelson")

Untimely as the swords-and-ploughshares theme may then have been, it was at least being mouthed from pulpits on Sunday mornings; generosity toward the foe, however, was another matter, and Melville expresses this unforgivable sentiment throughout *Battle-Pieces,* as well as in later works. Primary in importance is his admiration for the guerilla chieftain, Mosby, implicit throughout his lengthy ballad "The Scout Toward Aldie." By the constant reminder of his name and of his genius for ambush, Mosby achieves for the reader the rank of mythic hero, and the portrait of his followers in captivity dramatically shifts our sympathy toward them. One, a middle-aged father, remarks: "They shot at my heart when my hands were up." A young rebel, offered whiskey, replies: ". . . if you think we'll blab why, then/You don't know Mosby or his men." The description of these Confederates (as in "Iris," "Lee in the

Capitol," "Magnanimity Baffled," "The Released Rebel Prisoner," and "The Rebel Color-Bearers at Shiloh") is loving and magnanimous:

> Virginians; some of family-pride,
> And young, and full of fire, and fine
> In open feature and cheek that glowed;
> And here thralled vagabonds now they ride.

This sympathy, later to be enunciated in "Bridgroom Dick" and the prose passages of "Marquis de Grandvin," is far more remarkable for a Northern poet addressing a hate-wracked Northern audience soon after accompanying a Northern force and immediately after his own cousin, Col. Gansevoort, has captured Mosby's camp. In a note accompanying the poem Melville praises Mosby:

> In partisan warfare he proved himself shrewd, able, and enterprising, and always a wary fighter. . . . To our wounded on more than one occasion he showed considerate kindness.

The hunter of Mosby, on the other hand, declares openly what the Civil War means to him: "Names must be made and printed be!" This young Northern leader suffers from the blind, vainglorious mania of a Custer — who was nurtured in just such Civil War excursions and felt unemployed when they came to an end. In fact, Melville's narrative is a chillingly prophetic rehearsal of the Little Big Horn twelve years later, to which he refers in "John Marr" as "a war waged by the Red Man for their native soil and natural rights." Though a recent bridegroom, the protagonist fails to win our sympathy precisely because Melville has used him to anatomize the growing war-lust in the American spirit.

Perhaps the supreme example of lonely prophecy is offered by "The House Top." In July, 1863, mobs of anti-Lincoln, anti-draft rioters led, ironically, by longshoremen whose immigrant parents had themselves been mobbed in the '30's and '40's, attacked blacks, burned down an orphanage and church, looted, and caused almost a thousand casualties in dead and wounded. After three days Federal troops restored order to New York.

Bryant and Whitman, the other major New York poets, held true to their habitual stance. The *New York Post* editor, as usual, kept his poetry free from the issues of the day, satisfied to editorialize. Whitman had carefully taken form as the poet of both evil and good, of the cosmic embrace (including all but Mexicans and Irish, apparently), of democracy and Manahatta, who — looking out "upon all the oppression and shame," will remain "silent." Unsurprisingly, his response to the rioters is a refusal "to abuse the poor people, or call for a rope or bullets for them." Nor did any other American poet of note so much as express public regret. It was left for Melville to be the "Mad John" crying in the wilderness, just as Mortmain was to cry in *Clarel* ten years later, "The dire Vox Clamans of our day":

> Repent! repent in every land
> Or hell's hot kingdom is at hand!

From his roof the poet looked down into the streets, unshrinking, ready as always to examine his and Hawthorne's lifelong subject-matter: "The ever-upbubbling wickedness!"

"The House Top" is a remarkable poem — in sombre blank verse, a rare use of that medium for Melville, emphasizing a grimness of spirit that could not stop to play games with form, as he notes the tiger in man, "apt for ravage," once more supreme:

> The Town is taken by its rats — ship-rats
> And rats of the wharves . . .
> And man rebounds whole aeons back in nature.

Instead of bringing peace to his soul, the arrival of the Federal troops troubles him most of all — for it corroborates "Calvin's creed" that man is innately evil, in need of policing, and it contradicts the very core of Jefferson's thinking — the basic assumption on which the Declaration and Constitution were framed: "that Man is naturally good,/And . . . never to be scourged."

It is easy to see why, aside from its unconventionality of form, *Battle-Pieces* was received coldly by critics and sold poorly. On the same grounds, it is difficult to understand why poetry of such impact and relevance has not yet found the large audience that needs it. In its struggle toward maturity, America should take to heart its writers of conscience, who were driven to expose the reality of ugliness around them because they would not surrender their vision of the ideal.

Appendix I: Recent Scholarship on Melville's Poetry

It is noteworthy that, decades after Robert Penn Warren and Randall Jarrell placed Melville among the three greatest 19th century American poets, alongside Whitman and Dickinson, his poetry continued to be neglected by scholars and readers. But the breakthrough has finally come, and it is beautifully band-wagoning along. Here are some recent critical studies:

I. Volumes

Herbert Blair Long, *The Expressive and Representational Modes in Herman Melville's Collected Verse* (Dissertation, Claremont College, 1981)

In this ambitious, original, and remarkably fruitful study, Long undertakes to bring a huge, variegated body of work into manageable order. He places each poem in one or another of two opposing categories, which represent the poet's own duality of spirit and purpose. Long's approach is best defined as he examines *John Marr:* "Instead of trying to characterize or solve the problem of dualism, as he had in *Clarel* and much of *Battle-Pieces,* Melville in this volume uses the problem as material, the clay from which to mold poems. His concern here is less with the historical events, philosophical problems, and natural facts to which his words refer than with the verbal elements, processes, and relations of which the poem is composed ... meaning arises from the aesthetic relations among the words in the poem." Long's familiarity with Melville's poetry is total; his discussion is consistently fresh and apt. One good example among many is his treatment of the *Burgundy Club* poems (pp. 161–72, 180–84). This work deserves publication. It contributes as much to the study of Melville's poems and poetics as any book I know.

John Bryant, *A Companion to Melville Studies* (New York: Greenwood Press, 1986)

This 900–page symposium, representing a constellation of distinguished scholars, swarms with riches, but mostly on the fiction. In "Melville Biography" James Barbour includes a brief comment on

Clarel and a stanza from "Monody" (p. 12). Thomas F. Heffernan does far better in "Melville the Traveler," alluding (p. 50) to the Syra visits and quoting from the poem. To illustrate Melville's creative method as well as his mood, Heffernan offers a diary jotting, then 43 lines from "Naples in the Time of Bomba" as "a tidy and typical example of the journal's shorthand turning into a rounded literary statement." Finally he deals with "The Scout Toward Aldie" as "extensive and dramatic next to the shorter pieces based on travel." Hennig Cohen, in his "Israel Potter" essay, quotes from "Pontoosuce" in discussing ends and beginnings (p. 300). Although Merton M. Sealts focuses especially on the *John Marr* poems, including "Bridegroom Dick," in "Billy Budd, Sailor" (pp. 410–12), he also touches on several battle-pieces whose boy-warriors resemble Billy Budd, "an inexperienced moral innocent." In "Melville's Poems" William H. Shurr summarizes general critical responses beginning with Newton Arvin (1949), then turns to the poetry, with brief remarks on *Battle-Pieces* and its commentators, and more expansive treatment of *John Marr, Timoleon, Weeds and Wildings,* and the *Burgundy Club* poems. There is no discussion of either "Aldie" or "Bridegroom Dick." Especially helpful is Vincent Kenny's "*Clarel*" (375–406). With impeccable scholarship he presents the history of the poem — its creation, publication, early reception, and recent criticism; he also contributes a detailed elucidation of the poem: its story line, philosophic probings, and prosody. Edward H. Rosenberg, in "Melville's Comedy and Tragedy," offers tragic images from "The Berg," *Clarel,* three battle-pieces, and "The Aeolian Harp" (609–12). Shirley M. Detlaff, in the "Poetics" segment of "Melville's Aesthetics," limits herself to a survey of essays on "Melville's ideas about poetry and the poet" (650–52). She calls "for a comprehensive study ... of Melville's later ideas about art as presented in his poetry." Sanford E. Marovits' gargantuan survey of international scholarship, "Herman Melville: A Writer for the World" (741–80), underscores how little interest in the poetry has developed: a 1975 German dissertation on the short poems, three "recent" items by Ekaterini Georgoudaki, a chapter on *Clarel* in a 1976 Israeli volume, and "A Reading of 'After the Pleasure Party'" in a 1983 Japanese collection of of Melville essays.

Robert K. Wallace, *Melville and Turner: Spheres of Love and Fright* (Athens: Univ. of Georgia Press, 1992)

This exquisite 640–page comparative study offers much artistic and biographical background, focusing in detail on Melville's responses to artworks and exploring their impact on his writings. Unfortunately, while dealing in depth with the prose, he ignores the poetry completely, with the exception of "The Temeraire," which is quoted without comment alongside Turner's painting (pp. 53–54). The omission of "At the Hostelry," a major poem in which a score of great artists are imagined disputing aesthetic philosophy, is particularly disappointing.

Stanton Garner, *The Civil War World of Herman Melville* (Lawrence: Univ. Press of Kansas, 1993)

The magnitude and brilliance of this achievement cannot be overstated. To study both Melville's life during America's "most crucial period," and *Battle-Pieces*, "one of [his] most underestimated ... works," is made more difficult because 1) he did not officially participate, therefore is included in no archives or published records; 2) he left no journal; 3) few of his letters survived; 4) he discarded most of the letters he received; 5) he was "a compulsively private person," unnoted in newspapers and memoirs. But Garner rejects the conclusion "that there was essentially no Melville war experience." His goal is to discover "where the poet, who ... witnessed no battles, went for material to feed his imagination." One way is to examine the communities whose experience he shared: "his family, his friends, his neighbors," his fellow Northerners, and his literary peers. If Garner had accomplished nothing else, this superbly researched and documented volume (55 pages of valuable endnotes alone) would be a major contribution to our understanding of the war and its poet. But he goes much further. Every poem is given its exact place and significance in the nation's and Melville's developing history, often compared with the responses of other poets, large and small, to the same event. Best of all, Garner invests his apparently total knowledge of Melville as person, thinker, and artist in a splendid analysis of each poem, both within the total oeuvre and as a separate work of art.

David Kirby, *Herman Melville* (New York: Continuum, 1993)

The author claims that his "is the first general book on Melville based on the ... Northwestern-Newberry edition." If that is so, then that is the only "virtue" it can claim. Pretentious, shallow, and choked with echoes of genuine scholars, it offers little of value on the prose, nothing on the poems in only two pages (155–57) devoted to them. The introduction grants Melville's poetry "a permanent if minor position in United States literature." Elsewhere he mischaracterizes *Battle-Pieces* as "a volume of patriotic verse" and explains Melville's motive in visiting the Virginia front as a "hope of finding something to write about." When he dares to opine, the babbling is painful: "*Battle-Pieces* is good war poetry, if not the best Melville. Paul Fussel writes that these poems 'occasion the shock one always experiences upon seeing how badly a great writer can write.' This is excessive, surely, but not by much. Suffice it to say that Melville treated the Civil War better than it treated him. In *Battle-Pieces* he was less himself and, for what it is worth, more a man of his times." Only once is the poet allowed to be heard — but the six-line excerpt from "After the Pleasure-Party" is disguised as prose within a paragraph and its interpretation is lame. Kirby's stated goal was "to write a biography of Melville's career." A worthy goal.

J. O. Tate, ed., *Mosby's Memoirs* (Nashville: Southern Classics Series, 1995)

Making this autobiography available is a gift to any serious reader of "The Scout Toward Aldie" and, indeed, all the Civil War poems. In his foreword, Tate discusses "Aldie" ("a literary ballad of considerable merit") in some depth (pp. xiv–vi), and includes a long commentary on the poem from Edmund Wilson's *Patriotic Gore* (1962).

II. Essays in Volumes

Andrew Hook, "Melville's Poetry," *Herman Melville: Reassessments* (London: Vision Press Ltd., 1984) 176–98.

This frank and thoughtful essay discusses the sustained neglect of Melville's poetry on grounds that it is "bad," and the attention paid to it only because it illuminates the novelist's thinking. While agreeing "that Melville is not a truly great poet," Hook sides with those who see "the 'hobbled metrics,' 'stumbling rimes,' and 'contorted language' " as "part of a design," a rejection of "his genteel and complacent poetic contemporaries," a choice of "ugly discordance and incongruity . . . as indices of truth" (here, as too often, Hook quotes Wm. B. Stein). Turning to the four books of poetry, he judges *Battle-Pieces* "the best and most satisfying," finding "an emotional depth and fullness that sets it apart." He ignores "The Scout Toward Aldie," but touches on many of the shorter war poems as well as "Lee in the Capitol" and the seldom mentioned "Donelson," which he rightly calls an "inventively dramatic narrative." As for *Clarel,* while accepting Stein's charge of "countless infelicities of expression," Hook deems its "obscuring awkwardness" counterbalanced by "its earnestness and weight." For him "it overcomes its . . . deficiencies and imposes itself as a major creative act," its substance unequalled in post-war America and matched in England only by *In Memoriam* and Browning's "more philosophical . . . poems." He might add that Browning too was charged with obscurity: for decades Browning societies wrangled over his meanings. In *John Marr* "outrage at the human condition has been replaced by acceptance of his futility." The sea is "as treacherous as ever." Once again the book's major poem, "Bridegroom Dick," is bypassed, though two of its lines on wartime profiteering are elsewhere quoted. Neither of the last books receives adequate attention. From *Timoleon,* "a more varied and accomplished volume," only a couple of titles and one line are given. Of the numerous pieces found among his papers, only "Pontoosuce," which Hook ranks as "one of Melville's finest and most beautiful poems," is examined. Despite the promise of definitiveness, there is no mention of the two major *Burgundy Club* poems, "At the Hostelry" and "Naples in the Time of Bomba," whose time for careful study has long since arrived.

Gene Patterson-Black, "On Herman Melville,*" American Novelists Revisited: Essays in Feminist Criticism,* ed. Fritz Fleischmann (Boston: G. K. Hall, 1982) 109–42.

Losing his father at twelve caused Melville to crave thereafter a surrogate male relationship; and a "repressed self-hatred . . . led him to the verge of a nervous collapse." On these biographical premises Patterson-Black bases her study. But, while acknowledging his "lack of interest in women," she rejects the current Melville curriculum as "a disservice" overlooking "many of [his] superior pieces." Paying as much attention to the poetry as to the prose, she shows how "the confrontation with the self-hate . . . occurred in Rome in February 1857," and how far he came in the next twenty years, especially as evidenced in *Clarel,* where "fraternity and toleration" prevail. Along with the great verse-novel, several *Timoleon* pieces receive a vigorous new look: "Shelley's Vision," "Venice," "In a Bye-Canal," and "After the Pleasure-Party." Underscoring her earlier point that his "interest is directed primarily toward women as wives rather than . . . as autonomous and equal persons," she presents "The Figure-Head" (from *John Marr and Other Sailors*), which follows "a couple from marriage to death." But she gives away her bristling though usually controlled bias by quoting only five lines from *John Marr*'s major poem, "Bridegroom Dick," meanspiritedly twisting an exquisite tribute so that "the bridegroom seeks to soothe his bride with the gallantry typical of the inattentive husband." The essay ends with what may be Melville's last poem, a Bridegroom Dick-like tribute to his own wife. Unfortunately, there is not one word here about *Battle-Pieces.*

A. Robert Lee, " 'Eminently adapted for unpopularity'?: Melville's Poetry," *Nineteenth-Century American Poetry* (London: Vision Press, 1985) 118–45.

In an endnote, Prof. Lee points out that "Even in the highly influential study by Roy Harvey Pearce, *The Continuity of American Poetry* (Princeton, 1961), Melville as Poet is completely ignored." Lee, however, includes Melville among the five poets worth separate chapters, along with Whitman, Poe, Dickinson and Emerson. After discussing the critics' absorption with the prose, and the poet's personal circumstances, Lee turns to the poetry, which "marks Melville's refusal to be ignored into silence." The *Battle-Pieces* are examined as meditations on "the War as both the national House Divided and as a source of divided feeling within himself." The major war poems — "Donelson," "Aldie," and "Lee in the Capitol" — receive serious attention. The three collections that followed, particularly *Clarel,* are also meaningfully approached. But the considerable work left in manuscript, including the *Burgundy Club* poems, is ignored.

Jeanetta Boswell, "Herman Melville," *The American Renaissance and the Critics* (Wakefield, N. H.: Longwood Academic, 1990) 295–409

Boswell energetically summarizes 161 essays on Melville, many published in the fifteen years prior to the completion of her project. If one were to depend on her harvest, one could only conclude that the scholarly focus is still on *Moby-Dick* and a few other works of fiction, with hardly any attention paid to the poetry. There are two items on *Battle-Pieces:* Joyce Sparer Adler's "Melville and the Civil War," *New Letters,* XL (1973) 99–117, and Catherine Georgoudaki's "*Battle-Pieces and Aspects of the War:* Melville's Quest for Meaning and Form in a Fallen World," *American Transcendental Quarterly,* 1 (March 1987) 21–32. Only one essay deals with the 1876 verse-novel: Nina Baym's "The Erotic Motif in Melville's *Clarel,"* *Texas Studies in Language and Literature,* XVI (1974) 315–28. Three listings are given for the shorter poems: Lucy M. Freibert's " 'Weeds and Wildings': Herman Melville's Use of the Pastoral Voice," *Essays in Arts and Sciences,* XII (March 1983) 61–85; Robert Milder's "Melville's Late Poetry and Billy Budd: From Nostalgia to Transcendance," *Philological Quarterly,* LXVI (Fall, 1987) 493–507; and Lewis P. Turco's "American Novelists as Poets: The Schizophrenia of Mode," *English Review,* XXV (1974) 23–29.

In Turco's view "Poetry is language art, not narrative art"; he finds Melville's "an unsuccessful wrestle with the technique in his poems," pummeling the words to serve as a vehicle for his ideas. Perhaps since 1974 the lesser poet, despite his admirable devotion to "language art," has discovered why Melville is the hundredfold greater poet. Thirty years later, William Bysshe Stein's "Time, History, and Religion: A Glimpse of Melville's Late Poetry," in *Arizona Quarterly,* XXII, 136–45, remains — in Boswell's summary — a treasure: "This collection trumpets his radical estrangement from the systems of reference that made life purposeful for his contemporaries . . . he invokes an old man's sense of comedy to register his disgust with the social and moral mummery of the Victorian world. He laughingly exposes its dullness, insensitivity, and pretentiousness, its shallow materialism and grotesque piety. Focusing upon the sterile mechanization of Christianity in practice . . . he satirizes the arid platitudes of the popular poets of the day, especially their sentimental and pseudo-mystical resolutions of the problems of human destiny." Having written this, how could Boswell then ignore almost completely the tremendous burst of critical responses to Melville's poetry?

John McWilliams, "The Epic in the Nineteenth Century," *The Columbia History of American Poetry* (New York: Columbia Univ. Press, 1993) 59–60.

McWilliams focuses briefly on Melville's hope that the Civil War will instruct America "through terror and pity," and that "*Battle-Pieces* will further national reconciliation." But by stressing the Miltonic references to a Satanic South, he totally overlooks a major thrust of the volume: generous in praise and grief for the soldiers of the South. The reader, he blindly concludes, "can only wish to dismiss the serpent with a universal hiss, rejoicing that Right has finally conquered Wrong."

The huge volume, despite its pretentious title, has not a word to say about the rest of Melville's poetry except for one passing reference to *Clarel,* while narcissistically reserving hundreds of pages for several current poets. See "An Afterword."

III. Essays in Journals

Lucy Freibert, "The Influences of Elizabeth Barrett Browning on the Poetry of Herman Melville," *Studies in Browning and His Circle,* IX, 2 (Fall 1981) 69–78.

Based on his "comments about [her], his markings and annotations of her poems, and parallel passages in their works," Freibert concludes that "studying Browning may have helped Melville at a crucial point in the development of his own practise as a poet." Four of her poems

— "Catrina to Camoëns," "The Dead Pan," "A Drama of Exile," and "Casa Guidi Windows" — are of special pertinence. Freibert demonstrates convincingly their impact on *Clarel*.

John Updike, "Melville's Withdrawal," *The New Yorker* (May 10, 1982) 120–47.

In the first 21 pages of this overview, there is only one tiny mention of a poem, not even identified as such — *Clarel* — cited only with reference to the Vine/Hawthorne episode. But on page 141 Updike finally turns to the three poetry decades. Of *John Marr, Timoleon,* and the posthumous pieces he says nothing, but praises "The House-Top" (the draft-riot poem of 1863) without naming it. "Melville's poetry," he says, "has been some of the last of his production restored to favor." But it had never *been* in favor, nor does Updike make the most of his opportunity to do so in *The New Yorker*. He contrasts its "effect of muttering" with "the full-throated ease of the prose." He pairs Melville with "another novelist turned poet out of disgust," Hardy: both move us "with [their] effort to thrust honesty and complex insight toward us through the resistant slats of metre and rhyme." *Clarel* alone receives expanded, if often mocking, attention. As for "Melville's withdrawal," it was "not so instant or so complete as the mythic image of it," and "can be viewed as itself a necessary and therefore successful artistic gesture."

Stanton Garner, "Melville's Scout Toward Aldie,*" Melville Society Extracts,* LI (Sept. 1982) 5–16.

This mammoth, brilliantly researched account chronicles a complex and important historical event. Everyone involved is fully introduced, as is every aspect of Melville's participation in "the adventure he communicates in his poem." Fifteen photos of pertinent locales and what Garner calls the "Cast of Characters" further enrich an exciting and valuable contribution.

Stanton Garner, "Melville's Scout Toward Aldie, Part 2: The Scout and the Poem," *Melville Society Extracts,* LII (Nov. 1982) 1–14.

To illustrate the risk in depending "upon the poem at all as a source of fact," Garner first turns to "the historical incidents on which 'The College Colonel' is based." We find it in part accurate, in part imaginatively reshaped for good strategic reasons. In the case of "Aldie" too, "much of the minor detail" is "historically true," while "from the point . . . at which the larger action" moves "toward a poetic climax . . . Melville is reshaping experience in order to express his truth." The scout itself, and Melville's participation, unfold in extraordinary detail. Step by step, Garner matches fact and stanza, revealing the artist at work as pure narrator and conjecturing on the motives for every invention. Experience "becomes a medium through which his perceptions of and attitudes toward the War are expressed"; transforming events "from fact into truth, he made a 'shark' poem of the events." Garner calls it "an imaginative leap toward an immutable truth, about the Civil War, about war, and about the tragic nature of human experience."

Joyce Sparer Adler, "A Note on Melville's Concept of Mosby," *Melville Society Extracts,* LXII (May 1985) 114–15.

Using as her springboard Stanton Garner's point that Melville made "an imaginative leap [from historical fact] toward an immutable truth," Adler argues that Mosby is the poet's "anti-war symbol," to be seen "not as war itself but as Death in war . . . the sudden ending of life at its most vital and promising time." Despite an ingenious choice of quotations, her reading diminishes Melville and is unconvincing. What Mosby means to his Union adversaries, and to Adler, is far less than what he means to the poet.

Paul Metcalf, "Manacle Your Icicle," *Ironwood,* XXVIII (1986) 92–103.

This unorganized series of comparative examples re Melville and Emily Dickinson is lively and clever, but there is only one reference to his poetry, when Metcalf discusses the possibility that, like Pierre, "Melville himelf had experienced syncope." A contemporary critic is quoted: "His poetry runs into the epileptic. His rhymes are fearful."

Bryan C. Short, "Memory's Mint: Melville's Parable of the Imagination in *John Marr and Other Sailors*," *Essays in Arts and Sciences*, XV (June 1986) 31–42.

This dense, provocative study ignores the craft in *John Marr* other than one comment on "The Haglets": "As in so much of Melville's late poetry, underneath a welter of florid imagery lies a delicate and psychologically acute exposition of artistic theory." Each poem is explored as an example of the poet's imaginative recoining of his past by which "his dark ironies give way" to "an optimistic partnership" of "art and sense." Of the four "personality poems" — "John Marr," "Bridegroom Dick," "Tom Deadlight," and "Jack Roy" — Short deals most fully with the third, which "speaks with the most distinctive voice in the collection, a highly metaphorical forecastle jargon superimposed upon the 'cadences' of a 'famous old sea-ditty.' " Indeed, the 'parable' told in this book is the parable of "Melville's own imaginative use of the sea," with which he is "more comfortable ... than he has been since *Moby-Dick*." The shorter pieces, also examined carefully, show Melville moving toward resolution through "images of suspension and interpenetration," combining the "inhuman" sea and the healing rose of love, the kelp — a bitter but pure trophy for which the artist must dive. Without such fusion, Melville's "extraordinary late creativity would ... be unimaginable."

Catherine Georgoudaki, "*Battle-Pieces and Aspects of the War*: Melville's Poetic Quest for Meaning and Form in a Fallen World," *The American Transcendental Quarterly*, I,1 (Mar. 1987) 21–32.

Though fewer than in *Clarel* and *Timoleon*, Georgoudaki finds "the transformed journal entries in *Battle-Pieces*" note-worthy, providing the poet "with some important themes and forms," contributing to his effort "to create aesthetic order and unity out of the disorder, division, and contradictions of the Civil War." She considers this volume "the climactic work" in the context of Melville's "disillusionment with the American Dream," the war being for him "the symbol of Edenic America's fall." He turns "more and more towards the socio-political, spiritual, and aesthetic values of the European past" for "meaning and inspiration." Deftly, she links to individual poems such diverse allusions as Lord Nelson, Henry V's knights, paintings by Rosa, Claude, Reni, and Carracci, the cemetery cypresses of Turkey, the Egyptian desert, and Vesuvius, pointing to their places of mention in the 1856 *Journal* and the specific effect of each in its poem.

Robert Milder, "Melville's Late Poetry and *Billy Budd:* From Nostalgia to Transcendence," *Philological Quarterly,* LXVI, 4 (Fall 1987) 493–507.

In his retirement Melville published *John Marr* and *Timoleon,* and moved *Billy Budd* from a "sailor monologue" like those in *John Marr,* through various stages "whose shifts of interest . . . reflect Melvillle's inward journey over the last five years of his life." Milder bypasses the poems left in manuscript, but gives *John Marr* a serious reading. He finds it divided not only "structurally between the sailor poems and the 'Sea-Pieces,'" but also "in vision and tone, consigning heroism to a romanticized past while facing the present neither reconciled to God's universe nor consoled by any victory of the human spirit." As for *Timoleon,* whose best pieces "explore the renunciations and rewards of truth's votaries," Milder stresses the title poem, "a compendium of Melville themes and a loose allegory of his emotional life" as in a Schopenhauer passage he marked: "The more a man belongs to posterity . . . the more of an alien he is to his contemporaries." In this volume the poet is still "fighting the battle of the spirit and the clay." But as *Billy Budd* evolves, Melville works through his "bitterness toward a remote Providence and a small-souled, neglectful world." Milder's analysis of the novel occupies the bulk of his essay. In its closing scenes the poet ventures "beyond both the nostalgia and despair of *John Marr* and the self-questioning of Timoleon," arriving at "a certainty of inward worth and, thereby, at a qualified peace."

Victor Strandberg, "The Frost-Melville Connection," *Dutch Quarterly Review of Anglo-American Letters,* XVII, 3, (1987) 171–81.

This essay typifies the continuing lack of interest abroad in Melville as poet. While Frost's poetry is related well to Melville's fiction, particularly *Moby-Dick,* only one poem is mentioned and briefly quoted, "The Conflict of Convictions," whose "stoic view of the agnostic dilemma" parallels Frost's.

Ronald Giles, "Melville's 'Malvern Hill,'" *The Explicator*, XLIII, 2 (Winter 1987) 27–29.

Giles presents the poem and explicates it. Here is the New Criticism at its finest: not a word about the battle, about the war, about Melville, about any other work, about Giles' judgment. What emerges is the poem itself, beautifully illuminated in terms of its construction, language, metrics, imagery, and rhetorical method, so that we return to the piece amazed at how blind we were the first time. This may be the ultimate way for Melville to win his place as a great poet.

Vernon Shetley, "Melville's 'Timoleon'," *ESQ*, XXXIII, 2 (1987) 82–93.

Though Melville subtitled *Timoleon* "and other Ventures in Minor Verse," Shetley deals with it as a major poem in this sensitive and thorough reading. Plutarch emphasized Timoleon's later triumphs; Melville concentrates on the politically noble murder of his tyrant-brother and his self-imposed exile, "bringing the story close to tragedy." Rather than being "healed of [his] hurt" by touching the ancient hero, Melville discovers a Timoleon too much like himself: "self-outcast ... as self-doubt destroys internal harmony." Like his poet, Timoleon turns "to doubting the reality of ... divine justice." Those who try to live "according to principle" become "fatherless shadows." If the gods do not exist, their statues represent nothing, and "Timoleon remains 'like a lost dog that for a master cries'." The hostile reception given to *Moby-Dick* and *Pierre* drove Melville into the self-exile of poetry. As Timoleon withdraws from the political culture of *his* moment, so Melville withdraws from the literary culture of his own. The extreme stylistic experimentation in this poem "rejects the norms by which verse in his time might acquire legibility." Its harsh quality is an index not of a failure of technique but of the poet's "alienation from his audience."

Turning to *Battle-Pieces*, Shetley finds the Civil War paralleling Timoleon's history. He too "commits fratricide, sacrificing natural ties to principles and duty." But postwar America, like ancient Corinth, "is a debased polis, men 'who knew not how to live in a democracy,' " as Plutarch puts it. From his vantage-point in the New York Custom House Melville saw all day, every day, the atrocious fruit of a four-year sacrifice, brother against brother, a political life of "patronage and corruption." Timoleon expressed "his disappointment in his city" by self-exile. Melville's outlet for his disappointment in Gilded Age America was "a poetry that turned its back on its age and its audience."

Robert Milder, "The Reader Of/In Melville's *Battle-Pieces*," *Melville Society Extracts*, LXXII (Feb. 1988) 12–15.

Perhaps the "much longer essay" of which this "is a preliminary version" paid some attention to the three major poems of *Battle-Pieces* ("Donelson," "Lee in the Capitol," "The Scout Toward Aldie"), the many short poems which pay tribute to Southern soldiers, and several masterpieces not listed here among "impressive performances" but passed over among the "flawed and repetitive commemoration of battles and heroes that constitutes the book's center." Still, Milder provides an exceptionally insightful reading of Melville's intentions and achievements. It was a hope of "converting his audience to the prospect of a wise and magnanimous America refounded on the bedrock of tragic vision." His prologue claims "desultory composition," but the book "shows a high degree of thematic order." This strategy invites the reader "to relive the war through what offers itself as ... a near-random poetic journal." Miltonically, Melville projects "two versions of the fall ... that contend for the reader's allegiance." The first fall, with which Northern readers agree, "is that of the rebel angels (the traitorous South)," and victory will reaffirm "America's status as a covenanted nation." The second fall, which his contemporaries would not care to consider, involves a "descent into violence and ... a knowledge of evil that cannot be expunged" even if America's crisis is survived. To Milder the book is shaped less by "the course of the war" than by a "play of voices." At first the Laureate, speaking for Melville's would-be readers, celebrates the Union cause and heroism; but undertones challenge their "pretensions to God's favor." A more "sober, authoritative" voice begins to emerge, that of the Reconciler (and Teacher), who would "gather the survivors on both sides round the bodies of sacrificed youth." Milder concludes that Melville's war poems convert a tragedy "to a source of ... strength," channeling it to "a sturdier and more compassionate democratic faith," summoning Americans "from materialism to sacrifice." His hope was "to guide the nation in a time of crisis and in so doing rescue himself from impotence and obscurity." But his "unreserved gesture" was rejected; "a failed poet," he withdrew to permanent isolation.

Ekaterini Georgoudaki, "Herman Melville's Trips to Syra in 1856–57," *Melville Society Extracts,* LXXIV (Sept. 1988) 1–8.

This University of Thessaloniki scholar explores the historical and biographical background of the very poem which climaxed my presentation at the 1983 Mediterranean Conference in Athens, attended by many Greek scholars (Chapter III of this book). Such travel writing as Melville's was also examined at an International Symposium held on Syra in July 1988. It would be pointless to conjecture whether my circulated but unpublished paper was involved in this sudden activity around a poem which went unnoticed in *American Poets and the Greek Revolution,* by Rouzis and Papas (Thessaloniki, 1971).

Georgoudaki does a fine job in researching the island's ancient and recent history, and its circumstances at the time of Melville's visits. She shows the large areas of inaccuracy in his 1856–1857 journals and in the poem based on them. Apparently he was unaware of how the port was founded, how it developed, the mass unemployment in which it was gripped as a result of the Crimean War, the cholera and diphtheria epidemics, and its decline as a shipbuilding center. He misunderstood "the natives' costumes, samples of a later folk tradition," as operatic, "outdated, unsuitable for work, and examples of the 'decayed picturesque.' " He misjudged the unemployed on the quay as childish, "vain and lazy." She concludes that his "impressions and conclusions ... reflect his own need to find another primitive, carefree society." He was "unfamiliar with [Syra's] long history and its rich intellectual and artistic life" at the moment, with "modern Greece's rich folk culture." He therefore saw Syran life "as a kind of relapse from the classical Greek civilization." The author might have noted that this theme pervaded dozens of Melville's poems, that evidence of this decline from glory was precisely what the poet sought and found on all his travels.

David Cody, " 'So, then, Solidity's a crust': Melville's 'The Apparition' and the Explosion of the Petersburg Mine," *Melville Society Extracts*, LXXVIII (Sept. 1989) 1, 4–8.

Cody summarizes and contradicts previous commentary on a significant *Battle-Pieces* poem, "The Apparition," i.e., that Melville is describing a volcano and that "the relationship between the poem and the Civil War is either tenuous or casual." First, the volcano image is a metaphor, related to his master Carlyle's recurrent theme: "the potentially devastating eruption of the irrational from the depths of the human psyche." It includes the poet's persistent fears for his own psychological stability, as well as his dominant concern "with the transient or illusory nature of apparent stability and order, and with the underlying 'darkness of reality.' " Second, it is profoundly a Civil War poem, dealing with "the volcanic anxieties inherent in American society — the lies which could not endure forever, and . . . the accumulated evils which, 'reaching a head,' inevitably brought on a Civil War."

But — even more specifically — the germ of the poem was the famous explosion of the Petersburg, Virginia mine on July 30, 1864, vividly described, with drawings, by Alfred Waud in *Harper's Weekly*. Disproving Hennig Cohen's assumption that "the relation between Melville's poems and the drawings . . . is tenuous" and that the drawings are not "the principal source of any particular poems," Cody reprints Waud's harrowing artwork and equally volcanic report in *Harper's*, to which Melville subscribed. Melville's imagination "was fired by Waud's graphic description of the manner in which, on a 'calm and clear' morning, two hundred apparently unsuspicious rebels . . . were instantaneously 'rushed into eternity' by an explosion which 'much resembled the eruption of a volcano.' " Thus, the poem gives "visible form to the shock, trauma, and terror, personal and national . . . inherent both in the sudden outbreak of war and on the prolonged struggle that followed," as well as the "overwhelming ... sense ... of ontological ... anxiety" that played a crucial role in Melville's life and work. It might be noted that "The College Colonel" also refers to Petersburg (see Appendix II).

R. D. Madison, "Melville's Sherman Poems: a Problem in Source Study," *Melville Society Extracts,* LXXVIII (Sept. 1989) 8–11.

Madison disputes Hennig Cohen's widely accepted belief that *The Rebellion Record* was "Melville's major source for his Civil War poems," at least in the case of the three Sherman pieces. But Cohen cites Nichols' *Story of the Great March* as the major source for "The March to the Sea," which Madison dismisses as uninspired in its use of source and "as a philosophical interpretation" of a major campaign, compared with "The Frenzy in the Wake," composed from the defeated rebels' viewpoint. As for "On Sherman's Men," it has nothing "to do with Sherman," could be "about anybody's men," and is remarkable only for reversing the position held in "A Utilitarian View" — here "war has not yet been made less grand than peace."

Unfortunately, Madison disappoints the interest he has engendered, and fails to expand on his strong responses to the three poems. Instead, he chooses to focus entirely on Melville's problematic use of his sources, for instance his adoption of "mostly isolated words" while uncharacteristically eschewing "nearly every dramatic element of Nichols' account." The heart of Madison's effort is a useful extract of passages that parallel "The March to the Sea" and "The Frenzy in the Wake." These poems show "nearly the same relation to Nichols' book," yet Melville says he wrote the second piece half a year before buying the book. Madison warns us to consider not only "books ... Melville owned" or elsewhere used, but also "the influence ... of general news of the day ... household gossip ... or the sharing of language and ideas ... among Melville's literary circle."

Robert A. Sandberg, " 'The Adjustment of Screens': Putative Narrators, Authors, and Editors in Melville's Unfinished *Burgundy Club Book*," *Texas Studies in Literature and Language*," XXXI, 3 (Fall 1989) 426–50.

Sandberg graciously credits me with "a brief but useful analysis of ['At the Hostelry' and 'Naples at the Time of Bomba'] in [my] editorial introduction to" *Melville's Poetry: Toward the Enlarged Heart* (1972), which was in the hands of publishers long before the appearance of Shurr's *Mystery of Inquiry* and Stein's *Poetry of Melville's Later Years,* books he also acknowledges. But what Sandberg contributes, based on the Melville Collection at Harvard, is a thorough history of Melville's thirty-year struggle to organize these two large poems and the prose pieces around them into a publishable *Burgundy Club* volume.

The key is "House of the Tragic Poet," a manuscript hitherto ignored but here summarized, which he feels Melville intended as the introduction, and by means of which the poems and sketches "can be now more readily analyzed as parts of a nearly completed book." Lacking "a clear story line," Melville finally created "an editorial persona — a member of the fictional Burgundy Club" motivated and talented enough to celebrate two great story-tellers and "methodize" each one's best story "into verse" (Melville's words). For many of his other stories Melville created narrators. Here we "contemplate and scrutinize a 'judiciously' lit portrait of two 'original' authors" — what makes the *Burgundy Club* unique is the introduction of "an editor that any aspiring author would consider ideal: one who endeavors to publish a book in spite of fears that it may prove unpopular." By assuming that persona near the end of his career, Melville found "the rhetorical and psychological means to prevail over" an uncomprehending public that had for decades "frustrated and disappointed him," a persona "for whom he must have continually longed: a sympathetic, understanding reader with the power and desire to publish him."

Joseph Fargnoli, "Archetype and History in Melville's 'The Scout Toward Aldie,'" *Forum for Modern Language Studies,* XXVII, 4 (1991) 333–47.

When James O. Tate generously proclaimed my discussion of this poem "the best commentary on it," he could not possibly have known Fargnoli's essay. The merit of my work was, in Tate's words, "to point us toward Melville's neglected poem" and make it generally "available" at last — an effort expanded the following year in my B.B.C. script, *Melville's Neglected Poems*. Fargnoli's masterful study places the poem squarely in the author's total *oeuvre:* "the motif of courageous action in the face of suffering and defeat ran through Melville's life as a writer." He sees *Battle-Pieces* as "the only poetry, besides Whitman's *Drum-Taps,* to evoke a national rather than partisan or regional" view of the war. And he sees "Aldie" as unlike the other war poems, since it was "shaped directly by experience with the war." He relates "Aldie" to specific early ballads, lyrics, and verse romances, including septet narratives by Shakespeare and Drayton. What "suggests its descending from the archetype of the quest myth is the story of the tragic downfall of an ambitious or noble character." He shows how Melville contrasts "the romance and chivalry of Lowell's style with Mosby's ... unconventional style of partisan warfare," often by means of imagery, such as the "strong chiaroscuro of light and dark, night and day." Fargnoli sees Melville's celebration of "the sabreless charge" as a "real tribute to ... Mosby's cavalry ... the first in history to mount accomplished charges with ... pistols." My own sense of Melville's contempt for Lowell's Custer-like arrogance ("he suffers from the blind, vainglorious mania of a Custer" — my words) is reinforced by Fargnoli's mention that Custer had in fact ordered the barbaric hanging of six captured Mosby-men. Major Forbes is seen as a Melville, whose "remarks to Lowell are often oracular and prophetic, though unheeded." There are valuable discussions of many incidents in the poem, but the main focus is, as it should be, on Mosby, whose "complex figure ... is replete with the tensions of man, life, firmament, transgression, suffering, fate, and death," an ambiguous metaphor "driven by the most consummate doubt" of where reality finally lay. The poem is "a carefully shaded monument" to him and his tragic cause.

Edward W. Goggin, "Confusion and Resolution in 'The Scout Toward Aldie,'" *Melville Society Extracts,* XCII (March 1993). 5–9.

Crediting my discussion of this poem as a primary source, Goggin turns my description of the Colonel as "vainglorious" into a persistently repeated epithet; but neither mine nor any of the other cited works can account for his original and valuable approach. His point is that "the world of unresolved, lethal confusion" Melville creates is not "a failed vision but a vision of perception doomed to failure." He scoffs at critics who try, as do the Union forces, to pin down the elusive Mosby; it is not Mosby but "the mystery, the unrealizable nature of the event that this poem ... is about." Many examples of Melville's masterfully plotted confusions are discussed — first of all Mosby, who represents both good and evil, or neither; other characters, who "appear and dissolve as if we experience them in a dream"; the forest itself, resembling Robin Hood's Sherwood, but more a maze leading to depth; its nocturnal sounds, animals, colors, and especially trees, including a metaphoric fallen one at the end, which imprisons both speaker and reader; even the relationship between the Colonel and his bride. "From early on, we are abandoned in a dark wood of dreams and nightmares without a Virgil for our guide." Like all great narrative poets, Melville has created a story which moves allegorically. Not only does "the journey to death at Aldie" suggest "the ultimate destiny of all," but there is the more desperate suggestion, reminiscent of other Melville works, that "all die for naught in a world where good and evil are inextricable." At the end the reader, like the Colonel's men, is left "essentially unarmed, defenseless, able only to peer into the obscurity that must overwhelm."

Basem L. Ra'ad, "Palm and Apple: Melville's Metaphor of the Trees," *Melville Society Extracts*, XCII (March 1995) 9–10.

This fascinating little study finds that various trees in Melville's works "represent moods and states of consciousness." Here the focus is on the palm of "the prelapsarian garden" and the apple of "the fallen garden." As he develops, he makes the apple "an accurate reflection of history and experience" in the "temporal, cultivated garden of the world." The palm, however, "in the eternal garden of hope," turns into "an increasingly isolated and threatened object ... Midway up a barren precipice," it becomes a particularly apt symbol of Melville's "artistic isolation." The apple-tree, "twisted and contorted," is a sign "of our despair." In artistic terms its grotesqueness expresses "the necessary complexity and abstraction of a modern art." The only poem directly referred to in this paper is *Clarel,* but we are told the "solitary Date-Palm" image "recurs in the late poems."

Warren F. Broderick, "Melville's First Five Poems?" *Melville Society Extracts,* XCII (March 1993) 13–16.

Move over, Whitman! The unimaginable has happened. Until recently, Melville's entire wealth of credited poems was ignored; now for five youthful pieces signed "H" serious attention is requested, pieces produced about the same time newspapers were publishing Walter Whitman's wretched stanzas that are now studied for hints of the greatness to come. The biographical evidence is persuasive; the "comparisons" with Melville's "poems and other writings" (particularly "The Death Craft") are not. Broderick, of the New York State Archives and Records Administration, claims no evaluative powers. He merely puts the five bits of hackneyed, sentimental verse into the laps of "Melville scholars" who may wish to "study them in depth and assess their possible place in Melville's formative writings."

Ernest Suarez, "Dickey on Melville,*" South Carolina Review,* XXVI, 2 (Spring 1994) 114–26.

The ever-expanding exploration of Melville's poetry takes surprising directions. Here Suarez examines James Dickey's *Symbol and Image in the Shorter Poems of Herman Melville* (Master's thesis, Vanderbilt Univ., May 1950). A two-page introduction supplies biographical background and declares that the thesis "provides insight into the literary culture [New Criticism and strong ghosts of the Fugitives] Dickey encountered at Vanderbilt" along with the "themes and techniques" in his own future work. Suarez shows whiteness — crucial throughout Melville — to be "a central motif" in Dickey as well. But he says not a word about Melville's poetry (except for passing reference to haglets and the Admiral of the White), nor does Dickey in the first part of the excerpt (6½ pages), turning to "the shorter poems" only in the second part (2 pages). Still, the comments on the novels prove useful as he finally approaches the poems offering "dozens of examples" that confirm his hypotheses. Almost none of his brief quotations are identified beyond their page in the *Collected Poems*. But they form an impressive crescendo of evidence. Along with whiteness, there are equally sinister images of calmness and of wreck. Together, they "make abundantly clear Melville's rejection ... of the Christian concept of the benevolent God." It is a brilliantly realized premise; but that the extraordinarily large bulk of riches offered by the shorter poems could be utterly ignored, demonstrates how successful the New Critics were in tunnel-visioning even so gifted a young follower as James Dickey.

The world of scholarship has changed since Nina Baym wrote of *Clarel:* "The poem receives only cursory treatment in most of the general studies of Melville and is omitted in several of them. There are not a half dozen published articles on the work." By now the field is swarming; I need only list a small number of books, dissertations, and journal articles.

Among the books are Harrison Hayford's 1990 *Melville's "Monody": Really For Hawthorne? A Keepsake to Celebrate the Publication of* Clarel *in the Writings of Herman Melville,* and Stan Goldman's 1993 *Melville's Protest Theism: The Hidden and Silent God in* Clarel (based on Goldman's 1987 dissertation). Other dissertations are Peter Joseph McGuire III's *Herman Melville's* Clarel: *The Repudiation of Myth* (1982), Warren Rosenberg's *Melville's Turn to Poetry: A Genre Approach to* Clarel (1982), and Will Steeds' *Herman Melville's* Clarel: *The Supreme Poem of the Faith-Doubt Crisis* (1990). The published essays include Joseph Flibbert's "The Dream and Religious Faith in Herman Melville's *Clarel*" (1981), Shirley M. Dettlaff's "Ionian Form and Esau's Waste: Melville's View of Art in *Clarel*" (1982), Douglas Robillard's "Melville's *Clarel* and the Parallel of Poetry and Painting" (1983), Ekaterini Georgoudaki's "Djekis Abbot of Thessaloniki and the Greek Merchant in Herman Melville's *Clarel*" (1985), four 1986 essays: Warren Rosenberg's "Poetry and Belief: *Clarel* as a Response to Modern Skepticism," Deborah Andrews' and Thomas Fahy's "*Clarel:* Holy and Land," Wyn Kelley's "Haunted Stone: Nature and City in *Clarel,*" and Hershel Parker's "The Character of Vine in Melville's *Clarel,*" two 1989 publications: "The Small Voice of Silence: Melville's Narrative Voices in *Clarel,*" by Stan Goldman, and "Recasting

Melville: *The Confidence-Man* and *Clarel* in Ed Dorn's *Gunslinger,"*
by Richard L. Blevins, and three recent pieces: James Duban's "From
Bethlehem to Tahiti: Trans-Cultural Hope in *Clarel* (1991)", Stan
Goldman's "A Source for *Clarel* and 'Fruit of Travel Long Ago':
Bellows' The Old World in Its New Face" (1992), and Zephyra
Porat's "Towards the Promethean Ledge: Varieties of Sceptic
Experience in Melville's *Clarel*" (1994).

Appendix II: A Selection of Melville's Poems

BATTLE-PIECES

Donelson (February, 1862) — excerpts
Later and Last
Shiloh: A Requiem (April, 1862)
Battle of Stone River, Tennessee (January, 1863) —
    excerpt
Stonewall Jackson (May, 1863)
The House-Top: A Night Piece (July, 1863)
In the Prison Pen (1864)
The College Colonel
Rebel Color-Bearers at Shiloh (After Appomattox)
Magnanimity Baffled
On the Slain Collegians
Commemorative of a Naval Victory — excerpt
Lee in the Capitol (April, 1866) — excerpts

SEA-PIECES

The Haglets — excerpts
To Ned

TIMOLEON

In a Garret
Lone Founts
The Enthusiast

FRUIT OF TRAVEL LONG AGO

Pausilippo (In the Time of Bomba)
Disinterment of the Hermes

THE GILDED AGE

When Forth the Shepherd Leads the Flock
The Rose Farmer — excerpts
The Rusty Man
Camoëns (Before)
Camoëns (After)
Fruit and Flower Painter
In the Hall of Marbles
Hearts-of-Gold
In Shards the Sylvan Vases Lie
The Dust-Layers
A Rail Road Cutting Near Alexandria in 1855

BATTLE-PIECES

DONELSON (February, 1862) — excerpts

Great suffering through the night —
A stinging one. Our heedless boys
Were nipped like blossoms. Some dozen
Hapless wounded men were frozen.
During day being struck down out of sight,
And help-cries drowned in roaring noise,
They were left just where the skirmish shifted —
Left in dense underbrush snow-drifted.
Some, seeking to crawl in crippled plight,
So stiffened — perished.

Yet in spite
Of pangs for these, no heart is lost.

Hungry, and clothing stiff with frost,
Our men declare a nearing sun
Shall see the fall of Donelson.
*   And this they say, yet not disown*
The dark redoubts round Donelson,
*   And ice-glazed corpses, each a stone —*
*   A sacrifice to Donelson;*
They swear it, and swerve not, gazing on
A flag, deemed black, flying from Donelson.

Some of the wounded in the wood
*   Were cared for by the foe last night,*
Though he could do them little needed good,
*   Himself being all in shivering plight.*
The rebel is wrong, but human yet;
He's got a heart, and thrusts a bayonet.
He gives us battle with wondrous will —
This bluff's a perverted Bunker Hill . . .

LATER AND LAST.
THE FORT IS OURS.

*   A flag came out at early morn*
Bringing surrender. From their towers
*   Floats out the banner late their scorn.*
In Dover, hut and house are full
*   Of rebels dead or dying.*
*   The National flag is flying*
From the crammed court-house pinnacle.
Great boat-loads of our wounded go
To-day to Nashville. The sleet-winds blow;
But all is right: the fight is won,
The winter-fight for Donelson.

*   Hurrah!*
The spell of old defeat is broke,
*   The habit of victory begun;*

Grant strikes the war's first sounding stroke
        At Donelson.
For lists of killed and wounded, see
The morrow's dispatch: to-day 'tis victory.

The man who read this to the crowd
        Shouted as the end he gained;
        And though the unflagging tempest rained,
            They answered him aloud.
And hand grasped hand, and glances met
In happy triumph; eyes grew wet.
O, to the punches brewed that night
Went little water. Windows bright
Beamed rosy on the sleet without,
And from the cross street came the frequent shout;
While some in prayer, as these in glee,
Blessed heaven for the winter-victory.
But others were who wakeful laid
        In midnight beds, and early rose,
        And, feverish in the foggy snows,
Snatched the damp paper — wife and maid.
        The death-list like a river flows
            Down the pale sheet,
        And there the whelming waters meet.
            Ah God! may Time with happy haste
            Bring wail and triumph to a waste,
                And war be done;
            The battle flag-staff fall athwart
The curs'd ravine, and wither; naught
Be left of trench or gun;
The bastion, let it ebb away,
Washed with the river bed; and Day
In vain seek Donelson.

SHILOH
A REQUIEM
(April, 1862)

Skimming lightly, wheeling still,
    The swallows fly low
Over the field in clouded days,
    The forest-field of Shiloh —
Over the field where April rain
Solaced the parched ones stretched in pain
Through the pause of night
That followed the Sunday fight
    Around the church of Shiloh —
The church so lone, the log-built one,
That echoed to many a parting groan
      And natural prayer
Of dying foemen mingled there —
Foemen at morn, but friends at eve —
    Fame or country least their care:
(What like a bullet can undeceive!)
    But now they lie low,
While over them the swallows skim,
    And all is hushed at Shiloh.

BATTLE OF STONE RIVER, TENNESSEE
A VIEW FROM OXFORD CLOISTERS
(January, 1863)

— excerpt —

With Tewksbury and Barnet heath
    In days to come the field shall blend,
The story dim and date obscure;
    In legend all shall end.
Even now, involved in forest shade
    A Druid-dream the strife appears,
The fray of yesterday assumes

The haziness of years.
    In North and South still beats the vein
    Of Yorkist and Lancastrian.

Our rival Roses warred for Sway —
    For Sway, but named the name of Right;
And Passion, scorning pain and death,
    Lent sacred fervor to the fight.
Each lifted up a broidered cross,
    While crossing blades profaned the sign;
Monks blessed the fratricidal lance,
    And sisters scarfs could twine.
        Do North and South the sin retain
        Of Yorkist and Lancastrian?

*　*　*　*

But where the sword has plunged so deep,
    And then been turned within the wound
By deadly Hate; where Climes contend
    On vasty ground —
No warning Alps or seas between,
    And small the curb of creed or law,
And blood is quick, and quick the brain;
    Shall North and South their rage deplore,
        And reunited thrive amain
        Like Yorkist and Lancastrian?

STONEWALL JACKSON
MORTALLY WOUNDED AT CHANCELLORSVILLE
(May, 1863)

The Man who fiercest charged in fight,
    Whose sword and prayer were long —
        Stonewall!
Even him who stoutly stood for Wrong,
How can we praise? Yet coming days
    Shall not forget him with this song.

Dead is the Man whose Cause is dead,
    Vainly he died and set his seal —
        Stonewall!
    Earnest in error, as we feel;
True to the thing he deemed was due,
    True as John Brown or steel.

Relentlessly he routed us;
    But *we* relent, for he is low —
        Stonewall!
    Justly his fame we outlaw; so
We drop a tear on the bold Virginian's bier,
    Because no wreath we owe.

THE HOUSE-TOP
A NIGHT PIECE
(July, 1863)

No sleep. The sultriness pervades the air
And binds the brain — a dense oppression, such
As tawny tigers feel in matted shades,
Vexing their blood and making apt for ravage.
Beneath the stars the roofy desert spreads
Vacant as Libya. All is hushed near by.
Yet fitfully from far breaks a mixed surge
Of muffled sound, the Atheist roar of riot.
Yonder, where parching Sirius set in drought,
Balefully glares red Arson — there — and there.
The Town is taken by its rats — ship-rats
And rats of the wharves. All civil charms
And priestly spells which late held hearts in awe —
Fear-bound, subjected to a better sway
Than sway of self; these like a dream dissolve,
And man rebounds whole aeons back in nature.
Hail to the low dull rumble, dull and dead,
And ponderous drag that jars the wall.

Wise Draco comes, deep in the midnight roll
Of black artillery; he comes, though late;
In code corroborating Calvin's creed
And cynic tyrannies of honest kings;
He comes, nor parlies; and the Town, redeemed,
Gives thanks devout; nor, being thankful, heeds
The grimy slur on the Republic's faith implied,
Which holds that Man is naturally good,
And — more, is Nature's Roman, never to be scourged.

IN THE PRISON PEN
(1864)

Listless he eyes the palisades
    And sentries in the glare;
'Tis barren as a pelican-beach —
But his world is ended there.

Nothing to do; and vacant hands
    Bring on the idiot-pain;
He tries to think — to recollect,
    But the blur is on his brain.

Around him swarm the plaining ghosts
    Like those on Virgil's shore —
A wilderness of faces dim,
    And pale ones gashed and hoar.

A smiting sun. No shed, no tree;
    He totters to his lair —
A den that sick hands dug in earth
    Ere famine wasted there,

Or, dropping in his place, he swoons,
    Walled in by throngs that press,
Till forth from the throngs they bear him dead —
Dead in his meagreness.

THE COLLEGE COLONEL

He rides at their head;
    A crutch by his saddle just slants in view,
One slung arm is in splints, you see,
    Yet he guides his strong steed — how coldly too.

He brings his regiment home —
    Not as they filed two years before,
But a remnant half-tattered, and battered, and worn,
Like castaway sailors, who — stunned
       By the surf's loud roar,
    Their mates dragged back and seen no more —
Again and again breast the surge,
    And at last crawl, spent, to shore.

A still rigidity and pale —
    An Indian aloofness lones his brow;
He has lived a thousand years
Compressed in battle's pains and prayers,
    Marches and watches slow.
There are welcoming shouts, and flags;
    Old men doff hat to the Boy,
Wreaths from gay balconies fall at his feet,
    But to *him* — there comes alloy.
It is not that a leg is lost,
    It is not that an arm is maimed,
It is not that the fever has racked —
    Self he has long disclaimed.
But all through the Seven Days' Fight,
    And deep in the Wilderness grim,
And in the field-hospital tent,
    And Petersburg crater, and dim
Lean brooding in Libby, there came —
    Ah heaven! — what *truth* to him.

REBEL COLOR-BEARERS AT SHILOH

A PLEA AGAINST THE VINDICTIVE CRY
RAISED BY CIVILIANS SHORTLY AFTER
THE SURRENDER AT APPOMATTOX

The color-bearers facing death
White in the whirling sulphurous wreath,
    Stand boldly out before the line;
Right and left their glances go,
Proud of each other, glorying in their show;
Their battle-flags about them blow,
    And fold them as in flame divine:
Such living robes are only seen
Round martyrs burning on the green —
And martyrs for the Wrong have been.

Perish their Cause! but mark the men —
Mark the planted statues, then
Draw trigger on them if you can.

The leader of a patriot-band
Even so could view rebels who so could stand;
    And this when peril pressed him sore,
Left aidless in the shivered front of war —
    Skulkers behind, defiant foes before,
And fighting with a broken brand.
The challenge in that courage rare —
Courage defenseless, proudly bare —
Never could tempt him; he could dare
Strike up the leveled rifle there.

Sunday at Shiloh, and the day
When Stonewall charged — McClellan's crimson May,
And Chickamauga's wave of death,
And of the Wilderness the cypress wreath —
    All these have passed away.
The life in the veins of Treason lags,

Her daring color-bearers drop their flags,
   And yield. *Now* shall we fire?
     Can poor spite be?
Shall nobleness in victory less aspire
Than in reverse? Spare Spleen her ire,
And think how Grant met Lee.

MAGNANIMITY BAFFLED

"Sharp words we had before the fight;
   But — now the fight is done —
Look, here's my hand," said the Victor bold,
   "Take it — an honest one!
What, holding back? I mean you well;
   Though worsted, you strove stoutly, man;
The odds were great; I honor you;
   Man honors man.

"Still silent, friend? can grudges be?
   Yet am I held a foe? —
Turned to the wall, on his cot he lies —
   Never I'll leave him so!
Brave one! I here implore your hand;
   Dumb still? all fellowship fled?
Nay, then, I'll have this stubborn hand!"
   He snatched it — it was dead.

ON THE SLAIN COLLEGIANS

Youth is the time when hearts are large,
   And stirring wars
Appeal to the spirit which appeals in turn
   To the blade it draws.
If woman incite, and duty show
   (Though made the mask of Cain),
Or whether it be Truth's sacred cause,

Who can aloof remain
That shares youth's ardor, uncooled by the snow
    Of wisdom or sordid gain?

The liberal arts and nurture sweet
Which give his gentleness to man —
    Train him to honor, lend him grace
Through bright examples meet —
That culture which makes never wan
With underminings deep, but holds
    The surface still, its fitting place,
    And so gives sunniness to the face
And bravery to the heart; what troops
    Of generous boys in happiness thus bred —
    Saturnians through life's Tempe led,
Went from the North and came from the South,
With golden mottoes in the mouth,
    To lie down midway on a bloody bed.
Woe for the homes of the North,
And woe for the seats of the South:
All who felt life's spring in prime,
And were swept by the wind of their place and time —
    All lavish hearts, on whichever side,
Of birth urbane or courage high,
Armed them for the stirring wars —
    Armed them — some to die.
        Apollo-like in pride,
Each would slay his Python — caught
The maxims in his temple taught —
    Aflame with sympathies whose blaze
Perforce enwrapped him — social laws,
    Friendship and kin, and by-gone days —
Vows, kisses — every heart unmoors,
And launches into the seas of wars.
What could they else — North or South?
Each went forth with blessings given
By priests and mothers in the name of Heaven;
    And honor in all was chief.

Warred one for Right, and one for Wrong?
So put it; but they both were young —
Each grape to his cluster clung,
All their elegies are sung.

The anguish of maternal hearts
    Must search for balm divine;
But well the striplings bore their fated parts
    (The heavens all parts assign) —
Never felt life's care or cloy.
Each bloomed and died an unabated Boy;
Nor dreamed what death was — thought it mere
Sliding into some vernal sphere.
They knew the joy, but leaped the grief,
Like plants that flower ere comes the leaf —
Which storms lay low in kindly doom,
And kill them in their flush of bloom.

COMMEMORATIVE OF A NAVAL VICTORY

(excerpt)

In social halls a favored guest
    In years that follow victory won,
How sweet to feel your festal fame
    In woman's glance instinctive thrown:
    Repose is yours — your deed is known,
It musks the amber wine;
It lives, and sheds a light from storied days
    Rich as October sunsets brown,
Which make the barren place to shine.
But seldom the laurel wreath is seen
    Unmixed with pensive pansies dark;
There's a light and a shadow on every man
    Who at last attains his lifted mark —
    Nursing through night the ethereal spark.
Elate he never can be;

He feels that spirit which glad had hailed his worth,
    Sleep in oblivion. — The shark
Glides white through the phosphorus sea.

LEE IN THE CAPITOL
(April, 1866)

— excerpts —

Hard pressed by numbers in his strait
    Rebellion's soldier-chief no more contends —
Feels that the hour is come of Fate,
    Lays down one sword, and widened warfare ends.
The captain who fierce armies led
Becomes a quiet seminary's head . . .

    But missives from the Senators ran;
Not that they now would gaze upon a swordless foe,
And power made powerless and brought low:
    Reasons of state 'tis claimed, require the man.
Demurring not, promptly he comes
By ways which show the blackened homes,
    And — last — the seat no more his own,
But Honor's; patriot grave-yards fill
The forfeit slopes of that patrician hill,
    And fling a shroud on Arlington . . .

The meeting follows. In his mien
The victor and the vanquished both are seen —
All that he is, and what he late has been.
Awhile, with curious eyes they scan
The Chief who led invasion's van . . .
    Their thoughts their questions well express:
"Does the sad South still cherish hate?
Freely will Southern men with Northern mate?
The blacks — should we our arm withdraw,
Would that betray them? some distrust your law.
And how if foreign fleets should come —

Would the South then drive her wedges home?"
And more hereof. The Virginian sees —
Replies to such anxieties.
Discreet his answers run — appear
Briefly straightforward, coldly clear.

"If now," the Senators, closing, say,
"Aught else remain, speak out, we pray."

They could not mark within his breast
The pang which pleading thought oppressed:
He spoke, nor felt the bitterness die.
"Our cause I followed, stood in field and gate —
All's over now, and now I follow Fate.
But this is naught. A People call —
A desolated land, and all
The brood of ills that press so sore,
The natural offspring of this civil war . . .

"How shall I speak? The South would fain
Feel peace, have quiet law again —
Replant the trees for homestead-shade.
     You ask if she recants: she yields.
Nay, and would more; would blend anew,
As the bones of the slain in her forests do,
Bewailed alike by us and you.
     A voice comes out from those charnel-fields,
A plaintive yet unheeded one:
'Died all in vain? both sides undone?'
Push not your triumph; do not urge
Submissiveness beyond the verge.
Intestine rancor would you bide,
Nursing eleven sliding daggers in your side?
Far from my thought to school or threat;
I speak the things which hard beset.
Where various hazards meet the eyes,
To elect in magnanimity is wise.
Reap victory's fruit while sound the core;

What sounder fruit than re-established law?
I know your partial thoughts do press
Solely on us for war's unhappy stress . . .

"But this I feel, that North and South were driven
By Fate to arms. For *our* unshriven,
What thousands, truest souls, were tried —
    As never may any be again —
All those who stemmed Secession's pride,
But at last were swept by the urgent tide
    Into the chasm. I know their pain . . .

"True to the home and to the heart,
Throngs cast their lot with kith and kin,
    Foreboding, cleaved to the natural part —
Was this the unforgivable sin?
These noble spirits are yet yours to win.
Shall the great North go Sylla's way?
Proscribe? prolong the evil day?
Confirm the curse? infix the hate?
In Union's name forever alienate?
When blood returns to the shrunken vein,
Shall the wound of the Nation bleed again?"

He ceased. His earnestness unforeseen
Moved, but not swayed their former mien;
    And they dismissed him.

SEA-PIECES

THE HAGLETS

(excerpts)

By open ports the Admiral sits,
And shares repose with guns that tell
Of power that smote the arm'd Plate Fleet

Whose sinking flag-ship's colors fell;
But over the Admiral floats in light
His squadron's flag, the red-cross Flag of the White.
    The eddying waters whirl astern,
The prow, a seedsman, sows the spray;
With bellying sails and buckling spars
The black hull leaves a Milky Way;
Her timbers thrill, her batteries roll,
She revelling speeds exulting with pennon at pole . . .

Ensigns and arms in trophy brave,
Braver for many a rent and scar,
The captor's naval hall bedeck,
Spoil that insures an earldom's star —
Toledoes great, grand draperies too,
Spain's steel and silk, and splendors from Peru . . .

By shot-chests grouped in bays 'tween guns
The gossips chat, the grizzled, sea-beat ones.
    And boyish dreams some graybeards blab:
"To sea, my lads, we go no more
Who share the Acapulco prize;
We'll all night in, and bang the door;
Our ingots red shall yield us bliss:
Lads, golden years begin to-night with this!"

Honor! our Admiral's aim foretold:
"*A tomb or a trophy,* and lo, 'tis a trophy and gold!"
    But he, a unit, sole in rank,
Apart needs keep his lonely state,
The sentry at his guarded door
Mute as by vault the sculptured Fate;
Belted he sits in drowsy light,
And, hatted, nods — the Admiral of the White . . .

    In dream at last his dozings merge,
In dream he reaps his victory's fruit:
The Flags-o'-the-Blue, the Flags-o'-the-Red,

Dipped flags of his country's fleets salute
His Flag-o'-the-White in harbor proud —
But why should it blench? Why turn to a painted shroud?

The hungry seas they hound the hull,
The sharks they dog the haglets' flight;
With one consent the winds, the waves
In hunt with fins and wings unite,
While drear the harps in cordage sound
Remindful wails for old Armadas drowned.

Ha — yonder! are they Northern Lights?
Or signals flashed to warn or ward?
Yea, signals lanced in breakers high;
But doom on warning follows hard:
While yet they veer in hope to shun,
They strike! and thumps of hull and heart are one . . .

Ah, what may live, who mighty swim,
Or boat-crew reach that shore forbid,
Or cable span? Must victors drown —
Perish, even as the vanquished did?
Man keeps from man the stifled moan;
They shouldering stand, yet each in heart how lone.
    Some heaven invoke; but rings of reefs
Prayer and despair alike deride
In dance of breakers forked or peaked,
Pale maniacs of the maddened tide;
While, strenuous yet some end to earn,
The haglets spin, though now no more astern.
    Like shuttles hurrying in the looms
Aloft through rigging frayed they ply —
Cross and recross — weave and inweave,
Then lock the web with clinching cry
Over the seas on seas that clasp
The weltering wreck where gurgling ends the gasp.

Ah for the Plate-Fleet trophy now,
The victor's voucher, flags and arms;
Never they'll hang in Abbey old
And take Time's dust with holier palms;
Nor less content, in liquid night,
Their captor sleeps — the Admiral of the White.

    Imbedded deep with shells
    And drifted treasure deep,
    Forever he sinks deeper in
    Unfathomable sleep —
    His cannon round him thrown,
    His sailors at his feet,
    The wizard sea enchanting them
    Where never haglets beat.

    On nights when meteors play
    And light the breakers dance,
    The Oreads from the caves
    With silvery elves advance;
    And up from ocean stream,
    And down from heaven far,
    The rays that blend in dream
    The abysm and the star.

TO NED

Ned, for our Pantheistic ports: —
Marquesas and glenned isles that be
Authentic Edens in a Pagan sea.
The charm of scenes untried shall lure,
    And, Ned, a legend urge the flight —
The Typee-truants under stars
    Unknown to Shakespere's *Midsummer Night;*
And man, if lost to Saturn's Age,
Yet feeling life no Syrian pilgrimage.

But, tell, shall he, the tourist, find
    Our isles the same in violet-glow
Enamoring us what years and years —
    Ah, Ned, what years and years ago!
Well, Adam advances, smart in pace,
But scarce by violets that advance you trace.

But we, in anchor-watches calm,
    The Indian Psyche's languor won,
And, musing, breathed primeval balm
    From Edens ere yet overrun;
Marvelling mild if mortal twice,
Here and hereafter, touch a Paradise.

TIMOLEON

IN A GARRET

Gems and jewels let them heap —
    Wax sumptuous as the Sophi:
For me, to grapple from Art's deep
    One dripping trophy!

LONE FOUNTS

Though fast youth's glorious fable flies,
View not the world with worldling's eyes;
Nor turn with weather of the time.
Foreclose the coming of surprise:
Stand where Posterity shall stand;
Stand where the Ancients stood before,
And, dipping in lone founts thy hand,
Drink of the never-varying lore:
Wise once, and wise thence evermore.

THE ENTHUSIAST
"THOUGH HE SLAY ME YET
WILL I TRUST IN HIM."

Shall hearts that beat no base retreat
    In youth's magnanimous years —
Ignoble hold it, if discreet
    When spirits that worship light
    Perfidious deem its sacred glow,
    Recant, and trudge where worldlings go,
Conform and own them right?
Shall Time with creeping influence cold
    Unnerve and cow? the heart
Pine for the heartless ones enrolled
    With palterers of the mart?
Shall faith abjure her skies,
    Or pale probation blench her down
    To shrink from Truth so still, so lone
Mid loud gregarious lies?

Each burning boat in Caesar's rear,
    Flames — No return through me!
So put the torch to ties though dear,
    If ties but tempters be.
Nor cringe if come the night:
    Walk through the cloud to meet the pall,
    Though light forsake thee, never fall
From fealty to light.

FRUIT OF TRAVEL LONG AGO

PAUSILIPPO
(IN THE TIME OF BOMBA)

A hill there is that laves its feet
In Naples' bay and lifts its head
In jovial season, curled with vines.

Its name, in pristine years conferred
By settling Greeks, imports that none
Who take the prospect thence can pine,
For such the charm of beauty shown
Even sorrow's self they cheerful weened
Surcease might find and thank good Pan.

Toward that hill my landeau drew;
And there, hard by the verge, were seen
Two faces with such meaning fraught
One scarce could mark and straight pass on.

A man it was less hoar with time
Than bleached through strange immurement long,
Retaining still, by doom depressed,
Dim trace of some aspiring prime.
Seated he tuned a homely harp
Watched by a girl, whose filial mien
Toward one almost a child again,
Took on a staid maternal tone.
Nor might one question that the locks
Which in smoothed natural silvery curls
Fell on the bowed one's thread-bare coat
Betrayed her ministering hand.
Anon, among some ramblers drawn,
A murmur rose " 'Tis Silvio, Silvio!"
With inklings more in tone suppressed
Touching his story, part recalled:
Clandestine arrest abrupt by night;
The sole conjecturable cause
The yearning in a patriot ode
Construed as treason; trial none;
Prolonged captivity profound;
Vain liberation late. All this,
With pity for impoverishment
And blight forestalling age's wane.

Hillward the quelled enthusiast turned,
Unmanned, made meek through strenuous wrong,
Preluding, faltering; then began,
But only thrilled the wire — no more,
The constant maid supplying voice,
Hinting by no ineloquent sign
That she was but his mouth-piece mere,
Himself too spiritless and spent.

Pausilippo, Pausilippo,
Pledging easement unto pain,
    Shall your beauty even solace
If one's sense of beauty wane?

Could light airs that round ye play
Waft heart-heaviness away
Or memory lull to sleep,
    Then, then indeed your balm
    Might Silvio becharm,
And life in fount would leap,
    Pausilippo!

Did not your spell invite,
    In moods that slip between,
    A dream of years serene,
And wake, to dash, delight —
    Evoking here in vision
    Fulfilment and fruition —

Nor mine, nor meant for man
    Did hope not frequent share
    The mirage when despair
Overtakes the caravan,
    Me then your scene might move
    To break from sorrow's snare,
    And apt your name would prove,
        Pausilippo!

But I've looked upon your revel —
　　It unravels not the pain:
Pausilippo, Pausilippo,
　　Named benignly if in vain!

　　It ceased. In low and languid tone
The tideless ripple lapped the passive shore;
As listlessly the bland untroubled heaven
Looked down as silver doled was silent given
In pity — futile as the ore!

DISINTERMENT OF THE HERMES

What forms divine in adamant fair —
Carven demigod and god,
And hero-marbles rivalling these,
Bide under Latium's sod,
Or lost in sediment and drift
Alluvial which the Grecian rivers sift.

　　To dig for these, O better far
Than raking arid sands
For gold more barren meetly theirs
Sterile, with brimming hands.

THE GILDED AGE

WHEN FORTH THE SHEPHERD LEADS
THE FLOCK

When forth the shepherd leads the flock,
White lamb and dingy ewe,
And there's dibbling in the garden,
Then the world begins anew.

When Buttercups make bright
The meadows up and down,

The Golden Age returns to fields
If never to the town.

When stir the freshening airs
   Forerunning showers to meads,
And Dandelions prance,
Then Heart-Free shares the dance —
   A Wilding with the Weeds!

   But alack and alas
For things of wilding feature!
   Since hearsed was Pan
Ill befalls each profitless creature —
   Profitless to man!

Buttercup and Dandelion,
Wildings, and the rest,
Commoners and holiday-makers,
   Note them in one test:

   The farmers scout them,
Yea, and would rout them,
Hay is better without them —
   Tares in the grass!
The florists pooh-pooh them;
Few but children do woo them,
Love them, reprieve them,
Retrieve and inweave them,
   Never sighing — *Alas!*

THE ROSE FARMER

(excerpts)

I chanced upon a Persian late,
A sort of gentleman-rose-farmer
On knees beside his garden-gate
Telling his beads, just like a palmer.

Beads? coins, I meant. Each golden one
Upon a wire of silver run;
And every time a coin he told
His brow he raised and eyes he rolled
Devout in grateful orison.

Surely, methought, this pious man,
A Florist, too, will solve my doubt.
Saluting him I straight began:
"Decide, I pray, a dubious matter —"
And put the Roses and the Attar . . .

"Attar? Go ask the Parsee yonder.
Lean as a rake with his distilling,
Cancel his debts, scarce worth a shilling!
How he exists I frequent wonder.
No neighbor loves him: sweet endeavor
Will get a nosegay from him never;
Of *me,* however, all speak well:
You see, my little coins I tell;
I give away, but more I sell,
In mossy pots, or bound in posies,
Always a market for my roses.
But attar, why, it comes so dear
Tis far from popular, that's clear.
I flourish, I; yon heavens they bless me,
My darlings cluster to caress me . . .
But now, Sir, for your urgent matter.
Every way — for wise employment,
Repute and profit, health, enjoyment,
I am for roses — *sink* the Attar!"

And hereupon the downright man
To tell his rosary re-began . . .
Discreet, in second thought's immersion
I wended from this prosperous Persian
Who, verily, seemed in life rewarded
For sapient prudence not amiss,

Nor transcendental essence hoarded
In hope of quintessential bliss:
No, never with painstaking throes
Essays to crystallize the rose.

THE RUSTY MAN
(BY A SOURED ONE)

In La Mancha he mopeth,
    With beard thin and dusty;
He doteth and mopeth
    In library fusty —
'Mong his old folios gropeth:
    Cites obsolete saws
    Of chivalry's laws —
    Be the wronged one's knight:
    Die, but do right.
So he rusts and musts,
While each grocer green
Thriveth apace with the fulsome face
Of a fool serene.

CAMOËNS
I
(BEFORE)

Restless, restless, craving rest,
Forever must I fan this fire,
Forever in flame on flame aspire?
Yea, for the God demands thy best.
The world with endless beauty teems,
And thought evokes new worlds of dreams:
Then hunt the flying herds of themes.
And fan, yet fan thy fervid fire
Until the crucibled ore shall show
That fire can purge, as well as glow.

In ordered ardor nobly strong,
Flame to the height of ancient song.

CAMOËNS
II
(AFTER)

What now avails the pageant verse,
Trophies and arms with music borne?
Base is the world; and some rehearse
How noblest meet ignoble scorn.
Vain now the ardor, vain thy fire,
Delirium mere, unsound desire:
Fate's knife hath ripped the chorded lyre.
Exhausted by the exacting lay,
Thou dost but fall a surer prey
To wile and guile ill understood;
While they who work them, fair in face,
Still keep their strength in prudent place,
And claim they worthier run life's race,
Serving high God with useful good.

FRUIT AND FLOWER PAINTER

She dens in a garret
    As void as a drum;
In lieu of plum-pudding —
    She paints the plum!

        No use in my grieving,
            The shops I must suit:
        Broken hearts are but potsherds —
            Paint flowers and fruit!

How whistles her garret,
    A seine for the snows:

She hums *Si fortuna,*
   And — paints the rose!

   December is howling,
     But feign it a flute:
   Help on the deceiving —
     Paint flowers and fruit!

IN THE HALL OF MARBLES
(LINES RECALLED FROM
A DESTROYED POEM)

If genius, turned to sordid ends
   Ye count to glory lost,
How with mankind that flouts the aims
   Time's Attic years engrossed?

Waxes the world so rich and old?
   Richer and narrower, age's way?
But, primal fervors all displaced
   Our arts but serve the clay.
This plaint the sibyls unconsoled renew:
Man fell from Eden, fall from Athens too.

HEARTS-OF-GOLD

Pity, if true,
What the pewterers said —
Hearts-of-gold be few.
Howbeit, when snug in my bed,
And the fire-light flickers and yellows,
I dream of the hearts-of-gold sped —
The Falernian fellows —
Hafiz and Horace,
And Beranger — all
Dexterous tumblers eluding the Fall,

Fled? can be sped?
But the marygold's morris
Is danced o'er their head;
And their memory mellows,
Enbalmed and becharmed,
Hearts-of-gold and good fellows!

IN SHARDS THE SYLVAN VASES LIE

In shards the sylvan vases lie,
Their links of dance undone;
And brambles wither by thy brim,
Choked Fountain of the Sun!
The spider in the laurel spins,
The weed exiles the flower,
And, flung to kiln, Apollo's bust
Makes lime for Mammon's tower.

THE DUST-LAYERS

Abreast through town by Nile they go
    With water-skins the dust to lay,
A soggy set in sorry row
    Squeezing their skins in bag-pipe way.
With droning rhyme that times the twitch
They squirt the water, squirt and switch
    In execrable play!

Osiris! what indignity,
    In open eye of day,
Offered the arch majesty
    Of Thotmes passed away;
The atoms of his pomp no prouder
Than to be blown about in powder,
    Or made a muddy clay!

A RAIL ROAD CUTTING NEAR
ALEXANDRIA IN 1855

Plump thro' tomb and catacomb
Rolls the Engine ripping;
   Egypt's ancient dust
   This before the gust,
The Pyramid is slipping!

Too long inurned, Sesostres's spurned,
   What glory left to Isis
Mid loud acclaim to Watts his name
   Alack for Miriam's spices!

Whitman

Five Approaches

I. Ever-Widening Network

W hitman's pervasiveness is self-evident; pointing it out yet again seems needless. 1981, however, offered an instance too remarkable to be bypassed. Those who saw *Reds*, the prize-winning epic, will recall a climactic episode in the stormy relationship between Louise Bryant and John Reed. Eugene O'Neill visits her in 1916 with a love poem and a proposition that they renew their affair. Having become Mrs. Reed, she rejects the proposition but keeps the poem, deliberately choosing *Leaves of Grass* as its home. Back from a difficult trip, in need of spiritual nourishment, Reed just as deliberately lifts the same volume from the shelf. No Hollywood coincidence has been concocted here. Whitman is indeed at the very core of their being. Both naturally seek out his book, as might anyone in their radical circle. What is not in the film is the interesting fact that in June 1917, through her friend Waldo Frank, Louise managed to get O'Neill's story "Tomorrow" published in *The Seven Arts* ("the first respectable sum he had earned from creative writing"). Frank, whose co-editors were James Oppenheim and Van Wyck Brooks, later wrote of their journal: "We were disciples of Walt Whitman and were creating the voice he wanted." Alfred Kreymborg had four months earlier published O'Neill's poem "Submarine" in his magazine *Others*. And it was Kreymborg who had just paid cogent tribute to Whitman in his first collection, *Mushrooms*:

> After we've had
> our age of gold
> and sung our song of brass,
> fingers will brush

> the age aside,
> fingers and leaves of grass.

Like Kreymborg, whose craft developed toward other kinds of mastery than Whitman's, Langston Hughes also shared his vision and humanity:

> Old Walt Whitman
> Went finding and seeking,
> Finding less than sought
> Seeking more than found,
> Every detail minding
> Of the seeking or the finding.

It was Hughes who supplied lyrics for the Kurt Weill setting of Elmer Rice's 1929 Pulitzer Prize play, *Street Scene*. Here, as in *Reds*, we meet Whitman without surprise, so thoroughly is he woven into the fabric of America's consciousness. In a climactic duet, a pair of tenement sweethearts challenge the sordidness and despair around them:

> I thought I'd walk to the office,
> So I cut through the park by the mall.
> Everything looked so fresh and green.
> Life seemed not so bad after all!
> What do you think I saw, Sam?
> A lilac-bush flowering bright.
> It made me think of that poem you said,
> Remember? When we sat in the Park one night.
> It was just like tonight,
> We were both feeling sort of low,
> And all of a sudden
> You began that poem.

[She then recites six lines from the elegy, beginning "In the door-yard . . . "]

> Yes, that's what I thought in the Park today,
> When I saw that bush, fresh and green.
> I wanted to break off a flower,
> But I was afraid I might be seen.

> Maybe a park policeman
> Might come and take me away.
> "Do not pick the flowers"
> The signs forever say.
> But in our dreams, Sam!
> A sprig with its flowers we break,
> And the lilac-bush is ours,
> Nothing can take it away.

The lovers' vow to keep the lilac-bush as their special symbol not only closes the first half of the opera but is also defiantly restated at the conclusion of the work. To set off the innocence and wholesomeness of a love that appears outmoded and doomed in our 20th century street scene, Langston Hughes could not have chosen a more appropriate focal point. For Whitman's sweetness and exuberance now carried an ironic, downright subversive undertone. The pristine world he'd celebrated was being laid waste, and the gorgeous evocations of his Paumanok — its earth, sea, air — now struck at our conscience: a powerful rebuke. The populist upsurge of the '30s finally brought Whitman his "great audiences," and what they heard in him was not so much the sweetness and exuberance of 1855 as his rage against the Gilded Age that followed. Edgar Lee Masters, a generation after *Spoon River*, defined both aspects in his 1937 biography:

> Whitman wrote for the American tribe and the American idea ... Whitman had the right idea, namely, that poetry, the real written word, must come out of life — not out of books or erudition. It must come out of the earth. When it speaks for a land and celebrates a tribe it has done the greatest work that poetry can do ...

> The definite and legalistic way in which a free government, such as America was before the War of the States, was turned into a despotic plutocracy and made a feeding place for swine has had no parallel in history. Whitman marked the beginning of this transformation and much of its consummation. He execrated it in *Democratic Vistas*. ... It is not strange that Whitman had no sons dedicated to carrying on his work. It is logical,

however, that he had sons bent on avenging the ruin of the America to which Whitman gave his life.

Some of those avenger-sons are today playing sensational roles in the history of their countries. Home from a showing of *Reds*, one opens the latest *American Book Review*. In a critique of Ernesto Cardenal's *Zero Hour and Other Documentary Poems*, Harold Jaffe credits Whitman as "principal forebear" of the great Nicaraguan, whose "moral nature ... closely resembles Whitman's." Stylistically:

> ... as with Whitman, there is less compression than extension in Cardenal's most successful poems. The effects usually depend on increment to uncover depth, and the poem is meant to be public, an open window baring the naked heart.

Nor have there been sons only. Erica Jong opens her latest book of poems, *Love-Root*, with "Testament (Or Homage to Walt Whitman)":

> I scorned you at twenty
> but turn to you now
> in the fourth decade of my life,
> having grown straight enough
> to praise your straightness,
> and plain enough
> to speak to you plain
> and simple enough
> to praise your simplicity ...
> The soul is contagious.
> One man catches another's
> like the plague;
> and we are all patient spiders to each other ...
>
> We meet on the pages of books and by beachwood fires.
> We meet scrawled blackly in many-folded letters.
> We know each other by free and generous hands.
> We swing like spiders on each other's souls.

Such full-throated expressions of affinity and fellowship testify year after year to Whitman's undiminished force, his ever-widening network by which "we swing" — intercontinentally — "on each other's souls."

II. A Mighty Charm

> O strong-willed soul with prophetic
>   Lips hot with the bloodbeats of song,
> With tremor of heartstrings magnetic,
>   With thoughts as thunders in throng,
> With consonant ardors of chords
> That pierce men's souls as with swords
>   And hale them hearing along . . .

It is well over a hundred years since Swinburne astonishingly hailed Whitman from across the Atlantic, at a time when most poets either ignored his existence or shuddered at the mention of his name. With the passing of years, many — like Swinburne — felt free to acknowledge their admiration, even their indebtedness, although no trace of the Whitman sound and structure could be found in their verses.

Others, beginning with his disciple Horace Traubel and the Tolstoyan Ernest Crosby, honored him by adopting his cadence, his long line, his cataloging, the sweep and crash of his oceanic passages. Early in the new century his distinguished heirs included Arturo Giovannitti and James Oppenheim. In the final two lines of "Petit, the Poet," Edgar Lee Masters definitively shattered the cult of prettiness that had long dominated literary America:

> Tick, tick, tick, what little iambics,
> While Homer and Whitman roared in the pines!

It was at this time that Whitman's greatest successor emerged. Carl Sandburg's life, and the total body of his work, can be looked at as a tribute to Whitman's unslackened power to inspire. A decade later, Robinson Jeffers seized upon Whitman's music, if not his affirmation. During the '30s a large number of new rebel poets claimed their heritage from him: Muriel Rukeyser, Kenneth Fearing and Kenneth Patchen were among the best.

Published in 1930, Hart Crane's *The Bridge* hinges on an extra-

ordinary series of apostrophes to "Walt," his spiritual ancestor and
Brooklyn's prime son. In "Cape Hatteras" it is Whitman's role as
fountainhead and guide that Crane stresses:

> O Saunterer on free ways still ahead! ...
> ... your eyes, like the Great Navigator's without ship ...
> But who has held the heights more sure than thou,
> O Walt! — Ascensions of thee hover in me now ...
>   ... O, upward from the dead
> Thou bringest tally, and a pact, new bound
> Of living brotherhood!
>
>   ... thy wand
> Has beat a song, O Walt, — there and beyond! ...
>
> When first I read thy lines, rife as the loam
> Of prairies, yet like breakers cliffward leaping!
> O, early following thee, I climbed the hill ...
>
> To course that span of consciousness thou'st named
> The Open Road — thy vision is reclaimed!
> What heritage thou'st signalled to our hands!
>
>   ... O joyous seer!
> Recorders ages hence, yes, they shall hear
> In their own veins uncancelled thy sure tread ...
>
>   ... yes, Walt,
> Afoot again, and onward without halt, —
> Not soon, not suddenly, — no, never to let go
>   My hand
>   in yours,
>   Walt Whitman —
>   so —

Crane demonstrates again Whitman's capacity to be absorbed en-
tirely into the souls of poets, even those who model their form on
other, more traditional, masters. This can be seen in some of our
finest post-World War II poets. The pattern of Randall Jarrell's work
bears no resemblance to Whitman's, yet he praises the older master as
"a poet of the greatest and oddest delicacy and originality and sensitiv-

ity," who expresses difficult concepts and complex emotions "with complete success, in language of the most dazzling originality." Above all, it is Whitman's universality that Jarrell honors:

> ... there is in him almost everything in the world, so that one responds to him, willingly or unwillingly, almost as one does to the world, that world which makes the hairs of one's flesh stand up, which seems both evil beyond any rejection and wonderful beyond any acceptance.

Almost a score of years later, another superb traditionalist poet, Richard Wilbur, extends the tribute:

> Whitman is ... a poet of psychic battle, and his great strength as a poet of ideas is that his conceptions are tested, contradicted, endangered, and so seem fairly earned ... he is the most inclusive of mystics, and he will not scorn the material, the physical, the urban, the vernacular, the particular and everyday. He leaves nothing out. How astonishing it is that a poetry aimed at the infinite should catch so unforgettably "the sluff of bootsoles" on the pavement ...

These responses, no less than the direct kinship of such giants as Neruda, testify to the sustained vigor of Whitman's presence. And the contributions to *West Hills Review: a Whitman Journal,* year after year, by poets famous and unknown, from every corner of the globe as well as from his own beloved Paumanok, bear ongoing witness to Whitman's seminal force. That they should encompass such an awesome range of themes and moods, yet all flow — either directly or indirectly — from the same wellspring, shows once again the fullness of Whitman's voice, the breadth of his vision.

> Bards of my own land ...
> Bards of the great Idea! bards of the peaceful
>   inventions! ...
> Bards with songs as from burning coals or the
>   lightning's fork'd stripes! ...
> You by my charm I invoke.

It is a mighty charm. The invocation continues to be heeded.

III. Whitmanesque Neruda

In 1950, aptly named "scoundrel time," the revolutionary senator-poet Pablo Neruda was in hiding: object of a nationwide manhunt by Chile's police. Two massive poems, "Let the Rail Splitter Awake" and "The Fugitive," sprang from this experience. *Let the Rail Splitter Awake*, a Neruda collection published that year, opens with these words: "Walt Whitman once wrote that the great poet enlisted in a people's cause 'can make every word he speaks draw blood.' This is true of Pablo Neruda." Further along in his preface, editor Samuel Sillen declares:

> Neruda speaks directly to the people of the United States in the title-poem of this volume, and his message has a life or death urgency.... This is a cry born of love for all that is good on this continent, love for the heritage of Lincoln and Whitman.

In the opening section of "Rail Splitter" Neruda identifies our shared literary roots, "what I was before being ... what we were":

> Melville is a marine yew tree,
> ... Whitman endless
> as the fields of grain ...

A far more remarkable reference occurs in Section III — remarkable because the context is so unlikely. Here Neruda achieves a peculiarly Whitmanesque vision, spanning oceans and continents with ease:

> ... in the Urals I pause
> and expand my soul permeated with solitude and resin.
> I love whatever man has created in space
> by blow of struggle and love.

His focus is on post-World War II Russia; but his description of the young returning from battle and of the agonized country rising from its million griefs toward reconstruction recalls a number of Civil War passages in Whitman. Perhaps it is with such lines in mind that Neruda suddenly invokes the revered ghost:

> Walt Whitman, lift up your grassy beard,
> look with me from this wood,
> from these fragrant heights.

What do you see, Walt Whitman?
I see, my wise brother tells me,
how factories are working in that city
remembered by the dead,
in pure resplendent Stalingrad.
I see how from the embattled plains,
from the suffering and the flames,
in the humid morning there is born
a tractor which clanks toward the fields.
Give me your voice and the strength of your buried breast,
Walt Whitman, and the solemn roots that are your face
so as to sing of these reconstructions!
Together we will pay homage to what arises
from all the grief, to what surges up
from the deep silence, from the somber victory.

More than anything else, it is a shared confidence in and love of humanity that Neruda acknowledges in these lines. There is also a shared reverence of Lincoln, "the Rail-splitter," embodiment for all time of the democratic idea:

Let Abe come with his axe
and his wooden plate
to eat with the farmers . . .
Let him bite into a yellow apple
and enter a moviehouse to converse
with all the simple people . . .
let him lift up his axe in his own town
against the new slaveholders
against the slave-lash . . .

As the poem ends, we hear a shared love of country. Just as Whitman, in his hottest wrath against the slave-catchers of Boston or the border-ruffians of Missouri and their "filthy Presidentiad," is careful to differentiate between the magnificent and the monstrous in America, never ceasing to celebrate "the great Idea," never ceasing to declare his love of homeland, so does the hunted Neruda sing:

. . . in my country they jail miners
and soldiers give orders to judges.

> But I love even the roots
> in my small cold country,
> if I had to die a thousand times over
> it is there I would die,
> if I had to be born a thousand times over
> it is there I would be born ...

Similarly, in "The Fugitive," we come upon a passage of well over a hundred lines — a paean to Valparaiso, the seaport in which he was stalked day and night. It is impossible not to think of Whitman's lusty love-chants to Manahatta, with all its sordidness and horror:

> Valparaiso, I love all that you enclose ...
> none but myself for your secrets;
> Queen of the world's sea-coasts,
> central hub of ships and waves,
> you are inside me like the moon ...
> I love your criminal alleys ...
> and your plazas where sailors ashore
> reclothe the spring in blue.
> I beg you, my harbor, understand
> that mine is the privilege to write
> of you, good and evil,
> for I am like a merciless lamp
> illuminating broken bottles ...
> Valparaiso, lone queen ...
> I felt your torrential pulse,
> your longshoreman hands embraced me
> as my soul required
> in the hour of night ...
> There is no other like you upon the sands ...

These poems reveal Whitman's inspiriting presence at the midpoint of Neruda's career — a time of extreme personal crisis. But the *Memoirs* underscore Whitman's crucial role in the shaping of Neruda's earliest standards — his very language:

> Our American stratum is dusty rock, crushed lava, clay mixed with blood. We don't know how to work in crystal. Our elegant poets sound hollow ... Spanish became a gilded lan-

guage after Cervantes, it took on a courtly elegance, it lost the wild power ... the genital fire.... This earlier well-spring had everything to do with the whole man, his freedom, his prolific nature, his excesses.

At least that was my problem, although I didn't put it in those terms, not even to myself. If my poetry has any meaning at all, it is this tendency to stretch out in space, without restrictions, and not be happy to stay in a room. I had to break out of my limited world by myself ... I had to be myself, striving to branch out like the very land where I was born. Another poet of this same hemisphere helped me along this road, Walt Whitman, my comrade from Manhattan.

Emerson had said as much: "The poets are liberating gods ... They are free, and they make free." He had sent out the call:

... our fisheries, our Negroes and Indians ... the wrath of rogues and the pusillanimity of honest men, the northern trade, the southern planting, the western clearing, Oregon and Texas, are yet unsung. Yet America is a poem in our eyes; its ample geography dazzles the imagination, and it will not wait long for metres.

Emerson, "demanding bards," had made Whitman free, free of "a mere tale ... a rhyme ... a prettiness," had turned the young newspaperman and his song into "earth, water, animals, trees":

> ... incarnating this land,
> Attracting its body and soul to himself, hanging on its
>   neck with incomparable love,
> Plunging his seminal muscle into its merits and demerits,
> Making its cities, beginnings, events, diversities, wars,
>   vocal in him ...
> If the Atlantic coast stretch or the Pacific coast stretch,
>   he stretching with them North or South ...
> Through him flights, whirls, screams, answering those of
>   the fish-hawk, mocking-bird, night-heron, and eagle,
> His spirit surrounding his country's spirit, unclosed to
>   good and evil.

Just so, Neruda was to be made free by his "comrade from Manhattan." But Neruda's relationship with Whitman was lifelong — more than gratitude to his liberator in youth, more than comradeship *in mezzo cammin*. In 1969, what translator Ben Belitt calls the "waning optimism" of the Chilean is reflected in "XIX" — a "left-handed compliment" to the 19th century giants who still have more to say to us than do most artists of our own time:

> Walt Whitman doesn't belong to us —
> that's called the nineteenth century! —
> yet he keeps tracking us down
> because no one else cares for our company . . .
>
> The twentieth century peters out
> with the century before on its shoulders,
> with all the colorless scribblers
> underneath the mouldering giants;
> we have climbed the long stair
> with a sack on our backs:
> the crushing precedence
> of more illustrious bones.
>
> Balzac weighs on us like an elephant,
> Victor Hugo comes on like a truck,
> Tolstoy looms, a horizon of mountains . . .
> all clobber us under their bulk.

Here, as in scores of passages throughout his work (often to the point of being downright interchangeable), Neruda parallels Whitman. In "Starting From Paumanok" Whitman also complains:

> Dead poets, philosophs, priests . . .
> Language-shapers on other shores . . .
> I dare not proceed till I respectfully credit what you
>   have left wafted hither . . .
> Think nothing can ever be greater, nothing can ever
>   deserve more than it deserves . . .

At last Whitman shakes himself loose:

> Regarding it all intently a long while, then dismissing it, I stand
> in my place with my own day here.

Such a "dismissal" is not particularly gracious, but necessary in order for a new poet to find himself. Neruda's declaration of independence from the well-loved voices — including Whitman's — is even more violent:

> They don't let us breathe
> or go on with our writing,
> they would never have left us alone
> unless old Uncle Ubu Dada spoke up
> and said: Shit on you all! in our name.

Much of this is, of course, tongue-in-cheek. "Rhymes and rhymers pass away, poems distill'd from poems pass away," declares Whitman in his credo-poem, "By Blue Ontario's Shore." But he knows that we know that he is not thus characterizing all the literature of the past. Whatever is great he absorbs. It happens to be necessary in America in 1855 to invoke "Bards for my own land ... Bards of the great Idea!" This he cannot accomplish without the inspiration of the past:

> And I saw the free souls of poets,
> The loftiest bards of past ages strode before me,
>
> Strange large men, long unwaked, undisclosed, were
>   disclosed to me.

In this poem of large definitions, to which Neruda surely harkened with special care, the bards Whitman requires are warriors and instigators of war. The poet "walks the States with a barb'd tongue." He "tauntingly compels men, women, nations,/Crying, Leap from your seats and contend." He must prepare "songs of stern defiance," unfold the "warlike flag of the great Idea," and "strike up the marches of Libertad ... marches henceforth triumphant and onward":

> ... bards of latent armies, a million soldiers waiting
>   ever-ready,
> Bards with songs as from burning coals or the lightning's
>   fork'd stripes!

Solemnly swearing, "I dare not shirk any part of myself," Whitman enlists — body and soul — in the war "to balance ranks ... complexions, creeds, and the sexes."

Neruda, in his *Memoirs*, after praising " 'the positive hero' found in the turbulent trenches of civil wars by the North American Walt Whitman," turns to the issue of a poet's personal involvement. The speaker might just as well have been Whitman:

> Perhaps the poet has always had the same obligations throughout history. It has been poetry's distinction to go out into the street, to take part in this or that combat. The poet didn't scare off when they said he was a rebel. Poetry is rebellion. The poet was not offended when he was called subversive. Life transcends all structures, and there are new rules of conduct for the soul. The seed sprouts everywhere; all ideas are exotic; we wait for enormous changes every day; we live through the mutation of human order avidly; spring is rebellious.
>
> I have given all I had. I have thrown my poetry into the ring, and I have often bled with it, suffering the agonies and praising the moments of glory I have witnessed and lived through.

How dear to Neruda's heart Whitman remained can best be seen in his eloquent remarks at a P. E. N. dinner in New York in 1972:

> I, who am now nearing 70, discovered Walt Whitman when I was just 15, and I hold him to be my greatest creditor. I stand before you feeling that I bear with me always this great and wonderful debt which has helped me to exist.
>
> I must start by acknowledging myself to be the humble servant of a poet who strode the earth with long, slow paces, pausing everywhere to love, to examine, to learn, to teach and to admire. The fact of the matter is that this great man, this lyric moralist, chose a hard path for himself: he was both a torrential and a didactic singer — qualities which appear posed, seeming also more appropriate to a leader than a writer. But what really counts is that Walt Whitman was not afraid to teach — which means to learn at the hands of life and undertake the responsibility of passing on the lesson! To speak frankly: he had no fear of either moralizing or immoralizing, nor did he seek to separate the fields of pure and impure poetry. He was the first totalitarian poet: his intention was not just to sing, but to impose on others his own total and wide-ranging vision of the relationships of men and nations. In this sense, his patent

nationalism forms part of a total and organic universal vision: he held himself to be the debtor of happiness and sorrow alike, and also of both the advanced cultures and more primitive societies.

There are many kinds of greatness, but let me say (though I be a poet of the Spanish tongue) that Walt Whitman has taught me more than Spain's Cervantes: in Walt Whitman's work one never finds the ignorant being humbled, nor is the human condition ever found offended.

Walt Whitman was the protagonist of a truly geographic personality: the first man in history to speak with a truly continental American voice, to bear a truly American name.

IV. "The Learn'd Astronomer"

Like Shakespeare, Whitman is colossal not so much for having introduced new ideas or episodes as for the resonance and dramatic emphasis with which he projected familiar ones. A case in point is the anti-academic stance taken throughout *Leaves of Grass*. Perhaps nowhere in literature is the lecture-room rejected as bitterly as in "When I Heard the Learn'd Astronomer," an eight-line satire that banishes "the proofs, the figures … the charts and diagrams" in favor of the "mystical moist night air" through which the poet "Look'd up in perfect silence at the stars."

Anyone familiar with the ascendancy of the Romantic temperament for over a century before these lines were written will recognize that Whitman was reformulating an old attack on the misshaping of young minds, an attack for which Rousseau's *Emile* was hailed as revolutionary in 1761 but which had already been devastatingly launched by Fielding in the Square/Thwackum segment of *Tom Jones*, and, even earlier, by Alexander Pope:

> Placed at the door of learning, youth to guide,
> We never suffer it to stand too wide.
> To ask, to guess, to know, as they commence,
> As fancy opens the quick springs of sense,
> We ply the memory, we load the brain,
> Bind rebel wit, and double chain on chain …

> Whate'er the talents, or howe'er designed,
> We hang one jingling padlock on the mind.
>
> *(The Dunciad,* 1743)

In 1772 John Trumbull's *Progress of Dulness* continued the trans-Atlantic assault, and in 1790 Philip Freneau's "The Indian Student" did for Harvard what Trumbull had done for Yale. Robert Burns' "Epistle to John Lapraik" pitted the poetry of instinct and heart against archaic patterns learned by rote:

> A set o' dull conceited hashes
> Confuse their brains in college classes! ...
> An' syne they think to climb Parnassus
>   By dint o' Greek!
>
> Gie me ae spark o' Nature's fire,
> That's a' the learning I desire ...
> My Muse, though hamely in attire,
>   May touch the heart.

In "Frost at Midnight" Coleridge expressed delight that his infant would "learn far other lore,/And in far other scenes" than the poet had learned "In the great city pent 'mid cloisters dim...." The boy would study Nature's "lovely shapes and sounds." Wordsworth exhorted his sister to "Come forth and feel the sun ... And bring no book," and warned the bookworm William Hazlitt against "Our meddling intellect" by which "We murder to dissect."

Wordsworth's greatest work, *The Prelude,* vividly depicted the spirit-dampening atmosphere of Cambridge in his own undergraduate days just as Edward Gibbon's autobiography had dealt with his drab years at Oxford. Wordsworth contrasted the damaged products of the schools with a "race of real children" allowed to grow freely in Nature, whose knowledge will not be "purchased by the loss of power!" In *Hard Times,* a year before *Leaves of Grass,* Dickens exposed the destructiveness of an anti-emotional, anti-imaginative educational system which brained the young into a monolithic intellectual anemia, teaching a child that her name was not Sissy Jupe but Girl Number Twenty, that the animals she had caressed and fed all her life were not horses but graminivorous quadrupeds.

It is first of all in this context that one should examine "When I

Heard the Learn'd Astronomer." More valuable, however, is to consider the "Astronomer" within the context of Whitman's total poetic output. Very soon one becomes aware of a recurrence that is almost obsessive, from the earliest to the last pieces. The smothering ambience of academe is deplored in several of the *Calamus* poems, always contrasted with the free world of nature and companionship: "in libraries I lie as one dumb, a gawk, or unborn, or dead," but not "with you on a high hill" or "with you sailing at sea." It does not "repay" him "to converse with learn'd persons," but to meet "eyes offering . . . love." His dread of stultification is emphasized in "Myself and Mine," a command that his admirers not "expound" him, that they found "no theory or school" on him, that they "leave all free."

Three of the big songs declare the same anti-academic bias. "Song of the Open Road" summons whoever would travel with him to escape "from all formules" promulgated by the "bat-eyed and materialistic priests." As if to underline the word "materialistic," that most despicable motive in Victorian education, Whitman climaxes the great song with a ringing cry of contempt. His Open Road is the ultimate rejection of the lecture-hall with its promise of diploma and career:

> Let the paper remain on the desk unwritten, and the book on
> the shelf unopen'd!
> . . . let the money remain unearn'd!
> Let the school stand! mind not the cry of the teacher! . . .
> I give you my love more precious than money . . .

"Song of the Broad-Axe" restates this sentiment, and with the same cluster of images. A great city is not "the place of the best libraries and schools, nor the place where money is plentiest," but where "the greatest men and women" live — individuals who "think lightly of the laws," whose gods are not Thrift and Prudence. "A Song for Occupations" concludes with the same juxtaposition of values, the same demotion of academic ikons — script, pulpit, books — in favor of men and women. "When a university course convinces as a slumbering woman and child convince," the poet will "make as much of it" as he now makes of ordinary people.

Age did not mellow Whitman on this theme. Near the beginning of *Drum-Taps* a Poet sneers: "Words! book-words! what are you? ... My song is there in the open air...." Toward war's end he remains the poet of *Calamus*, choking "In the learn'd coterie," reviving outdoors in the camp, amid the wounded. After the war, in "By Blue Ontario's Shore," he still advocates the Open Road, warning against "the decay of ruggedness" brought on by excessive schooling: "grace, elegance, civilization, delicatesse." At the close of "Passage to India" true learning is identified once and for all as exploration without fear or limits:

> Have we not darken'd and dazed ourselves with books long
>   enough?
> Sail forth — steer for the deep waters only,
> Reckless O soul, exploring, I with thee, and thou with me,
> For we are bound where mariner has not yet dared to go ...

* * * *

In *Autumn Rivulets* Whitman strips the masks off "persons arrived at high positions, ceremonies, wealth, scholarships, and the like," exposing them as often "gaunt and naked," whose "core of life, namely happiness, is full of the rotten excrement of maggots." This being so, we are not surprised to find life's wisest, most profoundly serene students in the opposite camp. Reminiscent of Wordsworth's unschooled heroes — the shepherd Michael, the leech-gatherer, the old Cumberland beggar, the solitary reaper — are Whitman's "offspring of ignorant and poor," whom he tenderly scolds for thinking less of themselves than of the President: "Is it you that thought ... the educated wiser than you...?"

In "By Blue Ontario's Shore" he claims the right "to teach or be a poet" on the grounds that he has "gone freely with powerful uneducated persons." "The Ox-Tamer" describes with reverence his "silent, illiterate friend." Most touchingly, in the final segment of "The Sleepers," he denies the supremacy of the diploma. In the democracy of slumber "Learn'd and unlearn'd" lie hand in hand. The question to be considered is therefore the way to genuine knowing, and on this subject Whitman supplies clues generously from first to last.

"Beginning My Studies" wittily promises practical advice to those preparing for tests. But the poet explains that for him "the first step" has been enough to last a lifetime. Not textbook studies, but loitering in an awed consciousness of forms and motions, has been so fruitful that he feels no need to go beyond it. Whitman here exactly parallels Wordsworth's famous defense of "wise passiveness" against Hazlitt's charge that he is wasting his time sitting on a stone without so much as a book. *Calamus* expands this point. The poet warns a would-be follower not to hope for learning from a book (including *Leaves of Grass*): "Nor is it by reading it you will acquire it." The process is "uncertain"; it involves indirection, silence, touch, an endless guessing at elusive hints:

> When the subtle air, the impalpable, the sense that words
>   and reason hold not, surround us and pervade us,
> Then I am charged with untold and untellable wisdom, I am
>   silent, I require nothing further ...

As with all transcendental poets, true personal growth — resulting from a moment of spiritual union with the Oversoul of the universe — requires a tearing loose from walls and roofs:

> I think heroic deeds were all conceiv'd in the open air, and
>   all free poems also ...
> Wisdom is not finally tested in schools,
> Wisdom cannot be pass'd from one having it to another not
>   having it ...
> Wisdom is of the soul, is not susceptible of proof, is its
>   own proof ...
> Now I reexamine philosophies and religions,
> They may prove well in lecture-rooms, yet not prove at all
>   under the spacious clouds ...

A generation earlier, the great Swiss educational reformer Pestalozzi had insisted that learning can begin only with what the pupil already knows. In "A Song of Occupations" Whitman goes even further:

> List close my scholars dear ...
> The gist of histories and statistics as far back as the records
>   reach is in you this hour, and myths and tales the same,
> If you were not breathing and walking here, where would
>   they all be?

> The most renown'd poems would be ashes, orations and
>   plays would be vacuums.

How to learn — how to teach? In "A Song of the Rolling Earth" the poet's conditions are merciless, the rewards wondrous. Not only the printed, but also the spoken word fails:

> All merges toward the presentation of the unspoken meanings
>   of the earth . . .
> Toward him who makes the dictionaries of words that print
>   cannot touch.
> I swear I see what is better than to tell the best,
> It is always to leave the best untold.

The poet's appetite for soul-learning is insatiable and contagious, unmatched under any roof, in any classroom. He ends "Myself and Mine" with a delicious shaft of wit:

> I must follow up these continual lessons of the air, water, earth,
> I perceive I have no time to lose.

But tireless as are his studies, he has as yet learned nothing, not even the primary textbook — himself — and he is ashamed of having "dared to open" his mouth at all. In "As I Ebb'd With the Ocean of Life" he confesses:

> . . . before all my arrogant poems the real Me stands yet
> untouch'd, untold, altogether unreach'd . . .
> I perceive I have not really understood any thing, not a single
>   object, and that no man ever can . . .

Many years later, in *Autumn Rivulets*, the process of education still obsesses him. For the miracle of true learning, Whitman's would-be pupil must prepare himself solemnly:

> Go, dear friend, if need be give up all else, and commence today
>   to inure yourself to pluck, reality, self-esteem,
>   definiteness, elevatedness,
> Rest not till you rivet and publish yourself of your own Personality.

Only from himself, the known, can the learner move toward the unknown: "Who out of the theory of the earth and of his or her own body understands by subtle analogies all other theories. ... " In the significantly titled "Tests" he uplifts those who have hitherto submitted themselves to be graded by the judgment of authority. "Who learns my lesson complete?" he asks. The answer is that he offers no fixed lesson: "It is no lesson — it lets down the bars to a good lesson,/And that to another, and every one to another still." The image remains that of the open road and the open sea. There is nothing before us but a tantalizingly withdrawing horizon. The true teacher can merely beckon to further exploration, letting down bars.

* * * *

To mock the astronomer's lecture-world is easiest. In "Song of Myself" one meets without surprise his "Trippers and askers" with their "art and argument." Outdoors are the oxen, whose eyes express "more than all the print" he has read in his life; outdoors is the bay mare, whose look "shames silliness out of him." To indicate how one learns, how one teaches, is less easy, but in "Song of Myself" more than anywhere else he shows the way, from the opening moment. While loafing and inviting one's soul, one observes "a spear of summer grass." What a simple key to the tremendous transcendental lesson this poem records!

But the lesson itself is least easy to verbalize, especially for a poet who confesses repeatedly that he understands nothing, leans toward "unspoken meanings," and chooses "always to leave the best untold." Still, throughout his work, often by hints and riddles, most spectacularly in "Song of Myself," Whitman demonstrates the courage and genius to tell the untellable. In seven lines, "To a Historian" encapsulates much of the lesson: not "bygones" "but the history of the future," not "the life that has exhibited itself" but "the pulse of life that has seldom exhibited itself," not "man as the creature of politics ... and priests" but "as he is in himself in his own rights."

In "Eidolons" the below-surface theme is expanded: under the apparent realities "The true realities"; under "the puzzling hour" waiting to be interpreted, "the permanent life of life"; under "segments, parts," beyond the lecture of the "learn'd professor," beyond "telescope or spectroscope ... beyond all mathematics" — the ultimate fact, the oneness of Being.

At times the "it" of what is to be learned does not emerge with such clarity. "When I Read the Book" limits itself almost teasingly to "a few hints, a few diffused faint clews and indirections." "A Riddle Song" invokes "That which eludes this verse and any verse … which you and I pursuing ever miss, open but still a secret … " In nine of the climactic final sixteen lines "it" is the last word; four times "it" comes at the caesura.

But in general Whitman does indicate what matters: "it" is within, beneath, beyond the visible, the measurable. "I Sing the Body Electric" points to the wonders within: the universal "red-running blood," the heart, whose "passions, desires, reachings, aspirations" are no less real because "they are not express'd in … lecture-rooms." "The Base of All Metaphysics" focuses on what finally counts: "underneath Socrates … and underneath Christ" the truest text: "The dear love of man for his comrade … / Of the well-married husband and wife, of children and parents.… " Similarly, "Song of the Exposition" would discard Troy, Jerusalem, Charlemagne and Arthur: "Away with themes of war … Away with love-verses sugar'd in rhyme." In their place Whitman offers superior themes: "To exalt the present and the real,/To teach the average man the glory of his daily walk and trade."

This revolutionary view is splendidly restated in "By Blue Ontario's Shore":

> Underneath all is the Expression of love for men and
>   women …
>
> Underneath the lessons of things, spirits, Nature, governments,
>   ownerships, I swear I perceive other lessons …
> I am for those that have never been master'd …
> For those whom laws, theories, conventions, can never
>   master …
> Who inaugurate one to inaugurate all.

Only a student willing to conform no longer, willing to grow thin and nettlesome, can consider such a dangerous new lesson:

> Piety and conformity to them that like.
> Peace, obesity, allegiance to them that like …

> I am he who walks ... with a barb'd tongue, questioning every
>   one I meet,
> Who are you that wanted only to be told what you knew
>   before?

As for America's would-be teachers:

> Have you not imported this or the spirit of it in some ship?
> Is it not a mere tale? a rhyme? a prettiness? ...
> Rhymes and rhymers pass away, poems distill'd from poems
>   pass away,
> The swarms of reflectors and the polite pass, and leave
>   ashes ...
> The blood of the brawn beloved of time is unconstraint ...

The crucial word is unconstraint. "Song of Prudence" is a frontal
assault on the "virtue" dearest to the heart of the Gilded Age and
most detested by that Age's greatest critics: Mark Twain, Herman
Melville, William Dean Howells. It is a poem about investments,
profits, interest — not for the sake of the bank account but the
account of the Soul:

> Charity and personal force are the only investments worth any-
>   thing ...
> Who has been wise receives interest ...
> Knows that the young man who composedly peril'd his life and
>   lost it has done exceedingly well for himself without a
>   doubt,
> That he who never peril'd his life, but retains it to old age in
>   riches and ease, has probably achiev'd nothing for himself
>   worth mentioning ...

At his most shimmeringly lyrical, however, Whitman turns without
his usual note of satire "away from books, away from art ... the
lesson done," to the Soul's favorite studies, achieved by its "free
flight into the wordless ... Night, sleep, death and the stars." As
great as "to penetrate the themes of mighty books" is what the soul
learns from a caged bird, to feel its "joyous warble," just as in "Out
of the Cradle Endlessly Rocking" Paumanok's boy learns bereave-
ment from the Alabama he-bird and in "When Lilacs Last in the

Dooryard Bloom'd" Lincoln's poet learns "lovely and soothing death" from the thrush. Whitman offers to barter all the beauties of Homer, Shakespeare and Tennyson if the sea would transfer to him "the undulation of one wave."

"Song of Myself" is Whitman's supreme elucidation of the *what* that the soul learns and teaches. Sometimes "it" is presented riddlingly, by innuendo: "... it is a word unsaid,/It is not in any dictionary or utterance or symbol." Elsewhere it is boldly declared as a credo: "I believe a leaf of grass is no less than the journey-work of the stars ..." And at moments it is transmitted with exquisite mysticism: "Logic and sermons never convince,/The damp of the night drives deeper into my soul." But above all, thanks to its scope and drama, in this poem Whitman is able to present his lesson paradigmatically, as only the greatest teachers do. Finding himself by losing himself, he seems to "celebrate" himself, but becomes in fact the mouthpiece of "many long dumb voices." By inviting his soul, by unleashing his empathic imagination, by undergoing an awesome act of self-transformation, Whitman is granted the ultimate vision available to everyone: the spiritual union of all creation. "I am the man ... I suffered ... I was there."

In "Song of Myself" our poet drolly covers himself from possible charges of inconsistency. "Do I contradict myself? Well, then I contradict myself." What is most astounding in this poem and throughout his work is the utter absence of contradiction on the question of true learning: "No shutter'd room or school can commune with me ... /If you would understand me go to the heights or water-shore,/The nearest gnat is an explanation...." No better evidence is needed of how basic and unswerving, from beginning to end, was Whitman's devotion to this cause.

V. Time's Revenges

About the time U.S. forces assaulted Cambodia, Norman Mailer's talk show host noted that the novelist was being widely condemned for obscenity. Mailer responded roughly that his function was to depict his world. Not his writing, but his world, was obscene, and it struck him as ironic that people who calmly stomached and even applauded the obcenities perpetrated around them were horrified by a truth-teller's tongue and pen.

What does this have to do with Whitman? Nothing and everything. In time it became clear to many of Mailer's critics where the obscenity of that decade lay. In time it also became clear that the recurrent obscenity charge against Whitman was unjustified. Those guardians of taste and honored poets of the day who vilified him while accepting the obscenities of Victorian life have in many cases become footnotes in literary history, wretchedly immortalized by their cruelty against *Leaves of Grass*.

Thomas Wentworth Higginson, who expressed regret that Whitman had not burned his book after writing it, was later involved in the District Attorney's successful drive to keep the seventh edition from being published in Boston. Then, in 1886, he helped defeat a Congressional bill "to award Whitman $25 a month in recognition of his hospital work during the war." Thomas Bailey Aldrich characterized Whitman as "a charlatan" whose work could survive only in "a glass case or a quart of spirits in an anatomical museum." Bayard Taylor, an early friend, mocked "the Kosmos, yawping abroad." And Josiah Gilbert Holland called him "a wretched old fraud . . . a pest and an abomination."

Justin Kaplan points out that William Cullen Bryant, like Taylor previously a friend, "turned cold and distant after he read *Leaves of Grass*." As Professor of Modern Languages at Harvard, James Russell Lowell promised to keep the book "out of the way of students"; possibly on his initiative (in Kaplan's words) it "was removed from the open shelves of the college library and kept under lock and key with other tabooed books." In *The Atlantic Monthly* Oliver Wendell Holmes satirized Whitman's "rhapsodies" as "figures played upon a big organ which has been struck by lightning," and placed them "among the most cynical instances of indecent exposure I recollect, outside what is sold as obscene literature."

Did John Greenleaf Whittier become so enraged that he hurled his copy into the fire? Whitman believed so. One thing is sure — thirty years later, when he and Holmes contributed ten dollars each to a fund for their ailing fellow-poet in Camden, Whittier apologized in a letter to the *Boston Transcript* that both gifts were "solely an act of kindness to a disabled author, implying no approval whatever of his writings." He privately sneered at Whitman's prosody as "the untamed, rough-jolting Pegasus he has been accustomed to ride — without check or snaffle." Longfellow found in *Drum-Taps* "a total want of education and of delicacy of feelings."

Fifteen years after greeting the first edition rapturously, Emerson mocked his disciple as "conceited," a "rather affected creature" without "good breeding," and resentful of criticism. A year later came his message of dissatisfaction: "I expect — him — to make — the songs of the — nation — but he seems contented to — make the inventories." Most stinging of all, as Kaplan notes, the Sage of Concord's massive 1874 anthology *Parnassus* favors a Forseythe Willson, whose "genius" is "akin to Dante's," but there is not a line by Whitman. In fact, the only Whitman poem anthologized in his lifetime in the U.S. was "O Captain! My Captain!"

Sidney Lanier, in an 1881 lecture, had good reason to point out, though he did so maliciously and viciously, that "the two English poets who have most exclusively laid claim to represent the people in poetry ... Wordsworth and Whitman," have an aristocratic audience only; "no preacher was ever so decisively rejected by his own" as Whitman, the declared enemy of dandyism, the "dandy-upside-down who ... throws away coat and vest, dons a slouch hat, opens his shirt so as to expose his breast...."

It is inevitable to compare Whitman's current standing with that of his once-towering critics, now that readers have had a century since theirs deaths to consider their relative gifts and significance. I am not suggesting that Emerson, Lanier, Whittier, Bryant, Lowell and Longfellow deserve the degree of neglect into which they have fallen. Part of their severe downgrading is due to the same fluctuating tyranny of taste which victimized Whitman during their days of fame and power. I suspect there will be further fluctuations, when today's utter dominance by free verse gives way to an appreciation of masterly poetry no matter what the form. In the case of such poetic pygmies as Higginson, Aldrich, Taylor and Holland, however, their oblivion as versifiers seems deserved and delicious.

How can one not enjoy the ironies bestowed by Time? Consider "O Captain! My Captain!" — in 1984 one of Whitman's least anthologized pieces, just as he would have wished. And consider Lanier's taunt that the mass-poet had no mass audience: is there a poet other than Shakespeare who matches Whitman's persistent best-seller status?

It must have been sweet for Whitman, marking the 22nd anniversary of Lincoln's assassination, to have in his New York audience such outstanding figures as poets John Hay, James Russell Lowell, and José Marti of Cuba, industrialist Andrew Carnegie, sculptor Saint-Gaudens, educators Norton of Harvard and Gilman of Johns Hopkins, novelists Mark Twain, Frank Stockton, Edward Eggleston and Mary Mapes Dodge.

But it would have been sweeter had he lived to 1900 and seen, in William Dean Howells' *Literary Friends and Acquaintances*, an illustration of the young novelist in 1860 almost reverently shaking his hand at Pfaff's beer cellar — the same Howells who, when it mattered, had judged Whitman's book "not poetry, but the materials of poetry," and condemned the "preponderant beastliness" of its content. And sweetest of all, perhaps, could he have witnessed the conversion of Henry James, who, now ranking "dear old Walt" as America's greatest poet, in 1903 ashamedly admitted authoring *The Nation's* unsigned 1865 assault on *Drum-Taps:* "This volume is an offense against art ... a medley of extravagances and commonplaces."

Matching the sardonic grin with which Feste the Clown ends *Twelfth Night,* Whitman might have murmured: "And thus the whirligig of time brings in his revenges."

The Poetic Career of Emma Lazarus[1]

I. A Notable Coming of Age

When the second collection of poems[2] by Emma Lazarus appeared, in 1871, it was clear to all who reviewed the volume that a new singer was on the scene: a woman just turned 21, who apparently had the lore of ancient Hellas and of medieval Germany on her fingertips — and who did not shrink from the use of verse-forms large enough to fit her heroic themes.

Today we are not particularly excited by such verses. At best, they strike us as skillful copies of Britain's Victorian poets. At worst they are banal and colorless exercises. Yet here and there we are struck by a flash of true feeling, as in the opening of "In Memoriam," a tribute to a dead friend:[3]

> O friend who passed away while flowers died,
> Now that the land bursts into bloom again . . .
> My thoughts revert to thee, who liest still
> Under the pulsing, stirring, glowing earth;
> Not rising with the lilac on the hill.

"Florence Nightingale," one of several war poems, has some moving stanzas — especially the fourth:

> And some of them arise,
> With eager, tearful eyes,
> From off their couch to see her passing by.
> Some, even too weak for this,[4]
> Can only stoop and kiss
> Her shadow, and fall back content to die.[5]

Even more impressive are the well-conceived, bitter verses titled "Dreams."[6] "Wings" (as well as "Florence Nightingale") employs the stanza form of Browning's "Rabbi Ben Ezra," published seven years earlier; the spirit and imagery, however, recall Shelley's "To a Skylark":

> It mounteth still, and sings:
> What soul yearns not for wings,
> To follow after, burst its prison bars,
> And learn the secret there,
> In those clear realms of air, —
> The secret of the rainbow and the stars.[7]

"Marjorie's Wooing"[8] suggests that she had lately been impressed by the old English ballads or by some of their numerous imitators.

Though less than memorable, these are pretty, facile pieces. Many had been written years earlier; her rhymes and rhythms show remarkable craftsmanship for an 18-year-old. She had mastered numerous classical forms, though giving them no new distinction.

Past adolescence, Emma Lazarus was not yet beyond an almost morbid obsession with death. "In a Swedish Graveyard," which opens with a motto from Longfellow's *Rural Life in Sweden*, expounds on the meaninglessness of life and ends with a half-longing for death:

> For all those who have toiled and are tired,
> Utter darkness and sleep may be best.[9]

"The Garden of Adonis,"[10] written a year later, continues in the same vein. This time her motto is from Spenser's *Faerie Queene*. Death strikes her as beautiful. It is merely a transformation. Nothing really dies. All that has lived and been beautiful is immortal.

The long title-poem, "Admetus,"[11] manages to hold one's attention throughout. Although hardly a passage is luminous from beginning to end, there is a certain high dignity, a purity of emotion, that gives this poem character and completeness. For a 20-year-old it was an unusual production, full of insights which must have had more behind them than books. Yet the diction remains artificial, unable to shake off the Old World's verse speech. The legend, too, is utterly removed from the life of her own time.[12]

The same strong points, to a lesser degree, and the same weaknesses, to a larger degree, are evident in three other lengthy poems which, with "Admetus," make up the bulk of the volume. "Orpheus"[13] echoes feebly the form and language of Shelley's *Prometheus Unbound*. Broken up into dialogue, this poem passes from blank verse to heroic couplet to Greek-style chorus.

From medieval Germany she took the legends of "Lohengrin"[14] and "Tannhäuser,"[15] which Wagner's operas had popularized for a score of years. Both of these huge blank verse poems were completed early in 1870, and too great facility is apparent on every page. Few lines contain vivid imagery; fewer still are enriched by living words. Rhetoric abounds, the stilted rhetoric of the past, which she and many in her time mistook for true poetry.[16]

In retrospect, her lines written "In the Jewish Synagogue" have a shocking effect. Here, as in others of her youthful pieces, she engages in conjuring up the dead. On this occasion they are Jewish worshippers; but, although she treats them with sympathy and respect, she expresses not a word of kinship. The Hebrew tongue she calls "a language dead," the Judaic idea "spent." Totally American in outlook, if not in expression, she sings:

> Now as we gaze, in this new world of light,
> Upon the relic of the days of old,
> The present vanishes, and tropic bloom
> And Eastern towns and temples we behold.[17]

The ending is sombre. She strikes a note of death.[18]

This volume, like her first, includes a group of translations, in which her talents are best displayed. Here she can be properly European, and her imitative genius might be called an asset. As in the earlier collection, Heine is represented,[19] along with such newcomers as Leopardi and Goethe. The Leopardi is a fragment of 28 lines, on the insignificance of mankind.[20] The Goethe consists of a big section from *Faust*[21] including the dedication, prologue for the theatre, and the entire first scene. The last four pages are an Easter hymn to the glory of Christ, a subject far from her mind in later years.

The critical success of *Admetus and Other Poems* was instantaneous throughout the English-speaking world. Henry Tuckerman wrote in the *Boston Transcript*: "Few recent volumes of verse compare favorably with the spirited and musical expression of . . . Emma Lazarus."[22] The *Galaxy of New York* "welcomed a genuine poetic talent,"[23] and considered passages of her "Tannhäuser" to be "finer" than similar passages in William Morris' "The Hill of Venus."

London bowed at her feet. The reviewer for the *Athenaeum* exclaimed: "The volume by Miss Lazarus is full of good things.... There is something — and not much — wanting to complete her success and place her alongside of the masters."[24] The *Illustrated London News* agreed: "Emma Lazarus must be hailed ... as a poet of rare original power. More force as well as grace than ... Browning.... It will be no surprise to us, after the present volume, if she hereafter take a high place among the best poets of this age."[25]

We may marvel at the generosity of these reviewers,[26] but on second thought Emma Lazarus can scarcely be blamed for the weaknesses of her early books. It is evident that she was doing extremely well within the standards set by her time; if the critic for the *Illustrated London News* could find more force in her poems than in those of Browning, she can be said to have absorbed with great success what the current literary world cherished.

Let it be remembered as well that those very lords of opinion had either ignored or condemned Whitman just a few years before — that the works of a Thoreau or a Melville would be granted scarcely a line of consideration in their journals of 1871 — that an Emily Dickinson would not attempt to submit poetry to them for publication — that a Gerard Manley Hopkins could hope for no better than bewilderment or disgust.[27]

Nevertheless, a new note can be heard, though faintly and rarely, in *Admetus and Other Poems*. "The Heroes" is a paean to America's builders: the 'common man' — from "Virginian woods" to "the broad Western plains" to "New England's fields."[28] "Sonnet," with a Maine setting, asserts:

> Our noble scenes have yet no history,
> All subtler charms than those that feed the eye
> Our lives must give them; 'tis an aim austere,
> But opes new vistas, and a pathway clear.[29]

"The Day of Dead Soldiers" celebrates Civil War heroes, who "left their land a fame so wide/So rich a page of thrilling histories." In this poem, written four years after "When Lilacs Last in the Dooryard Bloom'd," Emma Lazarus added her voice to that of Whitman in tribute to the martyred president:

> Who knows what tremulous, dusky hands set free
> Deck quaintly with gay flowers the graves unknown,
> What wealth of bloom is shed exuberantly
> On the far grave in Illinois alone,
> Where the last hero, sleeping peacefully,
> Beyond detraction and mistrust, doth lie,
> By the glad winds of prairies overblown?[30]

Her "Miscellaneous" section closes strongly indeed, with "How Long?" — a clarion call for liberation from the influences of Europe. Looking at "this fresh young world . . . with heroes, cities, legends of her own," she echoes Emerson's and Whitman's rejection of the Old World forms:

> The distant siren-song
> Of the green island in the eastern sea,
> Is not the lay for this new chivalry.
> It is not free and strong
> To chant our prairies 'neath this brilliant sky.
>
> The echo faints and fails;
> It suiteth not upon this western plain,
> Our voice or spirit; we should stir again
> The wilderness, and make the vales
> Resound unto a yet-unheard-of strain.[31]

It was a noble program; but where in Emma Lazarus' own poetry, even fifteen years later, could the "yet-unheard-of-strain" be heard?[32] She recognized it, earlier than most, in Whitman — as had her friend Emerson. But, like the Sage of Concord himself, she was apparently unable to break the despised bonds in her own work. Only in "Babylonian Sorrows," her last published poem, did she come to fulfilling the program charted by herself at the age of 21.

2. *Songs of a Semite*

In 1881 Emma Lazarus had been given to read, before its publication, an essay by Edmund C. Stedman on U.S. poetry.[33] In response she had criticized his explanation of the lack of great poets in America by stating: "Wherever there is humanity there is the theme for a great poem."[34]

At the closing exercises of the Temple Emanu-El Religious School, one year later, she proved that statement dramatically; for it was there, having at last come away from the bookshelves and entered the ranks of humanity, that she emerged as an inspired poet.[35] Her stirring clarion-call, "The Banner of the Jew," given its first reading on that day, displayed a simplicity, freshness and power beyond anything in her previous poetic work:

> Oh for Jerusalem's trumpet now,
> To blow a blast of shattering power,
> To wake the sleepers high and low,
> And rouse them to the urgent hour!
> No hand for vengeance — but to save,
> A million naked swords should wave.
>
> Oh deem not dead that martial fire,
> Say not the mystic flame is spent!
> With Moses' law and David's lyre,
> Your ancient strength remains unbent.
> Let but an Ezra rise anew,
> To lift the Banner of the Jew!
>
> A rag, a mock at first — erelong,
> When men have bled and women wept,
> To guard its precious folds from wrong,
> Even they who shrunk, even they who slept,
> Shall leap to bless it, and to save.
> Strike! for the brave revere the brave.

This poem was published in *The Critic*,[36] and six days later was reprinted in the *American Hebrew*.

The following week "An Epistle" appeared in the *American Hebrew*. "It has a strong bearing on the question of the day, besides having a curious historic interest," she wrote in submitting the poem.[37] This work may have been produced while she was steeped in Spanish research and translation. Based on an account in Graetz,[38] "An Epistle" dissects apostasy and bitterly attacks those who dissociate themselves from their people in time of oppression:

> Thine own lips tell . . .
> How thou midst panic nowise disconcerted

> By Thomas of Aquinas wast converted!
>
> Truly I know no more convincing way
> To read so wise an author, than was thine.
> When burning Synagogues changed night to day,
> And red swords underscored each word and line.
> That was a light to read by! Who'd gainsay
> Authority so clearly stamped divine?
> On this side, death and torture, flame and slaughter,
> On that, a harmless wafer and clean water.[39]

Among the poetic fruits of her research which she now thought proper to exhibit was a long blank-verse narrative, "Raschi in Prague,"[40] based on the life of a great eleventh-century rabbinical scholar, whose wisdom and bravery, according to the legend, won the favor of Prague's Duke and saved the Jewish population of that city. The frequent stiltedness of style here, as in much of "An Epistle," indicates that it may have been written several years before. If such is the case, it gives further credence to Schappes' contention that her interest in Jewish heroism, though perhaps academic, had been alive for some time before she was galvanized and transformed by the eastern European pogroms of 1881.[41]

Different in spirit and language were the new poems of 1882: rhapsodic, militant, deeply Jewish in imagery, classic in their simplicity. "In Exile"[42] paints a picture of a Russian refugee in a Texas farm colony. "The New Year — Rosh Hashanah 1882"[43] and "The Feast of Lights — Chanukah"[44] celebrate Jewish holidays which she had perhaps observed perfunctorily in previous years. Her verses gave new illumination to the ancient rituals, enflaming the discouraged hearts of her people with the Maccabean spirit:

> Blow, Israel, the sacred cornet! Call
> Back to thy courts whatever faint heart throb
> With thine ancestral blood, thy need craves all.
> The red, dark year is dead, the year just born
> Leads on from anguish wrought by priest and mob,
> To what undreamed-of morn?
>
> High above flood and fire ye held the scroll,
> Out of the depths ye published still the Word.

No bodily pang had power to swerve your soul:
Ye, in a cynic age of crumbling faiths,
Lived to bear witness to the living Lord,
Or died a thousand deaths.

(from "The New Year")

Kindle the taper like the steadfast star
Ablaze on evening's forehead o'er the earth,
And add each night a lustre till afar
An eightfold splendor shine above thy hearth.
Clash, Israel, the cymbals, touch the lyre,
Blow the brass trumpet and the harsh-tongued horn;
Chant psalms of victory till the heart take fire,
The Maccabean spirit leap new-born.

(from "The Feast of Lights")

For Christian ears her voice acquired a particularly stinging note. When had the conscience of a civilization been so violently shaken alive?

Across the Eastern sky has glowed
The flicker of a blood-red dawn,
Once more the clarion cock has crowed,
Once more the sword of Christ is drawn.
A million burning rooftrees light
The world-wide path of Israel's flight . . .

When the long roll of Christian guilt
Against his sires and kin is known,
The flood of tears, the life-blood spilt,
The agony of ages shown,
What oceans can the stain remove,
From Christian law and Christian love?[45]

These poems, and a number of others in a similar vein, were widely reprinted and recited. Becoming a regular contributor to the *American Hebrew* at this time, she published *The Dance to Death* in its pages. Immediately afterward, the American Hebrew Publishing Company issued a pamphlet of her poems on Jewish themes, together with her translations from the Jewish poets of medieval Spain, and *The Dance to Death*.

The title, *Songs of a Semite*, emphasized her identity, which none of her previous volumes had indicated. She now wanted to be known publicly as a member, a voice, of the Jewish people. Her insistence upon a low-priced pamphlet symbolized, as did her simplicity of language, a determination to reach large numbers of people.[46] In her effort to win an audience, however, she surrendered none of the earlier dignity and erudition. It became the dignity of an indestructible people instead of a precocious young recluse's lofty aloofness; it became the erudition of a people's scholar, supplying knowledge as ammunition for a great battle instead of the means by which a well-protected mind could escape into other lands and centuries. Words were no longer the be-all and end-all; they were brands intended to ignite a conflagration. And, in the process, they became infinitely richer and more effective:

> Her verse rang out as it had never rung before: a clarion note, calling a people to heroic action and unity, to the consciousness and fulfillment of a grand destiny.... The dead forms burst their bonds and lived again.[47]

Henry Ward Beecher's non-denominational weekly, *The Independent*, welcomed the appearance of *Songs of a Semite* sooner than any other journal.[48] Its critic described *The Dance to Death* as a "tragedy of remarkable finish and power." The following week a highly favorable notice appeared in the *New York Sun*.[49] A reviewer for *The Critic* wrote:

> Starting among the literary people of her own race, her reputation has grown steadily, spreading to a much wider circle, and reaching within the past five years the cultivated centres of scholarly life.... The monologue is sometimes too long, but the tone is elevated and strong, the diction fresh, and poetic, and vigorous.[50]

A *New York Times* critic, also spotlighting *The Dance to Death*, reminded his readers that "the ability to handle a matter of this scope is rare," and expressed the belief that "Miss Lazarus has come very near to making a masterpiece of it."[51] She herself made a number of efforts to bring the new volume to the attention of reviewers, and presented copies to at least a few key figures in the literary world.[52]

Part of the Jewish press seems to have been more critical than the non-Jewish press. London's *Jewish Chronicle* carped about metrical details and one or two "Americanisms," although the review was otherwise enthusiastic, and expressed the hope that she would, like Elizabeth Barrett Browning, achieve "actual fame."[53] The *Jewish Record* of Philadelphia inaccurately referred to several of the poems as "having been elaborated long after the first flush of genuine enthusiasm in the subject had disappeared." Yet the reviewer added, "We cannot but regard 'The Dance to Death' as the masterpiece of the 'greatest of living poetesses.' "[54] One newspaper in particular, the *Jewish Times*, showed itself to be completely unfamiliar with her work, including the volume under review, which was referred to as "her collected poems." Overlooking her earlier achievements, the reviewer welcomed "to the field of authorship Miss Emma Lazarus."[55]

The Century Magazine, on the other hand, while noting "weak parts," praised the plot and "fine passages" in *The Dance to Death*, and quoted extensively from several of the most militant lyrics, hailing her national fervor, for which it gave Heine partial credit.[56] *Lippincott's Magazine* also singled out the drama for special praise, speaking highly of her "rigid self-discipline" and "elevation of tone."[57]

That the book was a popular success, which had been among her chief concerns, is unquestionable. Only a month after publication, Emma Lazarus' name was trumpeted by the *American Hebrew* (against her wishes) "at the advertising illumination on the corner of 23rd Street and Broadway," as an inducement for readers to buy that magazine![58]

3. Contemporary Appraisals and a 20th Century View

At the height of her powers and commitment, Emma Lazarus was struck down by cancer. To gauge the immensity of her loss, one need only turn to the Memorial Issue of the *American Hebrew*, published on December 9, 1887, twenty days after her death. This greatly enlarged number was devoted entirely to tributes, both in prose and poetry (among the ten poems was one in German and one in Hebrew).[59] During the same week, *The Critic* honored her memory by devoting its lead article to her, presenting an estimate of her life from a Jewish point of view, and including a sonnet of praise.

The *American Hebrew* reprinted the sermon which Dr. Gottheil, long her friend and guide, had delivered at the funeral services in Temple Emanu-El. Several other prominent Jewish leaders, including the Rev. Dr. F. de Sola Mendes and Cyrus Sulzberger, lauded Emma Lazarus' unsurpassed contribution to Jewish thought in America. Testimonials to her great practical achievements on behalf of her people came from the President of the Montefiore Home for Chronic Invalids, the President of the Aguilar Free Library, and the President of the Philadelphia Young Men's Hebrew Association.

Some of the most prominent literary figures of the time added their eulogies. The titles of the articles themselves indicate what Emma Lazarus had come to symbolize: "A Brave Singer," by John G. Whittier; "Bryant Recognizes her Genius"; "A Woman of High Ideals and Noble Enthusiasms"; "Endowed with a Sensitivity Rich, Rare, and Poetic"; "A Vital Power for Beneficence and Light"; "An Absolutely Unaffected Character"; "A Loss to Lovers of High Literature"; "A Contagious Inspiration in her Ardor," by Edmund C. Stedman; "The Representative to the World of her People"; "Faithful to her Convictions"; "Capable of High Enthusiasm without Bigotry"; "She Gave an Impulse to Higher Things"; "Her Deeds will bear Rich Fruits," by Henrietta Szold; "A Poet by the Grace of God"; "Of Unusual Mental Power and Erudition"; "An Irreparable Loss to American Literature,"by John Hay; "Her Position in New York Society Unique," by E. L.. Godkin; "A True Friend Gone," by John Burroughs.

From London Robert Browning cabled that he "associates himself with the admiration for the genius and love of the character of his lamented friend, Emma Lazarus." Hjalmar Boyesen of Columbia described "the marvelous hospitality of her mind to great ideas, and her universal appreciation of all that is beautiful in art, in literature and in life." Whittier wrote:

Since Miriam sang of deliverance and triumph by the Red Sea,

the Semitic race has had no braver singer. "The Crowing of the
Red Cock," written when the Russian sky was red with blazing
Hebrew homes, is an indignant and forceful lyric worthy of the
Maccabean age. Her "Banner of the Jew" has the ring of Israel's
war trumpets.

Stedman offered an excellent evaluation of her qualities, and traced
her parallel development as person and poet:

> So warm a sense of regard and admiration was felt in my own
> home for our friend, Emma Lazarus, that I cannot hesitate to
> write, as you request, a few words of tribute to the memory of
> a noble woman, enthusiast, and poet. While thoroughly femi-
> nine, and a mistress of the social art and charm, she was —
> though without the slightest trace of pedantry — the natural
> companion of scholars and thinkers. Her emotional nature
> kept pace with her intellect; as she grew in learning and mental
> power, she became still more earnest, devoted, impassioned.
> These advances marked her writings — especially her poetry,
> which changed in later years from its early reflection of the
> Grecian ideals, and took on a lyrical and veritable Hebraic fire
> and imagination ... there was a contagious inspiration in her
> Semitic ardor, her satire, wrath and exaltation. That she was
> able to impart these qualities to sustained creative work is
> shown by her strangely powerful drama, *The Dance to Death*,
> unique in American poetry.

Almost a year later,[60] the *American Hebrew* published tributes from
three major figures whose letters had reached the editors too late for
inclusion in the Memorial Issue. The Southern novelist George W.
Cable wrote:

> ... she was the worthy daughter of a race to which the Chris-
> tian world owes a larger debt of gratitude, incurred from the
> days of Abraham until now, and from which it should ask
> more forgiveness than to any other people that ever trod the
> earth.

Harriet Beecher Stowe expressed grief, and added, "I am happy to
see that *The Century* and *The Critic* are doing justice to the fine

poetic gifts of Miss Lazarus." Thomas W. Higginson asserted that "she was certainly one of the most high-minded, the most gifted, and the most faithful of our younger poets."[61]

Nearly a score of years after her death, *The Critic* in January, 1906 celebrated its 25th anniversary by giving a front-page résumé of its history. Emma Lazarus was listed second only to Stedman on its "fine list of contributors." The same issue carried a sonnet by Richard Watson Gilder, "To Emma Lazarus — 1905," inspired by a new series of pogroms which was sweeping eastern Europe:

> Dear bard and prophet, that thy rest is deep
> Thanks be to God! Not now on thy breast falls
> Rumor intolerable. Sleep, O sleep!
> See not the blood of Israel that crawls,
> Warm yet, into the noon and night; that cries
> Even as of old, till all the world stands still
> At rapine that even to Israel's agonies
> Seems strange and monstrous, a mad dream of ill.
> Thou sleepest! Yes, but as in grief we said: —
> There is a spiritual life unconquerable;
> So, bard of the ancient people, though being dead
> Thou speakest, and thy voice we love full well.
> Never thy holy memory forsakes us;
> Thy spirit is the trumpet that awakes us![62]

These tributes were written by men and women who were not accustomed to making careless judgments and spouting extravagant praise. Were only half of them to be trusted, her long oblivion would still be inexplicable. Even an exploration of her accomplishments as sketchy as this (without even considering her novel on the young Goethe, *Alide*, her Shakespearean tragedy on the painter Ribera, *Spagnoletto*, her literary essays, her major 1881 volume of Heine translations, and her brilliant series, *Epistle to the Hebrews*) reveals what an amazing creative force and unique personality she became.[63] Even in the grip of a harrowing disease, as her final essays, poems, and letters from abroad testify, she demonstrated not only personal valor but an unfaded vitality both as thinker and writer.

To place her in the top rank of America's 19th century poets — alongside of Poe, Emerson, Melville, Whitman and Emily Dickinson

— would be as unjust to her as to them. Had she not dispersed her energies and talents in such a multitude of directions, had her life not ebbed precisely when her original power was at last manifesting itself, she might have ripened into a poet of major proportions. Imagination she had, but never dared nurture it toward the splendor of a Poe. Philosophic depth she had, but seldom allowed herself to break away from others, to be a pioneer, a creator in the world of thought, such as Emerson and Melville were. Prophetic zeal she had, but only at the last moment did the power of her vision burst through the ancient dikes of the stanza and turn her poetry into a flood as ecstatically free as Whitman's. Spiritual insight she had, but neither the time to await, nor the keenness to see, nor the nerve to lasso such galloping steeds of light as Emily Dickinson pulled from the clouds.

Not in a class with these five, she nevertheless bears up surprisingly well in comparison with others more widely favored than she. One must read patiently in Lowell, Bryant, Whittier, Longfellow, Holmes and Lanier, to find a passage finer than several in *The Dance to Death* or a lyric more stirring than three or four in *Songs of a Semite*. Indeed, much of her mature work can be ranked with much of theirs. Even some of the verses she composed at eighteen would, if signed by them, scarcely have harmed their reputations.

When one considers that in an extremely short span she also produced a large body of distinguished translations, a good first novel, a first play deserving of interest if not production, and a number of brave, provocative and eloquent essays, one cannot help being impressed by the richness and liveliness of her talent, and wondering, with regret, what further contributions she might have made, with a little more time.

NOTES

1. Emma Lazarus, *Admetus and Other Poems* (New York: Hurd and Houghton, 1871).

2. *Ibid.*, pp. 176–78. Perhaps this refers to her maternal uncle, Benjamin Nathan, murdered on the night of July 28, 1870. Emerson wrote her on August 19, 1870: "I have not known how to write to you since I received your painful note. . . . I think very sadly of the desolation which this shock must bring to your peaceful house and

to yourself." (R. L. Rusk, *The Letters of Emerson*, VI (New York: Columbia University Press, 1939) 128–29.

3. *Admetus*, pp. 153–54.

4. *Ibid.*, p. 155.

5. *Ibid.*, pp. 163–64.

6. *Ibid.*, pp. 168–69.

7. *Ibid.*, pp. 165–67.

8. *Ibid.*, pp. 171–73.

9. *Ibid.*, pp. 1–23. In 1869 Emerson had brought this poem to the *Atlantic Monthly*. When the editor, W. D. Howells, rejected it, Emerson wrote: "I should have printed it thankfully and proudly. We must believe that his *Atlantic* portfolio is very rich in poetry in these months, and shall frankly own it if Sparta hath worthier daughters. I am at a loss to find the imitation of Tennyson and Morris that the editor remarks." (Rusk, p. 90).

10. The famous Greek myth of Alcestis' devotion had also been used by William Morris, and was later to be taken up by Rilke. Fascination for the past, notable as it was in the case of Emma Lazarus, typified many artists of her time.

11. *Admetus*, pp. 25–59. Dedicated to her sister, Josephine.

12. *Ibid.*, pp. 61—82. Dedicated to Washington Nathan, her cousin.

13. *Ibid.*, pp. 83–132. Dedicated to her mother.

14. Heinrich E. Jacob, *The World of Emma Lazarus* (New York: Schocken Books, 1949) 41–42, calls "Lohengrin" an exceptionally feeble piece, toying with dreams without substance, half derived from Rossetti, "half-Wagneresque." His opinion of "Tannhäuser" is much higher. *Admetus*, p. 132, immediately following the four long poems, carries a defensive note in answer to "the imputation of plagiarism already made in private circles," explaining that "Admetus" and "Tannhäuser" had been completed before the publication of Morris' poems.

15. *Admetus*, pp. 160–62.

16. S. Wininger could not have read this volume, which he describes as being "shot through with love for her long-suffering people and with faith in its rebirth." (*Grosse Jüdische National-Biographie*, Cernauti, Germany, p. 611.)

17. *Admetus*, p. 230.

18. *Ibid.*, pp. 197–98. See Max I. Baym, "A Neglected Translator of Italian Poetry: Emma Lazarus," *Italica* (December, 1944) 175–85.

19. *Admetus*, pp. 200–228. H. E. Jacob, *op. cit.*, p. 43, points to this as "an extraordinarily successful translation."

20. Quoted in an advertisement for *Songs of a Semite*, which appeared in the *American Hebrew*, October 13, 1882, p. 105.

21. January, 1872, pp. 136–37.

22. September 23, 1871, pp. 395–96.

23. October 14, 1871, p. 359.

24. Excerpts from a few other reviews can be found on p. 12n of Morris U. Schappes' *The Letters of Emma Lazarus, 1868–1885* (New York: New York Public Library, 1949). It is noteworthy that the praise of American reviewers generally followed by several months the stamp of approval given by their British counterparts.

No record of unfavorable comment is indicated in the available sources, although Thomas W. Higginson wrote that "her volume of poems was better received in England than here." (Mary Thatcher Higginson, *The Letters and Journals of Thomas Wentworth Higginson* (Boston: Houghton Mifflin, 1921) 266.

25. Even as late as 1891, her contemporaries' lack of perspective is indicated in such an important literary encyclopedia as *Allibone's Dictionary of English Literature and British and American Authors* (Philadephia: J. B. Lippincott, 1892), where Emma Lazarus is given 58 lines, as compared with 57 for Lanier, 32 for Whittier, 28 for Bryant, 4 for Melville (as a writer of verse — with no mention of his novels!) and not a word for either Poe or Thoreau. Eight years later, a critic as advanced as Higginson, who knew the work of Emily Dickinson far better than did any of his contemporaries, could give the following estimate of Helen Hunt Jackson, remembered now, unfortunately, for little else besides the novel *Ramona*: "The poetry of Mrs. Jackson unquestionably takes rank above that of any other American woman, and its only rival would be found, curiously enough, in that of her early schoolmate, Emily Dickinson." *Contemporaries* (Boston: Houghton Mifflin, 1899) 162.

26. *Admetus*, pp. 182–85. Emerson had been urging her to use American themes, and she sent this to him in manuscript with the following note: "What seems of such mighty consequence to me — my mental journey from Greece to America, is of course quite an indifferent and unimportant matter to you — nevertheless I am going to ask you as a kindness to read the first production of my new style of thought." (Schappes, *op. cit.*, p. 10)

27. *Admetus*, p. 188.

28. *Ibid.*, pp. 191–92.

29. *Ibid.*, pp. 193–94.

30. Her prose, however, especially her letters and essays, underscores what Schappes terms "her advocacy of an American national literature" (*op. cit.*, pp. 4–5). He identifies for the first time (*Ibid.*, p. 29) an article in *The Critic* of June 18, 1881, titled "American Literature," as the work of Emma Lazarus.

31. According to Schappes (*op. cit.*, p. 67n), the only other critic to whom Stedman sent a chapter for comment in advance of publication seems to have been Edmund Gosse, who was asked to read the proofs of his article on Emerson. Schappes gives this fact as evidence of the "respect he entertained for her judgment." *Scribner's Monthly* published the article under the title of "Poetry in America," (August, 1881, pp. 540–50) and in 1885 it was reprinted as the opening chapter of Stedman's important volume, *Poets of America*.

32. Schappes, p. 68. This matter is explored in Appendix I.

33. The controversy on this evaluation is aired in Appendix II.

34. "The editors of that journal have marked as a red-letter day in its annals the date [June 3, 1882] when her ringing lyric was given to the world." With these words the editor of *The Critic*, Joseph B. Gilder, eulogized Emma Lazarus in the Memorial Issue of the *American Hebrew*, December 9, 1887.

35. Morris U. Schappes, *Emma Lazarus, Selections from Her Poetry and Prose* (New York: Cooperative Book League, 1944) 37n.

36. A note appears directly below the title: "In this poem I have done little more

than elaborate and versify the account given in Graetz' *History of the Jews* (Vol. VIII, page 77) of an Epistle actually written in the beginning of the 15th century by Joshua ben Joseph Ibn Vives to Paulus de Santa Maria."

37. *The Poems of Emma Lazarus*, II (Boston: Houghton Mifflin, 1889) 52–53.

38. *Ibid.*, pp. 25–40. See also "The Death of Raschi," *Ibid.*, pp. 40–44.

39. According to Josephine Lazarus (and most scholars before Schappes did not question her word) prior to the pogroms her sister "had been seeking heroic ideals in alien stock, soulless and far removed; in pagan mythology and mystic, medieval Christianity, ignoring her very birthright — the majestic vista of the past, down which . . . had been conveyed the precious scroll of the Moral Law . . . Judaism had been a dead letter to her." (*Poems*, I, 19). A well-documented contradiction of that statement is contained in an appendix to Schappes' *Selections*, pp. 103–05, under the heading, "Emma Lazarus's Interest in the Jews."

40. *Poems*, II, 5–7. It was Michael Heilprin, author of *Historical Poetry of the Ancient Hebrews*, who showed her the joyous letter from a refugee in his new home, which she uses as the motto of this poem. Heilprin had also taken her to visit the refuge on Ward's Island.

41. *Poems*, II, 1–3. Philip Cowen, in his "Recollections of Emma Lazarus," *American Hebrew* (July 5, 1929) 240–41, relates that he had asked her for a New Year poem, to which she replied that she "could not write poetry to order." The following day she sent him the poem.

42. *Poems*, II, 18–20. According to Annie Nathan Meyer, her cousin now "for the first time became devoutly religious." "Emma Lazarus — A Note on Her Background," *Common Ground* (Winter, 1944) 108.

43. *Poems*, II, 3–4.

44. In a letter to the editors of the *American Hebrew*, acquainting them with *The Dance to Death*, she wrote "to ask if the American Hebrew Publishing Company will undertake to print it in pamphlet form." Whether at the editors' suggestion, or on her own initiative, she later added her other Judaic lyrics and translations. (Schappes, *Letters*, pp. 37–38) The clothbound edition was priced at fifty cents per copy, and twenty-five cents was the price of the paper edition.

45. *Poems*, I, 20–22.

46. September 28, 1882, p. 13.

47. Reprinted in the *American Hebrew* (October 4, 1882) 98. Her drama was here likened to Lessing's *Nathan der Weise*.

48. October 7, 1882. Reprinted in the *American Hebrew* (October 13, 1882) 110.

49. October 8, 1882. Reprinted in the *American Hebrew* (November 10, 1882) 153.

50. She furnished the *Evening Post* with a copy; however, no review appeared there. (Schappes, *Letters*, p. 43). Samuel G. Ward thanked her with high praise (*Ibid.*, pp. 43–44). Senator S. S. Cox afterward remembered "a beautiful note from Miss Lazarus, asking my acceptance of a volume of poems, which I read with great interest and admiration for her genius." (*American Hebrew*, Memorial Issue, December 9, 1887) See also references to London journals (Schappes, *Letters*, pp. 39–40) and William Wetmore Story (*Ibid.*, p. 54).

51. October 20, 1882, p. 12.

52. November 10, 1882.

53. Excerpts in the *American Hebrew* (October 13, 1882) 110.

54. January, 1883. Reprinted in the *American Hebrew* (January 5, 1883) 89.

55. February, 1883, p. 216.

56. Schappes, *Letters*, p. 45. "Though quite a large edition has been printed, there is scarcely a doubt but that it will last only a short while.... The announcement that a volume of her poems was to be issued was received with delight, substantially evidenced by the number of copies ordered from all parts of the country in advance of publication." *American Hebrew* (September 22, 1882) 74.

57. The editors published this note of apology at the outset: "In spite of the twenty pages we have added to the *American Hebrew* this week, we find it necessary, at the last moment, to omit our Philadelphia and Baltimore letters, considerable local news, and several contributed articles of interest."

58. October 5, 1888, pp. 130–31.

59. This is a far cry from the characterization of Emma Lazarus he had sent his sisters from Newport in the summer of 1872: "It is curious to see how mentally famished a person may be in the very best society.... Less excluded from brains are the J. J. Astors whom I took tea with at Richard Hunt's." Thatcher, p. 266.

60. p. 75.

61. Whitman remarked, "She must have had a great, sweet, unusual nature." This, and other quotations from Horace Traubel's *Walt Whitman in Camden* relating to the great poet's admiration for her, are given in Jacob, *op. cit.*, pp. 198–99.

Appendix I: Her Attitude Toward American Literature

In the introduction to his collection of Emma Lazarus' letters, pp. 4–5, Schappes keynotes "her advocacy of an American national literature, which she defended against decriers in private and public." He writes:

> John Burroughs had exclaimed his delight in 1878 to learn that she was enthusiastic about Whitman's "Democratic Vistas," and revealed an indelicate sense of male superiority by confessing she was the only woman he knew of who was "equal to the task of appreciating" that book!

Schappes identifies for the first time (*Ibid.*, p. 29) an article in *The Critic* of June 18, 1881, titled "American Literature," as the work of Emma Lazarus. The writing of this unsigned editorial (which was rewarded with a "Memorial Ode" of praise from Col. Higginson) may have been spurred on by her reactions to the article Stedman had asked her to read prior to publication. She singles out for attack an essay by George E. Woodberry in the *Fortnightly Review* of the previous month, in which he had denied the development of any continuous national tradition in American writing. Overlooking the Victorian echoes in all but his dialect verses, she lists Bret Harte along with Emerson, Hawthorne, Thoreau, Burroughs, Whitman, Lowell, and Holmes as distinctively American.

Her letter to Stedman answers pungently many of his arguments. He had written: "Look at Scotland. Her national melodies were ready and waiting for Burns; her legends, history, traditions, for Walter Scott." To this she replied:

> Now that Burns and Scott have poetized all the Scotch legends, traditions and national songs, it is easy to say, these were ready at hand, waiting for their poet. But how long did they wait? Until these clear-eyed seers were born, whoever thought the rich patois of the grim old Highlander and the barbarous music of the bagpipes could be associated in our mind with romance and melody? I never have believed in the want of a theme.... I think it is the poet's fault if he do not know how to utilize the accessories and materials which surround him.

Schappes expresses the belief that her letter influenced Stedman to make certain changes in his chapter (*Letters*, p. 68n). It is difficult to imagine otherwise.

Appendix II: The Effect of Her Jewish Zeal on Her Poetic Work

The view that Emma Lazarus' poetry grew in merit as her zeal in the Jewish cause increased, is by no means universally accepted. Max Baym ("Emerson and Emma Lazarus," *American Jewish Historical Society Publications* June, 1949) 277–279 goes so far as to suggest that such development would not have taken place in the poet's attitude and work "had she attained a place in *Parnassus* — had she truly and actually been accepted by Lowell, Howells and Emerson." Baym speaks vaguely of "those who persisted in that doubt a score of years ago," without offering a single name or quotation.

Yet he introduces a letter from Venice, written by Emma's sister, the Anglo-Catholic Anne Humphreys Johnston, to prove what needs no proof: that at least within the poet's immediate family, if not among critics, there has always been some effort to tone down her reputation as a Jewish writer. Mrs. Johnston, the erstwhile Jew, declares:

> There has been a tendency on the part of some of her public to overemphasize the Hebraic strain in her work, giving it thus a quality of sectarian propaganda, which I greatly deplore, for I understood this to have been merely a phase in my sister's development.... Then, unfortunately, owing to her untimely death, this was destined to be her final word.

Philip Cowen ("Recollections of Emma Lazarus," p. 240) mentions a sister who referred mockingly to Emma's espousal of the Jewish cause, and speaks of another who, in later years, expressed a willingness to publish a definitive edition — on condition that all the Jewish work be kept out.

Baym rebukes those whose "estimate of her as a poet" emphasizes her Jewish writings, and claims that "as a result, she has fared ill indeed at the bar of accredited literary history.... It is high time, we submit," he concludes on p. 280, "that Emma Lazarus were saved ... from those zealots who throw her true worth out of historic focus in one way or another."

What her "true worth" is, Baym does not say. Shall her savior, then, be one whose article is filled with hypotheses based on hypotheses based on half-quotations, inaccuracies, and an overactive imagination? Albert Mordell, in "Some Final Words on Emma Lazarus," *American Jewish Historical Publications* (March, 1950) 324–27, exposes the complete absurdity of Baym's view, which he politely calls "unwarranted," and paraphrases the *Parnassus* theory with fitting irony: "If her vanity had been satisfied and a poem of hers included in the anthology, she would have let the Jews go hang!"

Actually, Emma Lazarus' true worth has been declared by a number of quite sober and "accredited" critics, none of whom can be thought of as zealots. The general feeling is that her outstanding, permanent contribution to American literature was produced in the period of her Jewish ardor. This opinion is perhaps best expressed by George F. Whicher in "Poetry After the Civil War," *American Writers on American Literature*, ed. John Macy (New York: Horace Liveright, 1931) 382. He uses the case of Emma Lazarus as an example of "special cause" writing versus the "ivory tower" brand:

> The difference can readily be illustrated if one compares the early verses of Emma Lazarus, written under the spell of Emerson, with the poetry she began to produce when the wrongs of her people fired her imagination and brought her forward as the champion of an oppressed race. The pogroms that were driving thousands of Jewish families from their homes in Russia served to concentrate her previously scattered ardors into a single effort. The desire to be heard stripped her verse of its finespun elaboration and brought to her lips the majestic accents of a racial past.... In the literary hothouse of the later nineteenth century the breath of a great cause blew through her verse with tonic effect.

Appendix III: Recent Scholarship on Emma Lazarus

My master's thesis (on which this chapter is based), *Emma Lazarus: Her Life and Work*, was submitted in 1951. Since that time there has not been an upsurge of critical interest nor a reversal of her omission from anthologies, despite the appearance of such formidable advocates as Charles Angoff and Edward Wagenknecht, a fine biography in Twayne's series of American poets, and reprints of *Songs of a Semite* and *Epistle to the Hebrews*. Much of what is currently being done seems motivated more by the discovery of poems and letters, or by occasions (i.e., the centennial of the Statue in 1986 and of the poet's death a year later), or by a women's studies agenda in which she serves as a useful example within a cluster.

The following are among the more interesting recent essays:

I. Chapters in Books

Edward Wagenknecht, *Daughters of the Covenant: Portraits of Six Jewish Women* (Amherst: Univ. of Massachusetts Press, 1983) 23–54, 174–76.

Wagenknecht focuses on "the work and more particularly ... the character and personality of the six women," who illustrate "various types of Jewish womanhood." Using Lazarus' work to create his portrait, he makes illuminating comments on her plays, her novel, her essays, many poems including uncollected ones uncovered from contemporary journals, and even a short story he found in *Scribner's.* He demonstrates her wide range of interest in music, painting, and literature. Only the last two of seven segments focus on her development as a Jewish activist. He asks: "Was the basic motivating force racial, religious, or humanitarian?" and concludes that ultimately "religious and humanitarian are one."

Diane Marilyn Lichtenstein, *On Whose Native Ground? Nineteenth Century Myths of American Womanhood and Jewish Women Writers* (Doctoral dissertation, Univ. of Pennsylvania, 1985) 21–22, 167–211.

Tracing the cultural myths of 19th century white, middle-class, Christian American women and of 19th century Jewish American women, the author explores how those myths affect individual writers, how they transform the myths for their own purposes, and how individuals who live in more than one culture reconcile the conflicting demands of the cultures. For such purposes Emma Lazarus proves a perfect choice of study, and Lichtenstein's approach results in fresh readings of many Lazarus works. Being outside Christian America, outside the male domain of poetry, and outside the traditional sphere of Jewish and American womanhood, but as a daughter of wealth and extraordinary culture, "she could forge a unique identity, defying stereotypes and traditional expectations." It was a "complex identity," often challenged and frustrated, but achieved with a fierce tenacity that belied the "quiet public demeanor" demanded of an upper-class Victorian woman; unswervingly, with words and actions, she affirmed her role — unmistakably, outstandingly "an American Jewish woman writer."

Carole S. Kessner, "Matrilineal Dissent: The Rhetoric of Zeal in Emma Lazarus, Marie Syrkin, and Cynthia Ozick," *Women of the Word: Jewish Women and Jewish Writing,* ed. Judith R. Baskin (Detroit: Wayne State Univ. Press, 1994) 197–204, 213–14.

Declaring Marie Syrkin and Cynthia Ozick Lazarus' "literary and spiritual descendants," Kessner shows the parallels in their lives and works. All chose "to assert an idiosyncratic feminism rather than to engage in sexual politics." All "are self-proclaimed Jewish autodidacts who did not begin to emphasize Jewishness in their writing until they were almost thirty." The "great gifts" of each "might have brought broad acclaim in a larger arena"; instead, each "discovered her true self through a life of passionate commitment in defense of the Jews and total dedication to her people's welfare." Most of the Emma Lazarus material is a rehash of earlier publications, but there is a fresh reading of "The New Colossus" as a rejection of "Western culture's Hellenistic glorification of male conquering power, of empty ceremony and aestheticism, and in its place she asserts the power of motherhood, and the Hebraic prophetic values of compassion and consolation."

II. Articles in Journals

George Gordh, "Emma Lazarus: A Poet of Exile and Freedom," *The Christian Century* (Nov. 19, 1986) 1033–36.

In the Statue of Liberty's centennial year, Gordh demands attention for "the woman who wrote" its sonnet. He offers a concise biographical study, focusing on "Epochs" as an example of her early thinking, and verses from *Songs of a Semite* to demonstrate the "profound change" she underwent. Since "exile and freedom" are at the heart of her work, Gordh uses them as a gauge of her growth. The early poems are addressed to all people; the later ones "address Jews specifically." The early poems are set in "the world of nature"; some later poems "take place in the world of . . . Hebrew history." These pieces are primarily political, "not psychological." The weeping by the waters of Babylon is recalled "to summon people to tears for present exile." And ancient struggles are recalled to inspire a new struggle for freedom. Finally, the professor of religion contrasts her "vague" and romantic early understanding of transcendence with what he sees as "The Transcendent One," as "Lord of Exodus and Sinai" in her later work.

This leads to the sonnet of the centennial itself, in which he feels "two Colossi" symbolizing two kinds of freedom — the old one offering "freedom for some through the denial of freedom for others," the new embodying "a freedom compatible with concern of people for one another." For Lazarus, such universal concern "was integral to her heritage."

Diane Lichtenstein, "Words and Worlds: Emma Lazarus' Conflicting Citizenships," *Tulsa Studies in Women's Literature*, VI, 2 (Fall 1987) 247–63.

To commemorate the centenaries of the Statue (1986) and Emma Lazarus' death (1987), Lichtenstein sharpens her dissertation chapter on Emma Lazarus (1985, above), beginning and ending with the premise that "The New Colossus" glorifies the Statue "to articulate ... the ideals that America believes it represents," transforming the outsider "into an insider who brings new vitality to her/his adopted nation." Ironically, "by valorizing the outsider," Lazarus "became the insider she wanted to be." Lichtenstein cites two uncollected 1884 poems, "The Choice" and an untitled sonnet for Emerson, as examples of her "publicly avowed Judaism" and "her own chosen vocation as an American author." Neither wife nor mother, she nevertheless "played the part of the Mother in Israel by using her pen" to educate and mediate. Through her imagination, the Statue becomes not only "the Victorian woman whose majestic strength supplied a nation with courage" but also "the nineteenth century Jewish woman who created for her family a refuge from a potentially hostile world."

Franz Link, "Pogromendramen," *Arcadia*, XXVI, 1 (1991) 50–71.

In this German essay, which warrants translation, Link organized four very different plays into a chain of responses to Jewish martyrdom in various countries and centuries. Emma Lazarus' *Dance to Death* comes first. Mastery of Lazarus' acknowledged German source, Richard Reinhard's 1875 "little narrative," allows Link to demonstrate her adaptive powers by comparing several of Reinhard's prose passages with her blank verse. Among the differences he stresses such "Ergänzungen" as her references to other pogrom episodes, her inclusion of Jewish ritual (i.e., Yom Kippur, *Kaddish*, and

Shibboleth), citations from Ezekiel and the *Talmud*, allusions to Esther and Jephthah's daughter, etc.

He finds in her drama echoes of Lessing's *Nathan der Weise* and Verdi's 1853 *Il Trovatore*. Interestingly, he hears specific vibrations from *Julius Caesar*, *Hamlet*, and *The Merchant of Venice* in certain passages. He suspects that the dedication to George Eliot, unlike the play itself, was composed after the Russian pogroms, and he points to Eliot's essay "The Modern Hep-Hep" as Lazarus' probable source in composing the anti-Semitic outcry: "Death to the Jews!/ Hep! hep!" He also finds a parallel between Heine's neglect of his *Rabbi of Bacherach* until the 1840 "Judenverfolgungen in Damaskus," and Lazarus' withholding of her play until the Russian pogroms. Dating the work 1879–81, prior to her radicalization by the pogroms, he finds the poetry somewhat removed from the horror of the situation and burdened by "die romantischen Klischeen ihrer Zeit" (as expressed in the Verdi opera and the Reinhard story).

Franz Link, "Emma Lazarus, Die jüdische Dichterin und ihr *Dance to Death*," *Literaturwissenschaftliches Jahrbuch* 32 (Berlin, 1991) 129–47.

As far as the play is concerned, this essay is little more than a rehash of "Pogromendramen," often repeating his material word for word, but expanding the citations from her sources, particularly the Middle German "authentic documents communicated by Professor Franz Delitzsch" on which, as Lazarus explains, Reinhard's narrative is based. He also deals with an 1863 novel by Carmoly, *Der Tanz zum Tod*, which contains much of the material, including characters, that appear in the Lazarus drama.

Most of the essay, however, deals with "Die jüdische Dichterin" aside from the play. Link is clearly familiar with much of the recent scholarship. He can also declare with assurance: "Ihr Name fehlt allerdings in fast allen verbreiteten Gesamtstellungen der amerikanischen Literatur und erscheint in kaum einer der bekannteren Anthologien." But such neglect is not likely to be reversed by Link's insidious performance in this essay. Challenging Van Wyck Brooks' belief that a great cause (the 1881–82 pogroms) had vitalized and magnified Emma Lazarus' talent, he praises instead her earlier poems, whose form and content, though not original, earn her a respectable place "auf dem Niveau ihrer Zeit." He suspects that her career benefited from her being the "erste Jüdin" in the poetic ranks.

Her familiar pre-1882 expressions of Jewish identity are cited, with some carping at a Heine translation and a frontal assault on her Raschi poems as "Klischeehaften Melodramatik." As for the anti-pogrom pieces of 1882, Link separates their "Bedeutung" from their "Qualität," quoting the nastiest judgments he can scrounge up, and dragging forth an unjust comparison by Philip Thody between "The New Colossus" and "Ozymandias." He finds "erstaunlich" the praise of her poem by a far better sonneteer, James Russell Lowell, and snidely conjectures that Lowell allowed his critical judgment to be blinded by his abolitionist sympathies.

With such friends Emma Lazarus has no need of enemies. Link may suppose his premise validated by H.E. Jacob's assertion that her *Songs of a Semite* (such an intentionally irksome title!) "were not really what she had formerly considered to be poetry. They were fanfare and appeals …" — and by D. B. Stauffer's judgment that they suffered "from the topicality of the subject and her emotional involvement with it." But for me these comments are valuable only as expressions of the critical snobbishness and sterility that have held sway throughout my lifetime: a contempt for any "topicality," any "emotional involvement" — above all, any tendency toward the prophetic; shunting aside, along with the best in Emma Lazarus, the best in other prophetic voices of her time as well as ours.

For his *piéce de résistance*, Link saves Philip Thody's demolition effort against "The New Colossus." This he considers "am treffend-sten." Thody reconstructs a powerful moment in Chaplin's early film, *The Immigrants*, when police are harassing the new arrivals and the camera zooms in "auf die zehnte Zeile des Sonnette." For Thody and his admirer Franz Link this is Chaplin's rebuke to "Emma Lazarus' hubristic sentimentality," and the point "is even more telling because of the contrast between the social reality and the richly self-confident rhetoric." But a less jaundiced reading may show Chaplin contrasting "the social reality" with the Great Ideal which summoned the immigrants here in the first place, and honor-ing Emma Lazarus as a prophet whose role was to redefine that Ideal as a reminder and a rebuke against its betrayal by a hubristic nation.

Mention should be made of the three full-length biographies, Eve Merriam's *Woman With a Torch* (New York: Citadel Press, 1956), Dan Vogel's *Emma Lazarus* (Boston: Twayne, 1980), praised by Edward Wagenknecht as "much the most comprehensive study of her work," and Bette Roth Young's *Emma Lazarus in her world* (Philadelphia: Jewish Publ. Society, 1995); also an unpublished dissertation (in which Arthur Zeiger discusses the unpublished sonnet "Assurance," suggesting it is "a lesbian fantasy"), and Charles Angoff's *Emma Lazarus: Poet, Jewish Activist, Pioneer Activist* (Jewish Historical Society of New York, 1979). She also receives serious attention from Saul J. Hurwitz in *Notable American Women, 1607–1950*, II (Cambridge: Harvard Univ. Press, 1971) and Louis Harap in *The Image of the Jew in American Literature* (Philadelphia: Jewish Publication Society of America, 1974).

Among the essays worth noting are Louis Ruchames' "New Light on the Religious Development of Emma Lazarus" in *Publications of the American Jewish Historical Society*, XLII (1952–53) 81–88, containing a discussion of her uncollected 1872 poem "Outside the Church"; Aaron Kramer's "The Link Between Heinrich Heine and Emma Lazarus," in *Publications of the American Jewish Historical Society*, XLV (1956–57) 248–57, excellently summarized by Wagenknecht (p. 176); Joseph Lyons' "In Two Divided Streams," in *Mainstream* VII (Autumn 1961) 78–85; George Monteiro's "Heine in America: The Efforts of Emma Lazarus and John Hay," in *Turn-of-the-Century Women*, II (1985) 51–55; Hans-Joachim Lang's "Mary Antin und das Vermächtnis von Emma Lazarus," *Women's Studies in Literature*, eds. F. Fleischmann and D. L. Schneider (Erlangen, 1987) 83–130; and Carol S. Kessner, "The Emma Lazarus—Henry James Connection: Eight Letters," *American Literary History* III, 1 (Spring, 1991) 46–62, which reveals that her old Newport acquaintance gave her letters of introduction to important friends in Britain.

Appendix IV: Selected Poems of Emma Lazarus

EARLY POEMS

In Memoriam
Dreams
Florence Nightingale
Wings
In a Swedish Graveyard
The Garden of Adonis
In the Jewish Synagogue at Newport
Sonnet
The Heroes
The Day of Dead Soldiers
How Long?

SONGS OF A SEMITE

The Crowing of the Red Cock
The Banner of the Jew
The New Year
In Exile
The Feast of Lights
Bar Kochba
The Dance to Death — excerpt
An Epistle — excerpts
The New Ezekiel

EARLY POEMS

IN MEMORIAM

O friend who passed away while flowers died,
Now that the land bursts into bloom again,
　　With vivid blossoms o'er the landscape wide,
　　Purple and white 'mongst grasses golden-eyed,
In beauteous resurrection o'er the plain, —

My thoughts revert to thee, who liest still,
Under the pulsing, stirring, glowing earth;
　　Not rising with the lilac on the hill,
　　Not waking with the sunny daffodil,
Living and breathing with no second birth.

In these sweet days I dream I see thy grave,
A mockery of death, alive with flowers.
　　The delicate sprays and tender grasses wave,
　　Blue violets and the hardy crocus brave,
Wooed back to life by sunshine, dew, and showers.

I cannot deem that thou art lying there,
Asleep through all these fervent days of spring;
　　For I perceive thy spirit in the air,
　　Around me ever in my dream and prayer,
Enskied and hallowed by thy suffering.

When thou didst walk upon the earth before,
My trivial words and deeds alone were thine;
　　But now my holiest dreams are evermore
　　Blended with thoughts of thee, on that far shore,
Where thy pale, girlish face has grown divine.

Through the dark shadows thou must go alone;
And lo! thou hast a dauntless bravery,
　　A most majestic resignation shown;
　　A valiant patience, a faith not overthrown
By the dread terror of uncertainty.

The day had fled, from thee for evermore,
Thy soul was ebbing with the waning light,
　　And still thou asked, aweary and heartsore,
　　The same pathetic question o'er and o'er, —
"O, I am tired! will I go tonight?"

Aye, thou didst go — and where? Thou knowest now.
Nature is innocent as well as fair;
　　Lilies, as well as amaranth, wreathe her brow.
　　She hath thy soul; because I cannot know
When it may be, I feel it everywhere.

And thus the spring hath brought me flowers of worth.
O mourners, come to weep o'er empty graves!
Open them all! no dead come trooping forth,
    To fill with ghastly hosts the living earth;
Only the flowers bloom, the green grass waves.

    Those ye laid low with solemn rites and tears,
Elude you; while ye weep, they all have flown.
    And so I lay aside my doubts and fears;
    My friend in day-dreams and at night appears,
And hovers near when I am most alone.

DREAMS

    A dream of lilies: all the blooming earth,
A garden full of fairies and of flowers;
    Its only music the glad cry of mirth,
While the warm sun weaves golden-tissued hours;
    Hope a bright angel, beautiful and true
As Truth herself, and life a lovely toy,
    Which ne'er will weary us, ne'er break, a new
Eternal source of pleasure and of joy.

    A dream of roses: vision of Love's tree,
Of beauty and of madness, and as bright
    As naught on earth save only dreams can be,
Made fair and odorous with flower and light;
    A dream that Love is strong to outlast Time,
That hearts are stronger than forgetulness,
    The slippery sand than changeful waves that climb,
The wind-blown foam than mighty waters' stress.

    A dream of laurels: after much is gone,
Much buried, much lamented, much forgot,
    With what remains to do and what is done,
With what yet is, and what, alas! is not,
    Man dreams a dream of laurel and of bays,
A dream of crowns and guerdons and rewards,

Wherein sounds sweet the hollow voice of praise,
And bright appears the wreath that it awards.

A dream of poppies, sad and true as Truth, —
That all these dreams were dreams of vanity;
    And full of bitter penitence and ruth,
In his last dream, man deems 'twere good to die;
    And weeping o'er the visions vain of yore,
In the sad vigils he doth nightly keep,
    He dreams it may be good to dream no more,
And life has nothing like Death's dreamless sleep.

FLORENCE NIGHTINGALE

Upon the whitewashed walls
    A woman's shadow falls,
A woman walketh o'er the darksome floors.
    A soft, angelic smile
    Lighteth her face the while,
In passing through the dismal corridors.

And now and then there slips
    A word from out her lips,
More sweet and grateful to those listening ears
    Than the most plaintive tale
    Of the sad nightingale,
Whose name and tenderness this woman bears.

Her presence in the room
    Of agony and gloom,
No fretful murmurs, no coarse words profane;
    For while she guardeth there,
    All words are hushed save prayer;
She seems God's angel weeping o'er man's pain.

And some of them arise,
    With eager, tearful eyes,
From off their couch to see her passing by.

Some, e'en too weak for this,
Can only stoop and kiss
Her shadow, and fall back content to die.

No monument of stone
Needs this heroic one, —
Her name is graven on each noble heart;
And in all after years
Her praise will be the tears
Which at that name from quivering lids will start.

And those who live not now,
To see the sainted brow,
And the angelic smile before it flits for aye,
They in the future age
Will kiss the storied page
Whereon the shadow of her life will lie.

WINGS

Dawn opes her pensive eyes,
In the yet starry skies,
A roseate blush upon her cheek and brows.
Her purple mantle still
Lies on the sky-kissed hill,
And a blue, solemn shade thereon it throws.

The earth lies hushed and calm,
No chant of praise, no psalm
Riseth to greet the rose-crowned queen of day.
Each blade of grass, each leaf,
Stands out in sharp relief,
Against the rayless blue and silver gray.

All nature seems to wait
For some new deed of Fate:
The silence is a sacred, reverent prayer, —
When hark! from some sweet throat
One thrilling, quivering note

Fills with its tremulous music all the air.

> Then from the dewy grass
> A tiny form doth pass,
A little soul all music and all wings.
> All nature's voice is heard,
> Embodied in this bird,
That darteth up and, rising, ever sings.

> It mounteth still and sings:
> What soul yearns not for wings,
To follow after, burst its prison bars,
> And learn the secret there,
> In those clear realms of air, —
The secret of the rainbow and the stars;

> To rush as swift as light,
> Within those regions bright
Of throbbing, scintillant, intensest blue;
> The air all breathless cleave,
> And far below to leave
Regrets and tears, the raindrop and the dew.

> Ah! caged 'mongst meaner things,
> The soul can use no wings,
And beats against the bars it cannot pass;
> But it might humbly turn,
> Essaying first to learn
The secret of the flowers and the grass.

IN A SWEDISH GRAVEYARD

"They all sleep with their heads to the westward. Each held a lighted taper in his hand when he died, and in his coffin were placed his little heart-treasures and a piece of money for his last journey."
— LONGFELLOW

After wearisome toil and much sorrow,
How quietly sleep they at last,

Neither dreading and fearing the morrow,
Nor vainly bemoaning the past!
  Shall we give them our envy or pity?
Shall we shun or yearn after such rest,
  So calm near the turbulent city,
With their heart stilled at length in their breast?

They all sleep with their heads lying westward,
  Where all suns and all days have gone down.
Do they long for the dawn, looking eastward?
  Do they dream of the strife and the crown?
Each one held a lit taper when dying:
  Where hath vanished the fugitive flame?
With his love, and his joy, and his sighing,
  Alas! and his youth and his name.

The living stands o'er him and dreameth,
  And wonders what dreams came to him.
While the tender, brief twilight still gleameth,
  With a light strangely mournful and dim.
And he wonders what lights and what shadows
  Passed over these dead long ago,
When their feet now at rest trod these meadows,
  And their hearts throbbed to pleasure or woe.

What dreams came to them in their living?
  The self-same that come now to thee.
If thou findest these dreams are deceiving,
  Then these lives thou wilt know and wilt see:
The same visions of love and of glory,
  The same vain regret for the past;
All the same poor and pitiful story,
  Till the taper's extinguished at last.

All the treasures on earth that they cherished,
  Now they care not to clasp nor to save;
And the poor little lights, how they perished,
  Slowly dying alone in the grave!
With a flickering faint on the features
  Of age, or of youth in its bloom:

Lighting up for grim Death his weak creatures,
  In the darkness and night of the tomb, —

With a radiance ghostly and mournful,
  On the good, on the just and unjust;
For a space, till the monarch, so scornful,
  Turned the light and the lighted to dust.
No taper of earth he desired
  In his halls where they quietly rest;
For all those who have toiled and are tired,
  Utter darkness and sleep may be best.

THE GARDEN OF ADONIS
(The Garden of Life in Spenser's "Faerie Queene")

It is no fabled garden in the skies,
  But bloometh here, — this is no world of death;
And nothing that once liveth, ever dies,
    And naught that breathes can ever cease to breathe,
    And naught that bloometh ever withereth.
The gods can ne'er take back their gifts from men,
They gave us life, — they cannot take again.

Who hath known Death, and who hath seen his face?
    On what high mountain have ye met with him?
Within what lowest valley is there trace
    Of his feared footsteps? in what forest dim,
    In what great city, in what lonely ways?
Nay, there is no such god, but one called Change,
And all he does is beautiful and strange.

It is but Change that lays our darlings low,
    And, though we doubt and fear, forsakes them not.
Where red lips smiled do sweetest roses blow,
    And star-flowers bloom above the lovely spot
    Where gleamed the eyes, with blue forget-me-not,
And through the grasses runs the same wave there
We knew of old within the golden hair.

Dig in the earth, — ye shall not surely find
    Death or death's semblance; only roots of flowers,
And all fair, goodly things there live enshrined,
    With the foundations of the glad green bowers,
    Through which the sunshine comes in golden showers.
And all the blossoms that this earth enwreathe,
Are for assurance that there is no death.

O mother, raise thy tear-bathed lids again:
    Thy child died not, he only liveth more, —
His soul is in the sunshine and the rain,
    His life is in the waters and the shore,
    He is around thee all the wide world o'er;
The daisy thou hast plucked smiles back at thee,
Because it doth again its mother see.

What noble deed that ever lived, is dead,
    Or yet hath lost its power to inspire
Courage in hearts that sicken, and to shed
    New faith and hope when hands and footsteps tire,
    And make sad, downcast eyes look upward higher?
Yea, all men see and know it, whence it came;
It purifies them like a burning flame.

And dreams? What dreams were ever lost and gone,
    But wandering in strange lands we found again?
When least we think of these dear birdlings flown,
    We find that bright and fresh they still remain.
    The garden of all life is round us then;
And he is blind who doth not know and see,
And praise the gods for immortality.

IN THE JEWISH SYNAGOGUE AT NEWPORT

Here where the noises of the busy town,
    The ocean's plunge and roar can enter not,
We stand and gaze around with tearful awe,
    And muse upon the consecrated spot.

No signs of life are here; the very prayers
    Inscribed around are in a language dead;
The light of the "perpetual lamp" is spent
    That an undying radiance was to shed.

What prayers were in this temple offered up,
    Wrung from sad hearts that knew no joy on earth,
By these lone exiles of a thousand years,
    From the fair sunrise land that gave them birth!

Now as we gaze, in this new world of light,
    Upon this relic of the days of old,
The present vanishes, and tropic bloom
    And Eastern towns and temples we behold.

Again we see the patriarch with his flocks,
    The purple seas, the hot blue sky o'er head,
The slaves of Egypt, — omens, mysteries, —
    Dark fleeing hosts by flaming angels led.

A wondrous light upon a sky-kissed mount,
    A man who reads Jehovah's written law,
'Midst blinding glory and effulgence rare,
    Unto a people prone with reverent awe.

The pride of luxury's barbaric pomp,
    In the rich court of royal Solomon —
Alas! we wake: one scene alone remains, —
    The exiles by the streams of Babylon.

Our softened voices send us back again
    But mournful echoes through the empty hall;
Our footsteps have a strange, unnatural sound,
    And with unwonted gentleness they fall.

The weary ones, the sad, the suffering,
    All found their comfort in the holy place,
And children's gladness and men's gratitude
    Took voice and mingled in the chant of praise.

The funeral and the marriage, now, alas!
    We know not which is sadder to recall;

For youth and happiness have followed age,
    And green grass lieth gently over all.

And still the sacred shrine is holy yet,
    With its lone floors where reverent feet once trod.
Take off your shoes as by the burning bush,
    Before the mystery of death and God.

SONNET

Still northward is the central mount of Maine,
    From whose high crown the rugged forests seem
    Like shaven lawns, and lakes with frequent gleam,
"Like broken mirrors," flash back light again.
Eastward the sea, with its majestic plain,
Endless, of radiant, restless blue, superb
With might and music, whether storms perturb
Its reckless waves, or halcyon winds that reign,
Make it serene as wisdom. Storied Spain
    Is the next coast, and yet we may not sigh
For lands beyond the inexorable main;
    Our noble scenes have yet no history.
    All subtler charms than those that feed the eye,
Our lives must give them; 'tis an aim austere,
But opes new vistas, and a pathway clear.

HEROES

    In rich Virginian woods,
The scarlet creeper reddens over graves,
Among the solemn trees enlooped with vines;
Heroic spirits haunt the solitudes, —
The noble souls of half a million braves,
    Amid the murmurous pines.

    Ah! who is left behind,
Earnest and eloquent, sincere and strong,

To consecrate their memories with words
Not all unmeet? with fitting dirge and song
To chant a requiem purer than the wind,
　　And sweeter than the birds?

　　Here, though all seems at peace,
The placid, measureless sky serenely fair,
The laughter of the breeze among the leaves,
The bars of sunlight slanting through the trees,
The reckless wild-flowers blooming everywhere,
　　The grasses' delicate sheaves, —

Nathless each breeze that blows,
Each tree that trembles to its leafy head
With nervous life, revives within our mind,
Tender as flowers of May, the thoughts of those
Who lie beneath the living beauty, dead, —
　　Beneath the sunshine, blind.

　　For brave dead soldiers, these:
Blessings and tears of aching thankfulness,
Soft flowers for the graves in wreaths enwove,
The odorous lilac of dear memories,
The heroic blossoms of the wilderness,
　　And the rich rose of love.

But who has sung their praise,
Not less illustrious, who are living yet?
Armies of heroes, satisfied to pass
Calmly, serenely from the whole world's gaze,
And cheerfully accept, without regret,
　　Their old life as it was,

With all its petty pain,
Its irritating littleness and care;
They who have scaled the mountain, with content
Sublime, descend to live upon the plain;
Steadfast as though they breathed the mountain-air
　　Still, wheresoe'er they went.

　　They who were brave to act,

And rich enough their action to forget;
Who, having filled their day with chivalry,
Withdraw and keep their simpleness intact,
And all unconscious add more lustre yet
    Unto their victory.

    On the broad Western plains
Their patriarchal life they live anew;
Hunters as mighty as the men of old,
Or harvesting the plenteous, yellow grains,
Gathering ripe vintage of dusk bunches blue,
    Or working mines of gold;

Or toiling in the town,
Armed against hindrance, weariness, defeat,
With dauntless purpose not to swerve or yield,
And calm, defiant strength, they struggle on,
As sturdy and as valiant in the street,
    As in the camp and field.

    And those condemned to live,
Maimed, helpless, lingering still through suffering years,
May they not envy now the restful sleep
Of the dear fellow-martyrs they survive?
Not o'er the dead, but over these, your tears,
    O brothers, ye may weep!

    New England fields I see,
The lovely, cultured landscape, waving grain,
Wide, haughty rivers, and pale, English skies,
And lo! a farmer ploughing busily,
Who lifts a swart face, looks upon the plain, —
    I see, in his frank eyes,

    The hero's soul appear.
Thus in the common fields and streets they stand;
The light that on the past and distant gleams,
They cast upon the present and the near,
With antique virtues from some mystic land,
    Of knightly deeds and dreams.

THE DAY OF DEAD SOLDIERS
May 30, 1869

Welcome, thou gray and fragrant Sabbath-day,
   To deathless love and valor dedicate!
Glorious with the richest flowers of May,
   With early roses, lingering lilacs late,
With vivid green of grass and leaf and spray,
Thou bringest memories that far outweigh
   The season's joy with thoughts of death and fate.

What words may paint the picture on the air
   Of this broad land to-day from sea to sea?
The rolling prairies, purple valleys rare,
   And royal mountains, endless rivers free,
Filled full with phantoms flitting everywhere,
Pale ghosts of buried armies, slowly there
   From countless graves uprising silently.

A calm, grave day, — the sunlight does not shine,
   But thin, gray clouds bedrape the sky o'erhead.
The delicate air is filled with spirits fine,
   The temperate breezes whisper of the dead.
What visions and what memories divine,
O holy Sabbath flower-day, are thine,
   Painted in light against a field of red!

Behold the fairest spots in all the land,
   To-day in this mid-season of fresh flowers,
Are heroes' graves, — by many a tender hand
   Sprinkled with odorous, radiant-colored showers;
By mild, moist breezes delicately fanned,
Sending o'er distant towns their perfumes bland,
   Loading with sweet aroma sunless hours.

Who knows what tremulous, dusky hands set free,
   Deck quaintly with gay flowers the graves unknown?
What wealth of bloom is shed exuberantly,
   On the far grave in Illinois alone,
Where the last hero, sleeping peacefully,

Beyond distraction and mistrust, doth lie,
   By the glad winds of prairies overblown?

With hymns and prayer be this day sanctified,
   And consecrate to heroes' memories;
Not with wild, violent grief for those who died,
   O wives and mothers, but with patience wise,
Calm resignation, and a thankful pride,
That they have left their land a fame so wide,
   So rich a page of thrilling histories.

HOW LONG?

How long and yet how long,
Our leaders will we hail from over seas,
Masters and kings from feudal monarchies,
   And mock their ancient song
With echoes weak of foreign melodies?

That distant isle mist-wreathed,
Mantled in unimaginable green,
Too long hath been our mistress and our queen.
   Our fathers have bequeathed
Too deep a love for her our hearts within.

She made the whole world ring
With the brave exploits of her children strong,
And with the matchless music of her song.
   Too late, too late we cling
To alien legends, and their strains prolong.

This fresh young world I see,
With heroes, cities, legends of her own;
With a new race of men, and overblown
   By winds from sea to sea,
Decked with the majesty of every zone.

I see the glittering tops
Of snow-peaked mounts, the wid'ning vale's expanse,

Large prairies where free herds of horses prance,
    Exhaustless wealth of crops,
In vast, magnificent extravagance.

    These grand, exuberant plains,
These stately rivers, each with many a mouth,
The exquisite beauty of the soft-aired south,
    The boundless seas of grain,
Luxuriant forests' lush and splendid growth.

    The distant siren-song
Of the green island in the eastern sea,
Is not the lay for this new chivalry.
    It is not free and strong
To chant on prairies 'neath this brilliant sky.

    The echo faints and fails;
It suiteth not, upon this western plain,
Our voice or spirit; we should stir again
    The wilderness, and make the plain
Resound unto a yet unheard-of strain.

SONGS OF A SEMITE

THE CROWING OF THE RED COCK

Across the Eastern sky has glowed
    The flicker of a blood-red dawn,
Once more the clarion cock has crowed,
    Once more the sword of Christ is drawn.
A million burning rooftrees light
The world-wide path of Israel's flight.

Where is the Hebrew's fatherland?
    The folk of Christ is sore bestead;
The Son of Man is bruised and banned,
    Nor finds whereon to lay his head.
His cup is gall, his meat is tears,
His passion lasts a thousand years.

Each crime that wakes in man the beast,
  Is visited upon his kind.
The lust of mobs, the greed of priest,
  The tyranny of kings, combined
To root his seed from earth again,
His record is one cry of pain.

When the long roll of Christian guilt
  Against his sires and kin is known,
The flood of tears, the life-blood spilt,
  The agony of ages shown,
What oceans can the stain remove,
From Christian law and Christian love?

Nay, close the book; not now, not here,
  The hideous tale of sin narrate,
Reechoing in the martyr's ear,
  Even he might nurse revengeful hate,
Even he might turn in wrath sublime,
With blood for blood and crime for crime.

Coward? Not he, who faces death,
  Who singly against worlds has fought,
For what? A name he may not breathe,
  For liberty of prayer and thought.
The angry sword he will not whet,
His nobler task is to forget.

THE BANNER OF THE JEW

Wake, Israel, wake! Recall to-day
  The glorious Maccabean rage,
The sire heroic, hoary-gray,
  His five-fold lion-lineage:
The Wise, the Elect, the Help-of-God,
The Burst-of-Spring, the Avenging Rod.

From Mizpah's mountain-ridge they saw
  Jerusalem's empty streets, her shrine

Laid waste where Greeks profaned the Law,
    With idol and with pagan sign.
Mourners in tattered black were there,
With ashes sprinkled on their hair.

Then from the stony peak there rang
    A blast to ope the graves: down poured
The Maccabean clan, who sang
    Their battle-anthem to the Lord.
Five heroes lead, and following, see,
Ten thousand rush to victory!

Oh for Jerusalem's trumpet now,
    To blow a blast of shattering power,
To wake the sleepers high and low,
    And rouse them to the urgent hour!
No hand for vengeance — but to save,
A million naked swords should wave.

O deem not dead that martial fire,
    Say not the mystic flame is spent!
With Moses' law and David's lyre,
    Your ancient strength remains unbent.
Let but an Ezra rise anew,
To lift the Banner of the Jew!

A rag, a mock at first — erelong,
    When men have bled and women wept,
To guard its precious folds from wrong,
    Even they who shrunk, even they who slept,
Shall leap to bless it, and to save.
Strike! for the brave revere the brave!

THE NEW YEAR
Rosh-Hashanah, 5643 (1882)

Not while the snow-shroud round dead earth is rolled,
    And naked branches point to frozen skies, —
When orchards burn their lamps of fiery gold,

The grape glows like a jewel, and the corn
A sea of beauty and abundance lies,
        Then the new year is born.

Look where the mother of the months uplifts
        In the green clearness of the unsunned West,
Her ivory horn of plenty, dropping gifts,
        Cool, harvest-feeding dews, fine-winnowed light;
Tired labor with fruition, joy and rest
        Profusely to requite.

Blow, Israel, the sacred cornet! Call
        Back to thy courts whatever faint heart throb
With thine ancestral blood, thy need craves all.
        The red, dark year is dead, the year just born
Leads on from anguish wrought by priest and mob,
        To what undreamed-of morn?

For never yet, since on the holy height,
        The Temple's marble walls of white and green
Carved like the sea-waves, fell, and the world's light
        Went out in darkness, — never was the year
Greater with portent and with promise seen,
        Than this eve now and here.

Even as the Prophet promised, so your tent
        Hath been enlarged unto earth's farthest rim.
To snow-capped Sierras from vast steppes ye went,
        Through fire and blood and tempest-tossing wave,
For freedom to proclaim and worship Him,
        Mighty to slay and save.

High above flood and fire ye held the scroll,
        Out of the depths ye published still the Word.
No bodily pang had power to swerve your soul:
        Ye, in a cynic age of crumbling faiths,
Lived to bear witness to the living Lord,
        Or died a thousand deaths.

In two divided streams the exiles part,
        One rolling homeward to its ancient source,

One rushing sunward with fresh will, new heart.
    By each the truth is spread, the law unfurled,
Each separate soul contains the nation's force,
    And both embrace the world.

Kindle the silver candle's seven rays,
    Offer the first fruits of the clustered bowers,
The garnered spoil of bees. With prayer and praise
    Rejoice that once more tried, once more we prove
How strength of supreme suffering still is ours
    For Truth and Law and Love.

IN EXILE

"Since that day till now our life is one unbroken para-
dise. We live a true brotherly life. Every evening after
supper we take a seat under the mighty oak and sing
our songs."

— FROM A LETTER OF A RUSSIAN REFUGEE IN TEXAS

Twilight is here, soft breezes bow the grass,
    Day's sounds of various toil break slowly off,
The yoke-freed oxen low, the patient ass
    Dips his dry nostril in the cool, deep trough.
Up from the prairie the tanned herdsmen pass
    With frothy pails, guiding with voices rough
Their udder-lightened kine. Fresh smells of earth,
The rich, black furrows of the glebe send forth.

After the Southern day of heavy toil,
    How good to lie, with limbs relaxed, brows bare
To evening's fan, and watch the smoke-wreaths coil
    Up from one's pipe-stem through the rayless air.
So deem these unused tillers of the soil,
    Who stretched beneath the shadowing oak-tree, stare
Peacefully on the star-unfolding skies,

And name their life unbroken paradise.

The hounded stag that has escaped the pack,
    And pants at ease within a thick-leaved dell;
The unimprisoned bird that finds the track
    Through sun-bathed space, to where his fellows dwell;
The martyr, granted respite from the rack,
    The death-doomed victim pardoned from his cell, —
Such only know the joy these exiles gain, —
Life's sharpest rapture is surcease of pain.

Strange faces theirs, wherethrough the Orient sun
    Gleams from the eyes and glows athwart the skin.
Grave lines of studious thought and purpose run
    From curl-crowned forehead to dark-bearded chin.
And over all the seal is stamped thereon
    Of anguish branded by a world of sin,
In fire and blood through ages on their name,
Their seal of glory and the Gentiles' shame.

Freedom to love the law that Moses brought,
    To sing the songs of David, and to think
The thoughts Gabirol to Spinoza taught,
    Freedom to dig the common earth, to drink
The universal air — for this they sought
    Refuge o'er wave and continent, to link
Egypt with Texas in their mystic chain,
And truth's perpetual lamp forbid to wane.

Hark! through the quiet evening air, their song
    Floats forth with wild sweet rhythm and glad refrain.
They sign the conquest of the spirit strong,
    The soul that wrests the victory from pain;
The noble joys of manhood that belong
    To comrades and to brothers. In their strain
Rustle of palms and Eastern streams one hears,
And the broad prairie melts in mist of tears.

THE FEAST OF LIGHTS

Kindle the taper like the steadfast star
    Ablaze on evening's forehead o'er the earth,
And add each night a lustre till afar
    An eightfold splendor shine above thy hearth.
Clash, Israel, the cymbals, touch the lyre,
    Blow the brass trumpet and the harsh-tongued horn;
Chant psalms of victory till the heart take fire,
    The Maccabean spirit leap new-born.

Remember how from wintry dawn till night,
    Such songs were sung in Zion, when again
On the high altar flamed the sacred light,
    And, purified from every Syrian stain,
The foam-white walls with golden shields were hung,
    With crowns and silken spoils, and at the shrine,
Stood, midst their conqueror-tribe, five chieftains sprung
    From one heroic stock, one seed divine.

Five branches grown from Mattathias' stem,
    The Blessed John, the Keen-Eyed Jonathan,
Simon, the fair, the Burst-of-Spring, the Gem,
Eleazar, Help-of-God; o'er all his clan
Judas the Lion-Prince, the Avenging Rod,
    Towered in warrior-beauty, uncrowned king,
Armed with the breastplate and the sword of God,
    Whose praise is: "He received the perishing."

They who had camped within the mountain-pass,
    Couched on the rock, and tented neath the sky,
Who saw from Mizpah's heights the tangled grass
    Choke the wide Temple-courts, the altar lie
Disfigured and polluted — who had flung
    Their faces on the stones, and mourned aloud
And rent their garments, wailing with one tongue,
    Crushed as a wind-swept bed of reeds is bowed,

Even they by one voice fired, one heart of flame,
    Though broken reeds, had risen, and were men,

They rushed upon the spoiler and o'ercame,
    Each arm for freedom had the strength of ten.
Now is their mourning into dancing turned,
    Their sackcloth doffed for garments of delight,
Week-long the festive torches shall be burned,
    Music and revelry wed day with night.

Still ours the dance, the feast, the glorious Psalm,
    The mystic lights of emblem, and the Word.
Where is our Judas? Where our five-branched palm?
    Where are the lion-warriors of the Lord?
Clash, Israel, the cymbals, touch the lyre,
    Sound the brass trumpet and the harsh-tongued horn,
Chant hymns of victory till the heart take fire,
    The Maccabean spirit leap new-born!

BAR KOCHBA

Weep, Israel! your tardy meed outpour
    Of grateful homage on his fallen head,
That never coronal of triumph wore,
    Untombed, dishonored, and unchapleted.
If Victory makes the hero, raw Success
    The stamp of virtue, unremembered
Be then the desperate strife, the storm and stress
    Of the last Warrior Jew. But if the man
Who dies for freedom, loving all things less,
    Against world-legions, mustering his poor clan;
The weak, the wronged, the miserable, to send
    Their death-cry's protest through the ages' span —
If such an one be worthy, ye shall lend
    Eternal thanks to him, eternal praise.
Nobler the conquered than the conqueror's end!

THE DANCE TO DEATH

This play is dedicated, in profound veneration, and respect, to the memory of George Eliot, the illustrious writer, who did most among the artists of our day toward elevating and ennobling the spirit of Jewish nationality.

The scene: Partly in Nordhausen, partly in Eisenach. Time: May 4th, 5th, 6th, 1349.

ACT V, Scene 3

Within the Synagogue. Above in the gallery, women sumptuously attired; some with children by the hand or infants in their arms. Below the men and boys with silken scarfs about their shoulders.

SÜSSKIND [*enters*]: Brethren, my cup is full!
Oh let us die as warriors of the Lord.
The Lord is great in Zion. Let our death
Bring no reproach to Jacob, no rebuke
To Israel. Hark ye! let us crave one boon
At our assassins' hands; beseech them build
Within God's acre where our fathers sleep,
A dancing-floor to hide the fagots stacked.
Then let the minstrels strike the harp and lute,
And we will dance and sing above the pile,
Fearless of death, until the flames engulf,
Even as David danced before the Lord,
As Miriam danced and sang beside the sea.
Great is our Lord! His name is glorious
In Judah, and extolled in Israel!
In Salem is his tent, his dwelling place
In Zion; let us chant the praise of God!
A JEW: Süsskind, thou speakest well! We will meet death
With dance and song. Embrace him as a bride.

So that the Lord receive us in His tent.
SEVERAL VOICES: Amen! amen! amen! we dance to
    death!
RABBI JACOB: Süsskind, go forth and beg this grace of
    them.
        [Exit Süsskind]
Punish us not in wrath, chastise us not
In anger, oh our God! Our sins o'erwhelm
Our smitten heads, they are a grievous load;
We look on our iniquities, we tremble,
Knowing our trespasses. Forsake us not.
Be thou not far from us. Haste to our aid,
Oh God, who art our Saviour and our Rock!
SÜSSKIND *[re-enters]*: Brethren, our prayer, being the last,
    is granted.
The hour approaches. Let our thoughts ascend
From mortal anguish to the ecstasy
Of martyrdom, the blessed death of those
Who perish in the Lord. I see, I see
How Israel's ever-crescent glory makes
These flames that would eclipse it, dark as blots
Of candle-light against the blazing sun.
We die a thousand deaths, — drown, bleed, and burn;
Our ashes are dispersed unto the winds.
Yet the wild winds cherish the sacred seed,
The waters guard it in their crystal heart,
The fire refuseth to consume. It springs,
A tree immortal, shadowing many lands,
Unvisited, unnamed, undreamed as yet.
Rather a vine, full-flowered, golden-branched,
Ambrosial-fruited, creeping on the earth,
Trod by the passer's foot, yet chosen to deck
Tables of princes. Israel now has fallen
Into the depths, he shall be great in time.
Even as we die in honor, from our death
Shall bloom a myriad heroic lives,
Brave through our bright example, virtuous
Lest our great memory fall in disrepute.

Is one among us brothers, would exchange
His doom against our tyrants, — lot for lot?
Let him go forth and live — he is no Jew.
Is one who would not die in Israel
Rather than live in Christ, — their Christ who smiles
On such a deed as this? Let him go forth —
He may die full of years upon his bed.
Ye who nurse rancor haply in your hearts,
Fear ye we perish unavenged? Not so!
To-day, no! nor to-morrow! but in God's time,
Our witnesses arise. Ours is the truth,
Ours is the power, the gift of Heaven. We hold
His Law, His lamp, His covenant, His pledge.
Wherever in the ages shall arise
Jew-priest, Jew-poet, Jew-singer, or Jew-saint —
And everywhere I see them star the gloom —
In each of these the martyrs are avenged!
RABBI JACOB: Bring from the Ark the bell-fringed, sil-
   ken-bound
Scrolls of the Law. Gather the silver vessels,
Dismantle the rich curtains of the doors,
Bring the Perpetual Lamp; all these shall burn,
For Israel's light is darkened, Israel's Law
Profaned by strangers. Thus the Lord hath said:
"The weapon formed against thee shall not prosper,
The tongue that shall contend with thee in judgment,
Thou shalt condemn. This is the heritage
Of the Lord's servants and their righteousness.
For thou shalt come to peoples yet unborn,
Declaring that which He hath done. Amen!"
   [The doors of the Synagogue are burst open with
   tumultuous noise. Citizens and officers rush in]
CITIZENS: Come forth! the sun sets! Come, the Council
   wait!
What! will ye teach your betters patience? Out!
The Governor is ready. Forth with you,
Curs! serpents! Judases! The bonfire burns! *[Exeunt]*

AN EPISTLE

*from Joshua ibn Vives of Allorqui to his former master,
Solomon Levi-Paul de Santa-Maria, Bishop of Carta-
gena, Chancellor of Castile, and Privy Councillor to
King Henry III of Spain*

Master and Sage, greetings and health to thee,
    From thy most meek disciple! Deign once more
Endure me at thy feet, enlighten me,
    As when upon my boyish head of yore,
Midst the rapt circle gathered round thy knee
    Thy sacred vials of learning thou didst pour.
By the large lustre of thy wisdom orbed
Be my black doubts illumined and absorbed.

Oft I recall that golden time when thou,
    Born for no second station, heldst with us
The Rabbi's chair, who art priest and bishop now;
    And we, the youth of Israel, curious,
Hung on thy counsels, lifted reverent brow
    Unto thy sanctity, would fain discuss
With thee our Talmud problems good and evil,
Till startled by the risen stars o'er Seville.

For on the Synagogue's high-pillared porch
    Thou didst hold session, till the sudden sun
Beyond day's purple limit dropped his torch.
    Then we, as dreamers, woke, to find outrun
Time's rapid sands. The flame that may not scorch,
    Our hearts caught from thine eyes, thou Shining One.
I scent not yet sweet lemon-groves in flower,
But I re-breathe the peace of that deep hour.

We kissed the sacred borders of thy gown,
    Brow-aureoled with thy blessing, we went forth
Through the hushed byways of the twilight town.
    Then in all life but one thing seemed of worth,
To seek, find, love the Truth. She set her crown

Upon thy head, our Master, at thy birth;
She bade thy lips drop honey, fired thine eyes
With the unclouded glow of sun-steeped skies.

Forgive me, if I dwell on that which, viewed
    From thy new vantage-ground, must seem a mist
Of error, by auroral youth endued
    With alien lustre. Still in me subsist
Those reeking vapors; faith and gratitude
    Still lead me to the hand my boy-lips kissed
For benison and guidance. Not in wrath,
Master, but in wise patience, point my path.

For I, thy servant, gather in one sheaf
    The venomed shafts of slander, which thy word
Shall shrivel to small dust. If haply grief,
    Or momentary pain, I deal, my Lord
Blame not thy servant's zeal, nor be thou deaf
    Unto my soul's blind cry for light. Accord —
Pitying my love, if too superb to care
For hate-soiled name — an answer to my prayer.

To me, who, vine to stone, clung close to thee,
    The very base of life appeared to quake
When first I knew thee fallen from us, to be
    A tower of strength among our foes, to make
'Twixt Jew and Jew deep-cloven enmity.
    I have wept gall and blood for thy dear sake,
But now with temperate soul I calmly search
Motive and cause that bound thee to the Church.

* * * *

Was Israel glad in Seville on the day
    Thou didst renounce him? Then mightst thou indeed
Snap finger at whate'er thy slanderers say.
    Lothly must I admit, just then the seed
Of Jacob chanced upon a grievous way.
    Still from the wounds of that red year we bleed,
The curse had fallen upon our heads — the sword

Was whetted for the chosen of the Lord.

There where we flourished like a fruitful palm,
  We were uprooted, spoiled, lopped limb from limb.
A bolt undreamed of out of heavens calm,
  So cracked our doom. We were destroyed by him
Whose hand since childhood we had clasped. With balm
  Our head had been anointed, at the brim
Our cup ran over — now our day was done,
Our blood flowed free as water in the sun.

Midst the four thousand of our tribe who held
  Glad homes in Seville, never a one was spared,
Some slaughtered at their hearthstones, some expelled
  To Moorish slavery. Cunningly ensnared,
Baited and trapped were we; their fierce monks yelled
  And thundered from our Synagogues, while flared
The Cross above the Ark. Ah, happiest they
Who fell unconquered martyrs on that day!

For some (I write it with flushed cheek, bowed head),
  Given free choice 'twixt death and shame, chose shame,
Denied the God, who visibly had led
  Their fathers, pillared in a cloud of flame,
Bathed in baptismal waters, ate the bread
  Which is their new Lord's body, took the name
Marranos the Accursed, whom equally
Jew, Moor, and Christian hate, despise, and flee.

Even one no less than an Abarbanel
  Prized miserable length of days, above
Integrity of soul. Midst such who fell,
  Far be it, however, from my duteous love,
Master, to reckon thee. Thine own lips tell
  How fear nor torture thy firm will could move.
How thou midst panic nowise disconcerted,
By Thomas of Aquinas wast converted!

Truly I know no more convincing way
  To read so wise an author, than was thine,

When burning Synagogues changed night to day,
    And red swords underscored each word and line.
That was a light to read by! Who'd gainsay
    Authority so clearly stamped divine?
On this side, death and torture, flame and slaughter,
On that, a harmless wafer and clean water.

Thou couldst not fear extinction for our race;
    Though Christian sword and fire from town to town
Flash double bladed lightning to efface
    Israel's image — though we bleed, burn, drown
Through Christendom — 'tis but a scanty space.
Still are we lords in Syria, still are free,
Nor doomed to be abolished utterly.

Where are the signs fulfilled whereby all men
    Should know the Christ? Where is the wide-winged
        peace
Shielding the lamb within the lion's den?
    The freedom broadening with the wars that cease?
Do foes clasp hands in brotherhood again?
    Where is the promised garden of increase,
When like a rose the wilderness should bloom?
Earth is a battlefield and Spain a tomb.

Our God of Sabaoth is an awful God
    Of lightnings and of vengeance, — Christians say.
Earth trembled, nations perished at his nod;
    His Law has yielded to a milder sway.
Theirs is the God of Love whose feet have trod
    Our common earth — draw near to him and pray,
Meek-faced, dove-eyed, pure-browed, the Lord of life,
Know him, and kneel, else at your throat the knife!

This is the God of Love, whose altars reek
    With human blood, who teaches men to hate;
Torture past words, or sins we may not speak
    Wrought by his priests behind the convent-grate . . .

* * * *

The God who balances the clouds, who spread
    The sky above us like a molten glass,
The God who shut the sea with doors, who laid
    The corner-stone of earth, who caused the grass
Spring forth upon the wilderness, and made
    The darkness scatter and the night to pass —
That he should clothe Himself with flesh, and move
Midst worms a worm — this, sun, moon, stars disprove.

Help me, O thou who wast my boyhood's guide,
    I bend my exile-weary feet to thee,
Teach me the indivisible to divide,
    Show me how three are one and One is three!
How Christ to save all men was crucified,
    Yet I and mine are damned eternally.
Instruct me, Sage, why Virtue starves alone,
While falsehood step by step ascends the throne.

THE NEW EZEKIEL

What, can these dead bones live, whose sap is dried
    By twenty scorching centuries of wrong?
Is this the House of Israel, whose pride
    Is as a tale that's told, an ancient song?
Are these ignoble relics all that live
    Of psalmist, priest, and prophet? Can the breath
Of very heaven bid these bones revive,
    Open the grave and clothe the ribs of death?

Yea, Prophecy, the Lord hath said. Again
    Say to the wind, Come forth and breathe afresh,
Even that they may live upon these slain,
    And bone to bone shall leap, and flesh to flesh.
The Spirit is not dead, proclaim the word,
    Where lay dead bones, a host of armed men stand!
I ope your graves, my people, saith the Lord,
    And I shall place you living in your land.

A Matter of Centennial Interest
(1894–1994)

In mid-'63, while a burgeoning wickedness gripped the States, including a series of civil rights assassinations and the beginnings of our Vietnam misadventure, it happened that I completed my Ph.D. examinations and needed to choose my dissertation topic. For many good reasons I decided that this, the most significant scholarly commitment of my life, should focus on what had never before been an area of special attention for me: American poetry, from 1835 to 1900. I wanted a chance to deal in depth with manifestations of several past iniquities that paralleled those of my time, and with the responses to each egregious episode by the poets then active, altogether about 150 poets, who knew very well and claimed to follow the ancient role of Isaiah and Jeremiah as moral sentinels.

For over two years, as the ugliness at home and abroad deepened, I did heavy research on the war with Mexico, the pursuit of fugitive slaves, the mobbing of unpopular sects and parties, the mistreatment of Native Americans, and the war with Spain. These studies formed the body of my dissertation, submitted in 1966. My book based on that dissertation, *The Prophetic Tradition in American Poetry, 1835–1900*, appeared two years later.

But an additional chapter, planned from the outset and for which I undertook a considerable amount of research, had to be scuttled in the end because my professors felt the work was too ambitious and already too long. Because 1894 was the year on which I chose to base my explorations, I believe it would be especially fitting for my preliminary and submitted statements of intentions to be made available now, in the hope that some young scholar may wish to use them as guides toward expanded study.

I. Government as Capital's Agent in Crushing Unions

As in the preceding chapters I have isolated a particular ethical crisis from a more general problem. Labor's long struggle for improved conditions and union recognition had called forth general responses from several poets including Halleck, Bryant, Whittier, Lowell, Emerson, Melville, Holmes and Whitman. The more immediate context, however, is the state of affairs in 1894 which made it possible not only for federal, state, and local authorities to crush organized labor on behalf of capital, but to win vocal support for their actions from a substantial segment of liberal opinion.

News media transmitted and enlarged among the public the fears of the wealthy. Populist gains; the marches on Washington by Coxey's and other industrial "armies"; the stirrings of immigrant labor; strike ferocity in coal, textiles, etc.; the anarchist and socialist upsurge at home and abroad; bomb plots and scares — whether all or any of these were actually related, the press and the pulpit succeeded in relating them.

The assassination of France's President Carnot on June 24th coincided with the start of the Pullman boycott; by July 1st the U.S. government was able to turn the Carnot Memorial into an anti-strike meeting; Debs' union was identified as part of a world-wide bomb-throwers' conspiracy. *The Nation* suggested that Debs was insane; others were less kind: his incarceration scarcely satisfied them. Unable to destroy the strike, capital found its task taken over by a lifelong enemy of unionism, Richard Olney, Attorney General of the United States. The railway workers, facing army regiments rather than company deputies, were suddenly engaged in an insurrection. [In the margin of this paragraph my generally sympathetic mentor penciled his comment: "Details could here be cut."]

The significant poets who had supported labor in the past and might have reacted indignantly now, were dead. The socially alert poets who remained were apparently silent. And those antagonistic to labor, like Thomas B. Aldrich, were content to rage in their private correspondence. What were they doing and thinking in July 1894? How much of the situation could have been clear to them at once? (The Attorney General's records were withheld until 1897.) Would fear of the anarchist label, in a year of nationwide frenzy, be pertinent? Were Europe's key poets silent in similar strike situations? Had such issues been placed beyond limits as poetic material by the literary leaders of the '80s and '90s? The prevailing innocuousness of theme in verse would seem to indicate such a proscription.

But the pro-labor writers of 1894 need to be examined — if not often in their poems, yet in their public prose and private papers, reverberations of the Pullman monstrosity may be heard, through Bierce's tone of bitter disenchantment; Howells' and Garland's social protest; the humanitarianism of John Burroughs, Richard W. Gilder, Edward E. Hale, Thomas W. Higginson and Father Tabb; Joaquin Miller's Coxeyite utopianism. Not less significant for this study is the work of the new poets — Edwin Markham, E. A. Robinson, Stephen Crane, William V. Moody — "haters of the national optimism" who voiced a "stiffening of the conscience" — and Richard Hovey, who celebrated Brotherhood.

In the shadow of Olympus were the anonymous makers of strike songs, and the anti-strike rhymers. Labor poets, immigrant and native-born, contributed to English and foreign-language periodicals, largely socialist and anarchist; I will offer samples of their work (in translation, when necessary) and discuss their poetic stature.

II. Thwarting Labor's Efforts to Win Bargaining Rights

In this area of investigation especially, many major poets turned from verse to prose as a means of expressing their support of organized labor. The long struggle for improved conditions and union recognition had been noted by poets as far back as Bryant's 1836 right-to-strike editorial. Emerson's sympathy toward European labor (*English Traits*) and Whitman's 1850 "Resurgemus," honoring the fallen revolutionists of 1848, are directly opposed by Holmes' anti-proletarian "Astraea" of the same year. Whitman's position, even stronger in his 1856 lecture, "The Eighteenth Presidency," culminated in the "Tramp and Strike Questions" lecture of 1879, after the shooting down of workers by federal troops.

Melville's tale, "The Tartarus of Maids," had exposed factory misery, and *Clarel* (1876) noted labor's grievances. Lanier's "The Symphony" (1875) criticized capital's power, while Holmes' "How

Not to Settle It" (1877) took a typical swipe at the vanquished Communards of Paris. Lowell, returning from abroad in 1874, had produced several poems sharply critical of his homeland: "Tempora Mutantur," "World's Fair," etc. Ten years later, in a London address, "Democracy," he defended unionism and even advocated socialism. Whittier's "The Problem" also gave prophetic warning to capital.

Of many German-American poets active during the 1874–1877 crackdown on unions, I have selected verses by Hermann Ihnen and Gustav Lyser. Many poems and songs were also spawned by the great mine and railroad strikes: some unsigned, others by obscure poets (Jonathan Vickers, James Monaghan). Opposing these are the exuberant Centennial Odes, with their euphoric view of labor.

In 1886 several anarchist union men were hanged in Chicago — ostensibly for a bombing, but actually for their beliefs. Governor Altgeld later exonerated them, and they had won the sympathy of Howells and Whitman while on trial. Still, just as poets like Emma Lazarus ("Sic Semper Liberatoribus!") had found anarchism itself guilty of Alexander II's assassination in 1881, Whittier now suggested a similar verdict in the last lines of his "Bartholdi Statue," as did Lowell in a letter to Howells after the hanging.

Aside from W. C. Marshall's prompt, Whittier-like rebuke to Whittier for his renegacy, the boldest poetic response came from two young Jewish immigrants, David Edelshtat and Morris Rosenfeld. Voltairine De Cleyre wrote "Light Upon Waldheim," a lofty and moving elegy. Soon afterward came Bierce's "Invocation," with clear 1886 references. Well-known poets like Duganne and O'Reilly dealt tangentially with the event.

In 1892 a midnight onslaught on Homestead's strikers produced a few songs which have lasted, and several poems. Rosenfeld's fiery "Shoot the Beast!" is opposed by Aldrich's anti-immigrant "Unguarded Gates." The stirrings of that time were voiced most notably by three poets — but, again, only in their prose: Hamlin Garland's *A Spoil of Office* (1892), Joaquin Miller's *The Building of the City Beautiful* (1893), and William D. Howells' *A Traveler From Altruria* (1894).

I shall focus on the Debs-led Pullman boycott of 1894. Capital — raising the specter of a bewhiskered and bomb-wielding Anarchy — crushed organized labor by enlisting not only federal, state, and local authorities, but also a substantial segment of liberal opinion. Among noted poets only Eugene Field and James Whitcomb Riley spoke up for the incarcerated Debs. The specifically Pullman verse came from unknowns (Emory Boyd, Horace Durant, Elizabeth Johnson). But several impassioned and luminous poems were inspired by the 1894 turmoil: Bovshover's Yiddish "To Those in Power," Clark's "If Christ Should Come Today," and Mrs. Gilman's "To Labor." These were countered by a slashing attack on "the mob" in Santayana's "Odes: I."

My touchstone does not yield impressive poetic returns. Yet literary historians who insist, after reading Gilder's, Stoddard's, and Aldrich's bloodless stanzas, that all the poetry of the mid-'90s lacked moral bite, have failed either to consider or properly to interpret such verses — among many others — as Stephen Crane's "The Trees in the Garden Rained Flowers," William Vaughn Moody's "Until the Troubling of the Waters," Vida Scudder's "A Sign of the Son of Man," Upton Sinclair's "On a Steamship," and Ambrose Bierce's savage rhymes throughout *The Devil's Dictionary*.

With aestheticism and symbolism in power, European poetry could not then boast a greater ethical alertness than ours. By 1900 the Central Pacific R.R. felt moved to offer a big prize for a rebuttal to the revolutionary masterpiece, "The Man With the Hoe." The winner — among five thousand entries — was Cheney's "Man With a Hoe," a direct appeal for Markham to abandon his trouble-making role as the bard of labor!

* * * *

It saddens me all these years later that my 1894 chapter never came into being. At least I was able to include several of the poems in the final section of my 1972 anthology, *On Freedom's Side*. On those pages I demonstrated that some American poets have indeed decried the mistreatment of the poor. That I chose to represent three of the Yiddish sweatshop poets — Rosenfeld, Edelshtat and Bovshover — should serve as a clue to my intentions when submitting the above statements. There is no question in my mind that the poetry produced by these and others prior to 1894 illuminates the incendiary mood then building, and that the catastrophic events of 1894 had a profound effect on their new poetry.

Among my discoveries while examining the German-language labor press of the day was a stirring poem by Johannes Most which the Yiddish choirs of my childhood sang as a revolutionary Yiddish folksong, scarcely a syllable changed from the original. Nothing can better illustrate the multiculturalism of 1894.

Obviously, as in most topical situations, it is hard to find poems of genuine artistic as well as rhetorical power, but some of the material should certainly be known. In the *Locomotive Firemen's Magazine*, for example, I found these ringing lines by John Boyle O'Reilly, known today only for one delicate love lyric:

> Beware with your classes!
> Men are men, and a cry in the night is a fearful teacher;
> When it reaches the hearts of the masses,
> Then they need but a sword for a judge and a preacher.
> Take heed! for your juggernaut pushes hard;
> God holds the doom that the day completes;
> It will dawn like a fire when the track is barred
> By a barricade in the city streets.

And in Edwin Markham I ran across lines that express more than the yearning of 1894:

> He comes to make the long injustice right;
> Comes to push back the shadow of the night.
> The gray Tradition full of flint and flaw
> Comes to wipe out the insults to the soul,
> The insults of the Few against the Whole,
> The insults they make righteous with a law.

Arturo Giovannitti

Poems of Italian Content

A great deal of lip-service is paid to exploring fresh fields of research; but the hollowness of such rhetoric is demonstrated by the annual lists of studies published and papers presented, in which the same cluster of currently fashionable authors is examined and re-examined, while the ever-swelling ranks of writers assigned to oblivion remain overlooked.

If it is at great professional risk nowadays that one admits a lingering admiration for Carl Sandburg or Vachel Lindsay or Edna St. Vincent Millay, how much more indiscreet would it be to trumpet the virtues of their once equally respected contemporaries — James Oppenheim, Alfred Kreymborg and Maxwell Bodenheim — whose reputations were shoved over the hill fifty years ago; and how utterly suicidal — let alone presumptuous — it must seem to proclaim the worth of a poet who, after some early hoopla, has been among the buried names for over seventy years.

There are many ways to approach Arturo Giovannitti: as an immigrant poet, an Italo-American poet, a socialist-syndicalist labor poet, an evangelical poet, a war poet, a city poet, a love poet, a prophetic poet. A comparative study of his free verse, once widely popular, and his far more numerous traditional poems, unpraised and unanthologized, might prove valuable. Such questions deserve investigation as his apparent decline in creative power after the Russian Revolution, or the relationship between his poems and his stage works, his poems and his life, or the possibility that admiration of his work depends on sharing his passions and visions, or the great similarities and greater differences between him and Whitman, or the Italian poems collected in his last years.

But these approaches can matter only after Giovannitti's significance has been established, and this would require more than merely quoting the extraordinary comments of Helen Keller in 1914 or Louis Untermeyer in 1919:[1] tomorrow's researchers tend to be impressed only by today's musclemen of culture. Still, one must start somewhere. Perhaps the best preliminary focus would be on his poems of Italian content, though they represent a very small portion of his achievement in English. The lyric which closes *Wind Before Dawn*, a posthumous collection, honors his heritage; its title is from Dante: "*Tre Donne Interno All Cor Mi Son Venute*" — and its first line is: "Three women came about my heart..."[2] Dante's sound also reverberates in three longer poems composed of tercets (two of them on Italian subjects),[3] and six condensed sonnets in an effective new form comprising three tercets and a solitary tenth line rhyming with the eighth.[4] As a sustaining spirit, Dante also appears in a fine free-verse elegy for Flavio Venanzi.

Giovannitti's unabashed "worship of Italy," the Italy of his youth, is expressed in "Pagan Spring"[5] (*pagan* because he declares his allegiance frankly to the pre-Christian gods of Rome):

> How holy the mountains looked bowing before the tall clouds,
> How frightened the chaste young streams awaking to puberty;
> How wondrous the trees regathered in solemnly waiting
>   crowds,
> How patient the rivers still working full time for the wise old
>   sea.
>
> I saw the olives black-hooded, white cowled like old monks,
>   chanting
> The matins, exhorting the vaporing plains and the mist-blue
>   hills.
> I saw the feast garmented almonds scolding the orchards and
>   granting
> A nod to the rival gardens and a broad grin to the sills.

His roots show proudly in "March 1919" and "The Senate of the Dead."[6] Here the newly-slain Karl Liebknecht, Germany's beloved Spartacist leader, is introduced to a host of earlier martyrs:

> This one, barefooted and ragged, is Masaniello, who assembled
> the councils of the rabble in the fishmarket of Naples, and
> made the holy emperor tremble, and the pope forget his curses

and remember his prayers. He was murdered like you, from
   behind.
That hooded one there is Bruno, who sits between Prometheus
and Lucifer, the third lighter of the unextinguishable fire, who
blew out the candles of the temple that men might see the
   greater light of thought. He disappeared in his own incan-
   descence, burned alive.

More than a score of years later, in "Italia Speaks,"[7] an appeal for
America to rescue Italy from "the vampire of Berlin," the poet again
recites his heritage:

Where are you now, Jupiter, Apollo, Minerva, Mars, Neptune,
Lords of the Thunder and Lords of the Waters and the
Mountains? See what they have made of me!

Where are you my sons? Where are you, Mutius, Camillus,
   Manlius, Marius, Julius, Scipio? Where are you Garibaldi?
   Look what they have done with me! . . .

Where are my other stalwart sons, the knights of the high seas,
   the challengers of the fog, the lightning and the gales?
   Where are you Christopher Columbus, Giovanni da Veraz-
   zano, Giovanni Caboto, Sebastiano Caboto, Amerigo Ves-
   pucci? Where are you, America, my daughter?

In a pair of arresting sonnets — "To Eleanora Duse" and "To
Mussolini"[8] — the poet touches what is best and worst in contem-
porary Italy. To the beloved artist he says:

Madonna, you are old as the first tear
Of woe, you are as young as the last smile
Of hope, ever renascent . . . the somni-eyed cortege
Stops at your feet by the footlights and asks
What is art's meaning, mistress of your age,
And you breathe back: Wait till the curtain drops
Then come and look upon the darkened stage.

Characterizing the dictator as one "who tries/With truth and fails,
and then wins fame with lies," he declares: "No man is great who
does not find/A poet who will hail him as he is . . ." and concludes:

> Duce, where is your bard? In all mankind
> The only poem you inspired is this.

Later, in "Battle Hymn of the New Italy,"[9] Giovannitti decries his motherland's union with Hitler Germany, "the Beast-born." Although little is left of the old poet here but bombast, there is some historic interest; after all, how many Italian or Italo-American poets were saying such things in 1942?

> Rise, our Mother, in your regal
> Armor and your shackles break!
> Roars the Lion, screams the Eagle,
> Growls the Bear: O Italia, awake!
> Where they hoisted noose and sabre,
> Where the chains of shame they wrought,
> Raise your hand, Italian Labor,
> Lift your voice, Italian thought!

Far greater is the value, both historic and literary, of his earlier poems. "The Death of Flavio Venanzi"[10] elegizes on a vast scale a Dante-like young East Side socialist whose hearse was followed by thousands on "the noblest of all May Days — MCMXX":

> [Like Dante] Flavio also was tall and lean and a bit bent in the shoulders through a long contemplation of the deeps and the little things of the earth, ants and man and wiggling wisdoms;
> and he also was sharp-nosed like Dante, whom he knew well and with whom he had been discoursing every night intimately and pleasantly as they visited each other — about the bitter bread of exile and the ingratitude of the People and the barrenness of revenge save through the unappealable sentence of a song . . .
> He was frail as a whispered word and as light as a seed, but like these he carried with him upheavals and everlastingness. For he had been born in Rome, where all things are made for the eternities . . .
> . . . there were many books on the shelves, old and new and terrible and meek and loud and soft-spoken . . . But the book I picked at random was the "Little Flowers" of Saint

Francis, and the page I opened was the Canticle of the Sun,
the first poem written in our gentle tongue:
"Blessed be Thou, for our Sister, Mother Earth!
"Blessed be Thou, O Lord, for our corporeal Sister Death!"
And lo! at that moment the Nurse came in slowly, her head
    down,
mourning the lifelong failure of Man, announcing without
    words the Mighty Visitress. And there She was, the sweet
    Sister of our Body, the Lonely One, the Silent One, the
    Sleepless One, the Liege-Mistress of all our endeavors, the
    Completer of all our tasks, the One forever shunned and
    misunderstood. There She was on the threshold tall and pale
    and august and full of grace.... Then with her entered into
    the room the Evening and the Children, weeping.
On the morning of May Day we drove the body of Flavio
    Venanzi through the East Side, and many men and many
    women walked behind the hearse in silence, though all the
    voices of Springtime and Mankind were pealing mightily in
    their hearts an ancient psalm of anger and deliverance. We
    walked for ten minutes and we passed six mounted police
    patrols with guns and cudgels and heavy frowns, and thus
    did the turbid world of the non-living pay its last homage of
    fear and hatred to the sweet Tribune that was dead....

Nothing underscores better the titanic force of Giovannitti in those
years than "Time's End,"[11] a restrained, rather hackneyed terza rima
elegy written a generation later, defining the dream he shared with
his fellow anti-fascist leader Carlo Tresca, gunned down in January,
1943:

> Strong hands will grip
> Soft hands in freedom's pact and there will rise
> New orders with the rule of brethrenship.

Unique among the early poems, "A Meeting at Astoria Hall"[12]
provides a dimensional view of the poet as organizer for the Amal-
gamated Clothing Workers, and records how a "hall full of Italians
after four months of lockout" responded to the sudden appearance
of "twenty-seven old men in long black robes":

The hall chairman leaped up to me on the platform and panted: "These are the old Jewish tailors who were discharged first before the lockout. You know the story — 'We are business-men not a charitable institution — we can't have pensioners in our shops.' Better say a few words in English even if they do not understand everything. Please!"

And then I who had come with a message of defiance and scorn for everything that was not new and young and impudent, I was suddenly taken back to the years of my boyhood when I was told to honor age next to the memory of the great dead....

And I thought that they, the eternal fugitives from persecution and servitude, had been toiling at all the true labors of life for six thousand years....

Yes, and I realized with a pang in my heart that none of them had achieved anything save the knowledge of numberless calvaries and the iron will to go up their pathways....

So I spoke and I spoke with my mouth and my eyes and my fisted hands, with whatever clamors and aches in the depth of me, and I was not conscious of anything but the dull feeling that I might be hanged for the things I was saying.

Then a mighty roar leaped up from the hall and a dazzling light beat upon the swaying white beards and reverberated in the dim walls and I retreated to my silence, but they still sat serene and inviolate.

And behold! They were no longer the beggar at the gate, the wailers by the ramparts of Babylon, the pleaders for life and mercy.

For they will be sitting at their high noon in the front stalls of the first and ultimate senate of Mankind when the great dawn breaks and mantles the world!

It is easy to recognize the sweep of Whitman's vision and cadence in such lines; the great anti-Metternich poem "Europe. The 72d and 73d Years of These States" instantly comes to mind. As for the city of Giovannitti and his fellow immigrants, however, it bore little resemblance to Whitman's somewhat rosily muralled "Manahatta." In "New York and I"[13] the poet declares both his hate and love:

> I shall sing of ...
> The singers you starve, the wastrels you fill,
> The thieves and the strumpets you honor, the cowards you
>   acclaim
> And the saints and the heroes you kill.
>
> I shall sing of your slums where you bleed,
> Your machines, iron claws of your greed,
> And your jails, viscid coils of your mind ...
> The Street where you buy and resell
> Each day the whole world and mankind,
> Your foundations that reach down to hell
> And your towers that rend the typhoons ...
> And the glory of your nameless dead,
> And the bitterness of your bread,
> And the sword that shall hallow your hand,
> And the dawn that shall garland your head!

That pledge is fulfilled in "Malebolge: a Glimpse of Mulberry Street,"[14] which in twenty-eight *Inferno*-like tercets portrays the tenement world of 1915 as harrowingly as Jacob Riis did a decade earlier in his matchless photographs and as Michael Gold did a decade later in *Jews Without Money.*

> ... The desolate houses lean,
> Hell's innest barbicans, against the skies
> Along the tortuous moat of this latreen.
>
> Hark now unto the creaking of their carts,
> The calls of ear-ringed bawlers, and the sturdy
> Whistles of your policeman who imparts
>
> Your penalties to them; list to their wordy
> Quarrels and bargains, and above the din
> The plaint of the sad-throated hurdy-gurdy.
>
> Smell the foul wind of woe that blows within
> Their cells, whence even the daylight recoils
> At the polluting stenches of their sin ...

> The crusty lips of babes that gasp for breath
> Torment them so, that tho' be great their guilt,
> So bitter is their doom that less is death.
>
> Mulberry Street is this. The domes they built
> Are not here. Despot! Here is where they mold
> And shall decay until their last seed wilt.
>
> Pursuing their mad dreams through ways untold,
> They spread through all your lands and all your seas,
> Eating black bread and lavishing bright gold . . .
>
> All that they made they never thought it good,
> All that they loved, they never could revere,
> All that they wished they never understood.
>
> Slothful and sleepless, lustful and austere,
> Gloried by death, made deathless by rebirth,
> The progeny of Rome, Despot, rots here!

Still, like Sandburg in *The People, Yes* twenty years later, Giovannitti prophesies that America will become what the immigrants dreamed. "Born of their indestructible desire/And nurtured with the bitter milk of wrong," the Hound of revolt

> Will lift them to their heritage of joy.
> He will heal all their wounds and blot their scars,
> And with red tongues of wrath he will destroy
>
> You, Despot, and the trophies of your wars,
> And lift the young Republic's head above
> The diadem of her reconquered stars!

Langston Hughes reaffirms this very vision in "Let America Be America Again," a much-anthologized and widely quoted poem.[15] One need merely place the two pieces side by side to appreciate the muscularity and lyric thrust of the unjustly neglected "Mulberry Street."

This study has not touched upon the poet's three best-known pieces — "The Walker," 1912, "The Cage," 1913, and "When the Cock Crows," 1917 — perhaps the crowning literary achievements of the I.W.W. movement.[16] Indeed, not a single line has been quoted from the volume on which his brief fame rested, *Arrows in the Gale*, 1914, which Helen Keller graced with a stirring introduction.[17] If nothing else, this fact should disprove the charge in *Italian-American Authors and Their Contribution to American Literature* that "After having given such a brilliant exhibition of his poetic ability with *Arrows in the Gale*, Arturo Giovannitti seems to be content to rest on his laurels."[18]

Even within the Italianism that is only a minor aspect of his work, the above-quoted passages give ample evidence of this poet's range in theme, feeling, and craft. Finally, although the focus here has not been on Giovannitti the Prophet, one cannot help but feel sweeping through most of these excerpts the great wind of prophecy — that brand of song which, anathematized by the high priests of 20th century American criticism, may yet be rediscovered with delight by a generation weary of sterile formalism and cerebral gymnastics, when the pendulum swings again.

Appendix I: Correspondence With the Poet's Son

While preparing this study, the writer sent Giovannitti's son Len a series of questions. Those questions, and his answers, follow.

1) Did your father ever acknowledge, in writing or in conversation, any stylistic indebtedness to a: the King James Bible, b: Blake's prophetic books, c: Whitman, d: Ernest Crosby,[19] e: such contemporary brother-socialists as Oppenheim and Sandburg?

My father never, in writing or conversation, admitted stylistic indebtedness to the sources you mention. However, he was an avid reader of the King James' Bible, much of William Blake, and probably all of Walt Whitman.[20] In my opinion, he was most influenced by Whitman. He was never greatly taken with the work of contemporary brother Socialists, with only rare exceptions.

2) Is it true, as the 1966 Mexican pamphlet claims, that "until his death ... he wrote a strange and powerful poetry"?[21] If so, has it remained in manuscript, or is it to be found in *Quando Canta Il Gallo*?

The claim, in the Mexican pamphlet, is invalid. He wrote very little poetry from about 1932 until his death in 1959. He left only fragments of work in manuscript and nothing of significance was left out of the *Collected Poems* in English or *Quando Canta Il Gallo*.

3) If not, then is it true that the Italian poems were written simultaneously with the English, during the decade 1912–1922 mostly, or did he return to Italian after more or less terminating his career as an English language poet, which the *Collected Poems* seems to indicate (and if so, why)?

The Italian poems were not written simultaneously with the English. His earliest poetry was written in English; collected in a volume, *Arrows in the Gale;* and published in 1914. After that book, he continued to write extensively in English and to a lesser extent in Italian, partly because he received more attention for his English poems and many offers requesting contributions to major literary magazines. It was in the late '20s and early '30s when my father began writing extensively in Italian, both in poetry and prose, primarily for a working-class audience. During that period, he headed the Italian Labor Education Council,* which produced a good deal of educational material for trade unionists, especially members of the Amalgamated Clothing Workers of America and the International Ladies' Garment Workers' Union. Aside from original work, my father translated important American historical documents into Italian, including the Declaration of Independence.

4) Some biographical sketches claim that he was among the socialists who became pro-war after "the Kaiser's atrocities";[22] if so, were there many war poems excluded from *Collected Poems?* That volume slants heavily against World War I.

My father certainly wanted the Kaiser's Germany to be defeated in World War I, but he never ceased to believe that it was a capitalistic war for the benefit of capitalism, and there are no war poems excluded from his collected poetry. The volume does slant heavily against World War I because it completely reflects his beliefs.

5) Are there any other politically or artistically meaningful omissions from that volume?

The answer to this question is, simply, "no."[23]

---

*I am not sure of the exact title of this organization.

6) I surmise, on the basis of the book, that your father produced very little in English after his great burst of poetry celebrating the Russian Revolution,[24] and that the few poems of World War II lack the earlier lyric fire; if so, is there a connection between his shifting appraisal of that Revolution — perhaps a shift in his political outlook altogether — and the loss of his impulse toward poetry (at least in English)?

There was no shift in my father's outlook following the Russian Revolution. The chief reason he produced very little in English or Italian, except what was necessary for his trade union work, after 1928 was because he was an alcoholic from then until about ten years before his death. In those last ten years of his life, his interests were as great and his mind as keen as ever, but he did not have the physical strength for sustained work.[25]

7) At what point did he stop being a field-organizer, in direct daily contact with workers? Can that have been a factor in the ebbing of his poetic activity (assuming that there was such an ebbing)?

He stopped being a Field Organizer in the early '30s and, though he still addressed labor mass meetings (he was considered a brilliant orator), he was no longer active in direct contact with the workers by the end of World War II. Of course, during the war, his voice was among the most eloquent against the forces of Fascism and Nazism. From the end of the war until his death, he withdrew from active participation in the labor movement and led a quiet life, mostly in the country.

8) Since I don't read Italian, I wonder if you can tell me whether the Italian poems, in form and content, parallel the English or are significantly different.

My father's poetry, in Italian, did parallel the English in form and content.

9) What was the fate of his stage-works: Were they performed? reviewed? published? How closely do they relate, in form and content, to the poetry? Do they contain any Italian or Italo-American elements?

His plays, almost solely in Italian, were performed chiefly by amateur labor groups. One or two of his short plays, in Italian, were published in obscure labor publications, long out of print and, to my knowledge, not available even in the main New York Public Library, which has quite a large body of his work.[26]

10) There are hints in the poetry of a tension between his political and personal selves. Did such a tension manifest itself in his life, in ways that ultimately affected him as a poet?

During the active period of his life as a writer, this does not appear to have been the case but, had he continued to write prodigiously after 1928, the tensions of his life might well have been reflected in his work.

11) Do you remember how he felt about the upsurge of proletarian poetry in the Thirties? Was he on friendly terms with "the new wave" who wrote for the *Masses*, *Dynamo*, etc.? Did he still, in fact, consider himself a proletarian poet during that decade?

My father maintained his interest in proletarian poetry in the '30s but, by then, he was no longer personally involved with leftist writers.

12) From internal evidence I am able to date most of the poems quoted in my essay (approximately). But I'd appreciate corroboration and help on a few:

a) The sonnets to Duse and Mussolini — around 1922–1923? (the Mussolini sonnet ignores D'Annunzio; did your father ever speak of him either as poet or political activist on behalf of Il Duce?)

I can't place the dates of the sonnets to Duse and Mussolini but my guess is that the Mussolini sonnet was probably at least two or three years after 1923. As for D'Annunzio, when my father spoke of him, it was always with condemnation and contempt for embracing Fascism.

b) "A Meeting at Astoria Hall" — unsure; I wish I could pinpoint this incident and look it up in the newspapers of the day; my guess, from the vigor of the lines and your father's role as portrayed here, is that it took place around 1920.

Your guess is undoubtedly more accurate than any I might suggest. In these areas, your research is better than my recollections.

NOTES

1. "It is epical; epochal. As an art-work, it is one of the most remarkable things our literature can boast. But it is something beyond that. It is a poetic epitome of a creed . . . I do not think that the growth of Socialism has produced . . . a more noble or inspired piece of literature." Louis Untermeyer, *The New Era in American Poetry* (New York: Henry Holt, 1919) 190-91.

2. *The Collected Poems of Arturo Giovannitti* (Chicago: E. Clemente & Sons, 1962) 131.

3. *Ibid.*, "At the Prayer Meeting," pp. 39-41; "Malebolge: Mulberry Street," pp. 78-81; "Time's End," pp. 130-31.

4. *Ibid.*, "Anniversary I," "Anniversary II," "Anniversary IV," "Anniversary V," "Anniversary VI," pp. 46-49, and "You Sing No Longer," p. 115.

5. *Ibid.*, pp. 36-38.

6. *Ibid.*, pp. 65-68, 50-57. These two poems are parallel in many ways. "March 1919," from which no lines are quoted, is done in iambic tetrameter and alternating rhyme. The rhyme pattern is shattered here and there as a result of someone's revisions: i.e., wrong/throng becomes wrong/mob; earth/worth becomes earth/freedom; noose/let loose becomes noose/unleash.

7. *Ibid.*, pp. 74-76.

8. *Ibid.*, pp. 64, 72.

9. *Ibid.*, p. 78.

10. *Ibid.*, pp. 102-09.

11. *Ibid.*, pp. 130-31.

12. *Ibid.*, pp. 82-84.

13. *Ibid.*, pp. 5-8.

14. *Ibid.*, pp. 78-81. The subtitle given here is as originally published in *Current Opinion* (Dec. 1915) 430-31. The title there was "Malabolgia," probably a dialect version of the word later abandoned.

15. I.e., *The Poetry of the Negro* (New York: Doubleday, 1949) 106-08.

16. *Collected Poems*, pp. 147-52, 206-12, 24-30. There is an egregious misprint on p. 29 — "Names" instead of "manes" — which is subsequently mistranslated into Spanish by Agusti Bartra, who followed this edition closely.

17. She wisely points out that "The laws of poetic beauty and power, not one's beliefs about the economic world, determine the excellence of his work." She links him with Homer, Virgil, Dante, Shakespeare, Shelley, and Isaiah. She dares, at the very height of the Chicago-based poetry renaissance, to declare him "a better poet than has come out of the privileged classes of America in our day." With astonishing insight, before he had written a single poem of Italian content, she recognized that "Behind Arturo Giovannitti stand the poets, prophets, wise men and patriots of Italy. Into him have been poured the fire and courage of a proud, energetic people."

18. Olga Peragallo, ed. by Anita Peragallo (New York: S. F. Vanni, 1949) 126. The inaccuracies in this well-intentioned sketch (pp. 124-28) include the creation of a new critic, Louis Kreymborg, blending Alfred Kreymborg and Louis Untermeyer. All the opinions she offers are a rehash of those two anthologists. Her

"bibliography" lists various poems under the heading "Short Stories." She also creates the false impression that Giovannitti is well-anthologized.

19. At the moment of Giovannitti's arrival in New York and entrance into socialist activity, Crosby's texts were included in the rebel songbooks, and his spectacular assaults on the war with Spain were deservedly well-known, especially a 1902 volume, *Swords and Ploughshares*. The visionary sweep of his long, denunciatory verse paragraphs immediately call Giovannitti to mind.

20. In response to Len Giovannitti's request for anything this author had written about his father, excerpts of several essays were sent. Among them was this sentence from "A Mighty Charm," *West Hills Review*, I (1979) 9: "Early in the new century Whitman's distinguished heirs included Arturo Giovannitti and James Oppenheim." The author added: "It is clear that I stand with you on the question of Whitman, unlike Untermeyer (*The New Era*, p. 189) who characterized your father's work as 'Utterly unlike Whitman's in structure (and Whitman's influence on Giovannitti is strangely small) . . .' What amazes me is the strength at the core of your father's voice, which made it possible for him to absorb completely so compelling a model as Whitman without surrendering one iota of his uniqueness."

21. *Poems/Poemas* (Mexico City: *el corno emplumado*, 1966) 70. This is a bilingual edition. Of the nine poems translated into Spanish by Agusti Bartra, seven are from *Wind Before Dawn*; this represents a radical departure from earlier approaches, which emphasize his first book. "The Walker" and "The Cage," predictably, are his choices from the 1914 volume.

22. In *The New Era in American Poetry*, pp. 195–96, Untermeyer declares: "Giovannitti was an impatient advocate of war against Germany long before his fellow-liberals were inflamed at the exposure of the Junkers' dishonor and the crime of Brest-Litovsk." On precisely this basis he calls the poet a "patriot." Stanley Kunitz echoes and embellishes Untermeyer on p. 537 of his presumably definitive *20th Century Authors*. What Untermeyer seems to be doing is defending his own aboutface on the war, along with many others in the previously internationalist ranks, so soon after the publication of his 1917 collection *These Times* (New York: Henry Holt), with its anti-war poems typified by "To a War Poet," pp. 135–38. It is puzzling that he could utterly ignore Giovannitti's greatest poem, "When the Cock Crows," produced in 1917 for Frank Little, an I.W.W. leader lynched for opposing America's entry into the war.

23. It would be worth examining such poems as "Revolution," in *Survey* (June 24, 1916) 335, "War Anthem of Labor," *Ibid.* (Sept. 16, 1916) 605, and "Lance of Max Eastman," in *Dial* (Feb. 8, 1919) 146. None of these appear to be in the *Collected Poems*.

24. See Appendix II: A Selection of Giovannitti's Poems. In "Dixi et Salvavi Animam Meam" he asks for this inscription on his tablet:

> . . . He did no thing but dream and boast,
> But when Russia arose he sang and wept
> And thereby saved his soul and won this stone.

In his 1961 introduction to the *Collected Poems*, Norman Thomas writes: "The Russian revolution which Giovannitti hymned and the violence which he extolled as the holy violence of release from bondage have contributed so mightily to this continuing crisis of mankind [the cold war] that it is hard to remember our earlier hopes or, perhaps, to be fair to some aspects of Russian achievement" (p. ix).

25. Yet Norman Thomas was permitted to give the opposite impression in his introduction: "Throughout the fifties he was bedridden by paralysis of the legs but continued to write despite this great hardship" (*Ibid.*, p. viii). What he did do was see to the publication of his Italian poems in 1957.

26. The 1949 Peragallo sketch, discussed above, concludes with the wild invention that "some of" his plays "had a fair amount of success on Broadway." Here, offered with some trepidation, is her listing of his dramatic works: "PLAYS: *Deliverance* — A play in one act, translated from the French of Rachilde, in *The Masses*, 1916; IN ITALIAN: *Come Era nel Principio; Il Rivale di Dio; L'Alfa e l'Omega; La Lanterna Verde.*"

Appendix II: A Selection of Giovannitti's Poems

POEMS OF ITALIAN CONTENT OR SPIRIT

Pagan Spring
To Eleonora Duse
To Helen Keller
March 1919 — excerpts
To Mussolini
Italia Speaks
Battle Hymn of the New Italy
Time's End
"*Tre Donne Interno All Cor Mi Son Venute*" (Dante)

SIX CONDENSED SONNETS

Anniversary I
Anniversary II
Anniversary IV
Anniversary V
Anniversary VI
You Sing No Longer

POEMS OF THE RUSSIAN REVOLUTION

When the Great Day Came
By the Kremlin Wall
On Lenin's Fiftieth Birthday
The Last Frontier
To Maria Spiridonova
John Reed
Moscow 1921

POEMS OF ITALIAN CONTENT OR SPIRIT

PAGAN SPRING

Beloved, Mid-March is here again, the day I have saved for my
    gods
(I know that one day they'll return), and for the confession of
    me
Before all the things that are humble: the flowers, the waters,
    the clouds
And for the praise of springtime and the worship of Italy.

For tho' I have given America a whole youth of hours and
    days,
And tho' I have all but forgotten the spell and the lore of my
    land,
This day my heart, a red eagle sated with lights and big preys,
Trembles like a young fledgling caught in the warmth of her
    hand.

And what if this song is disloyal to other songs that I sing?
What if I leave my new comrades one day for my ancient for-
    bears?
Beloved, once in the year it is a permissible thing
To grow insane with the dreams of our unlived yesteryears.

And so I arose with the dawn, as by the sacred old rite

And watched for the rooks that the cock crows out of the blue
      glen,
And when the first lark went up, I bowed like the acolite
And after each pause in their singing I humbly answered amen.

I went to the source by the hill to drink the earth-milk in the
      hollow
Of my cupped hands, and I washed the sleep off my eyes with
      the dew,
I turned down my quiver and each arrow became a wild swal-
      low
And when the yearling colts neighed I dashed with them to
      meet you.

How holy the mountains looked bowing before the tall clouds;
How frightened the chaste young streams awaking to
      puberty;
How wondrous the trees regathered in solemnly waiting
      crowds;
How patient the rivers still working full time for the wise old
      sea.

I saw the olives black-hooded, white-cowled like old monks,
      chanting
The matins, exhorting the vaporing plains and mist-blue hills.
I saw the feast garmented almonds scolding the orchards and
      granting
A nod to the rival gardens and a broad grin to the sills.

I heard again the old belfry awakening the flock of red roofs
To smoke and sparks, and the rattle of buckets and chains in
      the wells;
I heard the dogs yawning, the clanking of harness, the stamping
      of hoofs
And the smith's hammer resuming its quarrelsome brawl with
      the bells.

I heard the wind rustle through the ever-awake cypresses
And through the bays ever-dreaming, and over the palaces —
      and

Holding at once its chilled breath and hushing with sudden dis-
    tress
As it passed over the tombs with wings folded over its head.

I saw him raise up the meadows like mighty hosts in swift
    marches,
Soothe the stone faces of heroes and heal the wounds and the
    scars
Of broken statues, and ruins of temples and bridges and arches
Enbalmed with pollens and mosses and dust of the fallen stars.

TO ELEONORA DUSE

Madonna you are old as the first tear
Of woe, you are as young as the last smile
Of hope, ever renascent like the wile
Of love, self-raising the deadly spear

Of hatred, seeress, mistress messenger
Of hate and pity, passion, deadly guile,
Behold the ghostly pageant, up the aisle
Marshalled and led by Aeschylus and Shakespeare.

In masks, in rags, in ermine and in stocks
Painted bewigged, the somni-eyed cortege
Stops at your feet by the footlights and asks

What is art's meaning, mistress of your age,
And you breathe back: Wait till the curtain drops
Then come and look upon the darkened stage.

TO HELEN KELLER

On a youthful picture of Helen Keller
and her teacher Ann Sullivan Macy
framed with a laurel wreath

Madonna from whose eyes the world's tears flow,
When I behold you with your goddess-child

Resting her head against your undefiled
Maternal breast I turn mine eyes, and lo!

Along a flowered lane of Florence go
Beatrice and Laura, while among the tiled
Slim-pillared porticos, appeased and mild,
The sun-seared eyes of Alighieri glow.

I think then surely once this picture fell
From a cathedral vault while heaven bound
Flew up from it the babes of Raphael.

Till Benvenuto, seeking God's last grace,
Picked it and framed it with the wreath that bound
The lost head of the Nike of Samothrace.

MARCH 1919
(excerpts)

Holah! Awake! The horns, the drums
Are still, the war dogs crouch and snore,
But peace, the tyrants' harlot comes
Again atinseling with gore,
And from her ancient bag of tricks
Pulls out again the same foul hoard
The flag, the crown, the crucifix
The knout, the shackles and the sword . . .

. . . Look, on from Italy they press
The tribunes of the common herd,
The Gracchi and the Brutuses
The thought, the law, the ax, the sword,
And Masaniello, ragged, unshod
Who made the mob his justicer,
And Bruno, next to Lucifer,
The second enemy of God.

TO MUSSOLINI

A man may lose his soul for just one day
Of splendor and be still accounted wise,
Or he may waste his life in a disguise
Like kings and priests and jesters, and still may

Be saved and held a hero if the play
Is all he knew. But what of him who tries
With truth and fails, and then wins fame with lies?
How shall he know what history will say?

By this: No man is great who does not find
A poet who will hail him as he is
With an almighty song that will unbind

Through his exploits eternal silences.
Duce, where is your bard? In all mankind
The only poem you inspired is this.

ITALIA SPEAKS

Almighty God of the universe and ye Gods of my lands and my
seas, behold what they have done with me!

Where are you now, Jupiter, Apollo, Minerva, Mars, Neptune,
Lords of the Thunder and Lords of the Waters and the Moun-
tains? See what they have made of me!

Where are you my sons? Where are you, Mutius, Camillus,
Manlius, Marius, Julius, Scipio? Where are you Garibaldi? Look
what they have done with me!

They have struck me between my eyes and on my breasts with
spiked fists; they have weighted me down with chains, me, who
was ever ready to set the whole world free!

I am reduced to rags and tatters and filthy shreds, I who had
always worn the armor of the warrior, the mantle of the priest
and the robe of the lawgiver!

Who has made of me a scullion to the vampire of Berlin, of me, of me, an empress, a goddess, a mother of mankind?

Who had made of me the Cinderella of Nations, the starveling waif of the world?

I was the parent of fruits and grains — my chariots dashed all over the earth, not to hurt or subdue, but to teach men how to tame horses and drive plows, how to crush olives and grapes into oil and wine, how to weave cloth and how to read and write and think.

I laid roads, I raised aqueducts, I builded cities throughout Europe, I won and gave out empires and gave the world the first universal language.

Three time I arose from the dead, I did it alone, by myself, though I never really died. But always poets and troubadours came from all parts of the world to sit at my feet and to rest their heads on my knees — singing my praise and my glory in all the tongues of man — and artists came to paint my face only to be dazzled and awed by its splendor and always ended by painting my feet. And to me came the first Apostole of Jesus and reared his Temple in Rome.

Only a little more than a century ago, came Goethe to weep over my hands his Roman elegies, then came Heine, then Byron, Shelley, Keats, Browning, God, how many! To sing of me and to me, and to die and be buried in my bosom like my own, my very own.

Then came my grandchildren from America — the singers from across the Ocean Sea — Whittier, who smote down slavery and Lowell who buried it, and Longfellow who came to kiss Dante's brow on a slab of cold marble ...

Then, then my poor children went across the main in search of bread and honest toil, expecting new and greater sorrows, millions of them, millions of them and you, America, received and sheltered and fed them, and they were true to your motherliness and your pity.

And now, after compelling us to declare war on Greece, my mother, and France, my first born, the two monsters have compelled me to declare war against you, America, my youngest child, my fairest one!

Where are my other stalwart sons, the knights of the high seas, the challengers of the fog, the lightning and gales? Where are you Christopher Columbus, Giovanni da Verazzano, Giovanni Caboto, Sebastiano Caboto, Amerigo Vespucci? Where are you, America, my daughter?

The twin ogres in black and brown have polluted my gardens and befouled my palaces and besmirched my triumphal arches and my monuments, but they cannot scar my face nor shame me.

I am the purest essence of the earth. They can bludgeon me but they cannot defile me. I am forever young because I am eternal and I am intarnishably beautiful, because I am Art and Poetry and Music and sunlight.

My daughter, America, come to my rescue! Stab the one assassin, the renegade, to the heart and cleave in twain the other assassin of the North with your mighty broadsword and let him fall into two shadows into the earth, one to the East and one to the West, forevermore, forevermore, world without end.

BATTLE HYMN OF THE NEW ITALY

Freedom comes! Arise and greet her
Mine Italia fair and great!
From the wounded shrine of Peter
Where you crouch and weep and wait,
From your ruins your blood hallows,
From your desecrated graves,
From the dungeons, from the gallows
Rouse the legions of your slaves.

Toil-bound, bent with black disasters,
Hunger-mad to feed the Huns,
You gave mansions to your masters
And foul hovels to your sons;
Aye, through ages half forgotten
Ever wandering from your goal,
You the Empress God-begotten
To the Beast-born bowed your soul.

Rise, our Mother, in your regal
Armor and your shackles break!
Roars the Lion, screams the Eagle
Growls the Bear: O Italia, awake!
Where they hoisted noose and sabre,
Where the chains of shame they wrought,
Raise your hand, Italian Labor,
Lift your voice, Italian thought!

Rise and break into their revels
Flashing lightning from your eyes,
Hurl your hosts of famished devils
In their drunken paradise,
Till the outcast, till the lowly
Shall their bloody altars blast
And the damned shall be made holy
And the first shall be the last!

TIME'S END

To my martyred Brother, Carlo Tresca,
who dreamed thus with me

Thus shall it be. When after this long night
The Rebel Fiend at last clasps hands with God,
And his black wings become great fans of light;

When the last tyrant has been slain and trod
Into the loam with the last cursing priest,

And every liar lies in his foul blood —

Judge, soldier, legislator, journalist —
Life shall then burst into a gale of fire
And cleanse Man from the taint of saint and beast.

Beauty rewed at last to man's desire
Will make all laws her handmaids and will strip
Them naked of all weapons and attire

Like lovers and athletes. Strong hands will grip
Soft hands in freedom's pact and there will rise
New Orders with the rule of brethrenship.

Then will the meek stand girt with boundless ties
Of strength, and strength will boast a humbler name,
Then power will be a servant in disguise,

And pride will be the better side of shame;
Then art and thought will take the place of strife
And only toil will wear the wreath of fame.

Then shall it be. For should this prove less rife
A reaping of the gifts you promised me,
You whom I worshiped as the breath of life,

Had been its foulest curse, O Poetry!

"*Tre Donne Intorno All Cor
Mi Son Venute*" — DANTE

Three women came about my heart
As I leaped forth to live, to dare;
One gave me opulence, one art,
One taught me never to despair.

The first was she whose vast empires
A lustless flash of love unrolled,
The chastest flame of all my fires,
My unseduced sweetheart, Revolt.

The second one brought me no thing
Though she was dowered regally,
But when I wept she bade me sing,
My barren mistress, Poetry.

Then she, the third, who linked her name
Forever to my fruitless life,
The only claimant to my fame,
My lady Death, my pregnant wife.

SIX CONDENSED SONNETS

ANNIVERSARY I

Along the flocks of clouds that browse the firs
The moon goes like a mystic grail of light,
Between the bowed heads of the worshippers.

The branches of the oaks swing with a flight
Of censers and the poplars sing a psalm
Of ancient glory to the holy night.

Peace lies upon our roof, and in my palm
Your hand unclasped lies restful and secure,
And everything is strong and white and calm,

For we are still in love and are still poor.

ANNIVERSARY II

Three years we gnawed the bitter bread of war,
And now that peace is back from its vain quest,
The same mute beggar saints crowd up our door.

Come, Father Cold, sit by our hearth and rest;
Here, Sister Sickness, lie down on our bed;
Old Brother Hunger, be our honored guest.

Tomorrow all around the world shall spread
The tables of our feast, after this wake.
Tonight let us sit up and mourn our dead

For Russia and John Reed and Jesus' sake.

ANNIVERSARY IV

When dusk prolongs the agony of light
On the bowed hills, and prostrate shadows creep
Up the pavillioned stairway of the night;

When nothing is awake or dares to sleep
For fear of death, save love that broods and stares,
And clouds hold back their rain, and you can't weep;

If I but catch your eyes and unawares
Your lips twitch with the sobs of our lost years,
Your smile then opens like the book of prayers

In which my mother kept her secret tears.

ANNIVERSARY V

Three times blared forth the clarion of the sun,
His stallions neighed and trampled on the roofs
His crimson mantle as he galloped on.

Upon the lawn mad March had left new proofs
Of his most ancient sorcery, for there lay
Amidst the tracks of faun and centaur hoofs

The spoor of a new man on a new way.
And lo! across the cannon smoke that arched
The dawn, loaded with gifts for the new day,

Springtime and love and revolution marched.

ANNIVERSARY VI

The flag says to the wind amidst the green
Of oaks and beeches as the curious sky
Leans down to listen: "What is there between

You and me, despot, that I droop and fly
At every whim of your mad heart?" And he
Who never answers save with a deep sigh:

"There are the ancient lore and destiny
Of tides and clouds that have obeyed my breath
Long ere you came and made the law." — Thus be

With you, love, who came after song and death.

YOU SING NO LONGER

You sing no longer now at your machine
As you mend faded rags and faded days,
Nor do you seek the sunlit spot between

Your flowerless sill and my untilled bookcase.
You sew and sigh, and as you snap the thread
You seem to fear to break the wonted ways

Of our joined thoughts. And yet love is not dead,
Nor any of its pledges is defiled,
For we still sleep together in one bed

And in six months we'll have another child.

POEMS OF THE RUSSIAN REVOLUTION

WHEN THE GREAT DAY CAME

On the Anniversary of the Russian Revolution

In the beginning was the Thought, and the Thought was with Man, and the Thought was Man.

The same was in the beginning, before there was either god or law or the promise of things to be;

And life was the shadow of Man cast upon the land and the water by the light of Thought;

And death the defeated desire to lift that shadow onto the stars.

Now all the great beginnings engender two things, one male and one female, and so with Thought, which begat two things, and one was the Deed, which was male, and one the Ideal which was female.

And the Deed dwelled alone with himself and grew fierce and mighty and invincible, save by life which is multitude,

And the Ideal went forth to all things and grew weaker as it expanded, and easy to conquer, save by death which is solitude,

And the Deed became a sword, and the Ideal became a cross,

And lo! there was strife between them, and the Deed pre-vailed always, until the prophecy was fulfilled.

Now this was the prophecy which was heard rising out of the tumult and wailing of nations, out of the roar of the split-ting chaos,

Saying: When she who is twirling the spindle and swaying the loom shall go forth into the fields and goad the oxen and push the plow in the furrow;

And she who is washing the wounds of the warriors with the salve of her silent tears, shall seize a sword and wield it like a man,

Then will the great day come.

And when he who rides the earth astride his black stallion shall dismount by the well and bemoan the hardness of the road;

And he who now gores the heifers and hacks the fruit trees
in bloom shall seek the peace of his fury and knit by the hearth;
And he who warms his hairy hands in the entrails of his foe
shall croon a lullaby and rock a cradle at dusk,
Then will the Spokesman return, then the Ideal will tri-
umph and the Deed become her manservant forever,
Then will the great day come.

And lo! as the prophecy spake, so it came to pass, after a
million years, after a thousand doctrines, after a hundred gods,
Yes, even after the great flood of blood, in the least of all
nations, as it was foretold.
For the man who measured the earth by the length of his
knout is fallen from his chariot and babbles a prayer in the
dust,
And his crown which outshone the sun now lies on the
floor of the earth, a toy for the peasant's child,
·And his charger which trampled the nations is now har-
nessed onto a dungcart,
And his mastiff which tore the flesh of the saints now leads
the steps of a blind beggar;
And the hut of the hermit is now too large for him who
held a province too small for his kennels,
And a loaf of black bread is dearer to him now than a moun-
tain of gold;
For the People have got together,
For the People have got together and have risen,
For the People have got together and shattered his throne!

And behold! The woman hath risen and rent her garment of
mourning and she hath shaken the dust from her knees and
vested the armour,
She hath broken her distaff and made a spear, she hath torn
the bandage from her wounds and made a red pennant in the
fray,
She hath blown out the lamps of the temple and kindled a
fire on the hill and set a torch by the sea;
And her mouth which was stuffed with ashes and prayers
now shouts fierce orders to the storm.

Behold! Her hands have gathered in sheaves the white
arrows of the thunder
And she sits no longer on the threshold dreading the return
of her sons,
No longer she prays in the night for the peace of the dead,
nor does she rise in the dark to propitiate the cruel daybreak
with her brow on the hearthstone.
But she stands rigid and naked, most dreadful and beauteous
to behold,
In the noonday of the world, upon the ramparts of time,
Calling, calling, calling,
Calling to the east and the west, calling to the north and the
south,
Calling to the white man and the yellow man and the black
man with the wild shouts of her mouth
To rise and stand up together,
To rise and stand up together against nature and destiny,
To rise and stand up together in one holy fraternity,
To rise and conquer the earth
With labor and love and mirth,
One race, one tongue, one birth,
One dream of eternity.

BY THE KREMLIN WALL

At the foot of this wall
Which for five centuries cast the shadow and the terror of
    the Cross
Over one hundred million men
Lies the Envoy of the First Republic to the First Commune.
He arrived here in the fullness of time
To see the fulfillment of the last pledge of Liberty,
And he bore witness of its truth even unto the silence of
    this earth.
He died of hunger and passion at the age of Jesus
And by this grave he recorded another of your glories,
O Youth! O Romance!

Here,
Through the hacking of four boards of red pine
And the digging of a seven-foot furrow,
The axe of Abraham Lincoln
Met at last the spade of Leo Tolstoi;
And by the eternal spark struck by their united steel
The Russian Soviet Republic
Forgave and blessed the Workers of America
Burying with her own Heroes,
John Reed.

ON LENIN'S FIFTIETH BIRTHDAY

Victory, lightning-faced, flame-winged, has come
Just on the day it was told by your prophets and seers,
The harbingers of your great day, the builders of your
    highway,
The blazers of your world-trails!
Holah; ye the axmen of truth, blasters of lies and wrongs,
Torch-bearers of the sun, incendiaries, petroleurs,
Marshallers of the storms, thinkers and pioneers,
Hurlers of proclamations, bomb-throwers of song,
Raisers of mobs and altars, knights of the mad crusade,
Arise! Break from your chains, burst through your jails.
Tear through the noose of the gibbets — the day of days
    has come!
For lo! the Red Army has broken through the blockade,
And Russia that spoke with the Bible, now speaks through
    the cannonade
And her spokesmen that were in the dungeon are now on
    the barricade
In Berlin and Dublin and Rome!
    Gone are the days of despair,
    Come are the days of your glee;
    Debout les damnes de la terre!
    For Wilson rides a wheel chair
    And Trotsky has reached the Black Sea!

And now that Lenin is fifty and he can rest, as your law
Prescribes, and now that Brussiloff is crashing through to
    Warsaw,
Rest you also, Mother Russia, O full of glory and blood!
The rainbow is wreathing your head, your ark has con-
    quered the flood,
The fates are fulfilled; your task is done. You have labored
    enough!
For gone is the pale little father, a little wind blew him off,
And the big father also is caught in the rifts of the gale,
The holy synod is filling with the red wine of the grail
And the white bread of the host the peasants' bags and the
    gourds;
Saint Peter and Paul is full of bishops and ladies and lords;
The hangman is kicking the wind, strung down from a
    minaret,
The children that begged for kopecks, now beg for a bayo-
    net;
The ikons of the saints wear a red cap instead of the halo,
Grand dukes are in the mines and the miners in Tsarkoe
    Selo;
Kolchak, ripped in the belly is reeling and vomiting out
His guts and your gold, and Yudenich, like a boar stuck in
    the snout,
Is trailing his blood and his froth across the Esthonian
    lands,
And Denikin runs to his ships with his bowels in his hands;
The Letts and the Finns now own you have principles and
    fieldpieces
And you have four million soldiers to reclaim the Poles to
    Jesus,
Your teachers enlighten the people without any rest or stint,
And they give them one good rifle to explain every new
    book you print;
The workers now own everything, even their right to be
    born,
The peasants have taken in full, the flax and the wheat and
    the corn,

And in Moscow it is high noon, and in Europe it is the
  morn,
And the dawn is everywhere!
    Rest, then! Your dreams are all there!

THE LAST FRONTIER
On Crossing the Russian Border

Here where the old world died, the new began
Without a rule, a chart, a guide, a friend,
If this sign falls, here dies the last god — Man;
If it stands straight, he lives world without end.
To set him free we were obliged to bend
His passions to his freedom, for we ran
Against all what he was for what he can
Become when both immortally shall blend.

But not into a spurious soft alloy
That tolerance stirs like a shapeless clay,
But like a hard grief welded with fierce joy
Upon the anvil beaten with the sledge
Into one serried broadsword that will stay
Forever rustless with a double edge.

TO MARIA SPIRIDONOVA
On her deliverance from prison

O thou who art so frail and pure and white
Like the primsnows that fecundate thy sod,
Thou who hast seen the shadowed cross of God
Bow past thy cell in thy remorseless night.

O man-sent Maid to conquer hell, o rod
Of burning steel that flowered into light,
Maria, thou shalt see the holiest sight
Since woman saw her first child in her blood.

Fierce sister sweet, open thine eyes and see!

Behold dispelling the auroral mists,
The pentecostal flame of Liberty!

Flung out like thy distress against the skies,
Beating thy dungeon with thy shouts and fists
And fanning the young sun — the red flag flies!

JOHN REED

What difference does it make
Whether a few bricks have fallen off the Coliseum
Or another bolt has clipped the brow of the Jungfrau?
What difference does it make whether you are alive or
  dead,
So long as you stand like these, Jack?

Yesterday we were drinking wine together
Cracking nuts with our teeth,
You and Bill Chatoff and Bob Minor and Max and Bill
  Haywood and I;
Today — or is it tonight? — you are playing cards
And testing the edge of newly forged blades
With Benvenuto
And Cyrano
And Salvator Rosa,
While Francois Villon fills the glasses wishing hard that
  you would ask him to read his new ballade,
La Ballade des Copains du Beau Temps Jadis.

You are all right, Jack, wherever you are, with such a
  steady and goodly company,
And we are gladder and stronger because you went away
And you did it so splendidly.

There will be hardier seeds and mightier metals in the soil
  of Russia,

Now that you are there.

MOSCOW 1921

A rift of clouds and wings around each sentried steeple
Red flags licking like flames the gold of the great dome,
Silence and sunlight and the bared heads of the people ...
The Red Army is coming home.

John Hall Wheelock

"Grave Music ... to Capture You in Language"

The literary coup of the century: an essay by the Bard! Imagine the hysteria if it were discovered that — like Sidney and Jonson and Dryden — Shakespeare took one "breather" from creative production in order to formulate his definition of poetry. Would this writer's refusal to be caught up in the ensuing frenzy be forgiven? Sooner or later, of course, he would have to take a look at the piece — but how much could it possibly add to what we already know of the Master's poetics, offered by positive example passage after passage, and hilariously anti-illustrated in the Pyramus and Thisbe rhymes of *A Midsummer Night's Dream*, Act V?

This is how one feels after going through John Hall Wheelock's 75-year harvest. Others, no doubt, will do the conscientious thing: comb through letters and interviews for aesthetic clues, examine the *Poets of Today* series he headed to see what sorts of unpublished poets won his approval, and study his prose work, *What is Poetry?* This writer, however, afraid such exploration might prove anti-climactic and redundant, serving merely to reinforce what is already apparent, will stick with the poems, which define Wheelock's poetics with the consistency and stunning clarity of positive example, supplemented by the hilarious anti-illustrations of "Scherzo," a large group produced in mid-career, roughly equivalent to Shakespeare's Pyramus and Thisbe as a condemnation of bad poetry.

Sticking with the collected poems we find from beginning to end a persistence of music, especially singing. And the discovery is by no means surprising. From 1959 until shortly before her death in 1970, this writer attended salon-like gatherings at the home of Jean Starr Untermeyer. Among the other "regulars" were (at first) Mr. and Mrs. John Hall Wheelock; later his wife's poor health made it necessary for him to come alone. As related in a piece on Wheelock and Mrs. Untermeyer (*Long Pond Review*, 1976) the most memorable moment for this writer came the night he coaxed her (a former concert singer as well as a distinguished poet and translator) to the piano and turned the pages while she "belted out" several Schubert songs. Wheelock stood beside him throughout that phenomenally strong unscheduled performance by an ailing woman past 80, and the two men talked of nothing else while awaiting the elevator, riding down to the lobby, and shaking hands at the corner for what was to prove the last time.

That recollection remains sharp and sweet, but it was not this writer's reason (not on the conscious level, at any rate) for choosing to explore Wheelock as a poet of music. The most cursory glance at *By Daylight and in Dream: New and Collected Poems, 1904–1970* shows that this theme is central in his work. Look at the very titles — "Chant," "River Whistles," "Serenade," "An Old Song," "Song at Twilight," "Songs" (thirteen of them), "Triumph of the Singer," "Requiem," "The Moonlight Sonata," "All Love-Songs," "Ballad," "Lullaby," "Unison," "Scherzo," "Lullaby for Allison," "Aubade," "Symphony: First Movement," "Mozart, Perhaps," "Elegy," "Chanty," "The Cruel Song," "Drunken Song," "Song on Reaching Seventy," "Song," "Beethoven," "The Whisper of a Star." And among the "New Poems" in *This Blessed Earth*, 1978, there is "The Concert."

Looking more closely, we find within the poems references to Bach (including a subtitle: "Inspired by 'Melody for the G String' "), Beethoven, Mozart, Schubert, Brahms, Wagner, and (in "Noon — Amagansett Beach") an opening quotation from Handel's *Messiah*. In various poems we come across musical instruments. There are the "wheezing melodies and old, cracked tunes" of an organ-grinder, the "strangled cries" of flute and trumpet, an orchestra crying out "to a cheap and tawdry tune," a harper playing "veiled adagios, fading, fading," a siren mourning far-off, "the twang of a lone guitar," the "vile throb of castanets and strings," a "murmuring string,/Faint with one music," the "idle jigging of a fife," a "lone flute … warbling/Its desultory music," the "plaintive radio music" with its "choral blues," the silent French horn whose tones his father once produced — "tones so full and round you could almost touch them."

What interests us as much as the number and variety of these references is their frequent grimness. The same can generally be said of nature's music, as Wheelock hears it. We are asked to notice "how the lonely sea-bird screams," the "blind pain of speech" in "The cry of any woodland bird," a cricket that "sounds his tender note solemnly and slowly," crickets and cicadas joining to offer "a dim susurrus," a "twittering" of "timid things," the "gnawing of the mouse," a whip-poor-will's bleak cries "across the baleful country," a "cold wind" that "cries across the rolling dunes." The "babbling, babbling" of "pebbly brooks" makes as little sense as does the cricket, singing "Unendingly of unremembered things" when the "old house wakes to a frail/And timorous music."

In the nightmare-visions of "The Divine Fantasy" Wheelock relentlessly catalogs the "Warring and warred upon": "the squirrel moans/As the hawk strikes ... the worm's death is in the robin's song." We are made to experience "the mare's tremendous whinny," the "wail of whip-poor-wills," the "cry of the lone wolf." While "The tree-toad ... trills for joy," the "sliding waters grieve/Quietly." The "old wrong is done again" to "the hunted mouse" by the owl — ending in "A squeak! A scuffle! Beating of wings." Even "the eternal love-song ... Of grasshopper and cricket" now shakes "fiercely all around ... in shrill sound." The "nighthawk's scream" shatters "the startled silence," and the "owl's clear tremolo" of love is made lovelier by "The mouse's blood along his veins." The night is crowded with "small/Twittering things obscene."

In the resolution of this superb meditation, Wheelock comes to recognize a "brotherhood/Of all earth's living creatures" — predator and prey — reminiscent of Blake's tiger and lamb. Together, their "starry cry, across the darkness hurled,/Makes music in the silence of the world!" The ferocious duality of Earth is again the theme in "The Holy Earth," where "the owl with noiseless flight/Moves, peering craftily," until "The fledgling's bitter cry comes sharp." The planet is seen as a "vast cathedral" in which "the fierce hymn to life" reverberates: "shrill voices in triumph" and "mingled moans." Even when nature's melody is joyous, the joy often turns to sorrow.

Returning to his old home in "The Heart Grows Old," the poet aches at the cricket's unchanged song, "the screech-owl's cry," because they remind him of how far he has come from his "burning youth" when he "loved and sang." In "Hushed Midnight" the owlet's "little, quavering call" becomes the cry of a failed early love: "timidly, timidly, out of the dark it cried." Again, in "Reverberation," the cricket "sings for unimaginable joy," but the poet cannot respond to a "happy cry" that "makes music" of his "lost youth." Lacking love and song, he has become "a harp, silent to all those lovely things/That laid such hands upon him" in the past, and "in the solitude" of his "heart's forest a far horn sounds drowsily." Even the loveliness of some great old poem agonizes him in "Evening Contemplation": "What blood was shed for this! ... what brave things, have died/To feed the music of these words!"

Clearly, music has increasingly taken on a symbolic role. The crow's song, for example, serves Wheelock as both personal and universal metaphor in "The Answer." Three times the "guttural cry," the "raucous question," the "harsh, vehement caw" challenged the pre-dawn silence. Then, allowing a new day to open, bringing peace, "Faintly, from far away,/The answer came." Nature's voices as metaphor are defined even more sharply in "Evening." Here "The wind that sighed among the hemlock branches" and the "little screech-owl ... / Crying about the house his timorous cry" express "The sorrowful mystery of things" that "Flows on forever," though a person who once loved those sounds "Is missing now."

The "fun" poems grouped as "Scherzo," however, present several humanized animals in a very different light. A rabbit "enchants yet he seldom sings." An alligator is "gifted, though he neither paints nor sings." A bob-white, having "repeated the same note" for two hours, is asked to leave, perhaps as Jay Hubbell was asked to remove Wheelock from the 1949 edition of his anthology:

> Your note
> Lacks the subtlety that would give its overtones
> Implications worthy of the theme you essay.

"Requiescat," beginning with the title's wordplay, compares a tomcat's night-long sex howl with the once equally "unappreciated" love-duet in *Tristan und Isolde,* and equates his backyard "soprano" with the artistry at the Met:

> The cat who lives for song must learn to savor

The horrid truth: the artist's life is hard.

Wheelock, with exceptional verve and wit, is commenting on the punishments meted out by society, and by powerful critics ("random objects angry hands are flinging"), to the "distinguished cat" whose "lofty song" is "purely personal." This is immediately followed by "Please Turn Off the Moonlight," in which Wheelock demolishes the dominant trend in modern verse, "advising" poets who want to avoid his own and the tomcat serenader's fate:

> Never stoop to sing;
> Reject the human heart,
> Be witty, never lyric ...
> Follow the latest trend
> And leave yourself behind ...
> Contrive to be obscure ...
> Till you are reader-proof!

In the cunningly titled "Intra-Mural Art" a rodent joins Wheelock's outrageous night-choir. Though annoyed at being "kept awake," the poet grants that the rat's "art was penetrating, and unique/In its grasp of the essential material," and dubs him "The outstanding tooth of our time":

> For resonance, for sheer intensity,
> Distinction of tone and firmness of technique.

In "Variations on a Wall Street Favorite" he pretends to envy a "wise old bird" who "The more he spoke, the less he heard" — an abomination in a universe so rich with melody! — very much like a "friend" in "The Valetudinarian" (kin to Whitman's "learn'd astronomer"), who "thinks very loud and talks very loud/About Kierkegaard, Kafka, Rilke and Mallarmé ... Night and day," while, in juxtaposition: "... there's music perhaps .../And a voice somewhere singing, and one star/Not too far...."

That Wheelock is using animal-music to represent kinds of poetry, and that the "Scherzo" group does indeed contain his aesthetic credo, becomes more obvious with each poem. "Mourning Dove" sardonically paraphrases those smug guardians of taste who would belittle a Wheelock for crying his "two notes, over and over, the whole day long," who would wish him to "vary them" or "add just one other note to make it" what they consider "a song." It doesn't matter that "the notes he loves so are certainly all his own." Because his world-view isn't "especially pleasing," they accuse him of being humorless and curse him for bludgeoning them "with a notion" and calling "it song." Outlandishly, the poet invents the *Journal* of an arrogant persona, a "Countess Growlinska," and uses an "excerpt" as motto against both the mourning-dove and the true lyric poet: "I used to think that I didn't like music, but now — now that I've heard him sing — I know that I don't."

Once again, in "Catbird," Wheelock turns his formidable guns of satire against the over-intellectualized trend that has prevailed in 20th century American poetry and poetry criticism, contrasting its pompous juicelessness with the affirming music of the universe. His own credo emerges by innuendo:

> The ritual of dawn ended, the jubilant choirs
> That hailed the divine return ...
> He mounts the platform of the nearest tree
> And begins, almost too clearly perhaps,
> To explain everything —
> His argument rips the heart out of mystery.

One of his prime targets is delicately savaged in the poem that follows. "Hippopotamothalamium" employs T. S. Eliot's favorite device, literary quotation, against the ostentatious author of "The Hippopotamus" himself — having a hippo pair ridiculously drag into their bridal song some of the most angelic lines in English poetry.

Such fables remind us of Aesop and La Fontaine. They are not only about animals, but also about people, especially poets, and about the universe. After all, "The Grand Hierarchy" of nature does unite "Snakes and poets, bankers, swallows, skunks." That Eliot himself served at Lloyd's Bank was an allusion not likely to be overlooked. "The Big I," a four-part satire on poets such as Eliot, who cultivated a worshipful audience, and Pound, his even more contemptuously oligarchic fellow-émigré, examines the anti-social force of egotism, as "A bird with a big eye" (!) destroys the more modest poet's transcendental "I-dea" that "I am one in all, and all are one in me."

> ... I wondered, this being true,
> What made us feel so separate, so alone.
> "I did," shouted the bird,
> And I turned to strangle him, but he was flown.

"Scherzo" closes with "The Plumber as the Missing Letter." This frontal assault on Wallace Stevens, another obscurantist demi-god in America's current pantheon, takes the form of a devastating parodic medley. The poet of the Fictive Muse dreams of "mice that sing soprano ... The owl's oesophagus, the curlew's pharynx." Like Stevens, Wheelock focuses on musical imagery, but in his hands it becomes a lethal weapon:

> ... land of prime
> Poets, de jure some, some few de facto ...
> Snoring, he falls asleep all over again,
> As you, no doubt, dear reader, already have done.
> And so to bed. Enough of this pizzicato,
> Strumming of strings, Stradivarian agitation.
> Sir, the next music be cock-adoodle-doo.
> Explicit "The Plumber as the Missing Letter."

Through his fifties and sixties (1936–56), Wheelock ripens as man and poet; one gauge of that profound development is his approach to music, particularly the music of nature. The sounds of his childhood, like the childhood house in Bonac, on eastern Long Island, that "Bird-haunted, ocean haunted country" to which he annually, agingly returns, are both a frame of continuity and a reminder of how far he has traveled. More painfully than before, he understands the music of daybreak and sunset, of living and dying. As with Keats' nightingale, it is the "selfsame song" — what has changed is the hearer.

Silence has its own special music. Out of it a voice he "had never heard" asks "How is it with you?" He is ready to wrestle with the meaning of "the sea's monotone" and the "other music" that "threads it." How different the song of dawn, the "jubilation" of "half-awakened birds," from "Night's superseded voices; the whippoor-will's/Lamentation and farewell." In the sunny day he hears an incantation of "Robin and wren, catbird, phoebe and chat,/

Song-sparrow's music-box tune." But his spirit, at fifty, is pierced through when the "flute-like adagio or/Wild syrinx-cry and high raving of the thrush" reach him from the dark woods. He aches as dusk, the close of the cycle, brings "the whip-poor-will again,/And the owl's tremolo." Like dusk's, the changed music of autumn affects him:

> Now bird-song fails us, now an older music
> Is vibrant in the land — the drowsy cry
> Of grasshopper and cricket, earth's low cry
> Of sleepy love, her inarticulate cry
> Calling life downward, promising release
> From these vague longings, these immortal torments.

Perhaps Wheelock's ears were weakening in those years, as he indicated in a 1973 letter to Hope Stoddard, but "The alert spirit listens," his poetry tells us, to the song of night-birds and the ever-present, mysterious "Reverberations" of the sea, which he now translates darkly, as he himself slowly moves toward "the primal darkness."

On one level, "The Abandoned Nestling" mourns a short-lived bird. But its silence sings to Wheelock of the silence, the peace, which is his own destiny and that of all mortal creatures. A comparison with Robert Burns' equally compassionate "To a Mouse" is a good way to come at Wheelock's greatness. Tiny as its immediate subject, the poem deserves to be given in full:

> Now there is silence. Among the voices of the coming
>   spring
> Yours will be silent. What shall be said of you, who lie
> Propped here so still in your nest upon the swaying bough?
> Out of nothing there came a need, a mouth, a cry,
> Out of peace, a suffering,
> Drawn back into it now.

"Herring-Gull" is the other side of the coin. Rather than on an abandoned nestling, the poet focuses here on a bird launched seaward "upon the air," and wonders about its mission:

> Are there … beyond your call
> Young, ravenous beaks strained skyward, gaping to be fed?

> A need is on you, a great need is on us all.
>
> Balance upon the wind, send out your desolate cry
> To the four corners of the waste, your clamor is
> The clamor of life in bondage to the old necessities —
> Torment that is the thrust of some immortal joy.

That Wheelock can by now extract such vast undermeanings from the cry of a bird is a reflection of his own growth.

Perhaps thirty years separate "Serenade" and "Aubade." Since the relationship between nature's music and a slumbering beloved remains much the same, these poems afford a remarkable opportunity to study Wheelock's maturation. Twenty-seven lush, loose, rhymed hexameters are pared down to eleven lines of blank verse, taut despite several major repetitions, with almost total stress on the music of nature through which the poet's tenderness is subtly transmitted:

> O love, the little wood-doves call and call . . .
> But you sleep on . . .
> The thrushes sing of you, but you sleep on.
> You do not hear them, though the far-off sea
> Talks to herself and murmurs through your dream
> Her endless love, you do not hear, who lie
> One arm over your breast, in careless sleep.

Equally instructive is a comparison of his early and later treatment of Beethoven. Though about 45 years separate "Earth" and "Evening Contemplation II," both poems unite the songs of cricket, grasshopper, Wheelock and Beethoven. But the pieces show a dramatic shift from the diffusely cataloged variety of creatures that express and celebrate Earth, to the densely cataloged variety of reasons for which the "holy substance of things" is celebrated by "the oceanic/ Rhythm, the wild spring rain,/And the music of a Beethoven,/And of which I too am a part."

Even more telling is the contrast between his 1913 interpretation of "The Moonlight Sonata" and two poems written a quarter of a century later. The first, a tightly-rhymed, trochaic tetrameter serenade of 140 lines, has little content or depth, but much lovely ornamentation, including images of nature's music:

Silver tides of music flow
Round the world: the cricket's low
Harp, the starry ecstasy
Of the keen cicada's cry,
With "I love, I love, I love,"
To the cloudless moon above
Lift the old, the endless song . . .

The two later poems, with their deep, courageous probings and
equally brave form, need to be quoted in full:

SYMPHONY: FIRST MOVEMENT

Faintly at first, and low,
The horns sing lamentation; answering cries
From flute and oboe weave obscure replies;
Through the forest of the spirit
Old fretful winds and murmurs breathe and blow;
Secrets we all inherit,
Sorrow, deep at the core of Being grounded,
Well up again, and flow;
The truce that bound it
Is torn away, Time's wound is bared anew.
Hear, O my spirit!
The violins begin their proud complaint
In the desert of the world.

MOZART PERHAPS

Walking at night alone,
I heard in a house on a dune along the shore,
The tinkle of a piano lightly played —
Mozart perhaps, the music Man has made —
The little intricate tune
Spelled out its human pathos tenderly
Against the oceanic surge and roar,

> The barbarous choiring of the wind and sea,
> That here shall sound when Man is here no more,
> His plaintive music gone —
> While they rave on.

The aging poet's pain in the presence of great music, expressed so forcefully here, reminds us of his confession in another 1973 letter to Hope Stoddard:

> For me, music remains the supreme art. Great music is the nearest thing to God, or whatever that word stands for. I adore and fear it . . . All my life I have been trying to say what can only be said in music . . . Music is a torment that I shun — I resist the temptations of the exaltation it causes to well up in me, telling me where I came from, where I am going . . . and I have learned to mistrust the poems I am impelled to make while listening to music.

The clearest expression of that pain occurs in the final lines of "Last Sonnet," written well into his eighties, and referred to in the same letter:

> now and then . . .
> I hear those far, ineffable strains, as when
> Bows, dragged in unison over the strings,
> Drag music's tide to the very truth of things,
> Unbearably — and beyond — till the heart cries out.

In "Mozart Perhaps" Wheelock discovers in the sea's rhythm not an endless retelling of "old, oceanic secrets" but a "barbarous choiring" as "wind and sea . . . rave on." The music is less ferocious but more sorrowful in "Chanty." Here "The sea-wind crying/Makes drowsy moan." We hear "No sound save/For the waters sighing."

Still, although such images persist from beginning to end of his long career, it would be wrong to suggest that, like the maligned mourning-dove, Wheelock sings only in a minor key. Not all his landscapes are nocturnal, nor does he hear only the creatures of night. As "Morning Draws Near," "preludes to joy" greet the sun's return:

> . . . the robin first
> With frenzied caroling gives thanks; the wren,
> The oriole, chewink, flicker and chat
> Sound jubilant assent; the thrushes last
> With solemn chant antiphonal proclaim
> Resurrection and return.

But it is at night, on the very verge of his seventies, surrounded by beloved ghosts in the empty old house of his youth, that the poet triumphs at last in every sense of the word. His indomitable persistence has "paid off"; he is able now to translate, in superb song, the mysterious sounds and silences around him "in this leafy/Bird-singing, haunted, green, ancestral spot/Where time has made such music!" through its harp of silence.

> . . . garden and walk
> Are marvellous with ghosts, where so much love
> Dwelt for a little while and made such music,
> Before it too was taken by the tide
> That takes us all, of time's receding music.
> Oh, all is music! All has been turned to music!
> And these familiar rafters, that have known
> The child, the young man and the man, now shelter
> The aging man, who lies here, listening, listening . . .

His arrival at this resolution appears to be less calculated, less artful, than Eliot's escape from "The Hollow Men" to the sanctuary of "Ash Wednesday," or — for that matter — Wordsworth's ultimate achievement of the positive mood that made it possible for "Ode: Intimations of Immortality" to shake off its despair and conclude, two years later, on a high note of affirmation. One senses a large, genuine struggle, a great cost in blood, and one notes with admiration that the struggle was to continue into the poet's eighties and nineties, that the moments of resolution were to be rare. It is hard to believe that he could have been granted the radiant glimpse of his "holy grail" in "Night Thoughts in Age" (quoted above), had he not confronted himself head-on, music as always being the mirror of his mind and heart, in two exquisite lyrics produced just prior to that meditation. The creator of "Wood-Thrush" and "The Cruel Song" is blood-brother to Browning's stubborn, intrepid knight:

"Childe Roland to the Dark Tower *came*!"

Behind "the wild-bird's throat" Wheelock hears a paradise earlier than Adam's, "Lost, yet forever here . . . /A longing, a regret,/In which it has no part." What it cries into the poet's, into our own, "labyrinthine heart" are voices:

> Happy and innocent,
> Within whose singing are
> Troy lost and Hector slain,
> Judas and Golgotha,
> The longing and the pain,
> Sorrows of old that were
> And joy come back again
> From ages earlier,
> Before joy's course was run . . .

That song, "so clear, so cool," might have been able to save us, but as "the false heart raves on," the thrush "Falls silent as the grave." The door is shut on what we should have remembered.

For "The Cruel Song" Wheelock's motto, or instruction, is: "Move with a dancing step to a sad music." Here, more completely and more tellingly than anywhere else in his work, music serves as the central metaphor of universal reality: "Atom and man and star . . . Longingly, loathingly":

> Striving with one another,
> Dying, each of the other,
> In the bloody web of things
> Tangled, the carnal mesh . . .
> As the great song wheels round,
> (The primal dissonance),
> They tread the harsh measure through,
> Do as they have to do,
> And all dance, dance,
> In that great agony . . .
> In iron bondage held
> As the great song comes round;

> In agony compelled,
> Out of that agony
> "God! God!" they cry,
> "Joy! Joy!" they cry —
> Oh, the joy is agony,
> That agony is joy —
> "Dance, dance," they cry,
> "Dance, dance for joy,
> In the great agony!"

Almost fifteen years after these masterpieces, at 84, Wheelock was still dissatisfied, and no wonder, considering the awesomeness of his goal:

> Grave music, which to keep was all my care,
> To capture you in language my sole prayer . . .
> The hidden music sounding everywhere,
> The secret that has never yet been told.

That he was still waging his stubborn crusade at 84, and even past 90, attests to his undiminished vigor — spiritual as well as poetic. Gerontologists might suggest the reverse: that the vigor remained undiminished precisely because he kept grappling with "the hidden music," the untold secret. Others before this writer have noted that much of Wheelock's finest work came in his seventies and eighties, work so crowded with musical images, and so dazzlingly matched by the poet's own music, that it deserves a separate study.

For how many figures in the history of art can such a claim be made?

Robert Burns and Langston Hughes

At the stern a swarm of families sang in an unfamiliar tongue. It was the summer of 1932 or 1933. At the edge of the group a young man concentrated on a page of verses in a worn pamphlet. He explained that the songs were Magyar, and that his poet was Petofi, Hungary's beloved martyr of 1848. It seemed a marvelous fate for a poet to be taken along by working people on their Hudson picnic. That — at the age of ten or eleven — was this writer's first definition of a people's poet, and it became his secret goal.

In the same subjective, unpremeditated way he soon chose his heroes: memorized Robert Burns and Langston Hughes, recited and emulated them. Their impudence, vision, and warmth sustained his spirit while college cronies succumbed to cynicism or escaped into the tower; their clarity, earthiness, and melody reinforced his aesthetic principles, while Eliot's abstruse texture cowed the literary landscape. In later years he often returned to these poets as to a desperately needed landfall. Increasingly he felt that the relatedness of Robert Burns and Langston Hughes ought to be explored, that a definition of people's poetry was as likely to emerge from an examination of their qualities as from the study of any two poets.

Even biographically, there are significant parallels. Both experienced poverty and hopelessness as children; each was nurtured on the songs and legends, the frustration and fury, of a nation enslaved by a great power; each came to manhood at a moment of cultural renaissance for his people; both strove for non-dialect excellence and fame within the literary circles of the "master race" while preferring their own folk tradition; both worked intensively with folk music and musicians; each saw his role at the outset, and clung to it throughout life.

Burns defines himself as "A rustic Bard" pledged to preserve "the dignity of Man," celebrate Scotland's beauty, and revive the memory of her heroic past until the blood of his people "boils up in a spring-tide flood!" He repudiates the "Critic-folk" who challenge his capacity "To mak a sang." Against the barren "jargon" of the schools he sets the sustaining inspiration of those bards who preceded him, particularly Ramsay and Fergusson. And in a preface to his 1788 edition of Scottish songs he states his aesthetic standard clearly:

> Ignorance and Prejudice may perhaps affect to sneer at the simplicity ... of these pieces; but their having been for ages the favorites of Nature's Judges — the Common People, was to the Editor a sufficient test of their merit.

Nourished by Paul Lawrence Dunbar and James Weldon Johnson, Langston Hughes vows to "stand up and ... sing about" his "black and beautiful" people: Alabama daybreak songs "rising out of the ground like a swamp mist," blues and spirituals that will "sound like" his people. Years later, recalling the abuse hurled at *Fine Clothes to the Jew*, his second collection, by the Negro literati, Hughes calmly declares, "I didn't pay any attention to the critics who railed against the subject matter of my poems," and he singles out as the virtues of his book the very features that won him such titles as "The Sewer Dweller" and "The poet lowrate of Harlem":

> ... it was more impersonal, more about other people than myself ... made use of the Negro folk-song forms, and included poems about ... workers, roustabouts, and singers, and job-hunters on Lenox Avenue ... people up today and down to-morrow, working this week and fired the next, beaten and baffled, but determined not to be wholly beaten ...

Underlying the poetic principle of both Burns and Hughes is a fondness for the common man and a romantic belief in his goodness. With this as their fundamental tenet, it follows that they will favor folk material, preferring song and ballad and comic epigram to long narrative and ode, shunning the oblique and bookish, capturing instead the rhythms and phraseology of everyday speech. Burns' woman in love sings:

> Oh-hon! for Somebody!
> Oh-hey! for Somebody!
> I wad do — what wad I not —
> For the sake o' Somebody!

Hughes' mother warns her baby as trucks roar by:

> Albert!
> Hey, Albert!
> Don't you play in dat road.

Their locale is proletarian. Despite the frowns of Edinburgh snobs, Burns brings us to cotter's hut, alehouse, dance-hall, barley-ridge. His details include the squeak of "restless" rats, a toothache that makes "the slavers trickle" down his beard, a fart, the stump of a horse's tail. Among his personae are racers, whores, a highwayman, a drunken shoemaker, a lascivious landlady, a fiddler ("poor gut-scraper"), a veteran with "wooden arm and leg."

Hughes' landscape is equally unglamorous: park bench, poorhouse, pawnshop, Sloppy Joe's tavern, "the sinister shuttered houses" of a red light district, a furnished room "so small I can't whip a cat without getting fur in my mouth...." The details are presented familiarly, as segments of his own reality: switchblade, half-empty coal-bin, toothpick thrown from a window, abandoned boxcar, and a whole catalog of complaints for the Rent Man:

> The sink is broke,
> The water don't run ...
> Back window's cracked,
> Kitchen floor squeaks,
> There's rats in the cellar,
> And the attic leaks.

It is in such circumstances that the personae of Hughes find themselves: number runner, tamale man, blind accordionist, harborwhore "For ten shillings offering love," unprosperous pimps who "wear summer hats/into late fall," sharecroppers "plowing life away," a cook afraid she is being turned into a packhorse, a pregnant child about whom "nobody cares/anywhere."

To the critics such characters would be disgusting, or quaint, or at best uninteresting; but to this pair of poets they are clearly the salt of the earth. With their inextinguishable zest, their unpretentiousness and intrinsic dignity, they are set against the hypocrites and snobs, the cruel and selfish and corrupt — "icebergs/ Wrapped in checks" — who hold sway by virtue of wealth and name. On Judgment Day the "purse-proud, big wi' cent per cent" may not fare so well as those who "drudge and drive thro' wet and dry"; and "the corpse of a white multi-millionaire" will be worth no more "pennies of eternity/Than the black torso/Of a Negro cotton picker ..."

This is not to suggest that Burns and Hughes idealize the common man (as Wordsworth often does) to a point beyond recognition; on the contrary, his grotesqueries and follies are graphically delineated. But while they portray with ferocity the King's ministers, the "Laird" who squeezes exorbitant rents and taxes, the rascal who dispossesses his peasantry and squanders his father's lands to go "whore-hunting" on the continent, the lyncher, the boss man who "owns the world," the "Misters, Lords, Generals, Viceroys, Governors" who say "Shut up, Boy!" — these poems treat the blunderings of the poor with brotherly good humor.

Burns addresses his illegitimate daughter as the "Sweet fruit o' monie a merry dint," whose mother waits impatiently to be kissed again by "The ranting dog the Daddie o't." Hughes, narrating another such birth, answers the outraged community: "But mother and child/Thought it fun." Burns defends whiskey, too; for it "chears the heart o' drooping Care." With more poignancy, Hughes' "po' gal" emphasizes the same point: "I need a dime fo' beer." Burns pits his "lads an' lasses ... cozie i' the neuk ... forming assignations," against the preacher who publicly warns of hell though he privately "thinks it auld wives' fable." Similarly, Hughes' minister threatens poor sinners with damnation, while his mind is on "the collection basket."

Both poets empathize so fully with the downtrodden, that they frequently allow their personae to speak directly. It is as though, in order to spotlight the ignored and silenced, they have sacrificed their uniqueness and become oral instruments. But the creator is always implicit in the songs of his creatures. When we have absorbed them all, we are aware of having experienced the whole "human comedy."

Demonstrating Keats' program for greatness, these poets keep finding themselves by losing themselves, by becoming what they sing about. Poems which use the impersonal "I" effectively, dramatic songs like "Duncan Gray" or "McPherson's Farewell," produce total identification within the reader. Hughes, like Burns, is remarkable for the number and excellence of his dramatic songs, particularly those of women in love, women betrayed, women down but not out. In 1931, at Bethune-Cookman College, an amazing incident underscored this special power. With Mary McLeod Bethune presiding, the young poet read:

> God put a dream like steel in my soul.
> Now, through my children, I'm reaching my goal.

Years later he pictured the astonishing scene that followed: " 'My son, my son!' cried Mrs. Bethune, rising with tears in her eyes to embrace me on the platform."

Poets who feel so profoundly cannot help raging against the anguish of their people. On the landlord's court-day, "Poor tenant bodies, scant o' cash, must stand humble and trembling while a factor curses them, arrests them and seizes their goods for debt." This description is written in blood and gall, for Burns' own father was saved from debtor's prison "by a consumption which, after two years' promises, carried him away." Hughes responds with equal bitterness to a lynching:

> Way Down South in Dixie
> (Bruised body high in air)
> I asked the white Lord Jesus
> What was the use of prayer.

As in Burns, the tone is urgent and personal, crystallizing all the slavery tales poured into his soul in childhood, all the monstrosities his own generation endured.

These poets are actively rebellious, in their lives as well as their verses. Thus Burns becomes a Freemason, founds societies for the dissemination of new ideas, flaunts his sexual freedom before the Presbytery, and defends a neighbor threatened with Church censure. Hughes is no less passionate in embracing the movements for radical social change, especially during the turbulent '30s.

Not only do they personally join the battle for reform, but they fulfill the more subversive role of awakening and inciting others. Burns occasionally provokes his readers to rise up against his own ironic comment: "what right hae they/To meat or sleep or light o' day,/Far less to riches, pow'r, or freedom. . . ." He may irk the poor by asking "how it comes" that, despite their sufferings, "They're maistly wonderfu' contented." Or he may put incendiary ideas into their heads through the mouth of their foe:

> Some daring Hancock, or a Franklin,
> May set their Highland bluid a-ranklin;
> Some Washington again may head them . . .
> Till . . . dunghill sons of dirt and mire
> May to Patrician rights aspire!

It is with an open battle-cry, however, that this poet achieves a high watermark of political romanticism:

> A fig for those by law protected!
> Liberty's a glorious feast!
> Courts for cowards were erected,
> Churches built to please the priest!

Hughes also arouses by a variety of means. Sometimes he prods his reader into challenging his words: "Git on back there in the night,/You ain't white." Or he may issue an ambiguous lyric manifesto: "Reach up your hand, dark boy, and take a star." At other times he may suggest, through the cry of the oppressor: "He's trying to ruin the government/And overturn the land!" Frequently he achieves a sense of the ominous through nature symbols such as the wind: "Beware the hour/It uproots trees!" or "Freedom/Is a strong seed/Planted/ In a great need." There is a more violent symbolism too — of frustrated dreams exploding, a Jim Crow car "like an atom bomb" bursting apart. The reader identifies when the "people with no titles" in front of their names menacingly "look out on their world," sick of "The old,/Be patient," ready to "Move on over/To Park Avenue."

Each poet, spokesman of a nation in bondage, subverts best by rekindling national pride. Burns refers to "old Scotia's grandeur," its heroes Wallace and Bruce, Mary Stuart and "Bonny Prince Charlie."

During the Edinburgh sedition trials of 1793 he pleads for a new Bannockburn:

> Lay the proud usurpers low!
> Tyrants fall in every foe!
> Liberty's in every blow! —
> Let us do, or die!

With equal persistence and power, Hughes invokes such "ghosts of former glory" as Toussaint L'Ouverture, Denmark Vesey, and Nat Turner; Sojourner Truth avenging "her children/all sold down the river"; Harriet Tubman scolding a frightened runaway: "You old fool! Even on your way to freedom, you might at least look at Niagara Falls." Against the lynch-terror he hurls the image of a new "Harper's Ferry alive with ghosts today,/Immortal raiders...."

Although their central focus never ceases to be national, both Burns and Hughes recognize the struggle of their own people as part of a worldwide confrontation. In a 1788 public letter Burns risks his reputation by declaring the American Congress of 1776 "as able and as enlightened... as the English Convention of 1688." Nor does he, although on the King's payroll, mute his joy in the French Revolution, even after Britain and France are at war. Indeed, his lines — dangerous for 1795 — remain an international anthem: "It's coming yet for a' that,/That man to man the world o'er/Shall brithers be for a' that."

In *The Big Sea* Hughes describes the impact of the Russian Revolution upon him. An early ballad of Lenin concludes: "The world is our room!" *I Wonder As I Wander* tells unforgettably of his Spanish experiences during the Civil War, and he produces such fine anti-fascist poems as "Moonlight in Valencia," "The Underground," and "Stalingrad: 1942." One of his last poems, "The Backlash Blues," attacks the war in Vietnam.

We cannot, of course, ignore the many differences in these poets. Trapped by a society that compelled Johnson and Coleridge to fawn on patrons, that destroyed the gifted charity-boy Chatterton in 1770 and was soon to destroy Keats — trapped by farm catastrophes, by ever-increasing family duties, by censorious colleagues, by a need for solid employment — Burns ultimately suppressed some of his strongest works, censored himself, and died at

37 after a humiliating recantation had been wrung from him by his employer, the King.

Assisted by his father, set free and kept free by success in a literary world no longer based on patronage and caste, free of family responsibilities as well, Hughes continued to speak boldly on public issues, and died at 65 after a distinguished career, not only in poetry, but as novelist, autobiographer, playwright, humorist, translator, lecturer, and anthologist. [See Appendix]

There are other important differences. Both love social fun, but Burns usually sings when happy, surrounded by friends — Hughes when sad and alone. Both affirm life and hope, but across the work of Hughes there often falls a shadow of death, of despair, such as we hear only occasionally in Burns (i.e., the concluding stanzas of "To a Mouse" and "To a Mountain-Daisy"). Both turn to standard English, but the non-dialect verse of Burns (inspired by sententious Alexander Pope, sentimental Beattie and Shenstone) is generally bloodless, derivative, pompous; while Hughes (set aflame by Whitman, profiting from the tautness, naturalness, concreteness of Lindsay, Sandburg and Masters) creates many superlative non-dialect poems in free verse and rhyme.

Further dissimilarities could be pointed out. But it is their astonishing degree of relatedness in form and content that warrants special notice: the oneness, perhaps, of all such poets who emerge from time to time, giving voice to the agonies and aspirations of their people. "For neither Pension, Post, nor Place" will they betray their mission: "One handful of dream-dust/Not for sale."

A century ago Burns was esteemed by American critics, revered at the colleges, extolled in poems by Longfellow, Lowell, Whittier, Holmes and many others. There seemed no question of his rank among the great poets (though Matthew Arnold, the arbiter of Victorian aesthetic standards, bolted the Pantheon gates from him and Chaucer because they were funny rather than lofty). But a reversal has taken place. More and more, editors and professors specializing in the Romantic Movement minimize him or omit him altogether. At the same time, a severe critical downgrading has victimized the reputations of those 19th century American poets who most admired and emulated him. It is no accident that this anti-emotional, anti-melodic, anti-humanitarian trend has resulted in a similar omission of Langston Hughes from serious consideration as a major American poet. One need only seek him in anthologies of the past fifteen years to see how few compilers have withstood the pressures of the current cultural tyranny. [See Appendix]

It saddens one to think how many young poets of today, in order to achieve publication, may be squelching a folk-oriented lyricism within them, echoing instead the sterile cerebral cacophonies which are more marketable. There is reason to hope, however, that the truest among them, defying the aesthetic decrees of a dehumanized epoch, will eventually come to such older brothers as Robert Burns and Langston Hughes for a verification of their own best impulses, and will inherit the mantle of people's song. Only "Nature's Judges — the Common People" can ultimately decide which poet comes along on their Hudson picnic.

Appendix

Invited, soon after Langston Hughes' death, to participate in a commemorative symposium, this writer unhesitatingly chose a comparative approach, declaring by scholarly demonstration what he had always believed: that Langston Hughes ranks with Robert Burns among the world's greatest folk-poets. Over a quarter of a century has passed since the writing of this essay, all of which remains valid, in his opinion, except for two points.

1) What had seemed an area of difference between the poets turns out instead to be one more feature of similarity. True, it was common knowledge that Hughes had been among many leftwing figures summoned to testify in Washington during the McCarthy Era. But what had transpired there was unclear, at least to this writer, except that he had "named no names." It was also apparent that, during the last decade of his career, Hughes maintained a strictly unaffiliated stance. But that was not unusual for the time; many had become politically disaffected; at least Hughes, unlike Howard Fast and others, did not make a dramatic recantation. As for the severe omissions from his collected poems, they too were not uncommon,

although this writer regretted the banishment of several early jewels intrinsic to his total achievement, simply because their militancy may no longer have fitted his mood. Didn't Irwin Shaw, much earlier in his career, forbid the production of his masterpiece *Bury the Dead?* Didn't Robert Hayden similarly reject in toto his fine first collection, *Heart-Shape in the Dust* (1940), even before rising to the post of Poetry Consultant at the Library of Congress? And — in earlier epochs — hadn't Matthew Arnold withheld *Empedocles on Etna* from his collected poems, condemning its note of despair? hadn't Tolstoy excoriated his greatest works, *Anna Karenina* and *War and Peace,* for failing to fulfill his later definition of great art? It is only in recent times that the facts in Langston Hughes' case have become universally known, receiving full discussion in the *Voices and Visions* video series produced by the National Endowment for the Humanities. We are now aware of the "deal" made by Hughes in Washington so that he could continue to function as a professionally successful author without smear or blacklisting: like Burns, he was forced to renounce his radicalism. It is unlikely that the editors of *Freedomways,* had they known the facts in 1968, would have allowed this essay to be published without raising a question or an eyebrow; the same can be said of *Freedomways'* exceptionally sophisticated readers, not one of whom challenged the paragraph under scrutiny now.

2) Over a quarter of a century later, the penultimate paragraph appears dated indeed. As far as Burns is concerned, his loss of scholarly attention has deepened; those who celebrated him — Whittier, Holmes and the rest — have sunk further into the shadows of neglect. But a tremendous counter-motion has lifted Langston Hughes into a position of posthumous glory, as anyone perusing current anthologies and college curricula can testify. His apotheosis, though deserved and overdue, would be more satisfying if it were based on the tardy contriteness of the critical establishment; unfortunately, it seems to have been forced upon them by the march of history itself, a gauge of the triumph achieved by the Black revolution in the late '60s and early '70s. Langston Hughes is by no means the only Black poet whose work is at last respectfully represented in basic college texts; but his preeminence is clear. How many professors assign him is impossible to guess; but at least the poems are there for a curious

student to discover. In one case, at least, the tendency toward neglect has been reversed and a golden voice — unjustly muffled — is being heard.

Sons of Jeremiah

Sol Funaroff and Alexander F. Bergman

Early in the McCarthy period, Joy Davidman — formerly a Jewish girl from Brooklyn, formerly recipient of a Yale Younger Poets Award for her incendiary 1938 collection, formerly poetry editor of *New Masses*, formerly wife of an Abraham Lincoln Brigade veteran and mother of his sons — found High Episcopalianism and knelt on her kitchen floor, as she reported in a page one banner headline Hearst press confessional which proclaimed, among much else, that with one or two exceptions the poets of the Left amounted to nothing. Who at such a time would dare challenge her? Certainly, none of those embattled poets. Most assuredly, not Sol Funaroff and Alexander F. Bergman, formerly her favorites, by then long dead.

Shortly thereafter, more prudent than his by now thoroughly blacklisted fellow-anthologist Alfred Kreymborg, Louis Untermeyer discreetly omitted from the new edition of *Modern British and American Poetry* his lifelong comrades Genevieve Taggard, Maxwell Bodenheim, Alfred Kreymborg, Lola Ridge, and James Oppenheim. How many noticed?

Afterward the tyrannies of time and taste gradually deposited a thick layer of dust, not only over the entire lyric leftwing except for Kenneth Fearing, Langston Hughes and Muriel Rukeyser, but over many major figures who merely leaned leftward such as Millay, Sandburg, Lindsay, and the brothers Benét. By 1969, when the phenomenally influential Irving Howe dismissed without exception all the proletarian writers of the '30s "both in English and Yiddish" as "middle-class intellectuals engaged in poetic slumming," he seemed to be beating a dead horse.

Even if I were not myself a child of the '30s, familiar with and owing much to that vibrant, variegated group, I hope I would be imprudent and saucy enough to compel here in Hartford [the author was addressing an NEMLA conference panel] at least a modest focus on two of its most neglected voices. One can make a busy career of disinterring unjustly buried reputations — there have been so many, and the process never ends.

Sol Funaroff was born in the Near East in 1911. His parents had fled Russia and were penniless. His father died in Palestine. His mother brought her young sons to New York's Lower East Side and worked in a sweatshop. At four, Funaroff nearly died in a tenement fire. He had a short but active career, helping edit the *College Student Review* (1932), *New Masses (1933), Partisan Review* (1934), *Dynamo* (1934), and *New Theatre Magazine* (1936). He published some important poets for the first time. In 1933 he co-authored *We Gather Strength. The Spider and the Clock*, his first solo collection, appeared five years later. He died in 1942. *Exile From a Future Time* was issued the following year.

Genevieve Taggard, a somewhat older and still occasionally mentioned member of the *Dynamo* group, wrote of Funaroff: "He was Jewish, and aware of his people's experience." Yet it is veritably impossible to detect a trace of Jewishness in his early poems, often published under such desemitized pseudonyms as Charles Henry Newman, Steve Foster, and Sil Vnarov. His first volume is proletarian and internationalist to the core. Its sole Jewish reference is in the title poem: "Oh here's a Joshua set to tame the sun!/Blow your horn Joshua!/Blow!" But this is merely part of an ironic political commentary followed by "Congress will open with a prayer," as in another poem "The radio voice intones the Sunday prayer" and "the religious merchants" are "death's dealers."

Two passages seem to inherit the imagery and feeling of the Yiddish sweatshop poets of the 1890s; in "Time is Money" he sings:

> Tick-tock. Scabshops of starvation . . .
> Oh we work, work, work,
> time, time and overtime,
> until the dawn is feverish in our faces
> like the flush of a consumptive;
> and our thin fingers ache with needles stitching pain.

Very close to the music and atmosphere of his Yiddish contemporaries known as the Proletpen poets, is "Dusk of the Gods, Part II":

> I toiled twelve hours,
> they took the work of ten,
> I toiled ten hours,
> they took the work of eight.
> They took my bed
> and they took my books,
> the clothes from my back
> and the crust from my table
> and I walked, holes in my shoes,
> on the damp pavement.

But how Jewish are these lines? They certainly applied equally to and were equally welcomed by the non-Jewish poor of the '30s. Further, if Funaroff was influenced by the Yiddish revolutionary poets of his own and earlier times, it should be pointed out that in the main their work avoided specifically Jewish subjects; they managed to be Yiddish but not Jewish.

Nor was this accidental. In a series of 1982 interviews with this writer, the Proletpen leader Ber Green recited shamefacedly his group's unswerving program throughout the '20s and '30s: "*With our face toward today, with our face toward the working-class, with our face toward America!*" Thus forty or more extremely productive and popular writers deliberately censored a basic part of their being, as did a huge nationwide audience, omitting whatever smacked of childhood memories, life in the *shtetl*, and whatever might expose a tinge of national heritage, identity or yearning.

For them, as for the earlier sweatshop singers they emulated, to be truly Jewish a poet should decry wickedness in the prophetic tones of Isaiah and Jeremiah. This Funaroff does:

> I made of the truth
> my sword of need,
> I made of my anger
> a battlefield.

It took the unfolding Holocaust to Judaize the Proletpen poets and their readers. By 1942 Sol Funaroff was dead of what a slum doctor had diagnosed as a "poverty heart." But his posthumous collection, *Exile From a Future Time*, reveals that in his final years he too was moving toward public identification as a Jewish poet. One of his "Negro Songs" alludes to the Towers of Babylon, the Jordan River, the Children of Israel, and the Angel Gabriel. "Iron Calf," an unfinished poem, modernizes the golden calf legend:

> The flock in fold
> bow and pray
> to an iron god . . .
> Iron that governs the soul
> with iron laws.

Of his "Prose Poems" the most powerful is "Medieval Jew," an expanded metaphor:

> My soul is a tall, dark-haired medieval jew in a
> long, black cloak. And his face is powerfully featured and
> inquisitioned with strong emotions. And he chants *Kol Nidre* in
> a rich bass voice through a profound black beard.
>
> And his mourning is my soul crying — like the dark wind and
> waters flooding the silent rich black mountain of midnight with
> their awesome weeping.
>
> And this my song, my soul, becomes full-throated, stronger,
> more tortured, until, as I listen, alone, trembling in a cold black
> wind that whirls fear about me, I hear rushing loudly upon the
> night that surrounds me,
>
> > stronger, stronger!
> > the song of a
> stormy river surging, beating, tearing —
> O woe is me! — O woe is my world!

"My Winter Coat on the Battlefield," commemorating the Spanish Civil War, is a translation from Arn Kurtz, a leading Proletpen poet, and "Song of Fatigue" has the most astoundingly Yiddish tone, syllable by syllable, I have ever come across in an English poem. It should be pointed out that the speaker is a creation of Funaroff's imagination; the poet had neither wife nor child.

> The meal's long over. The room is strangely silent.
> My child sleeps. My wife is thinning thread.

Her gaze is sharpened upon the needle;
upon her lap the frugal cloth's outspread.

We once walked in the cool streets at evening.
Now I sit at the window, stars overhead.
The dark tenement walls are before me.
My mind is numb, my body chill, my day is dead.

Hitherto anti-fascist in a strictly international sense, Funaroff finally
became a great anti-Nazi poet in his Biblical cantata, "The Exiles,"
choreographed by Anna Sokolow:

The beast is in the garden,
the beast with claws of iron,
the beast with breath of fire,
the brown pestilence in the land ...

The branches are slashed with swords,
the limbs are lopped with terror,
there is burning instead of beauty,
there is no green thing.

Awake and sing, you that dwell in the dust.
Gather yourselves together,
gather together, o people not desired,
blow the trumpet ...

The brown beast shall perish,
the cities of his pestilence crumble,
you shall rise in the dust of their cities
as a people of grass,
as roots out of dry ground ...

Set up your banners,
wave them in the fields,
gather in the hills,
roll in the valleys,
from the crevices of earth
go forward,
march.

* * * * *

Born a year later and dead a year earlier, Alex Frankel paralleled Sol Funaroff's career in some important ways. His family, too, fled Russia after the 1905 revolution was crushed. In Brooklyn they occupied one dark room behind their laundry shop, then moved to a rural area of Connecticut where the youth developed a deep love for farming, but soon returned to Brooklyn. After high school he worked as a bookkeeper, but at 24 entered Montefiore Hospital with advanced tuberculosis, and from 1938 could not leave his bed. Yet he kept studying and writing, and such magazines as *Poetry* accepted his work. A posthumous collection, *They Look Like Men*, appeared in 1944. A few years later a central character based on him was vividly drawn in William Lindsay Gresham's novel *Limbo Tower*, most likely at the instigation of Gresham's wife Joy Davidman, whose style is recognizable in the poems attributed to the fictional hero.

Like Funaroff, he created a less Jewish pseudonym: Alexander F. Bergman. He too celebrated the "coming" proletarian revolution and denounced fascism in a voice devoid of Jewish identity other than the compassion and indignation that mark him as a son of Isaiah and Jeremiah. Death came to him in May 1941, a month before Hitler's tanks crossed the Soviet border and the climactic period of genocide began.

It was a horror of another kind that, in Bergman's final years, made him a Jewish poet. First, from the window of Montefiore's death ward, he wept with longing for the family nest on Pitkin Avenue: "my father ... /the poor little laundry man ... /and my tired mother beside him/as always, weeping too." Soon, however, he familiarized himself with the agonies of his fellow-inmates. "Many people in the hospital," his brother recalls, "came to him for advice ... But he could not talk much because of his scant breath; and he coughed incessantly." Still, this was the period of his flowering as a poet — in particular, a Jewish poet, the voice of those around him — scribbling in the dark "after the lights were turned out," still writing the day before he died, "although he was taking oxygen."

Among the most remarkable of his last poems is "Lament," a piece similar in tone to Funaroff's "Song of Fatigue." Here too, through the poet's ripening powers, his persona's history is chronicled and his emotional state harrowingly dimensionalized:

In this time of the year when leaves fall
yellow and dry with sickness and age,
the old men and the ailing die,
and some among us here must die.
I am ailing, I am old, ai ai ai.

The angel of death walks in the corridors,
the many-handed stalks all night.

Hear me; I was a baker once,
I labored at night while the populace slept;
when couples walked in the starlit streets
I saw their feet through the cellar grating ...

Twenty hard years I was buried there,
I buried my wife and my child there,
I buried my youth, I buried the sun,
I buried the dream of America there.

Even more excruciating is the duet, "Letter," in which the doomed
young poet's responses to the words of his old ward-mate are heard
only by us:

... Come closer please, I want to ask you
if you have some time to spare.
    I've got the time all right
    but not enough to sing, to love, to go away
    and never see that ugly face again.

To write for me a letter to my wife ...
And tell her this, but say it in your own words ...
Dear Rose;
Tonight I feel so bad I want to die.
    That's not the way I feel tonight,
    Dear Jane; That's not the way I feel at all.
    Dear God that's not the way.

Please try to come and don't be mad no more.
I didn't see you now a long time.
    In my own words, if she remembers

> anything that wasn't groaning, slobbering,
> unclean, she'd never come.
>
> And bring the boy. I want to talk to you before I die.
>   What can the old man have to say
>   that must be said, to them, to me
>   or anyone alive? What?
>
> Love,
>   Abraham.

Like Funaroff's Biblically cadenced "Exiles," Bergman's "Jerico" captures the incandescence of Jeremiah. The reader is inundated by an apocalyptic vision of the quarantined bursting loose:

> We cannot be kept within the walls.
> The false barriers will break at the shout
> of our anger free from its long silence . . .
>
> Out of our beds and our uniform cells
> out of the smelling, serried, crowded wards
> into the clean streets of little towns,
> the green fields that never saw our faces —
> we shall go — past the homes of the straight
> firm walkers into the cities that banished us.
>
> There are those who will fear our poison
> our twisted, sometimes bitter faces,
> our eyes of lizards strangers to the sun . . .

How would Bergman have responded to the hellish news from Europe? For most American poets apparently it took time to arrive and sink in. A couple of statistics may be apropos. *War Poems of the United Nations*, edited by Joy Davidman in 1943, is fiercely anti-fascist. Hundreds of translated poems from many countries are included, but not one from Yiddish. The largest number — 120 pages — are from the U.S. On the Holocaust that huge group offers two words in a David de Jong poem, four lines in a piece by Robert Whittington, an oblique reference by Alexander Laing, several stanzas in my own "Blood Donation," and Funaroff's "The Exiles."

A year later *Seven Poets in Search of an Answer* won international acclaim as a "fiery" anti-fascist compilation. Five of us, including Joy Davidman, were Jews. The others, Alfred Kreymborg and Langston Hughes, had long spoken out for the victims of fascism. Yet of the seventy poems in this collection, only "Poem to Gentiles," by Maxwell Bodenheim, focuses somewhat on the "butchering" of Jews, and there is a two-line reference in "Prelude," by Norman Rosten. By me there is nothing.

At best, a paper this brief can only provoke curiosity and raise questions. What makes a poem Jewish — must it be specifically national in theme? Did Funaroff and Bergman become better and deeper poets when they became consciously Jewish, as Heine did in *Hebrew Melodies* and as Emma Lazarus did, thirty years later, in *Songs of a Semite?*

What of the many Jewish *Dynamo* poets who lived past the Holocaust — did Jewish consciousness enter and enrich their work, as it did in the case of every Proletpen poet, whose Yiddish poems were finally Jewish too?

As for Joy Davidman, who dedicated her United Nations anthology to Bergman and Funaroff: "Poets of the American People," and who a year later edited Bergman's book, singling out "Letter" as "perhaps one of our great poems ... straightforward, unpretentious, towering ..." — is it an accident that, like Wordsworth and Coleridge, from the time of her political and religious conversion she failed as a poet?

Obviously, a great deal of research is called for; and, although Irving Howe thought otherwise, the findings may be of value not only on historical but also on aesthetic grounds.

[Some years after the presentation of this paper at the Hartford NEMLA Conference, a stirring began to take place among young scholars on several U.S. campuses, including Alan M. Wald at Michigan, Albert Filreis at Penn, Paul Buhle at Brown, and Cary Nelson at Illinois. Nelson's study of Edwin Rolfe has earned some attention, for example, and he is now contemplating a similar focus on the career of Don Gordon, who shared a joint volume of new poems with me in 1946. Douglas Wixson at Texas has just published a massive biography of novelist Jack Conroy which pays serious attention to some of the '30s poets in Conroy's midwest circle, notably the long-ignored H. H. Lewis. As for Joy Davidman, it remains to be seen whether Debra Winger's recent romanticized portrayal in *Shadowlands* will lead to the disinterment of her poetry.]

Muriel Rukeyser

A Memoir

In a century of American criticism and scholarship dominated by anti-prophetic tastes, the great proletarian wave of '30s poetry was scorned from the first and utterly obliterated from the McCarthy period onward. If an even deeper grave could be dug, it was reserved for the women poets — Lola Ridge, Genevieve Taggard, etc. Only Muriel Rukeyser was too gigantic a figure to be entirely ignored, but her stature was seldom acknowledged and until very recently, revived by the enthusiasm of several young academics, mostly women, her work had steadily faded from anthologies and college courses. Her 80th birthday this month [December 1993] seems an appropriate time to focus on her immense contributions to world literature and on her role — for almost half a century — as an inspired sentinel for human rights.

I. Personal Recollections

Before entering my teens, and when I was writing my own strident verses of protest against the frame-up of nine young Blacks in Alabama, Muriel Rukeyser entered my consciousness as a poet at the end of her teens jailed in Scottsboro on behalf of the same cause. Soon after, my father gifted me — *how* was a mystery, since he was unemployed at the time — with a copy of *Proletarian Literature in the United States*, the new anthology that was to be a treasure and a guidebook for years to come. A favorite poem was Muriel's "City of Monuments," whose last lines expanded my sense of what poetry could do: "Split by a tendril of revolt/stone cedes to blossom everywhere."

A few years later she was covering the war in Spain, a war that had become the central passion for socially aware youngsters like me, a passion we never outgrew. By late 1937, not yet 16, I was at college; but my heart and imagination were in Barcelona ... *and Spain sings*, issued that year, enhanced my trove of books — 50 Loyalist ballads translated by Edna St. Vincent Millay, Rukeyser, William Carlos Williams and others listed on the jacket, with many more inside such as Katherine Ann Porter, Rolfe Humphries and Stanley Kunitz. A good handful, including Jean Starr Untermeyer, Millen Brand and Shaemas O'Sheel, were to become lifelong personal friends.

By 1948, my new book, *The Thunder of the Grass*, and Muriel's *The Green Wave*, were reviewed together, and together our faces were presented. A year later I joined the Poetry Society of America, in which I played an increasingly active role for the next decade. From time to time I ran into Muriel at PSA meetings, always with warm mutual greetings. She generally sat with Mrs. Untermeyer.

In 1954 the worn, once-flamboyant Greenwich Village poet Maxwell Bodenheim and his young wife were murdered by a psychopath who asked the court to reward him for having "killed two reds." Since my employer would not allow me to attend the late-morning memorial service, my tribute had to be read by Alfred Kreymborg — as reported in the next day's press. At this point the Poetry Society, which had banished Bodenheim years before for discomfiting public behavior, decided to acknowledge his death. I was invited to speak briefly and read "four minutes' worth of his poetry." What I did was to read my memorial tribute, every word an arrow of defiance against the leaders of the Society in attendance; I then announced that I would add two minutes to the time allotted me. The applause for my presentation was not deafening, but Muriel made a point of shaking my hand vigorously and thanking me for what I had done.

Our most extended and personal conversation took place toward the end of the '50s in the Washington Heights post office near our homes. When I mentioned my excitement at finally entering the academic world (as a high school teacher), she narrated bitterly and at length her current tribulations at Sarah Lawrence College, where the once-leftist husband and wife team of Horace Gregory and Marya Zaturenska were making a career of poisoning her reputation and trying to turn the English Department against her. In fact, her job there was now under threat — as if the McCarthy period had never ended.

We finally read from the same platform on Jan. 13, 1967. A group calling itself New York Poets for Peace observed a 24-hour fast for world peace at St. Mark's Church in the Bouwerie. The sponsors of the unprecedented event included, along with Muriel and me, John Ashbury, Paul Blackburn, Allen Ginsberg, Barbara Guest, Kenneth Koch, Denise Levertov, Eve Merriam and Joel Oppenheimer. During the final three hours, witnessed by an audience of about 1,000, poets came forward in impressive numbers to read. Our work became the anthology *Poets for Peace* later that year. Muriel was represented by "The War Comes Into My Room," I by "Year of Shame." Among the almost 80 poets were W. H. Auden, Walter Lowenfels and Lenore Marshall.

From 1961 I had appeared annually for poetry readings at the Donnell Library in New York, each year paired with a different poet. None of us received payment, yet Muriel — whose usual honorarium probably averaged 1,000 — enthusiastically agreed to share the evening with me. In 1968 our rapport with each other and with the audience was so extraordinary as to demand a second — even better — program on Dec. 28, 1971, this time limited to our new work. Unlike many of the poets who joined me in the 30 years' duration of my Donnell series, decent and technically superb though they were, Muriel on both occasions made a point of showing that she had listened attentively to what I read, and named the poems that had moved her most.

I phoned her in 1976, when I was at Dowling College on Long Island, and invited her to participate in our visiting poets series, of which I was coordinator. She had just recently suffered a stroke, and was under doctor's orders not to do such things. Nevertheless, she was preparing for a trip to Vienna to speak out on behalf of Amnesty International for poets East and West who were being mistreated, imprisoned, silenced; and she came for peanuts to Dowling.

On April 16, 1980, I keynoted the Fifth Annual Long Island Writers' Conference at Suffolk Community College. My reading was dedicated to Muriel, who had died in February. I shared with the audience my idea for a new poem, which would, among other things, describe her reading at Dowling College. Here is an excerpt of those transcribed remarks:

My new poem is going to be called "The Chair." It tells how I come home and hear somebody talking about me. I feel very embarrassed. I'd like to walk out. But they're talking to my daughters, who happen to be many miles away. It turns out to be a furniture ad on the radio. A furniture company is telling my daughters that the best gift they can give me is a chair — or a recliner — or a love-seat — or even a rocking chair. . . . I'm so furious, I want to just kick the radio, and as I kick it, say to it: "Am I ready for the chair? To do nothing but sit and play Scrabble and do crossword puzzles and go through photo albums to find the missing faces in the jigsaw puzzles of my past — aunts and cousins? I'm not ready for that yet, damn you!" Then, as the afternoon wears on, I'm a little troubled by the extremity of my reaction: maybe there's something to it after all. Maybe I *am* reaching the chair phase . . . Then, at night, I'm in my recliner. As I lie back, the news of the day, the horrors, unfold in parade before me. I see the raping of the populations of the world by its leaders, which goes on and on — budgets for cannon and not for bread — people tormented, assassinated — the whole parade you and I know. But the years go by, and I'm no longer writng poems about it or participating in the resistance to it. I'm watching as if it's a show, a special, on t.v. night after night.

And as I sit in my chair realizing that indeed the furniture store was right, it suddenly comes back to me, the end of that day when I brought Muriel Rukeyser to speak at Dowling and didn't know how that creature, with buckling, thin legs, varicosed legs, was going to stand there and face a young audience who didn't care beans about poetry or the world. . . . How was she going to wake them up and stay alive and on her feet?

But she got up there at the podium; she held on to the podium. For an hour she read, and her voice came back with that magnificent organ-sound it had in 1940 when I first heard her. And as she read, out of her eyes and out of her mouth her poems and her visions, her sense of life, her militancy, her spiritual fervor, went into the bodies and minds of my students. Afterwards, for a second hour, she answered questions — every answer shaped like a beautiful poem. She didn't sit down; there was no tiredness at all — a big smile on her face. She got back in the car and I took her to Babylon, where she got the train back to Penn Station. And though my students went their separate thoughtful ways, they were marching, marching I hope, for the rest of their lives, with the live Muriel Rukeyser in them forever! — That's the poem. Now to write it.

These are among my personal recollections of a woman whose character and work remain a great force in my life.

* * * * *

II. Muriel Rukeyser Reads at Dowling College: Oct. 11, 1976

Aching since February 1980 at the loss of my friend, I never allowed myself to hear the recording of her program at my college. Now, listening and transcribing, I relive the matchless session I was privileged to experience. Her remarks strike me as being of tremendous value, not only in demonstrating Muriel Rukeyser's creative and personal qualities, but also in dramatizing the historic moment of which she was a part, and in showing her communicative powers, her capacity to connect with a throng of strangers not one third her age and untrained in either politics or poetry. Here are excerpts along with some brief recollections.

KRAMER: Once again I have great pleasure in welcoming you to a program presented by our Cultural Affairs Committee. In the past year we have heard such masters as Stanley Kunitz, David Ignatow and John Hollander. I think you'll agree that today's event will crown the series.

In my early teens Muriel Rukeyser literally flashed across the horizon with her first volume of poetry, *Theory of Flight*, in 1935. Three years later she produced *U.S. 1*, followed by *The Turning Wind* and a superb work rooted in both the American past and the pre-war world of 1940, *The Soul and Body of John Brown*. Since then she's been productive not only as a poet ever-gaining in strength and scope, but also as a splendid translator of Sweden's Ekalaf, Mexico's Octavio Paz, and Brecht. She's written a novel, *The Orgy*, brilliant biographies of Willard Gibbs and Wendell Willkie, and a juvenile, *Come Home, Paul*, which she herself illustrated. Her new collection is *The Gates*. Miss Rukeyser will read from it, and you'll find it in the bookstores very soon. It's an honor to present one of the great voices of the century, Muriel Rukeyser.

RUKEYSER: Good morning. It's a morning on which one wakes up having some odd feeling of discovery, because of the date's memorial [Columbus Day]; but like any other discovery, it's a recognition: the hemisphere was here, and it was called "discovered." And these poems that are in you and in me are recognized in the same way. We discover something that can hardly be spoken about, that can hardly be named. *The Times* this morning referred to education as a vague product, and spoke of you as consumers. It's vague, all right. It's precious because it's vague. It has no defined boundaries.

And perhaps what we are playing for is an effort to find boundaries. We have a center of what we do. We have, I think, a tension between two things, on which we work always, in ourselves and in the world around us. One is an unverifiable fact, be it dream, or love, or sex, or any of the things we can give each other only by the power and the skills by which we give them — the way of sharing that is the only thing that can make the truth of what we speak come through to the other person. The other is the actual document of the thing, the evidence: sometimes unverifiable, sometimes known to all. These are our materials. But the fact is that everything, everything, is our material; that the power of poetry, which cannot really be defined, is perhaps the power of bringing our entire life to this moment, which in a way is the only real, which we share with each other, which I share with you whom I do not know but from whom whatever I bring will come. In a very odd and wonderful way it comes from you — and the poems of this moment, that are still unwritten.

To write a poem is a good response to a poem, I think; to make love is a good response; to hold silence is a good response. I hope that we will come to another level after I read, and there will be things in your lives and things about you that are unverifiable facts that you have not been able to say or to write and that you want to ask about or talk about. And if it is silence, that is a perfectly good response.

I'd like to read very new poems, and recent poems. I've brought the last published book and the proofs of this new book that's going to be out this month. I'll read first from *Breaking Open*. [*Reads "This Morning": I want to make my touch poems, to find my morning, to find you entire, alive, moving among the anti-touch people.... Today once more I will try to be non-violent one more day, this morning, waking the world away in the violent day."*]

I think of myself as a violent woman who tries, as the alcoholics try, to be non-violent one more day, because of the robbing and devastation of our lives, even among the things that attempt to let us find and enrich our lives, which is to give us ourselves entire, so that we can give ourselves to each other, so that we can find the next place. And it seems to me that the devastation, and the rape of the self, and the rape of the city among the sky-scrapers, comes from a huge despisal that we have allowed to take over in many ways in our life. And I want to work against these despisals and to write the poems of despisal. This is one of them. It's called "Despisals." ["... *never to despise the homosexual who goes building another with touch, with touch ... not to despise any touch ... Never to despise in myself what I have been taught to despise...* "]

This one has been coming for a long time, because I'd been thinking, as all of us have, about that riddle given to us as a central riddle in our culture. It's called "Myth." [*Old and blind, Oedipus again meets the Sphinx. "Why didn't I recognize my mother?" he asks. She explains that he "gave the wrong answer" to the riddle. He defends himself for answering "man" and not including women: "When we say Man we include woman too; everyone knows that." The Sphinx replies: "That's what you think." Laughter and prolonged applause.*]

This was written while the young men were facing choices about the war, going into a war many of us would hold the responsibility to oppose ... that now, in the presidential campaign, they're saying was ended, as if the times ended it, as if the people in power had really ended it. It was the young who protested and refused to go and became more and more a strong force although singly they felt that they were not strong, that they could do very little, that it was almost impossible to hold these meanings. And in caring very much about what the United States did, they questioned everything. I thought of it at the opening of the film *Memory of Justice* the other evening, and in the discussion after it: whether the Holocaust in

Europe could possibly be equated with what happened in Vietnam. … Anything that is a horror to any one of us is equated with any of the others, anything in which we have lost ourselves and people who are dear to us. I have this about Spain, in which somebody very dear to me, a German, was killed by the Franco troops. The whole feeling of how the Resistance has been found out and killed, country after country, comes into this. And our wish for more life for each other and for ourselves is bound up with holding on to these meanings. [*Reads a number of short poems. Special applause for "Rational Man": "Anything you can imagine … rational man has done. Mercy, Lord, on every living life."*]

After going to Hanoi I was jailed briefly, very briefly here; it wasn't like those who got prison … it was by choice, and just a few days, and there were many good things in it, particularly the kindness of the other prisoners and the guards in the prison called D.C., D.C., which is Dept. of Correction in Washington. It's almost completely a Black prison, and they were very good to me because, oddly enough, they knew about a Scottsboro poem I had written years ago, and they wanted to talk about poetry, and about reasons people should not be in prison.

And just a year ago I went to Korea, to Seoul, where a poet is imprisoned because he has done what our poets have not, he has, in the fierceness of his writings, created in the line of Brecht and Robert Burns poems that have got under the skin of the government and under the skin of its President Park Chung Li. He was put in prison and condemned to death, but that verdict has been changed to life imprisonment. This is Kim Chi Ha, in prison now in Seoul. The title of the book, *The Gates*, is the title of a sequence of poems. It is the gates of perception and the gates of the body; it is also the inner gates of that prison, where I stood in the mud and the rain, as near as I could get to what is classically the house of the poet, on a visit, on what is called a vigil there. Those who helped me get there were the writers' organization I represented, P.E.N., and an international group called The Friends of Kim Chi Ha, as well as the university people, the Cardinal, and the officials of Korea's P.E.N., who we didn't think, for very good reasons, would be able to help us or would want to, and the many writers there.

[*Her throat is increasingly taxed, her voice weakening steadily.*] Not only writers, but students and working people of many kinds, and members of the government and of the academic communiity. I met with them at a place called the Church of Galilee. There was a chance to talk after the religious service; and they were introduced as Professor So-and-So, dismissed from his post at Such-and-Such College ... and somebody else dismissed, and somebody else dismissed. It became clear that Dismissed was an honorable academic degree, and that this is how it is moving there; the closeness of poetry, and of the work that is being done ... for us, actually, for everybody who shares a time of life. I'll read you some of the other poems in the book first, and then from that group.

This you know the scene of already. The night before our arrest in Washington, our meeting was very curious, because we found we didn't agree. We didn't have the same ideas at all about what we were doing and were going to do. And this is the poem of that, "How We Did It." [*Let some walk away, let some stand until they want to leave, let some lie down, and let some be arrested. Let each do tomorrow what he feels at that moment. The doctor spoke of friendships made in jail. We looked into each other's eyes and went all to our rooms to sleep, waiting for morning.*"]

Now that is a curious way, and it is very deeply traditional, a way of disagreeing and of going ahead with what is meant, being confident in the fact that what is being meant by any of us will be meant by all of us, and we will all be responsible. Actually, we were all responsible under the law, and our arrests were for what other people had done, although I was not aware of what we were charged with, which was blocking the passage of a senator to the Senate chamber. Actually, we were trying to get the senators into the Senate chambers to vote, and to vote against the war and what the war signified.

As I talk here, I hear myself talking in terms of war, but I do not only mean war; I mean the wastage of our people by these things and by the economic things and by the imaginative things by which we waste each other. It seems to me a tremendous attack on our lives and our inner lives; I do not believe in the separation between inner and outer. I believe that the inner is the outer — and the ways in which we imagine are the ways in which we live and act, and this speaks from a thousand years ago. Some of it comes out of dream itself. This poem comes from a dream and is called "Dream Running." [*Up to now her face had gradually drained of color, as had her utterly exhausted voice . . . so much so that I was alarmed, and guilt-ridden for not having insisted she sit. But this poem, perhaps chosen because she knew she needed to, had the effect of a transfusion; she beat time on the podium, and was in high gear by the time the final lines rang out to the farthest corner:*]

> *As I played, weakness went through me, weakness left me.*
> *I held my arms high . . .*
> *I drummed past my tiredness, vibrating weakness,*
> *past it into music, as in ragas, past exhaustion*
> *into the country of all music,*
> *held my arms high, became that vibration . . .*
> *with my arms up into music, at last turned into music,*
> *drumming on that possessed vibration,*
> *drumming my dream.*]

This is for Neruda, the last time I saw him in New York shortly before his death. It's called "Neruda: the Wine." You've never heard of Neruda? A great Chilean poet who stood up to tyranny all his life and stood for the kind of poetry he wrote and all the meanings connected with Republican Spain, with whatever in our lives works for that kind of imaginative freedom and work-freedom and the freedom of all people. The name Neruda has come to mean that. [*The poem describes their last meeting: she has spilled her wine at the table. Neruda dips his finger in it, then marks her forehead: "I go, a woman signed by you: 'The poems of the wine.'"*]

* * * *

This would have been a perfect place to end, and her body as well as throat must have ached for an ending. But clearly she was impelled to proceed: it was her new collection that mattered — the whole hour had marched toward it. More quickly than before, to get them all in, she now read half a dozen lyrics from *The Gates*. The image of the imprisoned poet's infant son beginning to run reminded her of her own son. This passage leapt out at me, because we'd discussed her son almost 20 years earlier, at the Washington Heights post office. "He runs toward me in Asia, crying. Flash gives me my own son, strong, and those years ago cut off from his own father and running toward me holding a strong flower." She then parallels the Korean child's loss of his imprisoned poet-father with her own child's loss of a father imprisoned "by his own fantasies." I lacked the courage to pursue this raw subject afterward. Also fascinating and painful was a reference to Anne Sexton "... saying ten days ago to that receptive friend: 'Muriel is serene.' Am I that in their sight? Word comes today of Anne's, of Anne's long-approaching, of Anne's overriding, overfalling suicide. Speak for, sing for, pray for everyone in solitary, every living life."

[Her final poem on the imprisoned poet ends with yet one more inner struggle, one more demanding of self and of humanity: "How shall we free him? How shall we speak to the infant beginning to run?" The applause is sustained. She murmurs "Thank you. Thank you very much." I explain that those about to leave will do so because they have classes to attend. But few go. She eagerly invites comments and questions. I again beg her to sit, but she is adamant, and truly has turned from a withered body into the giant of old. The questions are on aesthetics, politics, and matters much more personal: our guest's poetic development, for example, and their own difficulties as beginning poets. Every question draws from her a response utterly accessible and pertinent, but at the same time exquisitely shaped and full. Transfixed and galvanized, they give her a standing, sustained ovation. They can't have imagined that she's recently undergone major surgery and is (once more) defying her specialists' severest orders to slow down.]

During the ride back she praised the students for their extraordinary attention span (two hours) and for the depth of their questions. "You've given me my best audience in years." I could only thank her for introducing them to aspects of reality seldom mentioned in their classes and probably never at home. Above all, and altogether unlike the fine poets who had preceded her on campus, Muriel stood, and would stand forever in their memory, as an example of a poet not only large in language but ready to lay down her life wherever the place of greatest moral urgency and personal risk might be, whether in Scottsboro, or Spain, or Washington, or outside a prison in the mud and rain of Korea.

Remembering Owen Dodson

I

Back from holiday. A letter waits, not in Owen's handwriting but with his return address. I unseal it eagerly, hoping that it is his comment on my *In Wicked Times*, dictated to a secretary because of weakening sight. But no; it is a duplicate of the invitation received six months back to attend a service for Edith. *That* one came too late — the very afternoon of the memorial. Hating, but needing, to hear the details, I phone the number I should have dialed much more often. The young man who answers, Patrick Trujillo, recognizes my name, noting that Owen had kept *In Wicked Times* next to his bed.

Patrick, who moved in five months ago, does "not recall one day of Owen's which was not miserable." Not only had his sister's death six months back punished him beyond endurance. Apparently he was crushed by the death of Tennessee Williams as well, and asked Patrick to read him all that came out in the papers. "Most of the time he was drunk." I had received and pushed aside several such impressions when Owen phoned at an unreasonable hour; liquor might have become an anodyne for the spinal agony which had gradually pushed him into a wheelchair.

When I mention Owen's distress at the legal problems connected with Edith's estate, Patrick informs me that Owen's heart gave out at 8:30 a.m. on June 21st, two hours before a scheduled appointment with the lawyer to settle her estate at last. Now Patrick, a stranger, must "stay on until Owen's estate is settled." ("Though I only knew him for five months, I knew him intimately, as a close friend.") On Monday he will share with me his memories of Owen.

Monday. I ask for, but cannot locate, Patrick. Arriving early, since I must leave early, I break down at the sight of Owen's powerless photo on the altar above a big white bouquet. It does not help to remember his recently published funny lines:

Cease messin' around
And read me the messages
On the tags of my flowers.

Slowly the big hall fills — a very small proportion of the mourners below middle age. Quite a few whites, mostly middle-aged. I am bulwarked by the arrival of Raymond Patterson and his wife Boy die, and wish we could sit side by side.

The program unfolds in a low key. Reverend Harrington's young successor notes our diversity: united only in our having known Owen. Graham Browne focuses on "Mr. D." — his teacher at Howard — as an authoritative, demanding, inspiring figure who kept in touch with former students and held them true to their early commitments. Ted Shine gives a wide-ranging overview of Owen's gifts. David Amram recalls himself as an 18-year-old music student in Washington 35 years ago. Owen, a neighbor, used to hear his flute-playing, and one day invited him to provide the music for Howard's production of *Alcestis*. This was the beginning of Amram's career. Through Owen he met hundreds of interesting and important theatre people. To the end Owen remained a loving, inspiring friend, and in his memory Amram plays a flute solo as excruciatingly eloquent as a great poem, for which even the little boy in front of me lifts his eyes from the comic book that has kept him quiet.

After Owen's favorite psalm, the 23rd, Southworth leads all but me, it seems, in The Lord's Prayer and "Faith of Our Fathers." It is a soul-filling moment; I regret not believing. Next, Ossie Davis and Ruby Dee read excerpts from "The Confession Stone"; in a 1980 letter offered as preface, Owen told why he preferred this to any of his other poems. First as Jesus begging for rest, finally as Mary lullabying her boy, Ruby is ineffably fine. Her keening art comes from exactly the same part of her being that Owen's did; like him, she is willingly lifted beyond her personal self to become an instrument of something mysterious, elemental and timeless. Entering the church and seeing his likeness, I thought: After such a monumental struggle, is this what it all comes down to? But Amram and Ruby Dee have dimensionalized the portrait, just as Owen unfailingly transformed his fragile form, writhing inside the walker as he reached the stage and turned to face us.

Dr. Harrington, who so recently came East for Edith's service, closes each segment of his tribute with a telling quotation from Owen's work. He begins with an unidentified poem Owen of all people would have enjoyed most, Langston Hughes' wonderful "Dream Dust": "One handful of dream-dust/Not for sale." Closing with "When I Am Dead," he takes up its root-image ("The roots below will twine a crown/When I am dead") with words to the effect that even though Owen died too young, before all of his gifts had been given, we can see the power of his roots in generations of new artists that have sprung up through his example.

I wrench myself away, moving toward Penn Station, observing the rich diversity of city folk at rush hour as if through the eyes — half-blind but all-seeing — of the poet who loved and encompassed and expressed them.

II

A wintry afternoon. I am greeted by the unmistakable penmanship of Owen: Under the hint of shakiness, a granite fullness still. But inside, there is only a printed invitation to a service for Edith this very evening at the Community Church. No train could possibly get me there on time. Under the dignity of his silence is a raw howl. Edith — lifeline, protector, soul-mate.... In recent calls he described the collapse of her health, her massive heart attack, her deepening anguish, her utter dependency on him now — a complete turnabout after years in which she was *his* sustaining angel.

I take an early train and dial from Penn Station. A young man answers: No — this is not a good time; the memorial service took its toll; Mr. Dodson is receiving no visitors. But Owen breaks in: Aaron Kramer can come. Turning west onto 51st Street, I am smacked in the face and pierced through the coat by a Hudson gust, paying me back for having postponed the promised visit. On his floor, several superb posters commemorate Dodson productions. The young midwesterner, Patrick, leads me past a flower-filled room, the Christmas tree still standing. I've forgotten how short Owen's debilitating illness has made him — the voice on the phone, in letters, in books, is after all that of a giant. This morning, however, nothing but a bit of trunk stirs under the sheet, and almost nothing remains for the undershirt to cover. Even the once-grand head straining to lift itself from the pillow seems shrunken. Worst of all, the voice is smaller, and there is a frequent pausing for breath.

The young man describes Owen's extraordinary performance last night clearly: though the feat of dragging his body and his grief to the pulpit rocked him to the roots, in front of the mourners he once again rose to the great burst of song they expected of him. Owen tells me of his sister's heroism through the long dying, her determination to celebrate another Christmas, to which the tree she helped adorn bears witness. He speaks not of his own love for her, but of the love she evoked in others. A woman now in Hawaii sent an exotic bouquet, which he urges me to go inside and look at closely. It stands, with other floral gifts, around the urn. Still grieving for his own recently lost wife, Reverend Harrington flew in from California to deliver the eulogy. A number of well-known musicians combined their talents, and a gifted young street-musician, a girl she took under her wing, begged to participate.

Owen's friend Ivory phones to ask how he feels and to praise the service, especially the poet's role. He tactfully cuts short the conversation, explaining that he has company. Frequently his eyes overflow, and he says: "Yes, Aaron, but it's so hard to go on." Still his humor is unimpaired, and he enjoys confessing a long, complicated plan of how he and a few of Edith's dearest friends will outwit the atrocious mortuary world when spring comes, by holding a modest ceremony at home to be followed by a forbidden service late at night at the Brooklyn family plot. The "unfinished business" (still waiting to be accomplished at this writing — ashes of brother and sister still unburied) represents only one of several difficulties arising from Edith's death. Handling the modest estate has damaged him; his hope was that *she* would serve as *his* executor.

The setting of a new poem highlighted last night's program. He flails about in search of the manuscript, stretching his bit of body among a hundred books and papers near the bed. The hunt is further hampered by a sharp decline in his vision. Yet amazingly, he fishes out of a pile on the floor two lined sheets of paper. Although the writing is huge, his nose practically touches the page. As soon as he begins reading, however, the weakness and shakiness leave his voice and it is once again an organ of elemental power. His tone carries — as the words do — with their spiritual-like refrain of woe on earth to be overcome at last — the same compassion and defiance, both personal and universal, that have always marked his best work, in which, as if by a miracle, he keeps being transformed from poet to bard.

III

Late in 1980, under new ownership, A.S. Barnes finally issues *Carousel Parkway*, my first full collection in seven years. As the weeks go by without press notice, it becomes clear that the new people have neglected to send out a single review copy. The burden falls on me — no novelty in the American poetry world. Among the respondents, one distinguished quarterly allows me to suggest an outside reviewer. I instantly suggest Owen, not only because he is attuned to my work, but because no Black writer — even of the "new wave" — having appeared in its pages, its readers should experience the name and force of Owen Dodson. He accepts their deadline of several months and a limit of 750 words.

The deadline approaches — no review. The editor phones to "prod" Owen. Late one night, he phones to read me his essay, a generous piece with well-chosen quotations and several Dodsonesque lyric bursts. We chuckle over the last sentence: "This poet's incredible sense of humanity is a gift for us to share, read and reread instead of so many modern poets who pretend a toothpick can undo a pyramid." He predicts it will raise a few hackles among today's high-flying warblers and their adherents. Almost at once the editor writes, highly perturbed because Owen's approach clashes with the calm, analytic aestheticism of his publication. Might Owen rewrite the piece, or let them revise it? I express my doubts.

Owen phones again, to share the portions of the editor's diplomatic letter that most enrage him. He has also received a sample issue. While praising its high technical standard, he scalds what strikes him as a sterile infatuation with style at the expense of content, surface at the expense of soul. Convinced that the journal took his last sentence as a personal affront, he remarks: "The shoe fit too well." In subsequent phone conversations, he will renew his assault on what he perceives to be these prissy, two-faced, bloodless young

Anglo-Saxon academics who are uncomfortable in the presence of plainly expressed emotion. For him, this episode merely underscores a major theme in our conversations: how far from the force of true poetry the dominant circles have drifted. Still, he offers to rewrite it if told specifically what displeases them. Nothing will come of it.

If the editors judged that Owen's preoccupation was entirely with content and that he lacked concern for or knowledge of style, they were profoundly mistaken. In the first place, his own work, from beginning to end, demonstrates a seamless purity of craft. Second, former students attest gratefully to his insistence on artistic integrity and discipline. Third, he has hammered home this very theme in lectures on "The Definition and Use of Drama" at leading campuses across the country, and in a crucial recorded interview of 1971 he dared to challenge the young dramatists. Black playwrights, he declared, should learn from their classic predecessors and create works "in terms we may all understand without losing the healing and blessed presence of artistic values." In "Playwrights in Dark Glasses," he actually scolded them for the excessive strength of their content: "So many of our Negro playwrights are so saturated with the idea of Negro oppression, which of course they should be, that they have left out the lasting power, the universality, of their art."

But even more, he despised a worship of form and a hollowness in the marrow. This he saw as the pervasive sickness in contemporary culture, including poetry. Given only 750 words, he chose to emphasize that poetry, in order to live, must be human.

IV

Every month or two, sometimes at hair-raisingly late hours, Owen phoned. Within minutes he would hit his stride, renewing our chat from the times before with savage comments on the politics of a heartless society and the moral bankruptcy of its cultural spokesmen. We lamented the passing of poets we both loved, true poets of the people: Carl Sandburg, Langston Hughes, Alfred Kreymborg, Muriel Rukeyser. No matter which poet was named, ancient or modern, he had something incisive to say, and cited lines to illustrate his point.

Sometimes he called to mention an upcoming theatrical event, a concert, a broadcast, or to report on it afterward. But what roared up from under the hello was a loneliness like the howling of a wolf.

When I asked about his work, especially a project on the "bag-ladies," he recited the same *Inferno*-like passage. This made me surmise that the work had become mired since the time when those very lines, aired publicly for the first time, had made my blood run cold. But I surmised wrong. He was offering the lines again because I had especially liked them.

At Martinson Hall, on May 3, 1982, Joseph Papp presented *Life in the Streets*, "a journey in poetry, drawings, music and drama through the isolated worlds of the city's 'street people' who dwell in our society but are not of it." Owen's poems were read by Roscoe Lee Browne, Mia Dillon, Gloria Foster and himself, with music by David Amram, drawings by Penrod Scofield, and choreography by Colin Connor prepared with Anna Sokolow. The evening was dedicated to Muriel Rukeyser's memory.

V

On a rainy April evening in 1979, Owen slowly pulled his body down the long ramp and into the Donnell Library auditorium for my 18th annual program. I introduced him to the audience as a "colossus of our time." After the reading, a young lawyer asked for the privilege of helping him out to the street and calling a cab. In five minutes, the poet made him feel like an old friend, with no sense of difference in age, career or race. The card Owen sent the next morning, an apology, typifies him: "Had to rush after poetry reading to avoid theatre traffic." An astounding memory and an ear keen for nuances: "Of your new poems, 'Madrid' and 'Granada' were very alive, and the contrast between 'The tyrant lay in state' with 'Lorca needs no flower' — was ironic and moving." A hand open for friendship: "See you soon I hope." As soon as the date of the Donnell program for Spring 1980 was set, I invited Owen to join me. From the outset, it was clear that this year's event would differ from most of the previous eighteen. He asked for 100 copies of the program and waited impatiently to circulate them! Marvelous people had shared my programs — Millen Brand, Edward Field, David Ignatow, Eve Merriam, Norman Rosten, Muriel Rukeyser,

May Swenson, et al. Our collaborations had gone well, but in most cases the other poets had acted as guests reading to my audience. This time, due to Owen's supplementary promotion, as many new faces as familiar ones, black and white in equal numbers, filled the auditorium.

Each of us, through a long career, had built a very special following for poetry that was unfashionable in our time — clear and melodic, indignant and visionary. What happened was a double discovery. Despite surface variations in cadence and image, we spoke with one voice; and, listening, the crowd became *one.* Each of us commented on what the other read; each new "set" followed the preceding one like a higher wave.

Owen, immaculately dressed, arrived half an hour early and climbed onto the stage. No one could guess, during his tremendous performance, that he was crippled. There was astonishment at the end when he came down the steps to shake a hundred out-stretched hands, dragging his tormented little frame within the frame of a walker.

After the reading, I had the honor of being invited by Owen to dine at an elegant party that included Edith Dodson, Dr. King's attorney Ben Carruthers, and Ben's vibrant sister Sallee Hardy. Knowing that I faced a two-hour wait for the next Oakdale train, Owen shooed me off early from the celebration; but, however brief, it was "the real thing." An hour of sparkling talk — politics, history, art — flew by.

Two mornings later, before I could send my own note of appreciation, his arrived, succinct as always, witty, and carrying the full sense of what had occurred:

> The audience attention was held true and the sound of our poetry — the humanly heroic and the slow-pulse ones. Poets are not always a bore! Thanks for inviting me. The Muriel poems, the Robeson and Tito, were oaks. Am reworking "The Subway Ride." [I had asked for a copy.] This year at any rate: April was not the cruellest month.

His reference was to my elegy for Muriel Rukeyser, who had recently transformed that hall with her ferocity and tenderness, had just died, and to whom the Donnell program was dedicated. This

November the annual program will be dedicated to Owen, who on April 21, 1980, sent comets through the Donnell air. Quincy Troupe will read with me, living proof of Rev. Harrington's tribute to the power of Owen's roots.

VI

Since the mid-'60s, dozens of poets had visited Dowling College — John Hollander, Kenneth Koch, Stanley Kunitz, Muriel Rukeyser, Diane Wakoski, and James Wright among them. Clarence Major had read, and Raymond Patterson appeared twice. In 1979, it seemed long past time for a Black woman poet to be heard on our somewhat removed campus. Audre Lorde, who had been my friend when she was a teenager, agreed to come for much less than her usual fee. When at the last minute she was prevented from appearing by a huge midwest snowstorm, I was determined to use the earmarked funds for another Black poet.

Owen Dodson instantly came to mind. I wanted our "budding poets" and others to experience one of the few surviving bardic voices, who — along with Claude McKay, Countee Cullen and Langston Hughes — combined fury with discipline and wit, and who had (in Dodson's words) "the daring and the flair to infuse high vision with our present angry condition." I also wanted a giant not operating through an agency, not "in vogue," probably receiving one campus invitation to fifty for an Audre Lorde. But I was ashamed to give such short notice and to offer so slight a fee.

My trepidation proved unjustified. A 55–mile trip to the campus didn't bother him, nor did the short notice. As for the funding, he sounded eager to reach the unsophisticated but responsive audience I described, no matter what the fee. The transportation problem was solved by the arrangement of a door-to-door ride.

On a wet April morning, a young economics instructor called for him; when they arrived, the driver was grinning from ear to ear. Lacking any background in poetry, he had been petrified at the prospect of two 90–minute sessions alone with a poet! Now he could hardly wait for the trip back with his newfound pal. Owen's magic had converted him. I'm sorry I never asked what they talked about; my hunch is that it was economics, since Owen always enjoyed exploring the worlds of others. In any case, the economist made it his business to attend part of the reading, stating that the journey with Owen had been "one of the most extraordinary experiences" of his life.

I tried to disguise my shock as Owen slowly twisted himself out of the car and let go of the walker to grip my hand. His casual explanation had not prepared me for the extent of his disability. But his contagious joviality set the tone for our day together. At my home, with every ounce of his strength (or nerve), he struggled up the seven steps, not too out of breath to praise the lawn and the budding lilacs, and to express delight upon being introduced to "Sydney," an evergreen we'd planted whose sex was still a mystery.

We recounted our boyhood days in East New York. A teenage Owen and his sister had played games at recess in the Thomas Jefferson High School yard, which I could see, at age seven, from my Dumont Avenue stoop. We had Howard in common too — I had attended its graduate school in 1942 and studied drama with Owen's colleague and friend, the brilliant John Lovell.

We swapped personal anecdotes about Langston Hughes, the Robesons, Dr. Du Bois and Shirley Graham, Maxwell Bodenheim, Alfred Kreymborg, and others. We compared the roles of our families in our development. I spoke about Frank Silvera, the first reader of my *Denmark Vesey* when we were neighbors in Astoria. He, on the other hand, described Silvera's last years in Hollywood after leaving wife and children, and his nightmarish death in a bizarre incinerator accident.

He took note of the hanging plants, the Steinway upright, the paintings. He wanted to know about my wife, children, grand-children. The lushness returning to the woods behind the house moved him, and in later phone calls he sent greetings to "my" woods.

Our talk progressed with even more animation as we drove through the picturesque artists' colony (formerly the servants' quarters of the Vanderbilt estate) to lunch near the mouth of the Connetquot River at the Great South Bay. He responded to everything with an eye and a phrase as fresh as those of a particularly sensitive child not ashamed to express wonder — even at the waves of slate marching north from the Bay.

At the college, an expectant throng greeted him. Unlike the Donnell audience, they saw his disability in advance, and were thunderstruck by a thrilling stage presence that needed no stage. He offered early poems first, introducing them in a way that brought the pieces and himself to fascinating life. These introductions were history as it should be taught — the slavery years, the civil rights movement, World War II — as eloquently shaped as the poems they explained. The second half included work new to me, demonstrating an unslackened creative drive and an often angelic grace of expression. Two highlights were from *The Harlem Book of the Dead* — "Allegory of Seafaring Black Mothers" and "War Games," a classic.

Not one student complained afterward that the poet had been beyond them, as some usually do with good reason. Though his frame of reference was vastly different, even from that of the Black students, he and they were immediately able to enter each other's world. His answers at the end were full and to the point. On form, he stressed the value of discovering the right vehicle for one's content, the double power of passion when expressed with artistic control. Youngsters who had never read a poem lined up to shake his hand and buy his books. He asked each purchaser's name and wrote personal inscriptions. One student was broke, but Owen inscribed what must now be a treasure to that young man and refused to hear of money. Several stood quietly around him, savoring that rare aura of modesty and humanity, then followed him to the car as if he could readily be their Pied Piper.

Our final moment, as he was about to be driven away, was devoted to a brotherly barter of books. My inscription hailed the beauty and courage of his life's work. Refusing payment for the novels I wanted to buy, he inscribed one for each grandchild by name: To Nora, almost six: "We'll meet some April with lilacs." To Joanna, 14 months old: "In sixteen more years you must say hello."

VII

Perhaps when anyone dies, certainly so when it is a man as remarkable as Owen Dodson, a reassessment occurs. An idiosyncracy, a single act, hitherto taken for granted, is now seen as special. One is startled, as if discovering them for the first time, by facts Owen never referred to. He did after all work with Gielgud, Vivien Leigh, directed the premiere of Baldwin's *Amen Corner*, brought *Mamba's*

Daughters and *The Wild Duck* to Norway, Sweden, Denmark and Germany for three triumphant months, collaborated with Countee Cullen on *The Third Fourth of July*, received Rosenwald, Guggenheim and Rockefeller fellowships.

His works were performed by James Earl Jones, Lawrence Tibbett, Maureen Forrester, broadcast over BBC and CBS, produced at the Kennedy Center, Madison Square Garden, EXPO. Retiring after 31 years of master-teaching at Atlanta University, the Hampton Institute, and Howard, he brought Anouilh's *Antigone* to 25,000 high school students and 25,000 adults in Watts, Los Angeles, then headed the Drama Department at the Harlem School of the Arts.

One hearkens to others more profoundly bereaved — to Roxie Roker: "His imagination and creativity were boundless, and he made his actors feel that the seemingly impossible was within their reach. He made me try — then, he helped me to succeed"; Josephine Premice: "Owen Dodson loved people. He had a zest for life. He had the courage to give a seventeen-year-old girl without credentials the opportunity to do the choreography for *Jason and the Golden Fleece*"; Betty Gubert, Schomburg Center: "Owen Dodson was one of the theatre world's irreplaceable citizens.... His influence and works will be studied for years to come by all who love the African American Theatre"; Dr. Anne Cooke Reid: "Because Owen Dodson never lost his exuberant, child-like wonder, he ignited others to become increasingly sensitive to the eternal verities"; Earle Hyman: "Owen was one of the Great People, Owen was an Artist, and Owen was my friend. I shall miss him."

Printed words, once passed over, now have an eerie resonance:

> You come back to us with the truth
> Of your indignation, protest and irony.
> Also in your brave and tender singing
> We hear all mankind yearning
> For a new year without hemlock in our glasses.
>
> "Countee Cullen: 1903–1946"
> (*Powerful Long Ladder*, 1946)

Finally, handwritten words that illuminate and sustain ... private legacy:

"The dead shall rise each Easter. L., Owen"
(Back of *Harlem Book of the Dead* card, April 1981)

Yes, Owen, the dead shall rise.

An Afterword

That others share my resentment of unmerited neglect was most recently demonstrated by three contributors to Jay Parini's imposing 1993 *Columbia History of American Poetry*. Lynn Keller, in "The Twentieth-Century Long Poem" (p. 541), has this to say about the persistently underestimated Muriel Rukeyser in particular and political poetry as a whole:

> Her presentation of social ills involves analyzing power and its abuses, not just in general but in specific cases — Sacco and Vanzetti, Tom Mooney, the Scottsboro boys.... Her poetic sequences of the later 1930s, such as "The Book of the Dead" (1938), demonstrate skillful poetic application of the techniques of cinematic montage. But this poem, which is based on Rukeyser's investigation of events surrounding miners' deaths from silicosis in Fayette County, West Virginia, and others that followed, were pigeonholed as literature of social protest by an establishment that refused to see aesthetic merit in topical political work.

Jeanne Larson touches on a related issue in "Lowell, Teasdale, Wylie, Millay, and Bogan" (pp. 203–04):

> Passionate expression of emotion, revelation of personal sensibility, apparent delicacy overlaying sensuality and self-assertion, musicality created by diction and cadence, a vigorous grace of form: these qualities are characteristic of much work by a succession of American women poets.... Yet by mid-century all three [Teasdale, Wylie, and Millay] — like other successful female poets of their era — had fallen into critical disregard. A new assessment of such disregard, and of the poetry itself, has begun. Understanding the value of these poets' work, and the reasons behind the changing estimations of that value, restores

to us a fuller picture of a vital era in American poetry.... For
half a century Teasdale, Wylie, and Millay have generally been
ignored or treated as embarrassing
mistakes in vulgar taste.

And Dana Gioia, in his brave, brilliantly detailed "Longfellow in the
Aftermath of Modernism," has this to say (pp. 68–69):

Few recent books on American poetry mention Longfellow ex-
cept in passing ... 'Increasingly rare is the scholar who braves
ridicule to justify the art of Longfellow's popular rhymings,'
[Kermit] Vanderbilt [has] characteristically quipped. Contem-
porary taste does not esteem the genres Longfellow favored —
the ballad, idyll, pastoral romance, and moral fable — nor does
it highly regard the stylistic strengths his contemporaries
praised — clarity, grace, musicality, masterful versification, and
memorability. These are not attributes that fit easily into the
traditions of Emerson, Whitman, and Dickinson.

Ironically, Editor Parini could publish these paragraphs, yet he re-
serves at least half of his presumably encyclopedic work for a cluster
of today's "in" poets while including not a word on Freneau, a mere
handful of brief references to Bryant (such as a snide comment on
Thanatopsis: "a volume that critics of yesteryear often cited as the
first great book of American verse"), and nothing on Melville's
poetry aside from a brief misreading of *Battle-Pieces*.

One seeks in vain for such names as Sidney Lanier, Emma Laza-
rus, William Vaughn Moody, and Edwin Markham. Nor does
Stephen Crane appear, except as the unnamed author of *The Red
Badge of Courage*. Of this century's earlier figures, one notes such
omissions as Ridgely Torrence, Elizabeth Madox Roberts, Mark Van
Doren, Joseph Auslander, Robert Hillyer, John Hall Wheelock,
Arturo Giovannitti, James Oppenheim, Malcolm Cowley, Lola
Ridge, and the whole *Dynamo* group, along with Leonie Adams,
John Gould Fletcher, William Ellery Leonard, Merrill Moore, Jean
Starr Untermeyer, James Agee, David McCord, and George Dillon.

Lizette Woodworth Reese, Louise Imogen Guiney, Adelaide
Crapsey, Genevieve Taggard, Horace Gregory, Archibald Mac-
Leish, Kenneth Patchen, Witter Bynner (misspelled), and Maxwell

Bodenheim are named only in passing. William Rose Benét is noted only as the husband of Elinor Wylie; Kreymborg and Untermeyer appear only as anthologists.

Excluded among the somewhat more recent poets are Norman Rosten, Eve Merriam, David Ignatow, Erica Jong, May Sarton, Edward Field, James Schevill, Edwin Honig, William Stafford, and William Heyen. Richard Eberhart is mentioned once in passing, X. J. Kennedy only as an anthologist, and John Ciardi as essayist and translator.

Even more egregious is the treatment reserved for Black poets. Among the distinguished earlier figures utterly omitted are Owen Dodson, Pauli Murray, Richard Wright, Donald Jeffrey Hayes, Frank Marshall Davis, Margaret Danner, Margaret Walker, Frank Yerby, Bruce McWright, Myron O'Higgins, and M. Carl Holman; Dudley Randall is named only once — in terms of "Dudley Randall's Broadside Press."

As for the exciting new wave of Black '60s poets, there is no mention of Mari Evans, James Emanuel, Naomi Madgett, Ted Joans, Conrad Kent Rivers, June Jordan, Lucille Clifton, James W. Thompson, James A. Randall, Jr., and Everett Hoagland. Two lines by Bob Kaufman are quoted to help define the San Francisco beatnik school; Etheridge Knight is listed once and referred to once as the "drug-addicted" husband of Sonia Sanchez; Audre Lorde is listed once (misspelled) and elsewhere a poem of hers is named; Maya Angelou is listed once; Carolyn Rodgers is listed as co-founder of the Third World Press.

A powerful anthology, larger than the Parini volume, could be assembled including only the poets named above. Clearly, a serious student will have to seek elsewhere than in *The Columbia History of American Poetry* for the true history of American poetry.

Index

Aaron Kramer first gained national prominence with SEVEN POETS IN SEARCH OF AN ANSWER, 1944, and THE POETRY AND PROSE OF HEINRICH HEINE, 1948. He was a leading resistance poet throughout the McCarthy era, with such texts for music as DENMARK VESEY and such volumes as ROLL THE FORBIDDEN DRUMS! In 1958 he collaborated with a dozen artists on THE TUNE OF THE CALLIOPE: POEMS AND DRAWINGS OF NEW YORK. Professor of English at Dowling College since 1961, and founding co-editor of WEST HILLS REVIEW: A WHITMAN JOURNAL, he has produced such scholarly works as THE PROPHETIC TRADITION IN AMERICAN POETRY, 1968, and MELVILLE'S POETRY: TOWARD THE ENLARGED HEART, 1972. The same year he edited the Macmillan anthology, ON FREEDOM'S SIDE: AMERICAN POEMS OF PROTEST. Equally noted as a translator, Kramer produced RILKE: VISIONS OF CHRIST in 1967 and an English version of THE EMPEROR OF ATLANTIS in 1975; this work, created in the death-camp of Terezin, was premiered by the San Francisco Opera in 1977 and has subsequently been performed in many countries, most recently at Philadelphia's Curtis Institute. In 1989, 370 of his translations from the work of 135 Yiddish poets appeared in a widely praised anthology, A CENTURY OF YIDDISH POETRY, also edited by Dr. Kramer. The most recent collections of his own poems are CAROUSEL PARKWAY, 1980, two 1983 volumes, THE BURNING BUSH and IN WICKED TIMES, and INDIGO AND OTHER POEMS, 1991. He also has a chapter in LIFE GUIDANCE THROUGH LITERATURE, 1992, and has authored numerous articles on poetry for the disabled, a field in which he has pioneered. OBLOMOV, a musical play for which he provided the lyrics, was recently showcased at New York's Cubicolo Theatre by the National Shakespeare Company. Kramer has been a popular public reader on both coasts for decades; over 80 of his radio broadcasts are archived, and he has recorded for Folkways Records as well as for the Library of Congress. In 1993 he received a National Endowment for the Humanities grant. A volume of translations from many languages and essays on the art of translation, assembled in his honor, was published last summer. In April a selected edition of his poems, BORDER INCIDENT, translated into Russian, was issued in St. Petersburg, and a Bulgarian edition later appeared in Sofia.

Dowling College Press

Sponsor: Victor P. Meskill *(ex-officio)*; *Editor in Chief*: James E. Caraway; *Managing Editor*: Parviz Morewedge; *Editors*: Norman Holub, and Robert M. Berchman.

PUBLICATIONS

Dowling Series in the Humanities and Social Sciences

Sponsor: Victor P. Meskill *(ex-officio)*; *Editor in Chief*: Robert M. Berchman; *Managing Editor:* Parviz Morewedge; *Co-Editors*: Joan Boyle, Joseph Behar, James E. Caraway, Jeffery Cole, Andrew Karp, John D. Mullen, Susan Rosenstreich, Byron Roth, Martin Schoenhals, and James O. Tate.

Categories and Experience, Essays on Aristotelian Themes, by John P. Anton. Aristotle's Principle of Contradiction: Its Ontological Foundations and Platonic Antecedents. The Meaning of *O Logos tes Ousias* in the *Categories* 1a. The Aristotelian Doctrine of *Homonyma*. Observations on Aristotle's Theory of the Categories. Aristotle's Theory of Categories and Post-Classical Ontologies. The Unity of Scientific Inquiry: The Scope of *Ousia*. Revolutions and Reforms. *Politeia* and *Paideia*: The Structure of Constitutions. Aristotle on Justice and Equity. Ideal Values and Cultural Action. ISBN 1-883058-02-3.

Aquinas on Mind and Intellect: New Essays, edited by Jeremiah Hackett. Recognizing One of Aquinas' Debts to Neoplatonism (Joseph W. Koterski, S.J.); Aquinas, Roger Bacon and Latin Averroism: The Problem of the Intellective Soul (Jeremiah Hackett); Aquinas's Earliest Philosophy of Mind: *"Mens"* in the *Commentary on the Sentences* and Other Contemporaneous Writings (William E. Murnion); Intellectual Knowledge of Material Particulars in Thomas Aquinas: An Introduction (James B. South); Thomas Aquinas on Intellect, Infinity and Immateriality (Michael J. Sweeney); Defense of a Thomistic Argument for Subsistent Soul (John F. X. Knasas); Sense and Intentionality: Aristotle and Aquinas (James T. H. Martin); Aquinas and Freud on the Human Soul (Donald C. Abel). ISBN 1-883058-13-9.

Mapping Cyberspace: Social Research on the Electronic Frontier, edited by *Joseph E. Behar*. *Preface by Langdon Winner. Introduction: Social Research and Cyberspace (Joseph E.Behar)."They've Got the Whole World in their Hands:" A Case Study of Social Control on The Internet (Patricia J. Peterson); E-mail to Somalia: New Communication Media Between Home and War-Fronts(Morton G. Ender);Sanctuary: Social Support on the Internet (Janet Moursund); The Dialectics Between the Real and the Virtual: The Case of the Progressive Sociology Network (Martha E. Gimenez); Caught in the Web: The Phenomenon of "Cyberaddiction" (Myron Orleans); Sex and The Internet: Deviant behavior and the Shaping of Social Control (Steven R. Cornish & Craig B. Nerenberg); Social Transformation Through Spatial Transformation: From Geospaces to Cyberspaces? (Robert M.Kitchin); The End of Mass Society?: A Preface to Telecommunication Politics (Marc A. Triebwasser); Internet Insurrection: Chiapas and the Laptop (Paul Rich & Guillermo De Los Reyes); Cyberspace Democracy and Social Behavior: Reflections and Refutations (James Willson-Quayle);Coda: Beyond the Year 2000 in Cyberspace (Joseph E.Behar).* ISBN 1-883058-43-0.

Forthcoming:

Giovanni Rutini and the Classic Sonata, by Carlo Lombardi. ISBN 1-883-058-18-X

Mediterranean Perspectives

Sponsor: Victor P. Meskill *(ex-officio)*; *Editor in Chief*: James E. Caraway; *Managing Editor*: Parviz Morewedge; *Editor*: Norman Holub; *Co-editors*: Robert M. Berchman and Alain Saint- Saëns.

Mediterranean Perpsectives: Literature, Social Studies and Philosophy, edited by **James E. Caraway**. The Devil and Dionysus in *Melmoth the Wanderer* (Andrew Karp); Convergencias y Divergencias en la Obra de Gertrudis Gómez de Avellaneda y Carolina Coronado (Jesse Fernández); Mario Vargas Llosa: on Moral Fiction (James E. Caraway); Gertrudis Gómez de Avellaneda: Desde una Perspectiva Feminina (Raquel Romeu); Literature as Revolution in the 20th Century Mediterranean World (Theresa Mackey); Santones Guerreros en el Islam Occidental (Carmen Martínez Salvador); Household Material Culture and the Origins of Modern Consumerism in Spain (Jesus Cruz); Relaciones Económicas entre Omeyas y Fatimies en el Mediterráneo Occidental (Francisco J. Navarro Suárez & Carmen Martínez Salvador); Regulating Quality in the Mediterranean Region (Victor & Jerome Selman); Averroës of Cordoba and the Platonic Republic (Robert M. Helm); André Malraux, Charles de Gaulle, and Bernard de Clairvaux on Action and Contemplation (M. Burcht Pranger); Aesthetics as Philosophical *Ethos*: Plotinus and Foucault (Robert M. Berchman). ISBN. 1-883058-20-1.

For Submission of Manuscripts: For Dowling Series in the Humanities and Social Sciences, and Mediterranean Perspectives, contact Robert M. Berchman, Department of

Philosophy, Dowling College, Oakdale, NY 11769-1999, Tel (516) 244-3155, Fax (516) 589-6644.

For Journal and Book Orders: please contact Parviz Morewedge at (607) 777-4495, Fax (607)777-6132 or write to SSIPS, Institute of Global Cultural Studies, Binghamton University, Binghamton, NY 13902-6000.

Style: Authors should follow the Chicago Manual of Style and send two copies of each manuscript and a floppy disk in DOS/Windows versions in either Word Perfect or Microsoft Word. Authors should use endnotes for *Dowling Series in the Humanities* and *Social Sciences* and *Mediterranean Perspectives*.